HANDBOOKS

GATEWAY CLIPPER FLEET STATION SQUARE

PITTSBURGH

DAN ELDRIDGE

Contents

Maps

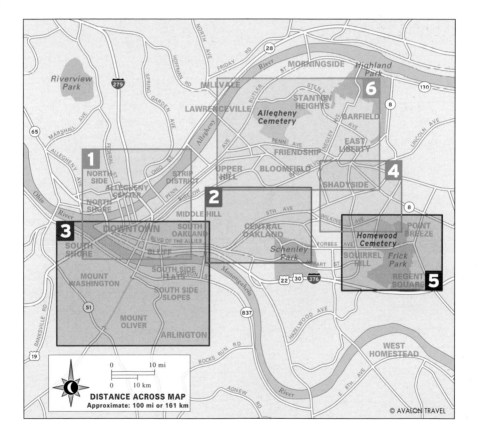

NIGHTLIFE
- 47 LITTLE E'S
- 80 ALTAR BAR
- 81 CLUB ZOO
- 94 EMBURY
- 94 FIREHOUSE LOUNGE
- 95 MULLANEY'S HARP & FIDDLE

SHOPS
- 13 ARTISTS IMAGE RESOURCE
- 65 LARRIMOR'S
- 71 THE COMIC BOOK INK!
- 74 EMPHATICS
- 74 THE SHOPS OF ONE OXFORD CENTER
- 86 PITTSBURGH PUBLIC MARKET
- 86 THE STORE AT THE SOCIETY FOR CONTEMPORARY CRAFT
- 91 PENN AVENUE
- 93 HOT HAUTE HOT

DISTANCE ACROSS MAP
Approximate: 2.2 mi or 3.6 km

© AVALON TRAVEL

MAP 1 · DOWNTOWN, STRIP DISTRICT, AND NORTH SIDE

STRIP DISTRICT

SEE MAP 6

SEE MAP 2

St. Patrick's Church

16th ST BRIDGE

VETERANS BRIDGE

Senator John Heinz Pittsburgh Regional History Center

David Lawrence Convention Center
Megabus Stop
Greyhound Station
Amtrak Station

August Wilson Center for African American Culture
ToonSeum

HILL DISTRICT

Civic Arena

Consol Energy Center

Allegheny County Courthouse

Duquesne

University

BOULEVARD OF THE ALLIES

★ SIGHTS
1 RANDYLAND
3 MATTRESS FACTORY
4 HOUSE POEM
8 CALVARY UNITED METHODIST CHURCH
10 NATIONAL AVIARY
11 CHILDREN'S MUSEUM OF PITTSBURGH
14 PHOTO ANTIQUITIES MUSEUM
17 RIVERS CASINO
20 CARNEGIE SCIENCE CENTER AND HIGHMARK SPORTSWORKS
27 THE ANDY WARHOL MUSEUM
28 THE THREE SISTERS
29 POINT STATE PARK
30 FORT PITT MUSEUM
40 THE CULTURAL DISTRICT
45 TOONSEUM
52 SENATOR JOHN HEINZ PITTSBURGH REGIONAL HISTORY CENTER
59 AUGUST WILSON CENTER FOR AFRICAN AMERICAN CULTURE
60 PPG PLACE
62 MARKET SQUARE
72 SMITHFIELD STREET BRIDGE
75 ALLEGHENY COUNTY COURTHOUSE
90 ST. PATRICK'S CHURCH

● RESTAURANTS
2 BUENA VISTA COFFEE
5 WILSON'S BAR-B-Q
6 HOI POLLOI VEGETARIAN CAFÉ AND COFFEEHOUSE
16 PENN BREWERY
32 LEMON GRASS CAFÉ
34 BRADDOCK'S AMERICAN BRASSERIE
43 NINE ON NINE
46 SEVICHE
48 ORIGINAL FISH MARKET
50 ELEVEN
53 SUSHI KIM
54 HABITAT
58 SREE'S INDIAN FOOD
63 ORIGINAL OYSTER HOUSE
66 FRANKTUARY
68 TAP ROOM
82 PRIMANTI BROTHERS
83 ROLAND'S SEAFOOD GRILL
84 PEACE, LOVE & LITTLE DONUTS
87 KAYA
88 PAMELA'S DINER
89 DELUCA'S RESTAURANT
92 LA PRIMA ESPRESSO COMPANY
97 KLAVON'S ICE CREAM PARLOR

● ARTS AND LEISURE
12 NEW HAZLETT THEATER
18 PITT PANTHERS
18 PITTSBURGH STEELERS
19 STAGE AE
21 CARNEGIE SCIENCE CENTER RANGOS OMNIMAX THEATER
22 THREE RIVERS HERITAGE TRAIL
24 PITTSBURGH PIRATES
24 PNC PARK TOURS
33 BYHAM THEATER
36 HEINZ HALL
37 PITTSBURGH PUBLIC THEATER (AT THE O'REILLY THEATER)
38 CABARET AT THEATER SQUARE
39 BENEDUM CENTER FOR THE PERFORMING ARTS
41 FUTURE TENANT
42 HARRIS THEATER
56 WOOD STREET GALLERIES
57 SPACE
61 THE RINK AT PPG PLACE
64 PNC YMCA
70 DOWNTOWN TRIANGLERS/ VENTURE OUTDOORS
73 ELIZA FURNACE TRAIL
77 CONSOL ENERGY CENTER
78 A. J. PALUMBO CENTER
78 DUQUESNE DUKES
78 PITTSBURGH PENGUINS
78 PITTSBURGH POWER
85 SOCIETY FOR CONTEMPORARY CRAFT
86 SCHOOLHOUSE YOGA

● HOTELS
7 THE INN ON THE MEXICAN WAR STREETS
9 THE PARADOR
15 THE PRIORY
23 HYATT PLACE PITTSBURGH-NORTH SHORE
25 RESIDENCE INN NORTH SHORE
26 MARRIOTT SPRINGHILL SUITES NORTH SHORE
31 WYNDHAM GRAND PITTSBURGH DOWNTOWN
35 RENAISSANCE PITTSBURGH HOTEL
44 COURTYARD MARRIOTT DOWNTOWN
49 WESTIN CONVENTION CENTER PITTSBURGH
51 HAMPTON INN & SUITES PITTSBURGH-DOWNTOWN
55 FAIRMONT PITTSBURGH
69 OMNI WILLIAM PENN
69 DOUBLETREE HOTEL & SUITES PITTSBURGH CITY CENTER
76 PITTSBURGH MARRIOTT CITY CENTER
79 CAMBRIA SUITES PITTSBURGH AT CONSOL ENERGY CENTER

☼ SIGHTS

2 SOLDIERS AND SAILORS MEMORIAL
4 ☾ CATHEDRAL OF LEARNING
7 SCHENLEY PLAZA
24 ST. PAUL CATHEDRAL
25 RODEF SHALOM BIBLICAL BOTANICAL GARDEN
36 ☾ CARNEGIE MUSEUM OF NATURAL HISTORY
36 CARNEGIE MUSEUM OF ART
38 CARNEGIE MELLON UNIVERSITY
40 ☾ PHIPPS CONSERVATORY AND BOTANICAL GARDENS
41 ☾ SCHENLEY PARK AND FLAGSTAFF HILL

☯ RESTAURANTS

8 HEMINGWAY'S
9 ☾ THE ORIGINAL HOT DOG SHOP
10 OISHII BENTO
12 SUSHI BOAT
13 DAVE & ANDY'S
14 FUEL AND FUDDLE
15 SPICE ISLAND TEA HOUSE
19 INDIA GARDEN
20 MAD MEX
28 LULU'S NOODLES
30 ALI BABA
32 LUCCA
33 STAR OF INDIA
34 UNION GRILL
35 KIVA HAN

☾ NIGHTLIFE

11 PETER'S PUB

☺ ARTS AND LEISURE

3 PETERSEN EVENTS CENTER
3 PITT PANTHERS
5 CHARITY RANDALL THEATRE
21 PITTSBURGH PLAYHOUSE
37 CARNEGIE MUSIC HALL
39 MILLER GALLERY AT CARNEGIE MELLON UNIVERSITY
42 SCHENLEY PARK
43 SCHENLEY PARK POOL
44 SCHENLEY PARK SKATING RINK
45 SCHENLEY PARK TENNIS COURTS

☯ SHOPS

6 UNIVERSITY OF PITTSBURGH BOOK CENTER
16 IRON CITY BIKES
26 SNOW LION IMPORTS
27 IRISH DESIGN CENTER
29 PHANTOM OF THE ATTIC COMICS
31 CALIBAN BOOKSHOP

☺ HOTELS

1 HOLIDAY INN SELECT AT UNIVERSITY CENTER
17 WYNDHAM GARDEN HOTEL
18 FORBES AVENUE SUITES
22 HAMPTON INN UNIVERSITY CENTER
23 QUALITY INN UNIVERSITY CENTER

NORTH OAKLAND

University of Pittsburgh

Soldiers and Sailors Memorial

Cathedral of Learning

Hillman Library

SEE MAP 1

CENTRAL OAKLAND

SEE MAP 3

Magee-Women's Hospital of UPMC

SOUTH OAKLAND

0   200 yds

0   200 m

DISTANCE ACROSS MAP
Approximate: 1.4 mi or 2.3 km

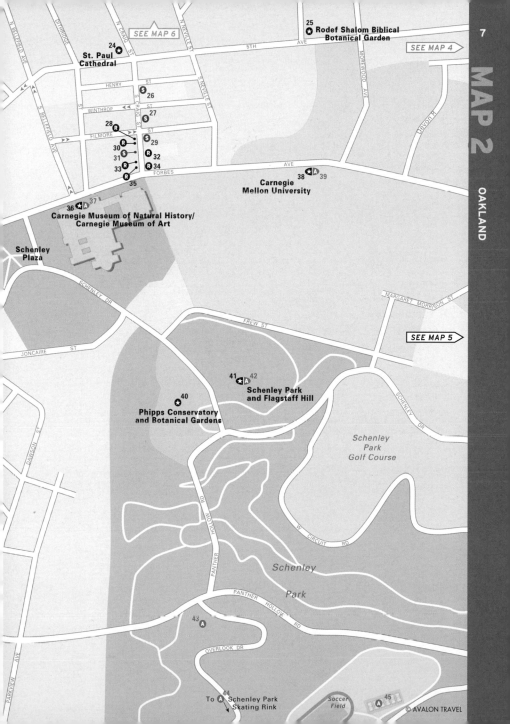

SEE MAP 6

25 Rodef Shalom Biblical Botanical Garden

SEE MAP 4

24 St. Paul Cathedral

HENRY ST

WINTHROP ST

S. CRAIG ST
S. NEVILLE ST
N. NEVILLE ST
N. CRAIG ST
DITHRIDGE ST

5TH AVE

MOREWOOD AVE

DEVON R

S 26

S 27

28 R

FILMORE ST

S 29

30
31 S

32 R

33 R

34 R

35 R

FORBES AVE

Carnegie Mellon University

38 39

36 37

Carnegie Museum of Natural History/
Carnegie Museum of Art

Schenley Plaza

SCHENLEY DR

JONCAIRE ST

FREW ST

MARGARET MORRISON ST

SEE MAP 5

41 42

Schenley Park and Flagstaff Hill

40

Phipps Conservatory and Botanical Gardens

SCHENLEY DR

Schenley Park Golf Course

DAWSON ST

PANTHER HOLLOW RD

W. CIRCUIT RD

Schenley

Park

PANTHER HOLLOW RD

43

OVERLOOK DR

PARKVIEW AVE

44 To Schenley Park Skating Rink

Soccer Field

45

© AVALON TRAVEL

Point State Park

The Duquesne and Monongahela Inclines

FORT PITT BRIDGE

DOWNTOWN

SEE MAP 1

DUQUESNE HEIGHTS

Gateway Clipper Fleet

SOUTH SHORE

Station Square

SMITHFIELD ST BRIDGE

LIBERTY BRIDGE

MOUNT WASHINGTON

Grandview Park

KNOXVILLE

○ SIGHTS

3 THE DUQUESNE AND MONONGAHELA INCLINES	9 GATEWAY CLIPPER FLEET	17 SOUTH SIDE SLOPES
	11 STATION SQUARE	

ⓡ RESTAURANTS

1 MONTEREY BAY FISH GROTTO	23 BIG DOG COFFEE	51 FAT HEAD'S SALOON
2 GEORGETOWNE INN	30 CAFE DU JOUR	54 THAI ME UP
4 GRANDVIEW SALOON	35 YO RITA	59 LE POMMIER
5 TIN ANGEL	38 GYPSY CAFÉ	65 TAQUERIA MEXICO CITY
6 LEMONT RESTAURANT	39 BEEHIVE	68 IBIZA TAPAS AND WINE BAR
12 GRAND CONCOURSE	43 PIZZA SOLA	69 MALLORCA
19 THE ZENITH	47 NAKAMA JAPANESE STEAK HOUSE	71 THE PRETZEL SHOP
22 HOFBRÄUHAUS	49 CAMBOD-ICAN KITCHEN	72 DOUBLE WIDE GRILL
		74 DISH

◎ NIGHTLIFE

8 BAR ROOM PITTSBURGH	33 CLUB CAFÉ	53 VILLA SOUTHSIDE
8 SADDLE RIDGE	34 JACK ROSE BAR	55 SMOKIN' JOE'S
8 WHIM	37 THE SMILING MOOSE	56 TIKI LOUNGE
13 ZEN SOCIAL CLUB	40 DEE'S CAFÉ	57 TOWN TAVERN
15 REDBEARD'S	45 DIESEL	60 Z LOUNGE
18 OVER THE BAR BICYCLE CAFÉ	48 REX THEATRE	64 LAVA LOUNGE
28 CHARLIE MURDOCH'S DUELING PIANO BAR	50 S BAR	73 BAR 11
	52 PIPER'S PUB	

◎ ARTS AND LEISURE

7 TRIB TOTAL MEDIA AMPHITHEATRE	20 THE PITTSBURGH TOUR COMPANY DOUBLE DECKER TOURS	32 BREATHE YOGA STUDIO
14 JUST DUCKY TOURS		36 CITY THEATRE
14 PITTSBURGH HISTORY AND LANDMARKS FOUNDATION TOURS	26 OLIVER BATH HOUSE	58 SOUTH SIDE ATHLETIC CLUB
	27 PITTSBURGH PASSION	62 RUGGERS PUB
16 DASANI BLUE BIKES PROGRAM	29 SILVER EYE CENTER FOR PHOTOGRAPHY	63 ORMSBY POOL

◎ SHOPS

21 SOUTHSIDE WORKS	44 E HOUSE	70 JUPE BOUTIQUE
21 SHOP 412	46 CULTURE SHOP	75 A DIAMOND IN THE RUFF
31 CITY BOOKS	66 PERLORA	76 FIREBORN STUDIOS
41 THICK BIKES	67 PITTSBURGH JEANS COMPANY	
42 ONE UP SKATE		

◎ HOTELS

10 SHERATON HOTEL STATION SQUARE	24 MARRIOTT SPRINGHILL SUITES SOUTHSIDE WORKS	25 HOLIDAY INN EXPRESS HOTEL & SUITES
		61 MORNING GLORY INN

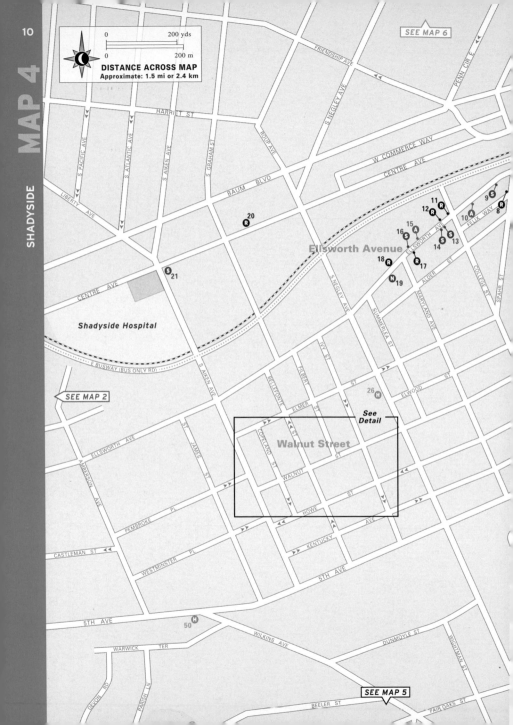

0   200 yds
0   200 m
DISTANCE ACROSS MAP
Approximate: 1.5 mi or 2.4 km

SEE MAP 6

FRIENDSHIP AVE

PENN CIR E

S. NEGLEY AVE

HARRIET ST

W. COMMERCE WAY

CENTRE   AVE

S. PACIFIC AVE

S. ATLANTIC AVE

S. AIKEN AVE

S. GRAHAM ST

BOUP AVE

BAUM   BLVD

LIBERTY   AVE

20 R

11 R
12 R
9 S
10 A
FELIX WAY
8 R

15 S
16 S
14
13 S

Ellsworth Avenue

ELLSWORTH AVE

18 R
17 R

S. NEGLEY AVE

CENTRE   AVE

21 S

N 19

ALDER   ST

MARYLAND AVE

COLLEGE ST

SPAHR ST

Shadyside Hospital

SUMMERLEA ST

IVY   ST

E. BUSWAY (BUS ONLY RD)

S. AIKEN AVE

HILBERT   ST

ST

ELWOOD   ST

26 H

SEE MAP 2

BELLEFONTE   ST

ELMER   ST

See Detail

COPELAND ST

Walnut Street

ELLSWORTH AVE

JAMES   ST

WALNUT   ST

ST

AMBERSON AVE

HOWE   ST

AVE

PEMBROKE   PL

KENTUCKY   ST

CASTLEMAN ST

WESTMINSTER   PL

5TH   AVE

5TH   AVE

50 H

WILKINS   AVE

DUNMOYLE ST

WARWICK   TER

WIGHTMAN ST

UPTON RD

PARISH LN

BEELER ST

SEE MAP 5

FAIR OAKS ST

RESTAURANTS

3	BUFFALO BLUES	11	UMI	33	LA FERIA
4	OH YEAH! ICE CREAM & COFFEE CO.	12	SOBA	35	COFFEE TREE ROASTERS
5	CASBAH	17	CRAZY MOCHA	40	SUSHI TOO
6	TYPHOON	18	HARRIS GRILL	42	GIRASOLE
8	CAFE ZINHO	20	AVENUE B	43	JUICE BOX CAFE
		31	THAI PLACE CAFÉ	44	PITTSBURGH DELI COMPANY

NIGHTLIFE

| 19 | SPIN BARTINI & ULTRA LOUNGE | 39 | DOC'S PLACE | 45 | ALTO LOUNGE |

ARTS AND LEISURE

1	FITNESS FACTORY	22	MELLON PARK	24	PITTSBURGH CENTER FOR THE ARTS
10	MENDELSON GALLERY	23	MELLON PARK TENNIS CENTER	27	X SHADYSIDE
15	AMAZING YOGA				

SHOPS

2	SMILEY'S PET PAD	25	PITTSBURGH CENTER FOR THE ARTS	37	TOADFLAX
7	WEISS HOUSE	28	TOTS & TWEEDS	38	FOOTLOOSE
9	LITTLE BLACK DRESS	29	TOURNESOL	41	MAXALTO
13	EONS FASHION ANTIQUE	30	S.W. RANDALL TOYS & GIFTS	46	EB PEPPER
14	DESIGNER DAYS BOUTIQUE	32	BONDSTREET SHOES	47	CHOICES
16	HIP'TIQUE	34	PURSUITS	48	MODA
21	DEAN OF SHADYSIDE	36	KARDS UNLIMITED	49	MARJIE ALLON FINE STATIONARY

HOTELS

| 26 | THE INN AT 714 NEGLEY | 50 | SUNNYLEDGE BOUTIQUE HOTEL |

South Highland Avenue

Mellon Park

SHADYSIDE

Walnut Street

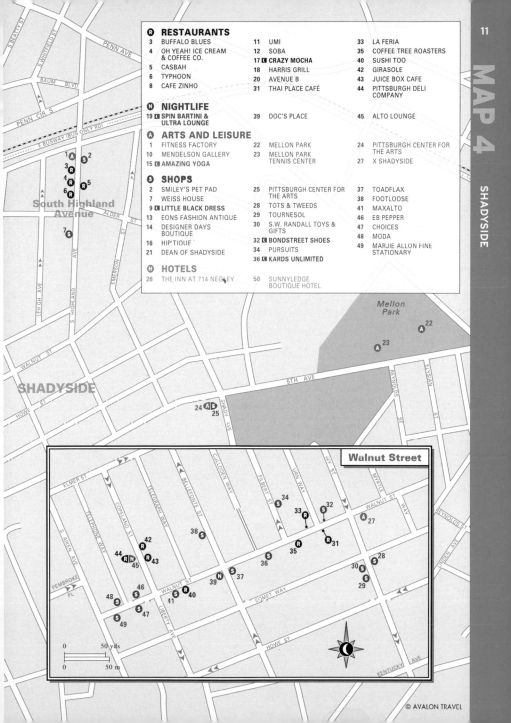

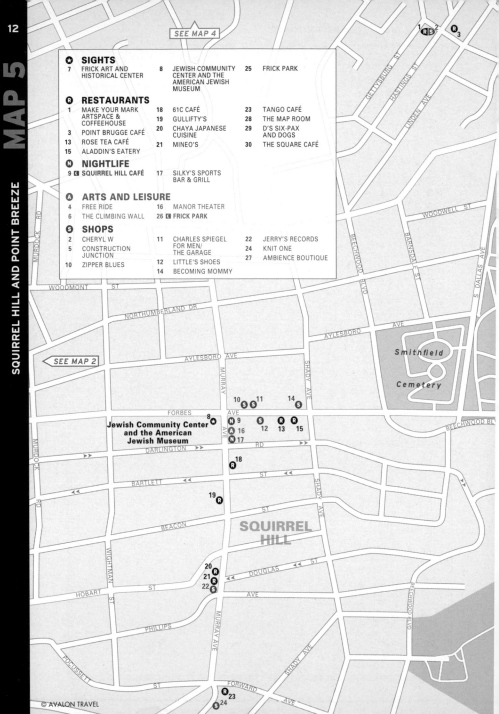

SEE MAP 4

✪ SIGHTS
7 FRICK ART AND HISTORICAL CENTER
8 JEWISH COMMUNITY CENTER AND THE AMERICAN JEWISH MUSEUM
25 FRICK PARK

ⓡ RESTAURANTS
1 MAKE YOUR MARK ARTSPACE & COFFEEHOUSE
3 POINT BRUGGE CAFÉ
13 ROSE TEA CAFÉ
15 ALADDIN'S EATERY
18 61C CAFÉ
19 GULLIFTY'S
20 CHAYA JAPANESE CUISINE
21 MINEO'S
23 TANGO CAFÉ
28 THE MAP ROOM
29 D'S SIX-PAX AND DOGS
30 THE SQUARE CAFÉ

ⓝ NIGHTLIFE
9 ⓒ SQUIRREL HILL CAFÉ
17 SILKY'S SPORTS BAR & GRILL

ⓐ ARTS AND LEISURE
4 FREE RIDE
6 THE CLIMBING WALL
16 MANOR THEATER
26 ⓒ FRICK PARK

ⓢ SHOPS
2 CHERYL W
5 CONSTRUCTION JUNCTION
10 ZIPPER BLUES
11 CHARLES SPIEGEL FOR MEN/ THE GARAGE
12 LITTLE'S SHOES
14 BECOMING MOMMY
22 JERRY'S RECORDS
24 KNIT ONE
27 AMBIENCE BOUTIQUE

SEE MAP 2

Smithfield

Cemetery

SQUIRREL HILL

Jewish Community Center and the American Jewish Museum

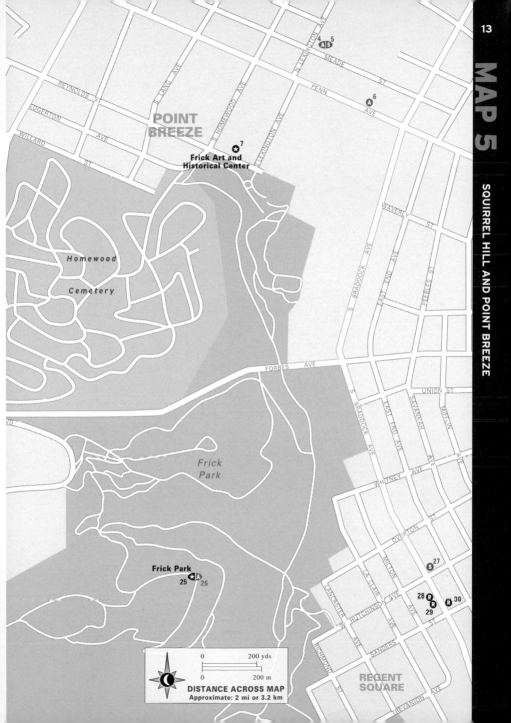

POINT BREEZE

Frick Art and Historical Center

Homewood

Cemetery

Frick Park

Frick Park

REGENT SQUARE

0   200 yds

0   200 m

DISTANCE ACROSS MAP
Approximate: 2 mi or 3.2 km

MAP 6

BLOOMFIELD, LAWRENCEVILLE, EAST LIBERTY, AND GARFIELD

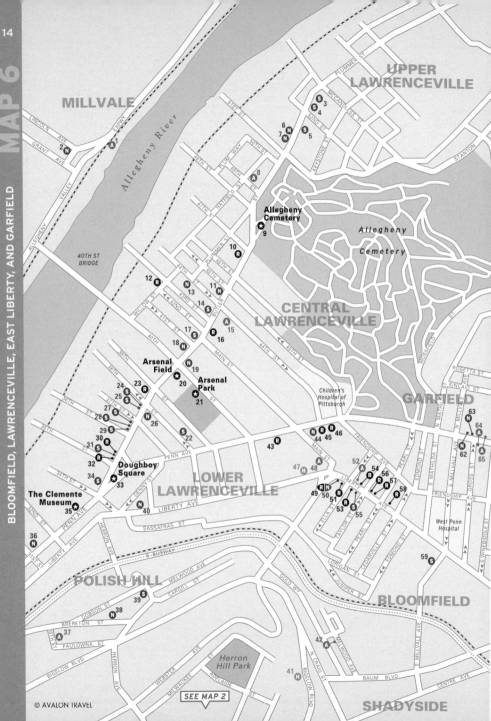

MILLVALE

UPPER LAWRENCEVILLE

CENTRAL LAWRENCEVILLE

GARFIELD

Allegheny River

Allegheny Cemetery

Allegheny Cemetery

40TH ST BRIDGE

Arsenal Field

Arsenal Park

Doughboy Square

The Clemente Museum

LOWER LAWRENCEVILLE

Children's Hospital of Pittsburgh

West Penn Hospital

POLISH HILL

BLOOMFIELD

Herron Hill Park

SEE MAP 2

SHADYSIDE

© AVALON TRAVEL

✪ SIGHTS

9	ALLEGHENY CEMETERY	20	ARSENAL FIELD	33	DOUGHBOY SQUARE	100	PITTSBURGH ZOO AND PPG AQUARIUM
		21	ARSENAL PARK	35	THE CLEMENTE MUSEUM		

® RESTAURANTS

10	LA GOURMANDINE	49	BLOOMFIELD BRIDGE TAVERN	68	PEOPLE'S INDIAN RESTAURANT	84	SPOON
12	RIVER MOON CAFÉ	51	DEL'S BAR & RISTORANTE DELPIZZO	69	THE QUIET STORM	85	DINETTE
16	ISTANBUL GRILLE			70	VOLUTO COFFEE	85	PLUM PAN-ASIAN KITCHEN
23 ☕	COCA CAFÉ	53	PIZZA ITALIA	72 ☕	SALT OF THE EARTH	89	VANILLA PASTRY STUDIO
30 ☕	TAMARI RESTAURANT AND LOUNGE	54 ☕	CRAZY MOCHA	77	TANA ETHIOPIAN CUISINE	90	PARIS 66 BISTRO
32	DOZEN BAKE SHOP	56	TESSARO'S	79	THE WAFFLE SHOP	97	E²
43	TRAM'S KITCHEN	57	THAI CUISINE	81	ROYAL CARIBBEAN	98	SMILING BANANA LEAF
45	J'EET	58	GRASSO ROBERTO	82	ABAY ETHIOPIAN CUISINE		
46	TASTE OF INDIA	66	SPAK BROTHERS PIZZA				

◎ NIGHTLIFE

2	MR. SMALL'S THEATRE	18	THUNDERBIRD CAFÉ	40	CHURCH BREW WORKS	63	GARFIELD ARTWORKS
6	REMEDY	19	BELVEDERE'S	44	BRILLOBOX	75	THE SHARP EDGE
7	BLUE MOON	26 ☕	ROUND CORNER CANTINA	50	BLOOMFIELD BRIDGE TAVERN	78	SHADOW LOUNGE
11	NEW AMSTERDAM	36	31ST STREET PUB	62	MODERNFORMATIONS GALLERY	80 ☕	AVA
13	CATTIVO	38 ☕	GOOSKI'S			88	KELLY'S BAR

◉ ARTS AND LEISURE

1	MR. SMALLS SKATEPARK	42	MELWOOD SCREENING ROOM	65	MOST WANTED FINE ART	91	CLUB ONE
8 ☕	ZOMBO GALLERY	48	THE SHOP	71	PITTSBURGH GLASS CENTER	92	URBAN ACTIVE FITNESS CLUB
15	ARSENAL LANES	52	BOX HEART	76	KELLY-STRAYHORN COMMUNITY PERFORMING ARTS CENTER	99	HIGHLAND PARK
37	WEST PENN SKATE PARK (POLISH HILL BOWL)	64	THE IRMA FREEMAN CENTER FOR IMAGINATION				

◎ SHOPS

3 ☕	BLOOM ORGANIC SKINCARE PARLOR	24 ☕	SUGAR BOUTIQUE	39	COPACETIC COMICS	86	THE GALLERY 4
4	FRESH HEIRLOOMS	25	DIVERTIDO	55	PAUL'S CDS	87	DAQUILA HAIR COLOR STUDIO
5	WHO NEW?	27	PAVEMENT	59	THE BIG IDEA INFOSHOP	93	BAKERY SQUARE
14	GALLERY ON 43RD STREET	28	PAGEBOY SALON & BOUTIQUE	60	BEST-MADE SHOES	95	GOLDEN BONE PET RESORT
17 ☕	WILD CARD	29 ☕	EQUITA	67	AWESOME BOOKS	96	THE DOG STOP
22	16:62 DESIGN ZONE	31	ASIAN INFLUENCES	73	BABYLAND		
		34	CLANKWORKS	83	MCN SALON		

⊞ HOTELS

41	RESIDENCE INN MARRIOTT	47 ☕	EDENHOUSE	74	FRIENDSHIP SUITES	94	MARRIOTT SPRINGHILL SUITES BAKERY SQUARE
		61	COURTYARD MARRIOTT				

✪ Pittsburgh Zoo and PPG Aquarium

Highland Park

HIGHLAND PARK

EAST LIBERTY

FRIENDSHIP

To ◎96 The Dog Stop

To ◎95 Golden Bone Pet Resort

Giant Eagle

UPMC Shadyside Hospital

SEE MAP 4

0   400 yds
0   400 m

DISTANCE ACROSS MAP
Approximate: 3.1 mi or 5 km

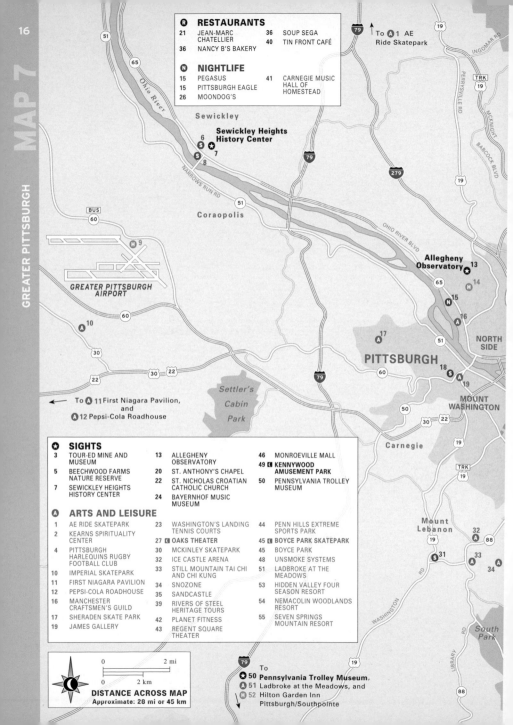

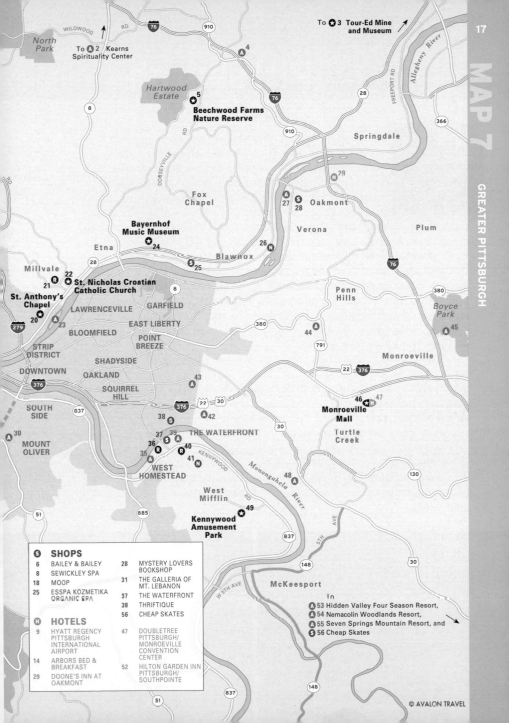

North Park

WILDWOOD RD

76

910

To 3 Tour-Ed Mine and Museum

To ⒶA 2 Kearns Spirituality Center

Ⓐ 4

8

Hartwood Estate

★ 5
Beechwood Farms Nature Reserve

76

28

910

366

FREEPORT RD

Allegheny River

Springdale

DORSEVILLE RD

Fox Chapel

Ⓗ 29

Ⓐ 27   Ⓢ 28   Oakmont

Bayernhof Music Museum
Ⓗ 24

Etna

28

Blawnox

26
Ⓝ

Ⓢ 25

Verona

Plum

76

Millvale

Ⓡ 22
21

St. Nicholas Croatian Catholic Church

8

St. Anthony's Chapel

LAWRENCEVILLE   GARFIELD

Penn Hills

380

Boyce Park

279
20   23

BLOOMFIELD   EAST LIBERTY

POINT BREEZE

STRIP DISTRICT

SHADYSIDE

DOWNTOWN   OAKLAND

376

SQUIRREL HILL

380

44   Ⓐ

791

Monroeville

22   376

43
Ⓐ

22   30
376

Ⓐ 42

46   47
Ⓗ

Monroeville Mall

SOUTH SIDE

837

38   Ⓢ

37   39
36   Ⓢ
Ⓡ
35   Ⓡ   40

THE WATERFRONT

30

Turtle Creek

Ⓐ 30

MOUNT OLIVER

41   Ⓝ

WEST HOMESTEAD

KENNYWOOD RD

Monongahela River

48
Ⓐ

130

West Mifflin

Ⓐ 45

51

885

★ 49
Kennywood Amusement Park

837

5TH AVE

30

148

51

McKeesport

W 5TH AVE

837

148

© AVALON TRAVEL

Discover Pittsburgh

Although the Steel City is still world-renowned for its industrial past, almost no vestiges of that era remain today. Instead, at the beginning of the 21st century, Pittsburgh is nothing less than a remarkable model of what might be called Rustbelt Renewal. While Pittsburgh was once called the Smoky City because of the pollution produced by its steel and iron mills, visitors today are often astonished to discover not only acres of green parkland and miles of biking and jogging trails, but also perfectly breathable air.

And yet, the renewed and revitalized Pittsburgh is about much more than just greener flora and healthier fauna. During your exploration of the city's distinct neighborhoods, you can expect to encounter contemporary art galleries, high-end eateries, and million-dollar sports stadiums. You'll experience all the same things you'd expect to in any mid-sized American metropolis.

Some of the sightseeing highlights include the Carnegie Museum of Natural History, famous for its Hall of Dinosaurs; The Andy Warhol Museum, a fascinating tribute to one of the city's most famous sons and the largest single-artist museum in the United States; and the city's historical funiculars, the Monongahela and the Duquesne Inclines, which continue to shuttle tourists and local commuters up and down Mount Washington.

Whether it's ancient history or postmodern culture you've come to explore, it's likely you'll find what you're looking for in today's Pittsburgh. This is a city that clearly doesn't care to let go of its blue-collar history, and continues to be one of America's most tenacious and unusual urban landscapes.

Planning Your Trip

▶ WHERE TO GO

Downtown

Also known as the Golden Triangle, Pittsburgh's Downtown is where you'll find the Cultural District, which offers Broadway-style entertainment and the occasional concert. Aside from the grandeur of Point State Park, however, Downtown is essentially utilitarian; this is where you'll find the bus and train stations, and probably your hotel.

Strip District

An industrial area filled with warehouses and loft buildings, the Strip District plays two separate but important roles in the life of the city. During the day, the area is visited largely for its produce dealers and ethnic restaurants, which line the parallel thoroughfares of Penn Avenue and Smallman Street. But once night falls, clubgoers fill the district's bars and dance clubs in full force. Saturday morning is the time to see the Strip at its best.

North Side

Just across the Allegheny River from Downtown, the North Side was originally an independent city known as Allegheny. The North Side is where you'll find the decidedly

The Andy Warhol Museum

upscale Mexican War Streets, as well as The Andy Warhol Museum and the world-class Mattress Factory museum. Sports fans will find the Pirates and Steelers battling it out on their respective fields here.

Oakland

Sometimes referred to as Pennsylvania's third-largest "downtown," Oakland is the city's

University of Pittsburgh in Oakland

Shepard Fairey wall poster on East Carson Street

main East End neighborhood and home to numerous institutions of higher learning, including Carnegie Mellon University and the University of Pittsburgh. The main branch of the Carnegie Library is here, as are the Carnegie Museums of Art and Natural History, behind which you'll find the urban playground of Schenley Park.

South Side

One of Pittsburgh's most eclectic and interesting areas, the South Side stretches along the Monongahela River from Station Square to SouthSide Works, a former steel mill turned shopping mall. East Carson Street, also known as the country's longest uninterrupted stretch of bars, runs the length of the district. Vintage clothing stores, art galleries, and ethnic eateries can also be found there.

Mount Washington

Sitting atop the city's South Side, Mount Washington exists in the mind of the average Pittsburgher for two reasons only: the breathtaking views along Grandview Avenue, which every visitor to the city should see, and the expensive eateries of Restaurant Row.

Near to the Monongahela Incline, which ferries its passengers from Station Square to Mount Washington, is the mini–commercial district of Shiloh Street.

Shadyside

Located just east of Oakland, Shadyside is one of the city's most prestigious and image-conscious neighborhoods. Walnut Street forms the area's commercial core; here you'll find both big-name and boutique shopping and a near-steady stream of pedestrian traffic. Running parallel to Walnut Street is Ellsworth Avenue, where most of Shadyside's better bars and restaurants can be found.

Squirrel Hill and Point Breeze

Home to one of the largest Jewish communities in the mid-Atlantic region, Squirrel Hill begins at the eastern end of Carnegie Mellon University and is sandwiched comfortably between Schenley Park and Frick Park. Its two major thoroughfares, Forbes Avenue and Murray Avenue, offer grocers, movie theaters, synagogues, and kosher eateries.

On the opposite side of Frick Park, Point Breeze and the small district of Regent Square

are Squirrel Hill's somewhat upscale neighbors to the east. Although largely residential, both areas have decent-sized commercial strips.

Bloomfield and Lawrenceville

Also known as Pittsburgh's Little Italy, the East End neighborhood of Bloomfield is a tightly knit residential community and a popular shopping district. Liberty Avenue, the neighborhood's heart and soul, is home to a charming medley of boutiques, cafés, grocery stores, and restaurants.

Lawrenceville, one of Pittsburgh's largest neighborhoods, stretches along the river from the Strip District to Morningside. The neighborhood is still largely working class, although a recent influx of artists and boutiques along the main drag of Butler Street has raised Lawrenceville's profile considerably.

Conflict Kitchen in East Liberty

East Liberty and Garfield

Formerly known only for their reputations as gang-inflicted danger zones, both East Liberty and Garfield have begun to gentrify over the past few years. Garfield is notable primarily for the art galleries and cafés that run the length of its Penn Avenue Arts Corridor, while East Liberty is home to a wide variety of popular bars, restaurants, and boutiques. East Liberty is also where you'll find Bakery Square and the EastSide retails complexes.

Greater Pittsburgh

The outlying suburbs and small towns of Greater Pittsburgh have much to offer the curious traveler, from the high-end retail district of Sewickley to the historic settlement of Old Economy Village. Other highlights include West Mifflin's Kennywood Amusement Park, the big-box shopping mecca of Monroeville, and the pioneering, DIY arts community being built in Braddock.

▶ WHEN TO GO

Choosing the perfect time to visit is really nothing more than a matter of personal inclination. When snow falls, the winter season here (late December–early April) is absolutely gorgeous, yet the months of January and February can be unbearably cold; even native Pittsburghers tend to hibernate during this time of the year.

Pittsburgh summers are often scorching hot and dripping with humidity, although this is also the season when the city comes alive with the most dynamism and excitement. What's more, a score of important festivals and events take place during the summer.

Fall is a particularly lovely time to visit Pittsburgh. The weather is pleasant, with days that are cool but not cold, and evenings that might best be described as light-jacket weather: sharp and brisk.

Explore Pittsburgh

▶ THE TWO-DAY BEST OF PITTSBURGH

the Duquesne Incline

John Heinz Pittsburgh Regional History Center. If it isn't a Saturday, treat yourself instead to a trip up Mount Washington on either the Duquesne Incline or the Monongahela Incline—and then to the best view of the city, from the lookout platforms along Grandview Avenue. If you take the Monongahela Incline back down to street level, you'll see Station Square just ahead—it's a perfect pit stop for coffee or lunch. Should you find yourself in the mood for fine dining, head to the historic Grand Concourse.

▶ Afterward, make your way down East Carson Street toward the South Side Flats for a bit of late-afternoon shopping.

Although a thorough exploration of Pittsburgh and its environs would require at least a week, the city is compact enough that its most important sights and activities can be experienced easily in two days. The following itinerary assumes a Saturday-morning arrival in Pittsburgh; with the exception of a visit to the Strip District, which is at its best on Saturday mornings, all of the following activities can easily be shuffled around at will.

Day 1

▶ Start your visit with an early-morning trip to the Strip District. Stop by Pamela's Diner for breakfast and then join the throngs of shoppers searching for kitschy souvenirs along Penn Avenue.

▶ Spend an hour or two at the Senator

▶ Head back to the heart of the South Side Flats and end your day with a nightcap. Dee's Café is one of Pittsburgh's best dive bars, but for a great selection of microbrews and a more clean-cut atmosphere, try Fat Heads, which also serves wonderful salads and sandwiches.

Day 2

▶ Locals will warn you not to miss DeLuca's Restaurant in the Strip District, which is without a doubt the city's most legendary breakfast spot. But if you're looking for a healthier alternative to the greasy spoon experience, try Pamela's Diner.

▶ Work off some of those carbs by taking a stroll through Downtown and into Point State Park. Use the pedestrian walkway

FUN AND CHEAP: PITTSBURGH ON A BUDGET

Operating strictly on a shoestring budget? You've come to exactly the right city. Budget living is practically a religion in some quarters of Pittsburgh, where a night on the town can be enjoyed for as little as $20, and a day exploring the urban jungle can be had for almost nothing at all.

SIGHTSEEING

For budget sightseeing, take a self-guided tour of the **Nationality Classrooms** inside Pitt's **Cathedral of Learning.** After exploring the nearby **Schenley Park,** stroll the length of the **Three Rivers Heritage Trail** on the North Shore, which has lately turned into something of an outdoor sculpture garden.

FOOD

Due to its dead-broke student population, Oakland is replete with restaurants serving half-priced food after 11 P.M. Try **Fuel and Fuddle** for American pub-grub, or **Mad Mex** for huge and toothsome burritos. **Sree's Indian Food** (in Squirrel Hill, Downtown, and on the CMU campus) serves up massive $4-5 plates of authentic Indian food.

SHOPPING

For shoestring-budget souvenir shopping, make the scene on **Penn Avenue** in the Strip District, where everything from fake Steelers T-shirts to Peruvian finger puppets are for sale.

THE ARTS

During the summer season, **free movies** are screened outdoors in seven different parks, including Schenley Park in Oakland and Grandview Park in Mount Washington. For movie listings and times, call **Cinema in the Park** (412/422-6426).

RECREATION

Kayak Pittsburgh offers a fantastic way to experience the city from a duck's-eye view; kayaks, canoes, and even hydrobikes can be rented by the hour. To tour Pittsburgh via bicycle, visit **Friends of the Riverfront** and sign up for the free **Dasani Blue Bikes Program.**

on the Fort Duquesne Bridge to cross over the Allegheny River.

► If you've got the energy for a long walk, follow the Three Rivers Heritage Trail. (The path ends near the 40th Street Bridge.) Descend the stairs at the opposite end of the Fort Duquesne Bridge, and you'll be at the North Shore. Head to the nearby Andy Warhol Museum, the largest single-artist museum in the United States. The museum also has a surprisingly good basement café, a great choice for lunch.

► Next, walk to the National Aviary in West Park, the only nonprofit bird zoo in the country. Before leaving the North Side, stop off at Rivers Casino to try your luck.

► Spend the rest of the afternoon exploring the Oakland neighborhood. Spend some time at the Carnegie Museums of Art and Natural History, and, if the sun

Eagle Owl at the National Aviary

is shining, visit Schenley Park and its Phipps Conservatory.

► For dinner, head back into Downtown. Take a cab if the weather is chilly, or if you're still on the North Side, go by foot across one of the Three Sisters Bridges. Your dining destination is Habitat, a contemporary Pan-Asian restaurant located inside Downtown's Fairmont Pittsburgh Hotel.

► After dinner, take in a show in the Cultural District. Pick up a free copy of *Pittsburgh City Paper* to see what's going on. If nothing grabs your interest or you'd prefer a less expensive and more intimate entertainment option, head back to the South Side via taxi and stop in at Club Café, which usually offers two pop or folk concerts nightly. (Ask your cabbie to take the 10th Street Bridge from Downtown, which can also be crossed on foot.)

BAR HOP LIKE A LOCAL

The Steel City doesn't call itself "a drinking town with a football problem" for no good reason: Most Pittsburghers like to drink. *A lot.* So if your aim is fitting in, you'll want to plan on regularly touring some of the city's finest taprooms and alehouses.

- Order a Mai Thai at the city's only Polynesian-themed bar, the **Tiki Lounge,** and then head down the street to its sister pub, the cavernous **Lava Lounge,** which seems to have been carved out of volcanic detritus.

- Head to Lawrenceville, where hipster outposts like **New Amsterdam, Brillobox,** and the **Round Corner Cantina** draw eclectic crowds on a nightly basis.

- The university district of Oakland is always good for a bit of late-night prowling. Wash down the big game with a microbrew at **Fuel and Fuddle,** or join the college kids for a mountain of French fries and a cheap six-pack at **The Original Hot Dog Shop.**

- Head to the **Sharp Edge** in Friendship for happy hour; it's known as one of the finest Belgian beer bars in the country. The pizza and pub grub is also a big draw.

- Take a trip to Deutschland without ever leaving the city limits: The South Side's **Hofbräuhaus** was modeled after an authentic Munich beer hall, while the North Side's **Penn Brewery** has authentic oompah music and some of the city's best beer, brewed right on the premises.

- **The Church Brew Works** in Lawrenceville is not only a top-notch brewpub serving phenomenal wood-fired pizzas – it's also located inside an actual church.

- Traveling on two wheels? Lock your bike to a metal rack outside the South Side's **Over the Bar Bicycle Café,** which acts as something of a clubhouse for the city's hardcore bicycle obsessives.

SIGHTS

Before beginning your exploration of the hilly and often-circuitous city of Pittsburgh, consider this: Even locals enjoy joking about how easy it is to get hopelessly lost on the town's twisting and turning roads. The war correspondent Ernie Pyle probably explained it best in a 1937 column that appeared in the *Pittsburgh Press:* "Pittsburgh is undoubtedly the cockeyedest city in the United States," he wrote. "Physically, it is absolutely irrational. It must have been laid out by a mountain goat."

There's a perfectly good reason for all this, of course: Pittsburgh's topography consists largely of steep hills, deep valleys, and three proud rivers—the Allegheny, the Monongahela, and the Ohio—all of which weave their way in and out of Pittsburgh's multihued quilt of neighborhoods, creating chaos and confusion for motorists and pedestrians alike. But spend a day or two exploring the nearly vertical neighborhood of the South Side Slopes, or strolling the historic bridges that span the Allegheny and Monongahela Rivers, or breathing in the natural beauty of Schenley and Frick Parks, and decide for yourself if all the confusion isn't actually worth it. While Pittsburgh's sights and scenery may at first appear to be little more than a jumbled-together collection of industrial-era ephemera, a closer inspection reveals something much more uncommon: one of America's most charming small cities that just happens to offer all the amenities of a major metropolitan town.

Which isn't to say that the Steel City's charms are intended to be any sort of a well-kept secret. On the contrary, since the early

SIGHTS

HIGHLIGHTS

LOOK FOR ◖◖ TO FIND RECOMMENDED SIGHTS.

◖◖ **Most Impressive Monument:** With its uniquely designed exterior and its impressively wide-ranging schedule of concerts, lectures, exhibits and more, Downtown's **August Wilson Center for African American Culture** is undoubtedly the city's most promising and inspirational new cultural endeavor (page 28).

◖◖ **Coolest Mini-Museum:** One of only three cartoon-art museums in the country, Downtown's **ToonSeum** is a fascinating tribute to the art of cartooning. Comic- and cartoon-themed workshops and educational programs take place here regularly (page 36).

◖◖ **Best History Lesson:** Most Pittsburghers agree that the **Senator John Heinz Pittsburgh Regional History Center** has done a fantastic job of documenting and presenting the history, culture, and attendant struggles of the Southwestern Pennsylvania region. And while much of the museum is serious business, there's more than enough here to keep kids amused (page 37).

◖◖ **Best Modern Art Museum:** Controversial, shocking, and endlessly entertaining, the North Side's **Andy Warhol Museum** is the largest official space dedicated to a single artist in the United States. The novelty-packed gift shop is practically a pop art museum in its own right (page 38).

◖◖ **Most Intimate Animal Experience:** Thanks to its recent multimillion-dollar renovation, the North Side's **National Aviary** is now even more exciting, educational, and interactive than ever. Kids can get up-close-and-personal with all manner of feathered and winged friends here (page 42).

◖◖ **Best Educational Museum:** Although Oakland's **Carnegie Museum of Natural History** is most famous for its Hall of Dinosaurs, it's also home to a staggering array of both permanent and changing exhibits that strive to educate visitors about the world and its many and varied inhabitants (page 47).

◖◖ **Best Gothic Landmark:** Certainly one of Pittsburgh's most beloved structures, the **Cathedral of Learning** is also the second-

COURTESY OF VISIT PITTSBURGH

The Lithuanian Room is one of the Cathedral of Learning's Nationality Classrooms.

tallest educational building in the world. Don't skip a visit to the Cathedral's multicultural classrooms, known as the Nationality Classrooms (page 47).

◖◖ **Best Way to Commune with Nature:** A truly peaceful and even meditative urban oasis, the Victorian greenhouse known as the **Phipps Conservatory and Botanical Gardens** is a 12,000-square-foot tropical forest wonderland, home to a mind-boggling array of plant life (page 48).

◖◖ **Best Park:** If you haven't been to **Schenley Park,** you haven't witnessed the full diversity of the student-filled district of Oakland. Free films are screened on the park's Flagstaff Hill throughout the summer, and walking and jogging paths are plentiful (page 49).

◖◖ **Best Mountainside Ride:** Pittsburgh's cable-powered **Duquesne and Monongahela Inclines** shuttle passengers back and forth between Mount Washington and the South Side. Definitely not a journey for the faint of heart (page 55).

◖◖ **Most Historic Amusement Park:** One of the oldest operating amusement parks in the United States – and now a designated National Historic Landmark – **Kennywood Amusement Park** features acres of thrill rides, an unmatched collection of wooden and steel coasters, and oodles of deep-fried junk food (page 63).

SIGHTS

1980s Pittsburgh has been consistently ranked as one of America's most livable towns. And much to the contentment of locals, who knew it all along, *USA Weekend* magazine recently graded the nighttime view from Mount Washington's Grandview Avenue as the second most beautiful sight in the country.

In fact, it might make sense to think of poking around Pittsburgh as something akin to an urban scavenger hunt. It's true that finding what you're looking for won't always be easy. Getting from here to there may be even tougher still. But once you arrive, your reward will almost always be singularly unique.

Downtown Map 1

ALLEGHENY COUNTY COURTHOUSE
436 Grant St., 412/350-4636
HOURS: Mon.-Fri. 8:30 A.M.-4:30 P.M.
COST: Free

Designed in 1883 by the much-imitated architect Henry Hobson Richardson, the Allegheny County Courthouse, which was the third courthouse to be built in the county, is one of Downtown Pittsburgh's most recognizable and historic sights. The granite structure is virtually impossible to miss—just keep your eyes peeled for the truly ancient-looking block building that sticks out like a sore thumb—albeit a very attractive and smartly designed thumb—among Grant Street's more modern skyscrapers.

One of the building's most interesting features is its arching stone bridge, which locals frequently refer to as the **Bridge of Sighs.** This bridge connects the courthouse to the adjoining jail, which is no longer in operation. Yet during its time, convicts were simply transferred to the jail by means of the bridge following their courthouse sentencing. It's also worth noting that some of the old jail's individual granite blocks weighed more than five tons each. Prison breaks, we can assume, were rare. (The new jail, should you care to see it, is also located Downtown, at 950 2nd Avenue, not far from the 1st Avenue "T" Station and the temporary Greyhound bus terminal.)

It's possible to enter the courthouse for a look-round, although you will be required to pass through a metal detector first. A model of the entire courthouse complex is on display beneath glass on the second floor; also take

note of the many rounded arches built into the courthouse's interior. Construction of the complex cost approximately $2.25 million; not a particularly small sum in the late nineteenth century.

Interestingly, the main building was designed with an interior courtyard at its center. Richardson considered this detail of his design to be particularly clever, as fresh air and light could then reach even the offices that weren't lucky enough to have street-facing windows. Today, the courthouse is a decent location for

Allegheny County Courthouse

© COURTESY OF VISITPITTSBURGH

a midday picnic; anyone is welcome to join the nine-to-fivers who gather around the outdoor fountain in the courtyard.

🄲 AUGUST WILSON CENTER FOR AFRICAN AMERICAN CULTURE

980 Liberty Ave., 412/258-2700, www.augustwilsoncenter.org

HOURS: Tues.-Sat. 11 A.M.–6 P.M.

COST: $5 adult, $3 senior and student, $2 child (ages 6-10), free for children ages 5 and under

For years, the August Wilson Center for African American Culture was, in actuality, a cultural center in name only. Since 2003, the group had been offering a wide-ranging schedule of educational and performance programs throughout the city—including dance, music, and spoken word—which celebrated the cultural advancements and achievements of all African Americans. But finally, after a number of financial false starts, the Center's architecturally stunning and LEED-certified building opened to the public in September 2009.

Located in the heart of the city's Cultural District, the Center's mission involves "preserving, presenting, interpreting, celebrating and shaping the art, culture and history of African Americans in Western Pennsylvania and people of African descent throughout the world."

To that end, the Center offers an impressively wide range of programming, events, and exhibitions. Live musical performances in the 486-seat theater range from jazz to hip-hop to experimental; lectures by African-American luminaries are regularly scheduled as well. The Center is also home to an impressive collection of ongoing and changing exhibits that document and celebrate the African American experience throughout Western Pennsylvania and beyond.

The 65,000-square-foot Center also sponsors a number of especially promising "cultivation" and family programs, during which members of the local African American community are encouraged to meet, mingle, and discuss the issues that most affect their populace today. Visit the Center's website to stay current on its regularly changing schedule of programs and events.

THE CULTURAL DISTRICT

Bordered by Fort Duquesne Blvd., 10th St., Liberty Ave., and Stanwix St.; www.pgharts.org

A 14-square-block area in the heart of the Golden Triangle, Pittsburgh's Cultural District encompasses a total of 47 restaurants, 88 retail establishments, and eight public parks. Yet none of those amenities have much to do with why tourists and locals alike flock here in droves on weekend afternoons and evenings. Instead, the expensively dressed crowds you'll spot clutching playbills in this compact region of Downtown come mostly to visit the area's four performing arts theaters. Each year, in fact, roughly 1,400 performances take place in the area—everything from chamber music and ballet performances to opera, drama, film screenings, and pop concerts.

Some of the district's most historically popular events are the concerts given by the Pittsburgh Symphony Orchestra at **Heinz Hall** (600 Penn Ave., 412/392-4900, www.pittsburghsymphony.org). The orchestra has long been noted by both stateside and international music critics as being one of the best orchestras in the country, and any visitor to Pittsburgh with the time and money would be wise to squeeze in a performance. In fact, merely sitting alone in an empty Heinz Hall could qualify as a cultural experience—the theater, which today has 2,261 seats, has a rather unique history.

The first structure to be built on the site was the St. Clair Hotel, which in 1880 changed its name to the Hotel Anderson. And although that hotel existed until 1927, during the end of the 19th century it was known for hosting mostly traveling theater companies, including Shakespearean actors.

The Anderson next became the Loews Penn Theater. One of the great American movie houses, the Penn Theater was known locally as the "Temple of the Cinema" and was considered the best and most ornate cinema between Chicago and New York City. But thanks in part to the invention of television, the theater was forced to close its doors in 1964. Slated to become a parking lot, the building was saved

PITTSBURGH: CITY OF FIRSTS

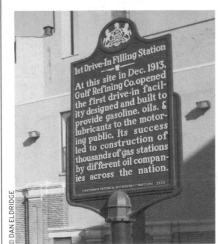

© DAN ELDRIDGE

The country's first drive-in gas station is now a parking lot behind the Spinning Plate Artist Lofts in Friendship.

When Pittsburgh bridge-builder George W. Ferris built his very first wheel – a Ferris wheel, for the 1893 Chicago World's Fair – he couldn't have possibly imagined that he'd given birth to a Steel City tradition of invention and innovation that continues today. A Latrobe-area pharmacist by the name of Dr. David Strickler, for instance, is responsible for creating the country's first banana split. That was way back in 1904. And Pittsburgh is also to blame for the now ubiquitous Big Mac – franchise owner Jim Delligatti debuted the sandwich at his Uniontown McDonald's store in 1967. Even the very first Internet emoticon, The Smiley, was created by a Carnegie Mellon University computer scientist in 1980. Here's a look at a few other Pittsburgh famous firsts:

FIRST WORLD SERIES – 1903

The Pirates were bested by the Boston Pilgrims in the eight-game series, four of which were played in a field not far from the current location of PNC Park.

FIRST MOTION PICTURE THEATER – 1905

The Nickelodeon on Smithfield Street, Downtown, was the world's first theater devoted exclusively to the moving motion picture.

FIRST GAS STATION – 1913

Gulf Refining Company built the country's first auto service station, which still sits in Friendship today. Look for it on Baum Boulevard.

FIRST COMMERCIAL RADIO STATION BROADCAST – 1920

After first installing a radio transmitter in his Wilkinsburg garage, a Westinghouse engineer sent a KDKA signal from a location in East Pittsburgh. The station still transmits today.

FIRST BINGO GAME – EARLY 1920S

After creating the game and then taking it to carnivals nationwide in 1924, Pittsburgher Hugh J. Ward penned an official book of bingo rules in 1933.

POLIO VACCINE – 1953

Dr. Jonas Salk and his staff developed the critical vaccine while at the University of Pittsburgh.

UNIVERSITY OF PITTSBURGH DIGITAL ARCHIVES

Dr. Jonas Salk developed the first polio vaccine while at the University of Pittsburgh.

only by the intervention of the Pittsburgh Symphony itself, which at the time was performing in too-small halls located in the university district of Oakland. Five years and $10 million later, construction was completed at the newly named Heinz Hall for the Performing Arts. An open-air Grand Plaza, complete with a small waterfall, was built adjacent to the hall in 1982. And then in 1995, the hall was given the gift of yet another facelift, during which it received a new orchestra shell, new wallpaper, paint and carpeting, and new acoustical risers, among other improvements. The total cost: $6.5 million.

Of course, the Cultural District doesn't consist of simply old and historical structures. Modern architecture buffs in particular will want to pay a visit to the recently built **O'Reilly Theater** (621 Penn Ave., 412/316-1600, www .pgharts.org/venues/oreilly.aspx), a $25 million state-of-the-art performance venue designed by the ultra famous Michael Graves, who has since given up on buildings and today focuses almost entirely on product design.

The O'Reilly sits on the former site of the Lyceum Theater, a vaudeville house that was deemed unusable following a 1936 flood. The new structure, where the Pittsburgh Public Theater as well as touring stage actors perform, is especially notable for its unique thrust stage, which is surrounded by the audience on three sides. The effect is such that shows here feel particularly intimate, sometimes uncomfortably so.

After observing the O'Reilly, followers of architect Michael Graves's work should examine the nearby **Agnes R. Katz Plaza,** which sits at the corner of Penn Avenue and 7th Street. Featuring possibly the most eclectic public sculptures in the Golden Triangle, the plaza is a striking example of Pittsburgh's ongoing bid to become a serious arts town. It's also rather tough to miss: Just look for the open square filled with a half dozen granite benches that resemble giant human eyes.

A collaboration with artist Louise Bourgeois (who created the eyeball seats), landscape architect Daniel Urban Kiley (who designed

bronze fountain and granite eyeball benches at Agnes R. Katz Plaza, designed by sculptor Louise Bourgeois

the plaza's backless granite benches), and the aforementioned Michael Graves, the square's focal point is a 25-foot bronze fountain, also designed by Bourgeois.

But even those who couldn't care less about fine art and design will find much to like about the plaza. Not only is it perfect for people-watching, it's also a convenient place to take a break or meet friends in between theater- or restaurant-going.

Also notable in the Cultural District is the **Byham Theater** (101 6th Ave., 412/456-6666, www.pgharts.org/venues/byham.aspx), a structure built in 1903 that was originally known as the Gayety Theater. Like the Lyceum, the Gayety was a vaudeville house—one of the country's most well known, in fact. Although somewhat faded, a masterfully designed tile mosaic featuring what must have been the Gayety's logo can still be seen on the floor of the Byham's entry. Sometime in the 1930s, the Gayety became known as the Fulton, which soon after transformed into a movie house. The building didn't become known as the Byham until the mid-1990s.

The Benedum Center for the Performing Arts (719 Liberty Ave., 412/456-2600, www .pgharts.org/venues/benedum.aspx), however, holds a distinction entirely unique from the district's other venues: After a $43 million restoration by I I. J. Heinz II (who restored the center to its former glory of 1928—it was then known as the Stanley Theater), the Benedum was added to the National Register of Historic Places.

Other venues located in the Cultural District include the **August Wilson Center for African American Culture,** a massive museum and cultural center celebrating the artistic contributions of African Americans nationwide; **SPACE** (812 Liberty Ave., 412/325-7723, www .spacepittsburgh.org), a contemporary arts gallery; the **ToonSeum** one of only three cartoon and comic art museums in the country, and the **Harris Theater** (809 Liberty Ave., 412/682-4111, www.pghfilmmakers.org), an independent cinema house where stage performances occasionally take place.

FORT PITT MUSEUM

101 Commonwealth Pl., Point State Park, 412/281-9285, www.heinzhistorycenter.org

HOURS: Daily 10 A.M.–5 P.M.

COST: $5 adult, $3 child (ages 4-17), $4 senior

It's certainly fitting that the two-story, 12,000-square-foot Fort Pitt Museum is located a stone's throw from the confluence of Pittsburgh's three rivers. As the site of the French and Indian War, the Point, as the confluence is known, is also where the history of Pittsburgh itself first began being written. The museum uses dioramas and historical artifacts to tell the story of the war, the outcome of which was much more important than most Americans realize. (If Fort Pitt had ultimately fallen to the French, guess what language this guide would probably be written in?) Next door is an authentic blockhouse; it's the city's oldest building.

MARKET SQUARE

Bordered by Stanwix, Wood, 4th, and 5th Sts.

Today, the relatively small area known as Market Square isn't much more than an

The Benedum Center for the Performing Arts has been added to the National Register of Historic Places.

open-air square-shaped block of restaurants and retail establishments with a small park at its center. What's more, the majority of the square's historic businesses have long since fled for the suburbs. And aside from the lunch hour, when business types descend upon Starbucks and Subway, the only returning visitors are a small gathering of homeless people and the occasional police officer on horseback.

The good news, however, is that the neglected and relatively unexciting Market Square that modern-day Pittsburghers have come to know is currently in the process of changing in a major way, thanks to a $5 million reconstruction process that officially kicked off in mid-August 2009. The crux of this seriously ambitious plan involves transforming Market Square into something of a European-style piazza, complete with a more pedestrian-friendly layout. Traffic, in other words, will no longer be a part of the decidedly relaxing and carefree Market Square plan, which is now open only to pedestrians, who are free to lounge at the Square's many outdoor tables and take advantage of the free Wi-Fi access. Visit http://marketsquarepgh.blogspot.com for news and updates.

Yet even while the construction is ongoing, the square is nevertheless worth a look, if only to imagine what it might have felt like to be a part of the action in the late 1700s, when John Campbell first designed the city's Downtown street plan.

The original market was a covered and enclosed building generally referred to as the Diamond. It soon became the commercial center of the city. The buying and selling of foodstuffs took place there, and the city's courthouse, its jail, and its first newspaper, *The Pittsburgh Gazette*, were also housed inside.

Business continued as usual until the early 1900s, when a fire permanently destroyed the Diamond. A new market house was soon built in its place; it encompassed 11,000 square feet and reached all the way to the road now known as Forbes Avenue. Yet five days after Christmas in 1960, the final enclosed market house was demolished, due largely to unbearable overhead expenses.

Thankfully, a small number of the market's older businesses have been restored and may be visited. If you have the time to visit only one, make it the 140-year-old **Original Oyster House** (20 Market Sq., 412/566-7925, www.originaloysterhousepittsburgh.com, Mon.–Sat. 10 A.M.–10 P.M.), a veritable Pittsburgh tradition offering enormous fish sandwiches and fried oysters. You might also try the much newer local legend known as **Primanti Brothers** (2 S. Market Pl., 412/261-1599, daily 10 A.M.–11 P.M., www.primantibros.com), where hearty meat sandwiches are served with french fries *inside*.

POINT STATE PARK

101 Commonwealth Pl., 412/471-0235 (park), 412/281-9284 (museum), www.fortpittmuseum.com, www.denr.state.pa.us/stateparks
HOURS: Wed.-Sun. 9 A.M.-5 P.M. (museum)
COST: $5 adult, $4 senior (museum)

It's easy enough to think of the triangle-shaped Point State Park as Pittsburgh's answer to Central Park: a grassy, seemingly secluded respite from the urban grind. But the 36-acre area now used solely as a recreational park—and also as an outdoor concert, theater, and visual arts gallery during Pittsburgh's annual Three Rivers Arts Festival—has a bloody history of some national significance.

Originally known as Fort Pitt, this was the site of the French and Indian War, which was won by General John Forbes (and an army of 6,000) for the British Empire in 1758. The **Fort Pitt Museum** and its accompanying **Fort Pitt Blockhouse** (Tues.–Sat. 9:30 A.M.–4 P.M., Sun. noon–4 P.M.), both located inside the park, tell the story of this crucial epoch in American history.

No interest in battlefield lore, however, is necessary to appreciate Point State Park's pivotal location at the axis of the city's three rivers: Not only do the Allegheny, the Monongahela, and the Ohio converge where the park begins, but a hidden "fourth river"—properly known as the Wisconsin Glacial Flow—streams lazily underneath them all. In fact, visitors who make their way to the westernmost tip of the park

SIGHTS

COURTESY OF ROB MATHENY

the Point State Park fountain

when its **fountain** is in operation will be able to view the fourth river themselves: That's it, shooting into a 30-foot-tall plume above the fountain's 200-foot-diameter concave bowl, in which children can often be seen frolicking. During the spring, summer, and fall, the fountain, which was dedicated in 1974, is in operation 7:30 A.M.–10 P.M., weather permitting.

The Point is also a place where Pittsburgh comes to play, especially during the summer months. Aside from the Three Rivers Arts Festival, the Three Rivers Regatta and the Fourth of July Fireworks take place here. During your exploration of the park, look out for the 23 monuments and commemorative markers detailing spots of historic importance within the park.

For much of 2007 and 2008, the park was closed and off-limits to visitors while it underwent an extensive multimillion-dollar renovation. And although only the first stage of the renovation was complete as of this writing, the park—which is now greener and more gorgeous than ever—has been reopened. New amenities

include bike racks, better lighting, and new park benches. Upcoming improvements are said to include Wi-Fi access, better seating around the fountain, much-needed repairs to the fountain's piping system, and the creation of new food-and-drinks kiosks throughout the park. The park's final renovations are scheduled to be completed by 2012.

PPG PLACE
200 Three PPG Place, 412/434-1900 (events), 412/394-3641 (ice skating rink), www.ppgplace.com
Completed in 1984 and designed by the legendarily influential architect Philip Johnson, PPG Place is easily the most noticeable and modern complex (some would say postmodern) located within the confines of the Golden Triangle. Wander toward Downtown's Market Square to separately view the six structures of PPG Place, or simply look skyward as you approach: PPG's massive tower, covered in a reflective glass skin, rises skyward. At its top are a series of jagged, "Glassy Gothic" spires with triangular and pointed tips. The remaining

SIGHTS

COURTESY OF VISITPITTSBURGH

PPG Place

five buildings, while of a much smaller stature, are also covered in a glass skin and sport gothic spires; in total, there are 231 spires in the complex.

PPG Place is an unusual and a somewhat bizarre series of edifices, to be sure, especially when considered with the immediate area's other corporate buildings, the majority of which are architecturally plain (except, of course, the few remaining historic structures, such as Henry Hobson Richardson's Allegheny County Courthouse).

So how exactly *did* the design for PPG Place come about? As critic Peter Blake put forth in the February 1984 issue of *Progressive Architecture:*

> If you are an architect asked to design a complex that will house the Corporate Headquarters of the Pittsburgh Plate Glass Company (plus other tenants), you will, obviously, design a glass building. The question is – what sort of glass building? And what sort of image will you try to project?

Blake goes on to suggest that Johnson might have designed something resembling one of Mies van der Rohe's sketches for skyscrapers in glass. But instead, Johnson chose to essentially create a miniature Rockefeller Center, complete with arcaded sidewalks that join all six buildings. Yet the complex also includes a magnificent, glass-enclosed Winter Garden, clearly a nod to the 17th-century gardens of Italy and France. And perhaps most exciting (and most interactive) for tourists are the 60- and 90-degree angles of glass that cover the facades of each face: Because of the way the plates of glass reflect upon each other, and upon the gritty scene of urban Pittsburgh surrounding them, the images appearing in the structure's reflections make for incredible photographs. Should you grow tired after exploring the structure, simply drop into any of the adjoining cafés, or descend to the ground floor of the complex where a food court can be found.

An interesting bit of trivia is that PPG Place almost became the mansion of the fictional vigilante Bruce Wayne, a.k.a. in the 1989 film

Batman, until the production company in charge decided not to shoot in the city.

SMITHFIELD STREET BRIDGE

www.pghbridges.com

COST: Free

Anyone walking from Downtown Pittsburgh to Station Square, which sits on the opposite side of the Monongahela River, does so by strolling along one of the two footpaths of the Smithfield Street Bridge, a span often referred to locally as the "Kissing Fish Bridge" (view the bridge from afar and you'll understand the reference). Yet even if the idea of a walk across the bridge doesn't necessarily appeal, anyone interested in viewing a particularly striking Pittsburgh city skyline should nonetheless give it a shot. As you cross, take the time to pause periodically along the way and observe the view in front of you, behind you, and even beneath you; assuming your timing is right, a tugboat or even a coal barge might pass.

Constructed between the years 1881 and 1883, the Smithfield Street Bridge is actually the third such structure to exist on the site. The first to be built here, in 1818, was the Monongahela Bridge, which was also the very first river crossing in Pittsburgh. Its construction put the city back only $102,000, although it was rendered unusable during the Great Fire of 1845.

The second bridge constructed on the site was designed by John Roebling, who also created both the Brooklyn Bridge and the span that was replaced by Pittsburgh's Roberto Clemente Bridge. Increasing loads of heavy traffic soon led to this second bridge's closure and then to the construction of the bridge we see today, which has been designated a Historic Landmark by the Department of the Interior, the American Society of Civil Engineers, and the Pittsburgh History and Landmarks Foundation.

Designed by Gustav Lindenthal—who was also responsible for creation of Hell Gate Bridge, which connects Astoria, Queens, to Randalls Island in New York City—the Smithfield Street Bridge is a truss-style span

Smithfield Street Bridge is known locally as the "Kissing Fish Bridge."

over which streetcars once passed. But in order to create room for more traffic flow, that practice ended in the summer of 1985, and the streetcars were moved to the nearby Panhandle Bridge, which you'll cross today should you ride the "T" from any of Downtown's four streetcar stops to Station Square.

As you cross beneath the portals of the Smithfield Street Bridge on foot, pay close attention to the detailed lamps, as well as to small, intricate moldings representing the city's legendary industrial prowess.

THE THREE SISTERS
www.pghbridges.com
COST: Free

Although nearly all of Pittsburgh's Downtown spans are visually striking and historically significant, probably no trio of bridges means more to the city than those known collectively as the Three Sisters. And because all are identically designed, it's quite likely that these bridges are the first you'll notice when exploring the Golden Triangle. The Three Sisters, in fact, all of them painted a rather striking shade of yellow known as Aztec gold, are the only identical trio of side-by-side bridges in the world. They were also the very first self-anchored suspension spans built in the United States.

Today known as the **Roberto Clemente Bridge** (formerly the 6th Street Bridge, built in 1928), **The Andy Warhol Bridge** (formerly the 7th Street Bridge, built in 1926), and **Rachel Carson Bridge** (formerly the 9th Street Bridge, built in 1927), all three bridges cross the Allegheny River to reach the North Side.

Renamed on March 18, 2005 was the Andy Warhol Bridge. It earned its new name as part of a 10th anniversary celebration for the Andy Warhol Museum, which sits just steps from the north end of the bridge. The celebration for its renaming was, appropriately enough, probably the most Dionysian of the three. A number of the city's most left-of-center artists were in attendance, and students from a nearby performing arts high school gave a brief drama and dance show.

Perhaps even more interesting, though, is

the Warhol Bridge's immediate neighbor to the west, the Roberto Clemente Bridge. The Roberto Clemente gained its new name on April 8, 1999, the day after a groundbreaking ceremony took place on the bridge's northern end for PNC Park, which became the new home of the Pittsburgh baseball club two years later (Clemente was a legendary Pirate who played from 1955 until his death in a plane crash in 1972). The bridge's proudest moment probably came in 1928, the year it was erected. This was when the American Institute of Steel Construction named it the year's most beautiful steel bridge. And while each of the Three Sisters replaced former bridges, the Roberto Clemente replaced a notable span built by the once-famous John Roebling, probably best known for creating New York City's Brooklyn Bridge.

The Rachel Carson Bridge was renamed on April 22, 2006, which was also Earth Day. It was quite an appropriate time for the renaming, as Carson was a pioneering environmentalist who authored the classic tome *Silent Spring* and remains known as one of Southwestern Pennsylvania's most influential natives. (Born in 1907, Carson was raised in Springdale at a site now known as the Rachel Carson Homestead, which is open to visitors.)

The renaming of the bridge happened largely due to the efforts of Esther Barazzone, the president of Chatham College, where Carson matriculated in the 1920s, when Chatham was still known as the Pennsylvania College for Women. Barazzone initially had her sights set on a statue of Carson, which would have been the city's first statue of a woman, but those plans were dashed due to Pittsburgh's financial problems.

◖ TOONSEUM
945 Liberty Ave., 412/232-0199, www.toonseum.org
HOURS: Wed., Thurs., and Sun. 10 A.M.–3 P.M.; Fri.–Sat. 10 A.M.–5 P.M.
COST: $4

As one of only three museums in the country dedicated exclusively to cartoon art (the other two are located in Manhattan and San

© DAN ELDRIDGE

ToonSeum

Francisco), the ToonSeum is a fairly small gallery that nevertheless manages to pack in an incredible amount of original comic and cartoon art. It was formerly located in a small corner of the Children's Museum of Pittsburgh on the North Side, but the ToonSeum now resides in the city's downtown Cultural District, where its smartly-curated exhibits change every two months. And because the museum's very mission involves promoting a deeper understanding of cartoon artists and their work, a wide range of original programming and hands-on educational workshops happen here on a regular basis. The gift shop is also worth a visit for its wonderful selection of comics, graphic novels, and cartoon-related ephemera.

Strip District Map 1

◖ SENATOR JOHN HEINZ PITTSBURGH REGIONAL HISTORY CENTER

1212 Smallman St., 412/454-6000,
www.heinzhistorycenter.org
HOURS: Daily 10 A.M.–5 P.M.
COST: $10 adult, $5 student, $5 child (ages 4-17), free for children ages 5 and under, $9 senior

Certainly one of the city's most educational and culturally viable additions to the museum scene, the seven-story Pittsburgh Regional History Center acts as a nearly exhaustive record of Western Pennsylvania life and culture spanning more than 250 years. And because so many exhibitions are hands-on and creatively curated, the museum—which is housed inside the former headquarters and warehouse of the Chautauqua Lake Ice Company—is also enjoyable for children. Young visitors will find much to capture their attention in the **Western Pennsylvania Sports Museum,** which celebrates the achievements of area athletes and allows youngsters to play along. And on the museum's third floor is Discovery Place, a hands-on historical exhibit specifically designed for younger guests. Kids also love sitting in the driver's seat of the restored 1949 streetcar trolley, which is located in the ground floor's Great Hall, which is also where you'll find Kidsburgh, a small play area built above Reymer's Old-Fashioned Deli. And yet the History Center might best be described as a can't-miss attraction for folks of any age, assuming they carry even a passing interest in the development of the region and its people.

Although the museum opened its doors to the public in 1996, it didn't come into its full glory until late 2004, when a new wing affiliated with the Smithsonian Institution was completed. That process also established the center as the largest history museum in the state. Two recent additions to the Smithsonian wing are the aforementioned Sports Museum and the superbly curated Special Collections Gallery, which takes an especially close look at the immigrant communities that flocked to Pittsburgh at the turn of the 20th century. Here you'll find artifacts used by the immigrant laborers, such as cigar-rolling supplies and tools that were used in the area's mines. There's also a life-size recreation of the inside of a typical laborer's home. Some of the more recent artifacts include the headgear and uniforms used by the steel miners of the 1970s; you'll also see an actual steel miner's locker, decorated in now-faded Pittsburgh Steelers stickers.

ST. PATRICK'S CHURCH
57 21st St., 412/471-4767
HOURS: Daily 8 A.M.-3:30 P.M.
COST: Free

Known to area residents as "Old St. Patrick's," this was Pittsburgh's very first Catholic parish. And while the church building itself wasn't constructed until 1936, the parish was founded way back in 1808 by a group of Irish immigrants. This most likely explains the structure's stone tower, built to resemble the towers of Irish monasteries in medieval times.

Today, St. Patrick's is probably best remembered by older generations of Pittsburghers because of Father Cox, an astonishingly altruistic man who acted as the church's priest throughout the Great Depression. Among other good deeds, Cox helped the city's homeless and unemployed population construct a ragged but livable Shantytown along stretches of Liberty Avenue.

Old St. Patrick's also has something of a national reputation; it's one of the very few churches in the world to own a replica of the famous **Holy Stairs,** which represent the number of steps Jesus climbed on the day Pontius Pilate condemned him to death. Visitors may climb the steps during normal church hours, except during the noon hour on Mondays and Thursdays, when Mass is held. Do keep in mind, however, that ascending the steps must be done on one's knees. (Walking *down* the steps is allowed.) The set of steps believed by many to be the authentic *Scala Pilati* (Pilate's Stairway), which is also known as the *Scala Sancti* (Holy Stairway), is located in a papal sanctuary next to the Basilica of St. John Lateran in Rome.

North Side   Map 1

€ THE ANDY WARHOL MUSEUM
117 Sandusky St., 412/237-8300, www.warhol.org
HOURS: Tues.-Thurs. and Sat.-Sun. 10 A.M.-5 P.M.,
Fri. 10 A.M.-10 P.M., closed Mon.
COST: $15 adult, $8 senior and student, $5 child 3-18

As the country's largest museum dedicated to a single artist, The Andy Warhol Museum is a particularly unique feather in Pittsburgh's cap. To explore the building properly, start on the top floor; this is where temporary exhibitions are generally held. As you work your way slowly down, you'll encounter work both obscure (Jesus punching bags, oxidation paintings made of urine) and familiar (Campbell's

ANDY WARHOL'S PITTSBURGH

So you've come from far and wide to visit The Andy Warhol Museum, and now you'd like to discover some of the sites that transformed the shy Pittsburgh boy into a pop art superstar? The following suggestions, adapted from a tour formerly offered by the Greater Pittsburgh Convention and Visitor's Bureau, will take you to a number of locations essential to young Andy's growth as an artist. For even more tips and ideas, visit the incredibly useful and comprehensive **Andy Warhol Family Album** at www.warhola.com.

Your first stop on the DIY Warhol Tour should absolutely be the **Warhola family home** in South Oakland, which still sits at 3252 Dawson Street. Don't expect much, just a typical rowhouse with a green and white striped awning and a collection of hedges. The Warholas were a family of especially modest means – Andy's father Andrei toiled as a construction worker during the Depression and was often without gainful employment.

An easy walk from the Warhola home is **Schenley High School**, at 4101 Bigelow Boulevard. Warhol was a student here, and this is also where some of his earlier artistic efforts first flourished.

Near the Jewish neighborhood of Squirrel Hill is Greenfield, where you'll find **St. John**

Chrysostom Byzantine Catholic Church. The church, at 506 Saline Street, is where the Warhola family worshipped regularly. Call 412/421-0243 for service schedules.

In between Oakland and Squirrel Hill is the campus of **Carnegie Mellon University,** which was known as Carnegie Tech when Andy Warhol attended as a student in the department of painting and design.

You'll need a car for this one: **St. John the Baptist Cemetery** is located in the South Hills neighborhood of Bethel Park, at the corner of Route 88 and Conner Road and not far from South Hills Village Mall. Warhol is buried here next to his parents. The tombstone, located on a sloping hillside, is very modest and is sometimes decorated with a Campbell's soup can or two.

In the somewhat rough-and-tumble neighborhood of McKees Rocks is the **Holy Ghost Byzantine Catholic Church,** where Warhol's funeral service took place. Feel the need to pay your own belated respects? The church is located at 1437 Superior Avenue.

Two of Andy Warhol's nephews, George and Marty Warhola, who both continue to live in Pittsburgh, are currently operating competing scrap metal businesses within three miles of each other on the North Side. Marty runs **Paul Warhola Scrap Metals** at 825 Pennsylvania Avenue, and George owns **A. J. Warhola Recycling Inc.,** located at 203 Chesboro Street.

On March 18, 2005, with much fanfare, the 7th Street Bridge was renamed the **Andy Warhol Bridge.** Start on the Downtown end and walk across for a beautiful view of the city and the Allegheny River. Once you reach the North Side you'll be within spitting distance of **The Andy Warhol Museum** (117 Sandusky St., 412/237-8300, www.warhol.org) itself.

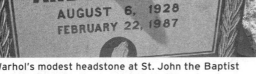

Warhol's modest headstone at St. John the Baptist Cemetery is sometimes decorated with cans of soup.

COURTESY OF ROB MATHENY

bus stop advertisement for The Andy Warhol Museum

soup cans, Brillo boxes). Definitely don't miss the Silver Cloud Room, where aluminum balloons are kept afloat by fans. A theater that regularly screens films by and about Warhol and his entourage is on the ground level; in the basement sits a café and the city's only vintage photo booth. An archival collection housing thousands of pieces of Warhol's personal ephemera is also on-site.

CALVARY UNITED METHODIST CHURCH

971 Beech Ave., 412/231-2007, www.calvarypgh.com

HOURS: Group tours given by appointment only

COST: Free

Built in 1890 by residents of the North Side's so-called Millionaires Row, which can still be visited today in the **Allegheny West Historic District** (www.city.pittsburgh.pa.us/wt/html/allegheny_west.html), Calvary United Methodist Church is probably best known

for its stained-glass windows. Large and wonderfully gorgeous, the triple-lancet, Tiffany-produced windows are still considered the finest and most elaborately detailed examples of religious stained glass ever created by the company. Calvary's exterior is also notable: Many claim its set of gargoyles to be among the city's best.

Also interesting is the architecture of the Gothic-styled church, which was constructed in the shape of a cross. The famous industrialist Charles Scaife, among scores of wealthy Pittsburgh merchants, was a member of the church's building committee. The uniquely curved pews, in fact, were constructed by the Joseph Horne Company, which sold dry goods in the city for decades.

Wrote Franklin Toker about Calvary United in *Pittsburgh: An Urban Portrait:* "Everything about the church inside and out is rich, textured, and above all, comfortable. To enter it is to intrude on a sumptuous private drawing room."

The **Allegheny Historic Preservation Society** is currently working to preserve the sections of this national landmark that have fallen into disrepair. To make a contribution, contact the AHPS at 412/323-1070.

CARNEGIE SCIENCE CENTER AND HIGHMARK SPORTSWORKS

1 Allegheny Ave., 412/237-3400, www.carnegiesciencecenter.org

HOURS: Sun.-Fri. 10 A.M.-5 P.M., Sat. 10 A.M.-7 P.M.

COST: $17.95 adult, $9.95 child and senior (including Science Center exhibits, Highmark SportsWorks, planetarium shows, and USS *Requin;* Omnimax films and laser shows are extra)

Filled with kid-friendly and hands-on exhibits, the Carnegie Science Center approaches an often-tedious subject with a rather honorable mission: "To [inspire] learning and curiosity by connecting science and technology with everyday life." In other words, gaining an understanding of the world in which we live can be a blast here, where permanent displays include the Kitchen Theater, which looks at science through the art of cooking, and SeaScape, a

2,000-square-foot aquarium. Visitors also flock to the Science Center for its four-story **Omnimax Theater,** as well as for its **Buhl Planetarium & Observatory,** regarded as one of the world's most technologically sophisticated. (On Friday and Saturday nights, the planetarium plays host to a series of laser shows accompanied by classic rock soundtracks.) And docked in the Allegheny River just behind the Science Center is the World War II–era USS *Requin,* a Navy submarine that can be boarded and explored.

The Center's newest attraction is the phenomenal Highmark SportsWorks facility, a wonderfully interactive experience where kids young and old are encouraged to learn about the mysterious workings of the body by engaging in physical activity. There are nearly 30 different interactive experiences here where visitors, for instance, can race a virtual Olympic sprinter, climb a 25-foot rock wall, or attempt to pitch a fastball. SportsWorks, in fact, is the very best sort of museum: It's practically a guaranteed good time.

CHILDREN'S MUSEUM OF PITTSBURGH
10 Children's Way, Allegheny Square, 412/322-5050, www.pittsburghkids.org
HOURS: Mon.-Sat. 10 A.M.–5 P.M., Sun. noon–5 P.M.
COST: $11 adult, $10 child and senior

After a recent expansion project transformed the Children's Museum of Pittsburgh from a relatively insignificant structure into something of a youth-oriented educational town square, Pittsburgh now has bragging rights to one of the most pioneering and novel museums for kids in the country. Even better is the building's environmentally friendly focus: Designed and constructed with sustainable materials, the museum is soon to become an officially LEED-certified "green building." Now four times as large as the previous museum, with part of the building located in a disused U.S. Post Office and part in the former Buhl Planetarium, there are nine permanent exhibits in total, including a replica of the television world seen on PBS's *Mister Rogers' Neighborhood* and a room known as the

Nursery, which is a uniquely creative space for infants, toddlers, and their parents.

For the remainder of the museum's intended demographic, there is an excellent collection of interactive exhibits built around a philosophy quite similar to that of the Carnegie Science Museum: The house's official mantra is "Play with Real Stuff," and it means that by playing and experimenting, as opposed to simply looking and listening, kids will be more excited to learn about the world that surrounds them. For instance, the museum includes an art studio offering printmaking, papermaking, and painting. There's a garage where machinery and engines can be tinkered with. And definitely don't miss the Attic, with its oddly tilted Gravity Room.

HOUSE POEM
408 Sampsonia Way
COST: Free

This tiny wooden rowhome is owned by the Pittsburgh chapter of the international City of Asylum organization, which provides sanctuary

The exterior of House Poem is decorated with a poem in Chinese by poet Huang Xiang.

to writers who have been persecuted in their own countries. The Chinese poet Huang Xiang was this house's first writer-in-residence, and he's also the person responsible for the striking Chinese characters that cover the home's façade, literally from the curb to the roof.

Down the road, at **324 Sampsonia Way,** is yet another unusually painted house that came about because of the City of Asylum project. At the time of this writing, 324 Sampsonia was the refuge of the Burmese writer Khet Mar and her husband, the painter Than Htay Muang, who plans to eventually cover the entire surface of their home with one giant, wrap-around mural featuring Pittsburgh cityscapes and traditional Burmese images.

MATTRESS FACTORY

500 Sampsonia Way, 412/231-3169, www.mattress.org

HOURS: Tues.-Sat. 10 A.M.–5 P.M., Sun. 1–5 P.M.

COST: $10 adult, $7 student, $8 senior

Not only is the Mattress Factory an internationally recognized organization that focuses singularly on installation art, it also hosts a truly unique residency program. Over the

Repetitive Vision, an installation by Yayoi Kusama at the Mattress Factory

past three decades, more than 250 artists have lived at the museum while creating new work. And while any given year sees a regular rotation of such new (and temporary) installations, the museum owns many permanent pieces as well. Some of the most stunning are James Turrell's odd and unsettling works of neon and light. Don't miss *Pleiades,* an entirely dark room where a presence of light may or may not appear. Another can't-miss is Yayoi Kusama's *Infinity Dots Mirrored Room;* entering it may just change your perspective on reality itself.

Admission is free for children under 6 and CMU students. University of Pittsburgh students can get in free during the fall and spring semesters. Every Thursday the museum offers half off the admission price (with the exception of group tours).

NATIONAL AVIARY

Allegheny Commons West Park, 412/323-7235, www.aviary.org

HOURS: Mon.-Sat. 10 A.M.–5 P.M., Sun. noon–5 P.M.

COST: $12 adult, $9.50 child 2-12, $11 senior

As home to more than 600 exotic birds of more than 200 species—many of them endangered—it's no wonder the National Aviary is known as one of the most important bird zoos in the country. Along with its extensive and many-hued flock, however, much of the Aviary's deserved popularity is derived from the glass building's interior design: Visitors can choose to stroll through the two open rooms where birds fly freely among them, or they can venture into a more traditional viewing locale where birds and humans don't mix. (In these areas, a thin mesh-wire sheet is used to cage the creatures.) Yet completely unlike the traditional zoo environment, it is possible here to literally get face-to-beak with a flamingo or a parrot. And while some visitors may find this setup surprising, or even frightening, young children often seem to mix quite naturally with the animals. What could possibly be a more exciting way to educate a preschooler or elementary school–age child about the wonders of the natural world?

Some of the many birds you may see here include the bald eagle, the gray-winged

an archive of more than 100,000 negatives and prints. Beginning with the very earliest days of photography, the collection spans not only images, of which roughly 3,000 are always on display, but also cameras and other photographic accessories. The era of the earliest Daguerreotype (roughly 1839) is documented, as is every important photographic era including the digital cameras of the 21st century. The relatively small museum has literally hundreds of historical photographs on display, and at the on-site gift shop, visitors can purchase reproductions—from 8 by 10 to mural-sized—of any of the museum's images. Lectures and tours are occasionally given by volunteers; call for upcoming schedules.

© DAVID FULMER

parrot at the National Aviary

trumpeter, the king vulture, the military macaw, the toco toucan, the African penguin, the speckled mousebird, and the white-crested laughing thrush. Feedings and various demonstrations take place throughout the day; especially curious visitors may even inspect specific menu items prior to mealtime.

The Aviary is currently in the midst of a massive, $18.5 million renovation and expansion, with new projects and exhibitions being unveiled at a surprisingly rapid clip, so be sure to check the website if you're planning a visit. Don't miss the new FliteZone Theater, for instance, where free-flight bird demonstrations will take place. A new café with both indoor and outdoor seating is also in the works.

PHOTO ANTIQUITIES MUSEUM
531 E. Ohio St., 412/231-7881, www.photoantiquities.org
HOURS: Mon., Wed.–Sat. 10 A.M.–4 P.M.
COST: $8 adult, $3 child, $6.50 senior and student
A 2,500-square-foot museum dedicated to the preservation of historical photography, the Photo Antiquities Museum is decorated with a quaint Victorian interior and boasts

RANDYLAND
1507 Arch St., www.visualvitamin.com
COST: Free
Although he claims not to be an artist, Pittsburgh native Randy Gilson has nevertheless spent more than 20 years transforming his three-story North Side home into what is commonly referred to as the most colorful building in the city. Indeed, stumbling across this improbably cheerful parcel of land, which sits smack-dab in the heart of the rough-and-tumble Central North Side, is certainly one of Pittsburgh's happiest surprises. The house itself is coated in shining-bright primary colors, and covered in murals, vintage signs, and random tchotchkes of all sorts, including a handmade 3-D map of the North Side. Over the years, Gilson has also painstakingly applied his creative touch to a roughly 30-block area around his home, a process that has resulted in more than 800 day-glo street gardens and 50 vegetable gardens cropping up around the Mexican War Streets neighborhood.

But what exactly *is* Randyland? For the time being, at least, it's nothing more than a seriously unusual corner of Pittsburgh; there's nothing to buy here, in other words, and nothing much to do. Gilson has flirted with the idea of opening a restaurant or coffee shop on his home's first floor.

The house at Randyland is covered in murals, vintage signs, and random tchotchkes.

COURTESY OF ROB MATHENY

RIVERS CASINO

777 Casino Dr., 412/231-7777, www.theriverscasino.com
HOURS: Daily 24 hours

Located right on the shores of the Ohio River, roughly halfway between Heinz Field and the West End Bridge, the always-open, steel-and-glass-encased Rivers Casino has been home to a certain degree of controversy for a number of years now—long before its license to operate had even been granted by the city, in fact.

Its most vehement detractors, predictably enough, cited the many negative ramifications such a business would almost certainly stir up in an economically-teetering city such as Pittsburgh: gambling addiction, growing levels of crime and prostitution, increased poverty. But despite the years of political hard-balling and liberal hand-wringing that preceded its arrival in August 2009, River Casino is now a seemingly permanent addition to the North Side's landscape. And what a truly enormous and world-class addition it is, reminiscent of the glamorous and higher-end mega-casinos that line the length of the Las Vegas strip.

The 120,000-square-foot gaming floor, for instance, features nearly 3,000 slot machines,

and the covered parking lot has spaces for 3,800 visitors. There's also an outdoor amphitheater, a half-dozen contemporary lounges and eateries, and a private club for high rollers. There are special ventilation units that clean and refresh the casino's air every 12 minutes. Penny slots are abundant, and Pennsylvania's solitary $500 slot machine can be found here. The only bad news, it seems, is that table games here are all electronic; standard table games are still outlawed within the confines of the Commonwealth.

There are, in fact, a number of casino anomalies here: The gaming floor features a massive wall of windows, which offers a brilliant view of the Ohio River outside. And LCD TV screens, mostly featuring professional sports, are abundant. And yet it's anyone's guess whether or not Rivers will actually manage to become a permanent part of the Pittsburgh story; first-year revenues have been disappointingly off-the-mark. For the time being, however, Rivers is nothing if not a fascinating cultural addition to a city that has always been lacking in extravagances. Don't leave Pittsburgh without at least paying it a quick visit.

Oakland

Map 2

CARNEGIE MELLON UNIVERSITY

5000 Forbes Ave., 412/268-2000, www.cmu.edu

COST: Free

After Scottish immigrant Andrew Carnegie made his fortune in the steel industry and then became one of the world's most famous philanthropists, he gave quite a bit back to the city of Pittsburgh, where buildings and institutions named after him seem nearly ubiquitous in some quarters.

Carnegie Mellon University was founded by Carnegie himself in 1900, who first dubbed it Carnegie Technical School; it later became known as the Carnegie Institute of Technology. Today, the university is considered a worldwide leader in the fields of robotics and computer engineering and, to a lesser extent, in fine arts and business administration.

To pay a visit to the campus, which is located on Forbes Avenue just up the hill from the University of Pittsburgh, start by wandering the grassy, parklike expanse known as "the cut"; to its left sits the **University Center,** where a convenience store, the student bookstore, a food court, and a café can be found. Once inside the University Center, the **Information Desk** (412/268-2107, daily 8 A.M.–10 P.M.), which is actually a walk-up window, should be your very first stop. Here you can speak to an actual CMU student who will respond to queries about where to go, what to see, and what to do while on campus. Detailed campus maps and handbills advertising upcoming events are available here. To view an even wider collection of notices, such as flyers announcing upcoming rock concerts, cars for sale, and roommates wanted, ask the Info Desk student to point you in the direction of the bulletin board down the hall.

In total, CMU has a collection of seven colleges and schools, and since the campus is relatively small and quite walkable, a stroll across the grounds shouldn't take much longer than a half hour.

Carnegie Mellon University

Should you care to extend your stay, you might consider taking in a performance by the world-renowned **School of Drama** (www .cmu.edu/cfa/drama). Not only was CMU the first university in the country to offer academic drama degrees, but the majority of performances today receive high marks from local theater critics. Carnegie Mellon Drama School graduates include Ted Danson, Holly Hunter, George Peppard, Blair Underwood, and Steven Bochco. Tickets can be purchased at the box office of the **Purnell Center** (412/268-2407) noon–5 P.M. Mondays and Fridays, and 6–8 P.M. on weekdays when a performance takes place, and two hours before curtain on Saturdays prior to a performance.

Visitors interested in computer technology might be interested in strolling the halls of Carnegie Mellon's **School of Computer Science** (www.cs.cmu.edu); its graduate program was ranked the top such program in the country by *U.S. News & World Report*. In 2000 and 2001, *Yahoo! Internet Life* magazine ranked CMU the "most wired" university in the United States. The university's **Robotics**

Institute (www.ri.cmu.edu) is also notable. Founded in 1979, it's the largest college research facility of its type in the United States, and its faculty, students, and the innovations of both frequently appear in the local and national press.

Any visitor to the Carnegie Mellon campus not particularly impressed by technological advancements should consider this: Beginning in 1937 with physics professor Clinton Davisson, 15 graduates or faculty members of Carnegie Mellon have had the very prestigious honor of being awarded the Nobel Prize.

CARNEGIE MUSEUM OF ART
4400 Forbes Ave., 412/622-3131, www.cmoa.org
HOURS: Tues., Wed., Fri., Sat. 10 A.M.–5 P.M., Thurs. 10 A.M.–8 P.M., Sun. noon–5 P.M., closed Mon.
COST: $15 adult, $11 student and child 3-18, $12 senior

Pittsburgh's premiere museum of modern art, the Carnegie Museum of Art also maintains a noted collection of contemporary pieces, post-Impressionist paintings, late 19th-century American art, and both European and American decorative arts from the past 200

one of the many statues outside the Carnegie Museum of Art

THE RUINS OF FORBES FIELD

Long before the existence of PNC Park and even the historic Three Rivers Stadium – which was imploded and turned into a parking lot in 2001 – the Pittsburgh Pirates baseball club battled its rivals at Forbes Field, a park located in South Oakland. Not much remains of the old field, which saw its first match in 1909 and its last on June 28, 1970. Nonetheless, baseball history buffs may appreciate seeing the park's original home plate; it lies under a slightly foggy slab of plastic on the ground floor of the University of Pittsburgh's Wesley Posvar Hall, just outside the men's restroom. (Posvar itself sits next door to the Hillman Library, where employees at the checkout counter will be more than happy to provide you with a campus map.)

Even more exciting is the remaining portion of the right field wall, which sits just across the street from Posvar and stretches all the way to the building that houses that Katz Graduate School of Business. Even though the wall is slightly vine-covered, it's fairly easy to find: Just look for the hand-painted numbers indicating the distance in feet between the wall and home plate. And while you won't often find fans gathered around the historic artifact inside Posvar, hardcore Pirates obsessives do occasionally set up shop – complete with patio chairs and radios – alongside the old stadium wall. It's a rather moving sight to see the fans, most of them old-timers, sitting perfectly still with wool blankets over their legs and battered boomboxes atop their laps.

Whitney Biennial. The next show is scheduled to open in October 2013; if you can't make it, you'll have to satiate yourself instead by perusing the museum's Scaife Gallery, where all manner of Warhols, Pollacks, and de Koonings can be found.

CARNEGIE MUSEUM OF NATURAL HISTORY

4400 Forbes Ave., 412/622-3131, www.carnegiemnh.org
HOURS: Tues., Wed., Fri., Sat. 10 A.M.–5 P.M.; Thurs. 10 A.M.–8 P.M.; Sun. noon–5 P.M.; closed Mon.
COST: $15 adult, $11 student and child 3-18, $12 senior

Located underneath the same roof as the affiliated Carnegie Museum of Art, the Carnegie Museum of Natural History is home to a wealth of scientific and environmental exhibitions, including the world-renowned Dinosaur Hall (which you may recognize from its cameo in *Silence of the Lambs*). Some of the museum's other permanent displays include the Walton Hall of Ancient Egypt (mummies!); the Hall of African Wildlife, which is complete with stunning lifelike dioramas and jungle creatures; and the Botany Hall, where plant life can be contemplated. Area scientists and archaeologists work daily in the museum's on-site PaleoLab.

CATHEDRAL OF LEARNING

Corner of 5th Ave. and Bigelow Blvd., 412/624-4141, www.pitt.edu
COST: Free

Aside from its hallowed status as one of the most majestic structures in the city, the Gothic-style Cathedral of Learning, which acts as the symbolic nucleus of the University of Pittsburgh campus, is also the second-tallest educational building in the world. (A structure at Moscow State University, in Russia, currently holds the title.)

Appropriately enough, the story of the Cathedral's construction is substantially grandiose. In 1925, Chancellor John Bowman divulged his vision of a tower whose soaring-to-the-heavens architecture would send a subtle message to the varied citizens of Pittsburgh: namely, that a higher education could be considered just as essential and dignified as a

years. Paintings and furniture certainly aren't the entire story, however. There's also the Hall of Sculpture, filled with Greek and Roman reproductions (including a scaled-down Parthenon). There's the Hall of Architecture and the Heinz Architectural Center, both of which see a good number of special exhibitions featuring modern masters. The acclaimed Carnegie International takes place here every three years—it's Pittsburgh's version of the

COURTESY OF ROB MATHENY

The impressive Cathedral of Learning is on the University of Pittsburgh campus.

higher power. Bowman enlisted a virtual army to raise the $10 million necessary to complete the project; during the Great Depression, when charitable contributions dried up, area schoolchildren took to kicking in a dime each to "buy a brick for Pitt."

The Cathedral was finally dedicated in 1937, and even today it cuts an impressive sight. A 42-story Indiana-limestone structure on the outside, the building's inside denotes a considerably more intimate feel. Filling a cavernous but churchly first floor is the 100-foot-wide-by-200-foot-long Commons Room; students can be found tapping on laptops and sipping coffee at its long wooden benches all hours of the day and night.

Running a ring around the first floor are the fabled **Nationality Classrooms** (1209 Cathedral of Learning, 412/624-6000, www.pitt.edu/~natrooms); collectively they are easily the building's most fascinating feature. Designed

to represent specific periods from various nations of the world—including many whose citizens have created enclaves in Pittsburgh—both original and recreated accoutrements were joined together as each successive room was built.

Twenty-six rooms in all can be viewed independently or as part of a guided or taped tour, including a 10th-century Armenian classroom, a folk-style Norwegian classroom, and a Byzantine-era Romanian classroom. Take care not to miss the resplendent Damascus-style Syria-Lebanon room (which unfortunately can only be viewed through a glass partition) or the many rooms on the third floor, especially the Minka-style Japanese classroom and the Israeli and African Heritage classrooms. Tours take place Monday–Saturday 9 A.M.–2:30 P.M. and on Sunday and holidays 11 A.M.–2:30 P.M. No tours are offered on Thanksgiving Day, December 24–26, or January 1. Tours are $3 for adults and $1 for children ages 8–18.

◖ PHIPPS CONSERVATORY AND BOTANICAL GARDENS

1 Schenley Park, 412/622-6914,
www.phipps.conservatory.org
HOURS: Sat.-Thurs. 9:30 A.M.-5 P.M., Fri. 9:30 A.M.-10 P.M.
COST: $12 adult, $9 child 2-18, $11 senior and student

Since its opening in 1893, Phipps Conservatory has been the nerve center of horticulture education in Southwestern Pennsylvania. Located just past the main entrance of Schenley Park in Oakland, the 13 rooms of the conservatory sit inside a Victorian-style glasshouse, where orchids, palm trees, ferns, a Japanese garden, a medicinal plant garden, and an assortment of floating water plants—to name just a sampling of the varieties on-site—await your discovery. Staying true to its fundamental mission as an education center, Phipps also hosts annual flower shows as well as occasional exhibits, lectures, and events.

Henry Phipps, a close friend of Andrew Carnegie's and, in his later years, a philanthropist, built the conservatory as a gift to the city of Pittsburgh. His explanation? He wanted to "erect something that will prove a source of instruction as well as pleasure to the people." Phipps even took pains to ensure that the

COURTESY OF VISITPITTSBURGH

Phipps Conservatory and Botanical Gardens in Schenley Park

scene depicting the Biblical lands from Lake Galilee to the Dead Sea, the Biblical Botanical Garden at Rodef Shalom Temple is meant to symbolize universal love and the Bible. Many of the plants here have Biblical names (Moses in a Basket, Biblical Coat), and during each season, the garden focuses on a differing theme of Near Eastern horticulture. The experience of wandering the garden is meant to be something akin to a stroll through the Holy Land of ancient Israel, but even nonbelievers will enjoy relaxing among the beauty of nature here; the Temple is within walking distance of both the Carnegie Mellon and Pitt campuses and sits across the street from the WQED studios.

New special displays and educational programs are scheduled most seasons; call or visit the garden's website for updated information. Free public tours are given with a trained docent on the first Wednesday of June, July, August, and September; tours can also be arranged for groups of eight or more, although it is highly recommended to make reservations two weeks in advance. A number of educational books and brochures about the art of horticulture are available for purchase on-site.

conservatory would remain open on Sundays so that workers could stop by on what was their only day off.

From 2005–2006, the conservatory underwent a massive, $36 million renovation and expansion project resulting in an environmentally friendly welcome center and the Tropical Forest Conservatory, a 12,000-square-foot display room that features a different horticultural theme every two years.

RODEF SHALOM BIBLICAL BOTANICAL GARDEN

4905 5th Ave., 412/621-6566, www.biblicalgardenpittsburgh.org
HOURS: Sun.-Thurs. 10 A.M.-2 P.M., Sat. noon-1 P.M., closed during winter
COST: Free

With a collection of more than 100 temperate and tropical plants, a small waterfall, a stream representing the River Jordan, and a desert

SCHENLEY PARK AND FLAGSTAFF HILL

Schenley Park Café and Visitors Center, Panther Hollow Rd., 412/687-1800, www.pittsburghparks.org
HOURS: Daily 10 A.M.-4 P.M.
COST: Free

A virtual oasis in the center of the city, the 456-acre Schenley Park sits on hundreds of acres of prime urban real estate in between Oakland's university district and Squirrel Hill. The park, which was donated to the city by Mary Schenley in 1889, features wooded trails that are particularly popular with after-work and weekend joggers. The park also boasts a soccer field, an ice skating rink, 13 tennis courts, a public swimming pool, and its very own lake. You'll also find **Phipps Conservatory and Botanical Gardens** here and, across the street, another perennial favorite, Flagstaff Hill.

From the beginning of June through the end of August each year, free movies are shown on

Flagstaff Hill, projected onto a jumbo outdoor screen. Show up on Wednesdays at sundown (usually around 9 P.M.) with a blanket and picnic foods. No alcohol is allowed. On Sundays at sundown, family-friendly films are screened.

If your plans include exploring the park in depth, stop first at the informative Schenley Park Visitors Center, where a guide can suggest walking routes or jogging trails. Ask about free historical walks of Schenley Park, which are led on the first and third Sunday of every month at 1 P.M. The visitors center will also have scheduling information about the free kids programs—storytelling, puppet shows—and the free National Geographic Film Festival, both of which take place throughout the summer.

Right next door is the **Schenley Park Cafe** (101 Panther Hollow Rd., 412/687-1800, www.pittsburghparks.org/schenleyparkcafe, 10 A.M.–4 P.M. with extended summer hours), which offers free wireless Internet access and live folk and blues music on Sundays 12:30–3:30 P.M. (July 2–Oct. 15 only). The café offers trail maps of the park as well as coffee, light lunches, desserts, and a gift shop.

SCHENLEY PLAZA
4100 Forbes Ave., www.schenleyplaza.org
COST: Free

Modeled after Manhattan's Bryant Park and quickly on its way to becoming the Oakland area's most popular outdoor socializing spot, it's hard to believe that Schenley Plaza—which sits directly in between the main branch of the Carnegie Library and Pitt's Hillman Library—was a medium-sized parking lot just a few years back. Now a lush and inviting town square of sorts with a one-acre lawn, the plaza acts as a gateway to Schenley Park itself. Coincidentally, that was exactly the land's intended use when Mary Schenley donated the acreage to the city in 1890.

The plaza today is filled with movable chairs and café tables designed for socializing, food vendors, free wireless Internet access, a large tented area to provide protection from the elements, 24-hour security, and an entertainment

schedule that includes author appearances and live music year-round. Perhaps the plaza's most exciting amenity, however, is its Victorian-style **PNC Carousel** (Mon.–Fri. 10 A.M.–8 P.M., Sat. 10 A.M.–6 P.M., and Sun. 11 A.M.–6 P.M., tickets $1.25). Featuring a colorful herd of animals that round the carousel to the accompaniment of old-fashioned pipe organ music, the ride is open to all ages and is wheelchair accessible.

SOLDIERS AND SAILORS MEMORIAL
4141 5th Ave., 412/621-4253,
www.soldiersandsailorshall.org
HOURS: Mon.-Sat. 10 A.M.-4 P.M.
COST: $8 adult, $5 child and senior, free to veterans and current military

One of America's largest museums dedicated to honoring and remembering its veterans, Soldiers and Sailors Memorial started out in the early 1900s with a much more local focus: It was originally intended only to recognize the sacrifice and patriotism of the Civil War veterans of Allegheny County. Today however, the memorial represents all wars and all branches of service.

The building's massive Greco-Roman grand edifice—look for it on the corner of 5th and Bigelow across from Pitt's student union—was designed to resemble the mausoleum of Halicarnassus, one of the Seven Wonders of the Ancient World. It's the memorial's museum, however, that will be of most interest to guests. Curios, uniforms, bric-a-brac, and other assorted gewgaws related to American-led battles—starting with the Civil War era and stretching all the way to Operation Iraqi Freedom—are displayed in glass cases. A special exhibition is dedicated to area women who've served in American wars.

ST. PAUL CATHEDRAL
Corner of Craig St. and Fifth Ave., 412/621-4951,
www.catholic-church.org/st.paulcathedralpgh
HOURS: Masses Sun. 6:30 A.M., 8 A.M., 10 A.M., noon, and 6 P.M.; Mon.-Sat. 6:45 A.M., 8:15 A.M., and 12:05 P.M.; call for tours
COST: Free

Known as the Mother Church of the Diocese

of Pittsburgh, the Gothic-style St. Paul Cathedral in Oakland celebrated its 100th birthday in 2006. The 1,800-capacity church, with a 75-foot ceiling designed to resemble the hull of a ship, is undoubtedly one of Pittsburgh's most breathtaking. But the cathedral's true treasure is its massive organ, manufactured by the Rudolf von Beckerath Co. of Germany and generally considered to be one of the finest pipe organs in the world. At the time of writing, however, St. Paul was undergoing a massive reconstruction project that included a restoration of the organ and its pipes. Once the instrument is fully repaired, a schedule of free-to-the-public organ concerts will resume; call for updated information.

Also impressive are the church's stained-glass windows, some of which represent Bible stories and the church's history in pictures. Take note of the large windows above the side doors, which document the life—and eventual martyrdom—of St. Paul himself.

To schedule a free tour of the cathedral, call the parish office at 412/621-4951 between 8 A.M. and 4 P.M. (Tour guides will only be granted to groups of five or more.)

St. Paul Cathedral is known as the Mother Church of the Diocese of Pittsburgh.

South Side

Map 3

GATEWAY CLIPPER FLEET

Near Station Square, 412/355-7980,
www.gatewayclipper.com

COST: Cruise prices vary

Located next to Station Square's Sheraton Hotel is a sloping dock that leads to the Gateway Clipper Fleet, a riverboat operation that for nearly 50 years has been providing cruise tours both luxuriously elaborate and relatively simple along the city's three rivers.

As the most popular attraction in Pittsburgh, the Gateway Clipper Fleet claims to be the largest inland riverboat fleet in the country today. Yet the company began in 1958 with just one solitary boat—a vessel

purchased in Erie for $50. By 1959, the river tours on the 100-passenger capacity *Gateway Clipper* had proved so popular that two more 100-passenger vessels, the *Good Ship Lollipop* and the *Gateway Clipper II,* were added.

The fleet now contains five boats, all of them authentic reproductions of old working riverboats. Cruises happen throughout the year and in all sorts of weather. Passengers can experience a cruise tailored specifically for children, a formal evening cruise with dinner included, or dozens of other voyages. Visit the fleet online for more detailed information or to learn about chartering an entire ship.

COURTESY OF ROB MATHENY

view of the Monongahela River from the South Side Slopes

SOUTH SIDE SLOPES

South of South Side Flats, www.southsideslopes.org

Just minutes away from the bustle and energy of East Carson Street, the South Side Slopes sub-neighborhood is Pittsburgh to the core. A winding maze of narrow traffic lanes and hillside steps weaves throughout this mostly blue-collar neighborhood, which was originally built for the immigrant workers who labored at the steel mills along the Monongahela River below.

The main attraction on the slopes is the view itself; many roads rival even the view of Downtown seen from Mount Washington's Grandview Avenue; beautiful views of Oakland and the South Side can also be had. To experience the various views for yourself, simply wander up 18th Street and poke around. The dozens of differing views will become clearly apparent as you stroll higher into the Upper Slopes, where you'll also see mixed-use development and upscale condos being built alongside the decrepit and decades-old row houses. Built mostly in the mid-1800s, the majority of houses in this particularly cramped region of Pittsburgh are

only one room wide, two rooms deep, and up to three or four stories high. Should you find yourself truly turned around while exploring, simply head down any hill; nearly all roads lead back to East Carson Street. And as you climb up 18th Street, take note of the mural on the road's right-hand-side retaining wall by local artist Rick Bach, who is also responsible for many of the metal sculptures and interiors found in the city's Mad Mex restaurants, as well as illustration work inside many of the older bars and restaurants of the South Side Flats.

The **St. Paul of the Cross Retreat Center** (148 Monastery Ave., 412/381-7676, www .catholic-church.org/stpaulsretreatcenter) is one of the more curious points of interest on the Slopes. The church was founded in the mid-1800s by four members of the Passionist Congregation who traveled to Pittsburgh from Italy. Today it acts as a spiritual facility open to anyone interested in deeply studying the Christian relationship with God. Traditional weekend retreats cost $160 and cover two nights' accommodations, six meals, and all

SIGHTS

programs. Call for scheduling information, as men's and women's retreats take place on differing weekends throughout the year.

St. Michael's Rectory (44 Pius St., 412/431-5550, www.veronicasveilplayers.org), also located in the Slopes, is the location where the historical Lenten drama *Veronica's Veil* has been staged on and off since 1910. The play explores the passion and death of Jesus Christ.

Another particularly popular event is the annual **Pittsburgh Step Trek** (www.steptrek.org), a leisurely but organized walk through some of the most picturesque reaches of the Slopes. The trek takes place every autumn; you can register online. To take a self-guided tour, purchase a copy of Bob Regan's *The Steps of Pittsburgh* (The Local History Co.), available from most local booksellers.

STATION SQUARE

Carson St. at the Smithfield Street Bridge, www.stationsquare.com

Previously a cluster of railroad yards utilized by the Pittsburgh & Lake Erie Railroad Company, the 52-acre indoor shopping center and open-air entertainment complex known collectively as Station Square was converted into a center of commerce thanks to the midcentury decline in railway usage. The **Pittsburgh History and Landmarks Foundation** (100 W. Station Square Dr., Ste. 450, 412/471-5808, Mon.–Fri. 9 A.M.–5 P.M., www.phlf.org) spearheaded the renewal, which is likely the sole reason so many historic artifacts remain on-site. Of particular interest to those fascinated by Pittsburgh's industrial past is the massive, steel-purifying **Bessemer converter;** only two such converters exist in the United States. Look for Bessemer Court behind the Hard Rock Cafe. A fascinating selection of archival photographs can be viewed in the lobbies of the **Grand Concourse** restaurant and its adjacent **Gandy Dancer Saloon** (412/261-1717, www.stationsquare.com/grandconcourse). The main entrance of the restaurant is located on what was once the lower level of the P&LE Railroad Station, while the Gandy Dancer itself was formerly the P&LE's waiting room.

COURTESY OF ROB MATHENY

Station Square, with the steel-purifying Bessemer converter on the right

SIGHTS

COURTESY OF ROB MATHENY

a Just Ducky Tours vintage World War II vehicle

The complex's **Guest Services booth** is located inside the Freight House Shops building and next to the **Station Square Express** (Mon.–Thurs. 4–9 P.M., Fri.–Sat. noon–9 P.M., Sun. noon–5 P.M., ticket $1), a small train ride for kids. A wealth of brochures containing information about the Greater Pittsburgh area can be picked up for free at the booth.

Although still a relatively popular shopping and entertainment complex, Station Square has certainly seen happier days. Retail establishments and eateries in the main terminus have lately been closing with a depressing frequency, although across the Smithfield Street Bridge in the square's nightlife sphere, new businesses appear to open just as quickly as old ones fade away. Currently, club-hoppers can visit various dance clubs, including a country-and-western club complete with line dancing and a mechanical bull.

At Station Square's outdoor **Bessemer Court,** you'll find the usual assortment of suburban chain restaurants. Those looking for an affordable and somewhat goofy way to explore Pittsburgh's waterways should stop by the **Just Ducky Tours booth** (125 W. Station Square Dr., 412/402-3825, Apr. 10–Oct., weekends only in Nov., $19 general, $18 senior, $15 child, www.justduckytours.com), also in Bessemer Court. The company's vintage World War II amphibious vehicles circle through the historical sites of Downtown before plunging into the water.

Mount Washington

Map 3

◖ THE DUQUESNE AND MONONGAHELA INCLINES

Duquesne Incline: 1220 Grandview Ave., 412/381-1665, www.incline.cc

Monongahela Incline: Carson St. at Smithfield Street Bridge, 412/442-2000, www.ridegold.com/ride/pgincline.asp

DUQUESNE INCLINE HOURS:
Mon.-Sat. 5:30 A.M.-12:45 A.M.,
Sun. and holidays 7 A.M.-12:45 A.M.

MONONGAHELA INCLINE HOURS:
Mon.-Sat. 5:30 A.M.-12:45 A.M.
Sun. and holidays 8:45 A.M.-midnight

COST: Tickets $2, $2.75 with a transfer

Definitely skip the taxi if you're planning an outing to Mount Washington; the most interesting way to arrive is certainly via one of the city's two remaining inclines—the hillside cable cars you may have seen inching up and down the mountain.

The Monongahela Incline is the easier of the two to reach on foot. The incline will scurry you up the hill and deposit you atop Grandview Avenue. Just a block away is Shiloh Street, home to a charming assortment of informal restaurants and cafés. From the corner of Grandview Avenue and Shiloh Street, make your way along the pedestrian path and look for the entrance to the Duquesne Incline, which would have been demolished in the mid-1960s if not for the efforts of the nonprofit Society for the Preservation of the Duquesne Incline; the society's volunteers have been operating the station since 1963.

Even if you don't plan to ride the Duquesne back down to Carson Street, don't miss the station itself, which is filled with historical newspaper accounts of Pittsburgh's incline system and archival photos and postcards of funiculars around the world. The view from the station's observation deck is absolutely jaw dropping, and also worth a look is the Gear Room, where $0.50 gets you up-close-and-personal with the machinery that makes the incline go 'round.

The Duquesne Incline makes its way down Mount Washington.

PITTSBURGH'S DISAPPEARING INCLINES

It was the late 1800s, and as the population of Pittsburgh's mill workers and coal miners quickly began to grow in number, the city also began to recognize a troubling site-specific problem. Because the land along the Monongahela River consisted mostly of mills and factories, the European migrants who worked there found it necessary to make their homes on the hills above. The precipitously steep hilltop neighborhoods – especially those above the South Side – were virtually inaccessible by either foot or horse. So in 1870, the two-car Monongahela Incline was constructed.

It rose from the base of the Smithfield Street Bridge and traveled up Mount Washington to what is now Grandview Avenue, operated by a relatively simple cable-pulley system: When one car traveled down, gravity pulled the other car up.

Eventually, more than 17 inclined planes – out-of-towners might refer to them as funiculars – were serving the city of Pittsburgh. But not only foot passengers utilized the hillside cable cars – light freight, horses, and wagons were also shuttled to and fro. Passenger fares ranged from one to five cents among the different inclines; heavy loads required extra payment.

The civil engineer responsible for the design and construction of the majority of the inclines in Pittsburgh was a Hungarian immigrant by the name of Samuel Diescher. After first settling in Cincinnati in 1866, where he built his first incline, Diescher eventually moved to Pittsburgh. He continued to build inclines elsewhere, however, including one in Johnstown, Pennsylvania, one in Wheeling, West Virginia, and two in South America.

Very few inclines exist today in the United States, although two shining examples remain in Pittsburgh: the Monongahela Incline and the Duquesne Incline. The Duquesne offers the superior view, although the Monongahela is much easier to access on foot; you'll find its entrance just across the street from Station Square on the South Side. Both inclines climb Mount Washington and dispatch passengers atop Grandview Avenue.

The inclines are certainly one of the city's most popular attractions for tourists, and for good reason. The two-minute, six-mile-per-hour ride, while a touch frightening for first-timers, is also exhilarating. As the cars slowly rise from their lower stations, Downtown Pittsburgh and the suburbs to the east and west appear into view. The Duquesne travels a total of 400 feet up the hillside to reach an elevation of 800 feet, while the Monongahela travels 635 feet to reach a much lower 369-foot elevation. And given their ages (the Monongahela Incline has existed since 1870, although it was renovated in 1983 and '94, while the Duquesne Incline was built in 1877), it's surprising to note just how smooth the experience is. Small children, however, often grow increasingly worried as the cars end their descent and gain traction toward the station houses; you might mention to any youngsters in your group that the car slows to a near dead stop about 10 feet from the bottom. It then easily inches its way home.

Keep in mind too that while the city refers to the inclines as "working museums," which is certainly an accurate descriptor, their primary function is that of public transport. You will almost always see more locals than tourists inside the cars, many of whom are Mount Washington residents who ride the inclines up and down the hillside each day (as this author did while briefly living on Mount Washington's Wyoming Street).

Bicycles may be taken on the Duquesne Incline only, although a double fare is required.

FRICK ART AND HISTORICAL CENTER

7227 Reynolds St., 412/371-0600, www.frickart.org

HOURS: Tues.-Sun. 10 A.M.-5 P.M.

COST: Center, museums, and greenhouse free; Clayton guided tours $12 adult, $10 student and senior, reservations recommended

A complex of historical museums and buildings located on the eastern stretch of **Frick Park,** the Frick Art and Historical Center is book-ended by its two most important structures. The **Frick Art Museum** displays a portion of the artworks collected by legendary Pittsburgh industrialist Henry Clay Frick, including paintings by Peter Paul Rubens (the majority of Frick's art investments can be found at the Frick Collection Museum in New York City). On the opposite end of the center is **Clayton;** it underwent a $6 million renovation in 1990 and can be explored on a guided tour.

Writing in *Architectural Digest,* the journalist Susan Mary enthused that Clayton is "a triumph of restoration." Indeed, when the Fricks left for New York City in 1905, they had spent 22 years in Pittsburgh, and Clayton, of course, was a well-lived-in house. Much to the delight of modern-day visitors and historians, the Fricks failed to bring the majority of their belongings with them to New York; 93 percent of the house's artifacts are originals. Visitors can view children's toys in the nursery, bedroom furniture, and even the study.

Clayton was purchased for $25,000 in 1882, but at the time it boasted "only" 11 rooms. Less than a decade later, the architect Frederick J. Osterling was hired to spice up the building; he masterfully transformed it into the same 23-room mansion seen today.

Also located on the grounds is the popular **Car and Carriage Museum** where visitors can ogle 20 vintage automobiles, including Frick's 1914 Rolls Royce Silver Ghost and Howard Heinz's 1898 Panhard, which some say was Pittsburgh's first car.

FRICK

Corner of
www.pittsb

HOURS: Daily

COST: Free

Popular with walkers alike, only the city's lied. Stretching in of Squirrel Hill an ___reeze, the park is filled with playgrounds, various recreational facilities, dog runs, winding footpaths, red clay tennis counts, and even a bowling green.

Lesser known are the park's nearly two-dozen phenomenal mountain biking paths. With names like the Rollercoaster and the Worm Trail, it probably goes without saying that many of these routes are significantly challenging; even experienced cyclists are urged to stay away on rainy or poor-weather days.

JEWISH COMMUNITY CENTER AND THE AMERICAN JEWISH MUSEUM

5738 Forbes Ave., 412/521-8010, www.jccpgh.org

HOURS: Mon.-Thurs. 5:30 A.M.-10 P.M., Fri. 5:30 A.M.-6 P.M., Sat. 1-7 P.M., Sun. 7:45 A.M.-6 P.M.

COST: Free

Something of an all-inclusive recreational clubhouse where both Jews and non-Jews congregate, the Jewish Community Center features a state-of-the-art fitness center, a regular schedule of art classes, seminars, educational lectures, and theater performances, as well as the wonderfully contemporary American Jewish Museum, which is the only museum in the western half of the state dedicated to preserving the art, history, and culture of the Jewish diaspora.

The JCC, as it's often referred to locally, opened its doors way back in 1895 and was originally known as the Irene Kaufmann Settlement. The Kaufmann family and the National Council of Jewish Women were both

...ich was built in ...growing number of ...settling in Pittsburgh. ...all backgrounds are improv-...dies and their minds at the JCC. ...the center has proven so popular that a second facility now operates inside the **Henry Kaufmann Building** (345 Kane Blvd. off Bower Hill Rd., Scott Township) in the South Hills. Visit the JCC's website to download a coupon offering a one-week trial gym membership.

Bloomfield and Lawrenceville Map 6

ALLEGHENY CEMETERY
4734 Butler St., 412/682-1624,
www.alleghenycemetery.com
HOURS: Sept.-Apr. daily 7 A.M.-5:30 P.M.,
May daily 7 A.M.-8 P.M., June-Aug. daily 7 A.M.-7 P.M.
COST: Free

More than 120,000 dead are currently at rest in the gorgeously landscaped Allegheny Cemetery, which covers some 300 acres smack-dab in the middle of Bloomfield and Lawrenceville. Composer Stephen Foster ("Oh! Susanna," "My Old Kentucky Home") is undoubtedly the cemetery's most recognizable name; a collection of difficult-to-follow signs point the way to his grave, which can be found in Section

the 300-acre Allegheny Cemetery, where songwriter Stephen Foster is buried

© DAN ELDRIDGE

21, Lot 30. (Stephen Foster's boyhood home is located just a five-minute drive away at 3600 Penn Avenue, also in Lawrenceville, although it unfortunately is not open to the public. A historical marker can be seen on the house's front lawn.) Other Allegheny Cemetery notables include Don Brockett (Chef Brockett of *Mister Rogers' Neighborhood*), Thomas Mellon, and General Alexander Hays.

Chartered as a nonprofit organization in April 1844, Allegheny Cemetery is the country's sixth-oldest rural cemetery. And probably because it was modeled on the landscapes of fashionable English parks, the experience of strolling the grounds is rather pleasant, and during the sunlight hours, not the least bit creepy. Nonetheless, it's all too easy to get lost in the cemetery; even locals who jog or walk here sometimes find themselves turned around. The roads are winding and the grounds are quite hilly, so even though posted signs point the way to various plots and sections, things can get confusing. But not to worry: Both the Bloomfield and Lawrenceville ends of the cemetery have separate entry points, and groundskeepers patrol regularly in private cars.

ARSENAL FIELD
40th and Butler Sts., Arsenal Middle School
COST: Free

Talk about standing on the shoulders of a giant: The footballers at Lawrenceville's Arsenal Middle School must be some of the country's only students to have the privilege of playing on the same field as a former sports hero—in this case, NFL legend Johnny Unitas.

A Pittsburgh native who grew up in Brookline

MOVING THE LIVES OF KIDS COMMUNITY MURAL PROJECT

Founded and largely organized by local artist Kyle Holbrook, the owner of Homewood's KH Design, the MLK Community Mural Project was quite likely the single largest demonstration of public art-making the city had ever seen when it first launched in the summer of 2007. Guided by professional Pittsburgh-area artists, more than 100 at-risk urban youths created a series of truly eye-catching murals throughout the city's East End, including locations in Wilkinsburg, Swissvale, East Liberty, and Edgewood. The project was expanded considerably during the following summer, and murals featuring everything from abstract art to historical figures to photorealistic depictions of actual neighborhood faces can be now be seen as far afield as Carnegie, McKeesport, Mt. Oliver, and Blawnox. The vast majority of the murals, however, can be found within the city limits.

Visit the MLK website, www.mlkmural.com, to view a complete map of mural sites, and to learn about the occasional bus tours that visit the project's most important and impressive works of community art. Don't miss the 100-foot-long mural stretching along a portion of the Martin Luther King Jr. East Busway in East Liberty; it's at the corner of Ellsworth and Shady avenues.

and on Mount Washington, Unitas was recruited in the ninth round by the Pittsburgh Steelers in 1955 but, as a fourth-string quarterback, was never once given a chance to play. Eventually, he was cut from the team and soon after agreed to join the semi-pro Bloomfield Rams, who competed in puddles of oil on Arsenal Field. (The oil was sprayed on the field to keep dust off the players.)

Unitas, who passed away in September 2002, was offered a spot on the professional Baltimore Colts squad after leading the Bloomfield Rams to the Steel Bowl Conference championship. During his stint with Bloomfield, Unitas was paid the princely sum of $6 a game. A plaque outside the Arsenal Field fence on Butler Street commemorates Unitas's contribution to the city's sports legacy.

© DAN ELDRIDGE

an authentic IX Shell Gun Cannon in Arsenal Park

SIGHTS

ARSENAL PARK

40th and Butler Sts., behind Arsenal Middle School

HOURS: Daily dawn-dusk

COST: Free

Today it's a pleasant and sprawling green space filled with playgrounds, sporting facilities, and, of course, many of the young families who've been drawn to Lawrenceville because of its generally affordable real estate and convenient East End location. But Arsenal Park from 1814 until 1913 was known as the Allegheny Arsenal. Designed by Benjamin H. Latrobe, the arsenal functioned as a military barracks during the Civil War, the War of 1812, and the Mexican War. At one point during the Civil War, more that 1,100 civilian workers toiled here.

The arsenal was also a manufacturing site for weapons, and on September 17, 1862, somewhere between 70 and 100 men, women, and children perished when barrels of powder exploded. A bronze marker outside the park's restrooms now memorializes the victims of the blast, and next to the fence separating the park and the middle school sits an authentic IX Shell Gun Cannon that was constructed in 1865; a marker atop the cannon notes that it fired a total of 1,681 rounds. The arsenal's powder magazine now functions as a maintenance shed.

Popular with picnickers, area teenagers, and recreational sports leagues, Arsenal Park also offers tennis and basketball courts, two baseball fields, and plenty of space for a casual jog or walk.

THE CLEMENTE MUSEUM

3339 Penn Ave., 412/621-1268, www.clementemuseum.com

HOURS: Tours given by appointment only

COST: $20 adult, $10 child

Although tours of this truly passionate and loving monument to professional baseball legend Roberto Clemente, also know as "The Great One," can only be scheduled by making an advance reservation, the experience is nevertheless very much worth the trouble—especially for anyone with a serious interest in Major League Baseball or, for the matter, the immigrant experience in America.

© MATT STROUD

The Clemente Museum is housed in Lawrenceville's historic Engine House 25.

Clemente was a Puerto Rican athlete who spent all 18 of his pro baseball seasons, from 1955 until his untimely death in 1972, with the Pittsburgh Pirates. Not only is he still considered one of the finest to ever play the game, he was also one of its most honorable and altruistic—the exact opposite of many modern-day pros, you might say—and he was well-known for devoting much of his time off the field to serious humanitarian work.

At the two-story Clemente Museum, which is owned by the professional advertising photographer Duane Rieder, visitors will find literally thousands of pieces of Clemente memorabilia, including photographs and family snapshots, all manner of Clemente's former sporting gear, letters, telegraphs, and other personal curios, a large collection of bats, and even a set of actual seats from Oakland's Forbes Field.

DOUGHBOY SQUARE

East of 34th St., where Butler St. forks off from Penn Ave.

Doughboy Square, an arresting war monument

celebrating area soldiers who gave their lives in World War I, is actually a triangle. At its base stands a statue of—what else?—a Doughboy. Most war historians agree that the nickname for World War I soldiers was derived from the white adobe soil that often coated them during training at a camp in Texas.

There's also a plaque at the statue's base listing the names of hundreds who perished not only in World War I, but also in World War II, the Korean War, and the Vietnam War. And just behind the statue sits the historic **Pennsylvania National Bank** building, a beautiful beaux arts structure that was built in 1902 and restored in the early 1990s.

PITTSBURGH ZOO AND PPG AQUARIUM

1 Wild Pl., Highland Park, 412/365-3640, www.pittsburghzoo.com

HOURS: Summer daily 9:30 A.M.–6 P.M., fall and spring daily 9 A.M.–5 P.M., winter daily 9 A.M.–4 P.M.

COST: $13 adult, $11 child 2-13, $12 senior

Much more than just a randomly selected menagerie, the 77-acre Pittsburgh Zoo and PPG Aquarium has been renovating and upgrading its facilities since 1980, when the once-staid exhibits first began their transformation into natural habitats. As a result, you won't see an abundance of depressing cages here. Instead, winding pedestrian paths take visitors past the African Savanna and the Asian Forest, and even into a five-acre indoor rainforest housing 150 different plant species and more than 90 primates, including orangutans, cotton-top tamarins, and western lowland gorillas. Other naturalistic habitats include Cheetah Valley and a bear habitat, where Kodiak bears and black bears can be seen rummaging through rocky hills.

In fact, there are now literally thousands of animals representing hundreds of species here. Don't miss the rare komodo dragon and the gila monster, both of which can be found in the Reptile House. And if children are a part of your group, visit Kids Kingdom, an

© ROBERT PERNELL/123RF.COM

a Siberian tiger at the Pittsburgh Zoo

SIGHTS

interactive facility with playground equipment that replicates animal motions, thereby teaching children to play just as a mole rat or a penguin might play.

Take care not to miss the PPG Aquarium, where polar bears, sea otters, and walruses can be found frolicking underwater. Keep in mind that balloons, pets, and tobacco products of any sort are banned from zoo premises.

Greater Pittsburgh   Map 7

ALLEGHENY OBSERVATORY
159 Riverview Ave., Riverview Park, 412/321-2400, www.pitt.edu/~aobsvtry
HOURS: Tours May 1-late Aug. Thurs. 8-10 P.M., Apr. 1-Nov. 1 Fri. 8-10 P.M.
COST: Free

Although it was founded in 1859 for the purpose of educating the citizens of the City of Allegheny (which later became incorporated into the City of Pittsburgh), the Allegheny Observatory eventually ran out of funds and was donated to the University of Pittsburgh, which today uses it as a research lab for its Department of Physics and Astronomy.

Located four miles north of Downtown in the 251-acre **Riverview Park** (www.city.pittsburgh.pa.us/district1/html/riverview_park.html), free public tours of the observatory are offered from April through October of each year. Advance reservations are required. The highlight of the tour is a stop at the 13-inch Fitz-Clark refractor, through which visitors may view any number of celestial wonders, assuming the night sky is clear. Before gazing through the refractor, a short film is screened, and visitors are then taken on a walking tour of the building. Because of the private research going on at the observatory, visitors can only tour the facilities during the designated tour schedule. Once a year, however,

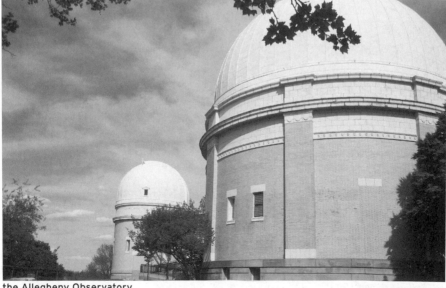

the Allegheny Observatory

COURTESY OF ROB MATHENY

an open house is held during which visitors are allowed to tour the observatory by following a designated path throughout the building; tour guides are not present. The event, which is also free and requires advance reservations, generally takes place toward the end of September.

The observatory also maintains a regular schedule of free astronomy lectures delivered by area scholars; regularly updated information is available at the observatory's website.

BAYERNHOF MUSIC MUSEUM

225 St. Charles Pl., O'Hara Township, 412/782-4231, www.bayernhofmuseum.com

HOURS: Tours given by appointment only

COST: $10

A gorgeous stone house overlooking the Highland Park lock and dam on the Allegheny River, Bayernhof was built by the late Charles B. Brown III, the founder and former CEO of Gas-Lite Manufacturing. Toward the end of Brown's life, he discovered the rather unique hobby of collecting rare automatic music machines. Before long, Brown got a bit carried away with his new obsession, and today, rare and antique machines can be found in every single one of Bayernhof's rooms. Thankfully, Brown had the foresight to add an amendment to his living will stating that upon his death, the instruments should be properly restored, and the house should be opened to the public as a museum. Brown passed away in 1999, and now all visitors to Pittsburgh can enjoy the Bayernhof Music Museum.

Some of the machines you'll see here include a massive Seeburg Pipe Organ orchestra, a Wurlitzer "Style A" Automatic Harp, an Encore Automatic Banjo, a Wurlitzer 125 Military Band Organ, and a combination phonograph and music box known as a Reginaphone Music Box. It's also worth mentioning that completely aside from the music machines, Bayernhof itself is a wonderfully unique house, if a bit on the unconventional side. A hidden passageway takes visitors to a cave, for instance, that winds past small waterfalls and pools. And the entire south side of the house is glass-lined, affording

beautiful views of Highland Park, Oakland, and Downtown.

BEECHWOOD FARMS NATURE RESERVE

614 Dorseyville Rd., Fox Chapel, 412/963-6100, www.aswp.org/beechwood.html

HOURS: Tues.-Sat. 9 A.M.-5 P.M., Sun. 1-5 P.M. (Evans Nature Center)

COST: Free

Considering it's the headquarters of the Audubon Society of Western Pennsylvania, it probably goes without saying that the Beechwood Farms Nature Reserve, which consists of five miles of walking trails and 134 acres of wilderness sanctuary, is a rather lovely and peaceful place. The trails here are open to the public from dawn until dusk every day of the year.

The reserve is also home to the 125-seat **Evans Nature Center auditorium,** an **Audubon Nature Store,** a **bird feeder observation room,** and a **Natural History and Teacher Resource Library.**

Wildlife exists in abundance on the reserve; be prepared to spot deer, screech owls, and even red fox. An artificially constructed pond built in 1981 is home to mallards and Canada geese. Visitors should also stop by the **Audubon Center for Native Plants,** a greenhouse and nursery complex whose mission is to educate gardeners and landscapers about the importance of working with native plants.

KENNYWOOD AMUSEMENT PARK

4800 Kennywood Blvd., West Mifflin, 412/461-0500, www.kennywood.com

HOURS: Memorial Day-Labor Day daily 10:30 A.M.-11 P.M.

COST: $35.99 adult, $22.99 child under 46 inches, $17.95 senior; Night Rider admission after 5 P.M. $20

Since its founding in 1898, the long-surviving and much-loved Kennywood Amusement Park has become practically synonymous with the city of Pittsburgh itself. Over the past century, the park has survived fierce corporate battles, major changes in the industry, and even the Great Depression. But good ol' fashioned fun trumps all, it seems, and today the park is still

SIGHTS

WELCOME TO BRADDOCK: WESTERN PENNSYLVANIA'S URBAN FRONTIER

The small town of Braddock, Pennsylvania, sits about ten miles southeast of downtown Pittsburgh, and viewing it on a map likely won't prompt you to pay the borough a visit. In fact, assuming you pay attention to Pittsburgh-area news, you might actually assume it's a place to avoid: High-profile murders happen there occasionally, while Braddock politicians make headlines due to all-too-common corruption charges and illogical governing decisions. Perhaps the biggest news story to come out of Braddock in the past decade was the closing of UPMC Braddock Hospital, which was located in the heart of town and which provided the place with much of its economic sustenance.

In total, since Pittsburgh's steel boom fully took hold in the early- to mid-20th century, Braddock has lost roughly 95 percent of its population. Approximately 2,000 people live there today, and both crime and decline have been at the center of Braddock's story for decades. However, for the first time since steel manufacturers lined the shores of Pittsburgh's three rivers, that story is beginning to change.

A new crop of do-it-yourselfers have turned Braddock's withered state into a type of industrial urban garden – a place where, as the borough's website (www.15104.cc) proudly proclaims, "reinvention is the only option." It's also a place where housing is so incredibly cheap that just about anyone can afford to live there, free to sow whatever seeds they so desire.

At the core of Braddock's DIY revolution is John Fetterman, a 6'8" giant weighing in at nearly 400 pounds. Back in 2005, Fetterman utilized his master's degree from Harvard's Kennedy School of Government, along with

PHOTO BY MICHAEL O'NEIL/COURTESY BRADDOCK OFFICE OF THE MAYOR

Braddock's mayor, John Fetterman

his history of working in the region as a community organizer, to make a run as Braddock's mayor. He defeated the incumbent by one vote. Literally.

Since then, he's used his family's independent wealth, the connections he's made with congressional politicians, and his unprecedented knack for grabbing people's attention to promote both Braddock's weaknesses and its potential for post-industrial urban opportunity nationwide. To remind himself of what and who he governs, he has Braddock's zip code, 15104, tattooed on his left arm. The date of every murder that has occurred in Braddock on his watch is tattooed on his right arm.

As of this writing, Fetterman's goateed mug has been featured in the pages of *The Atlantic* and *Rolling Stone* magazines, and he's spoken at length on TV programs including C-SPAN and *The Colbert Report*. Levi's clothing company recently donated more than $1 million to a number of Braddock-based charitable initiatives, and has also partnered with the Independent Film Channel to produce a series of mini-documentary films about the "urban pioneers" who have come from far and wide to make Braddock their home and, in some cases, their place of business.

Much of Braddock is still in tatters, of course. Many houses and some entire residential blocks are completely vacant. Buildings crumble into unoccupied space and squatters use the remaining structures as garbage receptacles. Astute observers have said certain quadrants of Braddock look like something out of David Fincher's *Fight Club*.

But that's understandable. After all, a sizeable corporate donation and a heap of media exposure can't undo years of neglect overnight. And yet a small group of concerned citizens have taken the initiative to establish such growing enterprises as **Braddock Farms** (www.growpittsburgh.org), for instance, which consists of ten acres of organic vegetable gardens grown in vacant urban lots. Area kids tend to the Braddock Farms plots, harvesting and supplying herbs and vegetables to regional eateries.

Another such altruistic project in Braddock is **UnSmoke Systems** (www.unsmokeartspace.com), a creative space within a reclaimed Catholic school. Unsmoke Systems offers art for sale in the building's repurposed auditorium, and expansive studio space is available for a share of the building's utility bills.

Another Braddock organization known as **Fossil Free Fuels** (www.fossilfreefuel.com) sells biodiesel gas that its employees have made out of fast food fryer oil. What's more, a growing number of artisans and craftsmen are now hawking their merchandise from once-forgotten Braddock storefronts. **New Guild Studio** (www.newguildstudio.com) offers "re-imagined liturgical art," according to its website, which blends "a respect for tradition with a healthy dose of modern techniques and materials." **Roadbourne Furniture** (www.roadbourne.com), meanwhile, makes and sells custom furniture using reclaimed materials.

In all, Braddock certainly isn't your typical tourist destination. But it's worth the visit if you're up for a history lesson that doesn't involve going to a museum, or a night out that doesn't involve bar hopping.

There are in fact bars on the borough's main drag, but you might find yourself in an awkward scenario if you order any kind of beverage that requires fruity flavoring.

Your best bet – if you find yourself at the **Elks Lodge** (424 Library St., 412/271-1335), or just down the street at **Lucky Frank's Irish Pub** (312 Braddock Ave., 412/351-3878) – would be to order an Iron City beer and work your way into a conversation. The result might be a kind of tourism you've never quite experienced before.

And who knows? You may even run into a very large man with numbers tattooed on his forearms.

(Contributed by Matt Stroud, a Pittsburgh-based freelance journalist.)

a hugely popular Pittsburgh-area attraction. New rides continue to be added each summer season, and, in 1987, Kennywood was awarded National Historic Landmark status.

History aside, however, Kennywood is a can't-miss choice for Pittsburgh visitors both young and old. Roller coasters continue to be a favorite here, especially the historical Thunderbolt and Jack Rabbit rides, as well as the terrifyingly fast Phantom's Revenge, which reaches speeds of 85 mph. The park also has its share of water rides and thrill rides, such as the catapulting SwingShot and the PittFall, a ride that simply drops its riders from a height of 251 feet to the ground below. But the fact that a decent number of classic rides are still in operation—like the paddleboats, the bumper cars, and the merry-go-round—probably lends the park its most authentic sense of classic greatness.

Live entertainment occasionally takes place at Kennywood, and operating hours and admission prices change according to season. Call or visit the park's website for the most up-to-date information.

MONROEVILLE MALL

200 Monroeville Mall Blvd. (Exit 57 on Business Rte. 22), Monroeville, 412/243-8511, www.monroevillemall.com
HOURS: Mon.-Sat. 10 A.M.-9 P.M., Sun. noon-6 P.M.

Cinephiles and horror fans in particular have for years been journeying to Pittsburgh with the intention of visiting just one solitary attraction: the Monroeville Mall. Built in 1969, the mall today consists of four anchor stores, more than 120 shops and restaurants, and 6,800 parking spots spread out over 1,128,747 square feet. But to splatter-film obsessives, it's more popularly known as the filming location of the original *Dawn of the Dead,* George Romero's hugely popular follow-up to his 1968 classic, *Night of the Living Dead.*

Generally agreed upon as Romero's best film, and certainly one of the best zombie movies ever produced, filming began in late 1977 and ended in February 1978. Romero's inspiration for the film happened during a visit to the

mall in the early 1970s, when it was still one of the largest shopping centers of its type in the United States. He noticed the vacant faces and glazed-over eyes of the mall's shoppers, dutifully marching from store to store, and couldn't help comparing them to the living dead. A deal was struck with the mall's development company: Filming could take place between the hours of 10 P.M. and 6 A.M., when the mall was closed to the public.

Thousands of fans visit what is essentially a historical film set each year, and mall security has responded by tightening up considerably. Some visitors have even had their film or cameras confiscated after photographing memorable film locations, so consider yourself forewarned. Should you still care to brave the wilds of Monroeville Mall, however, do yourself a favor by first doing a quick Internet search; numerous fan sites list the exact locations of the film's most memorable scenes.

Horror fans might also consider making a pilgrimage to the borough of Evans City in Butler County; the opening graveyard scene in Romero's *Night of the Living Dead* was shot at the Evans City Cemetery. Much closer to the center of town is the East End neighborhood of Bloomfield, where legendary makeup artist and special effects man Tom Savini hangs his hat. Savini, who can often be seen around town, has worked on nearly every one of George Romero's films and today is a horror-film actor and director as well.

PENNSYLVANIA TROLLEY MUSEUM

1 Museum Rd., Washington, 724/228-9256, www.pa-trolley.org
HOURS: Summer Mon.-Fri. 10 A.M.-4 P.M., Sat.-Sun. 10 A.M.-5 P.M.; call or visit website for off-season hours
COST: $9 adult, $8 senior, $5 child 3-15

Consisting of a historic trolley car house and a visitor education center, the Pennsylvania Trolley Museum is a documentation of the state's streetcars and of the era during which they were regularly traversing the Keystone State's urban areas.

The museum opened its doors in 1963, although the concept first dawned on the PTM founders in the early 1940s, when it seemed as if the cars—a truly quaint and important chapter of U.S. public transport history—were quickly disappearing from American cities. Today, a gift shop and a trolley car restoration site are a part of the facilities as well.

Admission includes a guided tour of the trolley car barn, which takes approximately 90 minutes to complete, as well as all the trolley rides you can handle along the museum's four-mile-long train track. Pictorial exhibits are always on display in the education center, and for an additional $2 charge ($1 children), visitors can tour the Trolley Display Building, a 28,000-square-foot site where 30 restored cars from the tri-state area are stored.

SEWICKLEY HEIGHTS HISTORY CENTER

1901 Glen Mitchell Rd., Sewickley Heights, 412/741-4487, www.sewickleyheightshistory.org

HOURS: Mon.-Fri. 3-5 P.M., Sat. noon-2 P.M.

COST: Free

Located on the former site of a working farm and surrounded by over 30 acres of gorgeous rolling pasturelands, the Sewickley Heights History Center is intended to be something of a reverential and historical monument to the upscale borough of Sewickley Heights. Ever since the Gilded Age of the early 1900s, in fact, when mill-owning industrialists relocated there from Pittsburgh in an effort to escape the city's omnipresent cloud of choking black smoke, Sewickley Heights has been well known as a haven for a small number of the city's wealthiest families.

The museum itself does a fine and respectable job of preserving the area's cultural and historical heritage, what with its decent collection of period photos, area artifacts, and antique carriages and automobiles. The museum also features a small theater where film footage of Sewickley's earliest days can be viewed. Educational lectures about what life was like in early-1900s Sewickley Heights are offered occasionally.

Perhaps the museum's most popular event is the annual Car, Carriage and Horse Show, a rather upscale nod to the many equestrian

events that once took place here. It generally happens at the end of the summer, although a good number of other family-friendly and educational events are scheduled throughout the year; visit the museum's website for details.

ST. ANTHONY'S CHAPEL

1700 Harpster St., Troy Hill, 412/323-9504, www.saintanthonyschapel.org

HOURS: Tues., Thurs., Sat., and Sun. tours conducted hourly at 1 P.M., 2 P.M., and 3 P.M.; call before visiting on Mon., Wed., or Fri., during which audio tours are available

COST: $3 donation

Although technically located in the northern neighborhood of Troy Hill, which isn't within walking distance of the North Side's more well-known attractions, the legendary St. Anthony's Chapel is nevertheless worth the trek. Tourists and other out-of-towners don't often come here to pray, but instead to examine the church's incredible collection of sacred Catholic relics.

St. Anthony's Chapel is known for its collection of Catholic relics.

The collection, in fact, is said to be the largest of its kind in the world, outside of the collection found at the Vatican in Rome. St. Anthony's now owns approximately 4,200 pieces that are kept in 800 separate cases.

The chapel was founded in 1883 by a Belgian known as Father Mollinger; the current collection began when he rescued a number of reliquaries from Germany. Some he discovered in European pawnshops in the late 1800s, a time when many monasteries had splintered, and the relics protected by those monasteries were stolen, lost, or otherwise misplaced.

The chapel itself is rather lovely, if not particularly large. Dark wood and stained-glass windows fill the interior, and the Stations of the Cross, beautifully carved out of wood, are remarkable.

As is the case with most collections of saints' relics, many of the pieces here come complete with a touch of creepiness: You'll see saints' teeth, skulls, and bone fragments, for instance, although it's worth noting that gnarly body parts do not make up the bulk of the

collection. There are also photographs, scraps of clothing, and other interesting bits.

Don't miss the small museum dedicated to Father Mollinger, which contains medicines and other items he used when curing the sick and dying. There's also a small gift shop. Tours, museum admission, and church admission are all free.

ST. NICHOLAS CROATIAN CATHOLIC CHURCH

24 Maryland Ave., Millvale, 412/821-3438 or 724/845-2907, www.stnicholascroatian.com

HOURS: Call to arrange personal or group tours

COST: Free

A tiny parish whose now-shuttered sister church on the North Side was the first Catholic Croatian church in the United States, St. Nicholas Croatian Catholic Church has since been awarded status as both a National Landmark and a Pittsburgh Historical Landmark. Twenty murals by the Croatian artist Maxo Vanka are the church's claim to fame; many critics consider them to be his greatest masterpieces.

The interior of St. Nicholas Croatian Catholic Church features murals by Croatian artist Maxo Vanka.

© TOM STEPLETON/COURTESY MATTRESS FACTORY

Painted in 1937 and 1941, and commissioned by the Rev. Albert Zagar, a fellow Croation who at the time worked as the church's pastor, the murals depict mostly secular scenes of cultural and political significance: Croatian mothers grieving over their war-dead sons and the images depicting the oppressed nations of Eastern Europe. According to Vanka, the majority of the images, of which only a few contain religious symbolism, were inspired by Hitler's Nazi occupation.

Oddly enough, St. Nicholas is equally famous for a rather unsettling reason: The church is widely believed to be haunted by the ghost of a former priest; church members and employees claim to have seen him tending the altar. When the North Side's St. Nicholas parish was closed and the congregation transferred to Millvale, many members refused to show up because of the rumored haunting. Even Vanka himself claimed to have spotted the priest while painting his famous murals.

TOUR-ED MINE AND MUSEUM

748 Bull Creek Rd., Tarentum, 724/244-4720, www.tour-edmine.com
HOURS: Memorial Day-Labor Day Wed.-Mon. 10 A.M.-4 P.M., closed Tues.
COST: $9 adult, $7.50 child 12 and under

With a collection of more than 9,000 authentic mining artifacts dating as far back as the 1850s, the Tour-Ed Mine and Museum wonderfully documents both the deep-mining and strip-mining histories of Southwestern Pennsylvania.

Schoolchildren especially enjoy the immersion experience of entering the Tour-Ed Mine, which was first mined for coal sometime around 1850 and eventually had its name changed to Avenue Mine. Since 1970, more than one million tours have been given at the site, each one led by experienced former miners. Tour groups will have a chance to examine mining tools and actual mining methods up close, and although the tour focuses partly on historical mining methods, modern advanced methods are also demonstrated and explained. Hydraulic machines are used to mine coal today, for instance, although in the mid-1800s it was largely dug by hand. Light jackets are recommended, as the mine's temperature remains steady at around 55°F year-round.

To ensure that every visitor has a chance to clearly view the demonstrations, tours never consist of more than 25 people. Visitors will also have a chance to view a working sawmill, as well as a reproduction of a 1900-era mine village, complete with a general store and a barbershop.

Just more than three miles away, you'll find the **Galleria at Pittsburgh Mills** (590 Pittsburgh Mills Circle, Tarentum, 724/904-9000, www.pittsburghmills.com, Mon.–Sat. 10 A.M.–9 P.M., Sun. noon–6 P.M., www.pitts burghmills.com), an indoor and outdoor shopping center with a bowling alley, a movie theater, and numerous retailers, including H&M, American Eagle, and Borders Books & Music.

RESTAURANTS

In Pittsburgh, hunting down more refined dining options can sometimes feel like a bit of an uphill battle. It's not exactly a foodie's paradise; eating well here often means embracing calories and comfort food. Historically, this makes good sense: You wouldn't have expected those mill workers to tackle their jobs on a diet of haute cuisine and foie gras, would you?

This is a town where both salads and sandwiches are frequently served with french fries on top, and where the double-carb nightmare known as a pierogi—a pasta dumpling filled with mashed potatoes—is considered something of a delicacy.

Which isn't to say that no interesting options exist. On the contrary, Pittsburgh today is rich in ethnic eateries, and not only of the Italian and Eastern European varieties. A number of master sushi chefs now call Pittsburgh home, for instance, and throughout the East End alone, locals flock on a daily basis to affordable Thai, Vietnamese, Indian, Ethiopian, and Filipino restaurants. Contemporary cuisine was relatively sparse within the city's limits just a few years ago, but today it's surprisingly easy to find. The best bets for contemporary cuisine can be found in restaurants on the main drags of the Lawrenceville and East Liberty neighborhoods.

Your best bet, however, is to think of each neighborhood as a separate and unique dining experience: Bloomfield for Italian restaurants, Oakland for ethnic and late-night bites, and

COURTESY OF ROB MATHENY

HIGHLIGHTS

LOOK FOR 《 TO FIND RECOMMENDED RESTAURANTS.

《 Cheapest Indian Food: Whenever you're in need of an incredibly cheap but immensely filling meal, head to an outpost of the vegan-friendly **Sree's Indian Food,** a no-frills joint that piles on the rice and lentils for just $5 (page 74).

《 Best Breakfast Spot: For an old-school, completely authentic Pittsburgh breakfast, go clog your arteries at **DeLuca's Restaurant** in the Strip District, where Pittsburgh accents and gum-snapping waitresses are still delightfully in style (page 75).

《 Most Authentic Pittsburgh Dining Experience: Yes, Pittsburghers really do eat sandwiches with French fries inside. Join the locals at the original **Primanti Brothers** (page 76) in the Strip District, and try one for yourself. And while in Oakland, don't miss a visit to **The Original Hot Dog Shop** (page 81), a.k.a. "The O," a time-honored Pittsburgh junk food tradition.

《 Best Microbrew Selection on Tap: The sandwiches and salads at **Fat Head's Saloon** on the South Side are top-notch, but nothing beats this spot's draft import and microbrew selection, generally a list of more than two dozen (page 87).

《 Best Themed Restaurant: Designed to resemble the 400-year-old Munich *bier* hall of the same name, **Hofbräuhaus** is a lively German brewpub with a truly authentic menu to match (page 91).

《 Most Satisfying Slice: A slice of plain isn't exactly cheap at **Pizza Sola,** which now has three locations in the city — but just wait until you see the size of these New York-style slices (page 92).

《 Most Creative Interpretation of Mexican Street Food: Culinary genius meets the simple Mexican street taco at the South Side's **Yo Rita,** easily the city's most inventive finger-food outpost (page 93).

《 Best Local Coffee Chains: With 26 Pittsburgh locations (and growing), free Wi-Fi,

and wonderfully eclectic atmospheres, locals flock to the nearest **Crazy Mocha** (pages 99 and 106). For a more refined and artistic experience, hit **COCA Café** (page 105), which serves an upscale Sunday brunch.

《 Best Restaurant for a First Date: Complete with unique sushi dishes and spicy, Latin-flavored small plates, it's no wonder Lawrenceville's warmly romantic **Tamari Restaurant and Lounge** has been getting consistent rave reviews (page 107).

《 Best New Restaurant: Pittsburgh's foodie scene is currently having its Contemporary American moment, and chef Kevin Sousa, of **Salt of the Earth,** is one of the community's biggest names. SOTE is one of the area's hottest culinary attractions (page 113).

Don't pass up the legendary sandwiches at Primanti Brothers, a Pittsburgh institution.

Mount Washington for romantic fine dining. And on the South Side you can always head to a bar after dinner if it's not quite time for the evening to end.

In other words, gastronomic delights can be found in even the furthest reaches of Pittsburgh, as long as you're willing to peek around the proverbial corner.

PRICE KEY

⑤ Entrées less than $10

⑤⑤ Entrées $10-20

⑤⑤⑤ Entrées more than $20

Downtown
Map 1

RESTAURANTS

Attempting to eat Downtown with any sort of creativity can be a difficult exercise; there simply isn't a lot to choose from. And should you find yourself working nine to five and searching out budget lunch options, things get even stickier still. If you're truly in a bind, there's an abundance of fast-food joints, chain cafés, and sandwich shops in the area. You'll also find that a good number of the Cultural District's pricier places stay open late on weekends—and some weekdays—for the theater crowd.

AMERICAN
BRADDOCK'S AMERICAN BRASSERIE ⑤⑤⑤
107 6th St., 412/992-2005,
www.braddocksrestaurant.com
HOURS: Mon.-Sat. 7 A.M.-11 P.M., Sun. 7 A.M.-2 P.M.
Located in the lobby of Downtown's Renaissance Pittsburgh Hotel, the opening of Braddock's American Brasserie was clearly the hotel's attempt to compete head-on with the notable contemporary dining scene that has cropped up in the city's Cultural District recently. Self-described as "French comfort food with a Pittsburgh twist," and with a name intended to reference its wide selection of whiskeys (nearby Braddock's Field was the site of the Whiskey Rebellion in 1794), Braddock's hasn't exactly become the trendy dining destination it was clearly meant to be. And yet the modern interpretations of local favorites (pierogies, kielbasa) are certainly solid enough, especially for hotel guests on a tight schedule. If nothing else, sample one of the bar's inventive cocktails.

FRANKTUARY ⑤
325 Oliver Ave., 412/288-0322, www.franktuary.com
HOURS: Mon.-Fri. 10 A.M.-3 P.M.
Located on the ground floor of Trinity Episcopal Cathedral, the pious-minded young entrepreneurs of Franktuary serve a beguiling blend of New York–style hot dogs, gourmet dogs, and fruit shakes. The prices lean a bit toward the steep side, but the quality simply speaks for itself, and only 100 percent beef franks and Boar's Head meats are sold. You might as well try something creative, like the The Mexico (a dog served in a tortilla with guacamole) or The El Greco (with feta and artichoke hearts). Soups, salads, and veggie dogs are on offer for vegetarians, and delivery by bicycle is free within the Downtown corridor.

ORIGINAL OYSTER HOUSE ⑤
20 Market Sq., 412/566-7925,
www.originaloysterhousepittsburgh.com
HOURS: Mon.-Sat. 10 A.M.-10 P.M.
The men behind the counter at the historic Original Oyster House have been serving up giant fish sandwiches, breaded oysters, and cold mugs of beer for more than 140 years. This eatery is in fact the oldest bar and restaurant in the city; it's even been designated a historic landmark by the Pittsburgh History and Landmarks Foundation. With its location in the heart of Market Square, the atmosphere here—and the speedy service—remains much as it has been since the Oyster House's opening in 1870. Even Hollywood considers the restaurant particularly quaint: Scenes from 25 films,

MAKING SENSE OF PITTSBURGH CUISINE

Yes, there really is such a thing as Pittsburgh-specific cuisine. And while none of it is particularly good for you, all of it is nearly addictively delicious. For starters, there's the legendary **Primanti Brothers sandwich,** which comes complete with french fries and coleslaw *inside.* Gnawing on a roast beef sandwich at the counter and washing it down with a pint of Iron City is a truly authentic Pittsburgh experience. According to Primanti's lore, the sandwich was created specifically for the hardworking men who unload produce trucks in the Strip District in the middle of the night. The idea was that they could eat an entire meal with one hand while still continuing to work with the other.

Pierogi and **kielbasa** are also considered regional staples. Both are of Polish origin; a pierogi is a boiled potato dumpling deep-fried in butter, and a kielbasa (pronounced "kiel-BAH-see" in Pittsburghese) is a smoked sausage, usually made of pork. The **Bloomfield Bridge Tavern** is the place to go to sample locally prepared Polish food at its finest – try the sampler dish known as the Polish Platter.

Order a steak salad at just about any restaurant in Southwestern Pennsylvania, and you'll likely find a generous bed of fries scattered atop. This is a regional riddle that even local culinary experts don't understand, but how can you not love a city that loads its salads with red meat and fried carbs?

And speaking of beef, what better time than now to order your next T-bone or porterhouse steak **"Pittsburgh rare?"** Do just that, and your meat will come charred on the outside and blood red on the inside. Allegedly, this trend reaches all the way back to Pittsburgh's steel-making era, when steelworkers would bring raw steaks to work, and then sear them on the nearest piece of burning hot metal just before lunchtime.

If you'd rather try lighter local lunch fare, go for a **Devonshire sandwich.** The open-faced sandwich, made with either chicken or turkey, was invented here in 1936 by restaurateur Frank Blandi. Blandi is also responsible for the creation of Mount Washington's swanky Le Mont eatery.

Most folks are aware that **Heinz Ketchup** has its roots in the Steel City. H. J. Heinz himself even taught Sunday School at the Grace Methodist Church in Sharpsburg. But few are aware that the **Clark Bar** and the **Klondike Bar** were born here as well. The Clark Bar was invented way back in 1886 on the city's North Side, where the Clark Building still stands. Today it houses the editorial team of the *Pittsburgh Tribune-Review.* The Klondike Bar was created by **Isaly's,** a company whose ice cream in particular remains legendary throughout the region. And should you care to pass yourself off as a local, order another Islay's creation – **chipped ham** – the next time you're at the deli counter in a Pittsburgh grocery store. Chipped ham is very thinly sliced; you can also order it "chipped chopped," meaning small clumps of the thinly sliced stuff. Enjoy!

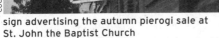

COURTESY OF ROB MATHENY

sign advertising the autumn pierogi sale at St. John the Baptist Church

including *Striking Distance* and *Innocent Blood,* have been shot here.

TAP ROOM $$

530 William Penn Pl., 412/281-7100, www.omnihotels.com

HOURS: Sun.-Thurs. 11:30 A.M.-1 A.M., Fri.-Sat. 11:30 A.M.-2 A.M.

An English-style pub located in the lobby of the upmarket Omni William Penn Hotel, the Tap Room is the perfect spot to hold a casual business meeting. The fare here isn't anything unusual—just typical tavern-style food and plenty of beer—but the cozy ambience is unlike anything else Downtown. If it's chilly outside, try a bowl of the locally legendary chili.

ASIAN

HABITAT $$$

510 Market St., 412/773-8848, www.habitatrestaurant.com

HOURS: Sun.-Thurs. 6:30 A.M.-2 P.M. and 5:30-10 P.M., Fri.-Sat. 6:30 A.M.-2 P.M. and 5:30-10:30 P.M.

It's certainly a bit unusual for a hotel restaurant, of all things, to feature an oversized chef's table with a perfect view of a wide-open kitchen. But then again, Habitat, which is located within the city's best-known new hotel, The Fairmont, is anything but average. The menu, for instance, featuring dishes from around the globe, might be thought of as the compliment to the hotel's guests, who hail from around the globe themselves. And although many of the entrées with roots in Asian, Indian, and even European cooking are prepared in the kitchen's tandoor oven, or in a wok (pad thai, chicken tikka masala, Maine lobster curry), standard domestic fare (with an inevitable fusion twist) is also available. Try the Elysian Fields lamb loin or the half-pound Habitat burger for something special but simple.

LEMON GRASS CAFÉ $$

124 6th St., 412/765-2222

HOURS: Mon.-Fri. 11 A.M.-9 P.M., Sat. 11 A.M.-1 P.M., Sun. 4-9 P.M.

No need to shed a tear about the closing of the crosstown Cambodian restaurant Phnom Penh; Lemon Grass Café is its sister restaurant and offers essentially the same menu but in a somewhat classier setting. (And with somewhat pricier entrées.) Curries seem to win the popularity contest here, but it's definitely worth the effort to try something slightly more adventurous, like the spicy mussels or the Haw Mook (steamed fish with coconut milk). Some Chinese and Thai entrées are also on offer here; the pad thai frequently earns approving nods. Don't fancy a sit-down meal? Try the take-away stand out front, which is always open for business during Pittsburgh Pirates home games.

CONTEMPORARY AND NEW AMERICAN

NINE ON NINE $$$

900 Penn Ave., 412/338-6463, www.nineonnine.com

HOURS: Mon. 11:30 A.M.-2 P.M., Tues.-Fri. 11:30 A.M.-2 P.M. and 5-10 P.M., Sat. 5-10 P.M.

One of the most recent (and most welcome) additions to the Cultural District's contemporary dining scene, Nine on Nine is the sort of elegant establishment not often found in Midwestern or Rust Belt locales. Both the menu and the ambience here are striking; grilled quail, wing of stingray, and Amish chicken are just a few of the unusual offerings. The wine list is 29 names long, and the artfully prepared desserts are said to be just as majestic as the entrées.

INDIAN

◖ SREE'S INDIAN FOOD $

701 Smithfield St., 412/860-9181, www.srees.com

HOURS: Mon.-Fri. 11:30 A.M.-3 P.M.

It doesn't get much simpler—or much cheaper—than Sree's, where flavorful and all-vegan South Indian food is served cafeteria-style. All vegetarian meals are $4 and include a choice of three veggie selections on top of a massive bed of rice. The menu rotates daily, and chicken is available for an extra dollar. Finishing a Sree's lunch in one sitting is no easy task, and because of its substantial value, dining here daily has become a habit for many Downtown desk jockeys, not to mention half the city's fleet of bike messengers. Sree's also has locations in Squirrel Hill

(2103 Murray Ave., 412/860-9181, Mon.–Fri. 5–9 P.M.) and on CMU's campus (trailer on Margaret Morrison St., 412/860-9181, Mon.–Fri. 11 A.M.–3 P.M.).

LATIN AMERICAN
SEVICHE $$

930 Penn Ave., 412/697-3120, www.seviche.com
HOURS: Mon.-Thurs. 5 P.M.-midnight, Fri.-Sat. 5 P.M.-1 A.M.

Operated under the direction of chef Yves Carreau, who also oversees the menu at the nearby Sonoma Grille (947 Penn Ave.), Seviche is nothing less than a cultural anomaly in Pittsburgh: If Latin American–style seafood tapas are what you're after, this is currently the city's solitary locale at which to track them down. As for the seviche itself—fresh seafood marinated in citrus fruit juices—more than a dozen varieties are available, including Bahamian conch and Scottish salmon. Seviche's happy hour is also hugely popular (Mon.–Thurs.

5–7 P.M. and Sat. 10 P.M.–midnight; try the mojitos), as are the restaurant's weekly salsa nights (Mondays at 9:30 P.M.), where beginners' dance lessons are on the house.

SEAFOOD
ORIGINAL FISH MARKET $$$

1001 Liberty Ave., 412/227-3657, www.originalfishmarketpgh.com
HOURS: Mon.-Fri. 11 A.M.-1 A.M., Sat.-Sun. 4 P.M.-1 A.M.

Tucked deep inside Downtown's Westin Hotel, the Original Fish Market serves what many claim to be the city's best sushi. (And for what it's worth, this author concurs.) A fantastic fresh seafood menu is also on offer—on it you'll find grouper, seared king salmon, ahi tuna, grilled swordfish, and the daily catch, among other house specialties. Better still is the fact that the Fish Market keeps such late hours; aside from a few greasy spoons on the South Side and the East End, this is one of Pittsburgh's very few late-night dining options.

Strip District   Map 1

Pittsburgh may not have a Chinatown, but it does have the Strip District—an international neighborhood brimming with everything from Asian grocery stores to Italian delis.

AMERICAN
DELUCA'S RESTAURANT $$

2015 Penn Ave., 412/566-2195
HOURS: Mon.-Sat. 6 A.M.-3 P.M., Sun. 7 A.M.-3 P.M.

A truly rough-around-the-edges diner in the finest greasy spoon tradition, DeLuca's has held legendary status among Pittsburgh's breakfast aficionados for eons now, this is the place to bring an out-of-town visitor who wants to experience the *real* Steel City. The menu is exactly what you'd expect: massive plates full of eggs, bacon, and buttered toast. For something a bit different, try the fruit-filled pancakes; a regular order is so large you may not be able to finish it in one sitting. Or go for the breakfast burrito, but try not to snicker at the slices

of processed American cheese melted on top. Remember: You've come for the *experience*.

PAMELA'S DINER $$

60 21st St., 412/281-6366, www.pamelasdiner.com
HOURS: Mon.-Sat. 7 A.M.-3 P.M., Sun. 8 A.M.-3 P.M.

A much loved mini-chain, Pamela's Diner is your best bet for a quality, even-tempered breakfast experience; last night's date will feel just as comfortable munching on toast here as will your visiting parents. Truthfully though, the fare at any given Pamela's isn't much different than your average greasy spoon—it's the crowd you'll run into here that makes the difference: students, hipsters, and young parents, mostly. The pancakes here are what most folks rave about, although take care not to miss the omelets, which are some of the most satisfying in the city. There are five other locations throughout the city in Shadyside (5527 Walnut St., 412/683-1003), Squirrel Hill (5813 Forbes

RESTAURANTS

You can expect to see interesting wall decor at Pamela's Diner.

Ave., 412/422-9457), Oakland (3703 Forbes Ave., 412/683-4066), Millvale (232 North Ave., 412/821-4655), and Mt. Lebanon (427 Washington Rd., 412/343-3344).

【 PRIMANTI BROTHERS ❸
46 18th St., 412/263-2142, www.primantibros.com
HOURS: Daily 24 hours

Much more than just a restaurant, the original Primanti Brothers location in the Strip is a destination, a tourist attraction, and a staple of Pittsburgh's history. The rumors you've heard are true: A huge pile of french fries, and sometimes a fried egg, go *inside* the sandwich, which is already stacked sky-high with coleslaw and your choice of artery-clogging meat (roast beef and pastrami are favorites). Soups and salads can also be ordered, but most folks don't bother. With five city locations in the

Strip District (46 18th St., 412/263-2142), South Side (1832 E. Carson St., 412/381-2583), Oakland (3803 Forbes Ave., 412/621-4444), and Downtown (11 Cherry Way, 412/566-8051; 2 S. Market Pl., 412/261-1599), and six more in the suburbs, you've got few excuses to miss this venerable Pittsburgh institution. And yes, vegetarians can always order sandwiches without meat.

ROLAND'S SEAFOOD GRILL ❸❸
1904 Penn Ave., 412/261-3401,
www.rolandsseafoodgrill.com
HOURS: Sun.-Thurs. 11 A.M.-1 A.M., Fri.-Sat. 11 A.M.-2 A.M.

A little nervous to try seafood in a land-locked locale like the 'Burgh? Don't be. Roland's serves an especially fresh and varied selection of all things oceanic at its nearly always-packed seafood bar—everything from lobster tails to the universally popular beer-battered fish sandwich. Arrive later in the evening, and you'll find Roland's transformed into a rowdy nightspot. The two-level deck is especially popular; wander by on a weekend night and you won't be able to miss the roaring hoards holding court high above Penn Avenue.

ASIAN
SUSHI KIM ❸❸
1241 Penn Ave., 412/281-9956, www.sushikim.com
HOURS: Mon. 5-9 P.M., Tues.-Thurs. 11:30 A.M.-2:30 P.M. and 5-10 P.M., Fri.-Sat. 11:30 A.M.-10:30 P.M., Sun. noon-9 P.M.

Tucked away on a battered stretch of Penn Avenue between Downtown and the Strip, Sushi Kim is a local diamond in the rough: The decor exists somewhere between Asian pop culture and hipster kitsch, and the entrée list is split evenly between traditional Japanese and Korean dishes—about 40 in all. But most come here for the sushi, which is some of the best in the Strip. (Other smart options include the take-away counter at Wholey's on Penn Avenue and at Benkovitz Seafoods on Smallman Street.) Particularly amusing are the massive sushi boats, a sort of combo platter for the young-at-heart fresh-fish lover.

THE GOODIE TRUCK

At some sad and strange point in the history of Americana, the cultural icon known throughout suburbia as the Ice Cream Man somehow transformed from "charming fellow in a pressed white uniform delivering old-fashioned sweets" to the stuff of kitsch, innuendo, and cheap horror movies.

Need an example? Do a search on YouTube for the Smashing Pumpkins video for "Today." Or track down the awful Paul Norman horror film *Ice Cream Man*, which featured the groan-worthy tagline, "I scream, you scream, we all scream for ice cream!" And then, of course, there are the rumors of low-level crime. Who among you, after all, hasn't heard of ice cream truck professionals who aren't merely selling cold treats from those vans? So someone, it seems, had to bring the profession back to good-hearted prominence.

Enter The Goodie Truck (412/404-6626, the goodietruck@gmail.com). Two Pittsburgh residents by the names of Millie Gregor and Jajean Morgan decided in 2008 that they would not only sanctify the ice cream profession, but would also improve on the very concept itself. To wit: Instead of serving mass-produced ice cream sandwiches, generic red white-and blue

popsicles and Choco Tacos, they'd spice things up a bit with authentic baked goods and occasional creations from their unique baking repertoire: Chocolate-covered spicy tortillas, for instance, and a thick, mouth-watering chocolate mousse.

And to subtract a further element of eccentricity, the women of The Goodie Truck (which, by the way, can be hired to appear at private events) don't rove the streets of Pittsburgh seeking to lure children from their very homes. Instead, they encourage people to follow the Goodie Truck's frequent Facebook and Twitter feeds (www.twitter.com/thegoodietruck), on which the truck's upcoming locations are posted. (A partial menu is available online at www.myspace.com/thegoodietruck.)

Essentially, the Goodie Truck is all about providing adults with fresh-baked sweets, and letting folks know where to find them beforehand. It's a novel concept. And maybe one that legitimate ice cream folk should consider mimicking in the future.

(Contributed by Matt Stroud, a Pittsburgh-based freelance journalist.)

CAFÉS
LA PRIMA ESPRESSO COMPANY ⑤
205 21st St., 412/281-1922, www.laprima.com

HOURS: Mon.-Sat. 6 A.M.-4 P.M., Sun. 8 A.M.-3 P.M.

Some call La Prima the most authentic espresso shop in Pittsburgh, and if you show up during the morning rush, you'll see why. Clusters of middle-aged men gather around the front counter with espresso and Italian-language newspapers, and the baristas busily craft specialty drinks with speed and skill. (Look for the leaf or heart design that'll likely be etched atop your latte or cappuccino.) Even drip coffee is something special here; there's almost always a Central American fair-trade or shade-grown selection on offer.

CARIBBEAN
KAYA ⑤⑤
2000 Smallman St., 412/261-6565, www.bigburrito.com/kaya

HOURS: Mon.-Wed. 11:30 A.M.-10 P.M., Thurs.-Sat. 11:30 A.M.-11 P.M., Sun. 11 A.M.-9 P.M.

An island paradise in the heart of the Strip's warehouse district, Kaya represents the Caribbean arm of the local Big Burrito restaurant group. This is certainly Pittsburgh's premiere locale for Jamaican jerk chicken and Cuban sandwiches, and what's more, the menu changes daily, so dining here often feels as much like a vicarious travel experience as it does a culinary adventure. The clientele leans toward the young, beautiful, and trust-funded, and the happy hour is a scene unto itself; saddle up for tropical island drinks or a martini.

CONTEMPORARY AND NEW AMERICAN
ELEVEN ⑤⑤⑤
1150 Smallman St., 412/201-5656, www.bigburrito.com/eleven

HOURS: Mon.-Thurs. 11:30 A.M.-10 P.M., Fri. 11:30 A.M.-11 P.M., Sat. 5-11 P.M., Sun. 11 A.M.-9 P.M.

The aptly named Eleven (it's the 11th creation of the Big Burrito restaurant group) has lately become a particularly strong cornerstone of the fine contemporary dining scene in Pittsburgh. The philosophy is contemporary, too: As a serious adherent to the slow food movement, Chef Greg Alauzen and his four-star charges take pains to include seasonal, regional ingredients in most dishes. You can expect all the usual suspects, of course: Elysian Fields lamb, pulled pork. But it's the gracefully prepared plates that truly make dining here a high-art experience. The wine list here is nearly 150 names long.

SNACKS AND DESSERTS
KLAVON'S ICE CREAM PARLOR ⑤
2801 Penn Ave., 412-434/0451, www.klavonsicecream.com

HOURS: Mon.-Tues. 10 A.M.-5 P.M., Wed.-Fri. 10 A.M.-9 P.M., Sat.-Sun. noon-9 P.M.

You wouldn't necessarily know it from walking past the uninspiring facade, but this art deco drugstore and ice cream shop is the real deal. It opened way back in 1925, and all the trimmings are original, including the marble soda fountain and its attendant swivel stools, which are designed to look like soda bottle caps. Along with the regular assortment of sundaes

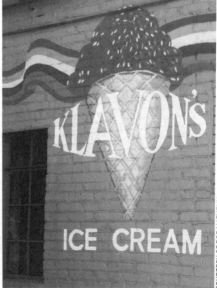

Klavon's Ice Cream Parlor has been serving ice cream since 1925.

and banana splits, Klavon's also stocks a wide array of old school–style candy and even boasts a sandwich and soup menu for the sugar-phobic. Brooklynites, by the way, swear by the New York Egg Cream here, so don't miss it.

PEACE, LOVE & LITTLE DONUTS $
2018 Smallman St., 412/489-7693,
www.peaceloveandlittledonuts.com
HOURS: Mon.-Fri. 6 A.M.-2 P.M., Sat. 8 A.M.-4 P.M.,
Sun. 9 A.M.-2 P.M.

It was only a matter of time before a family-friendly sweets shop like Peace, Love & Little Donuts opened up in the Strip, which transforms into one of city's busiest tourist attractions on the weekend. The bite-sized confections sold here are offered with a staggering array of creative and candy-heavy toppings, most of them variations on the same sort of old-school donuts that Dunkin' once specialized in. A second, smaller location recently opened inside Fernando's Café (963 Liberty Ave., Downtown, 412/281-4522, www.fernandoscafe.com), and a third is in the works.

North Side — Map 1

Some of the North Side's more interesting restaurants have recently closed, although the majority of tourists who come to this part of town find themselves in the so-called North Shore area surrounding PNC Park; a good number of chain restaurants and cafés serving bar food can be found there. Wander up to the commercial strip of East Ohio Street to find more restaurants, including old taverns where patrons still toss their peanut shells on the floor. And when visiting The Andy Warhol Museum, don't hesitate to grab a bite in the downstairs cafeteria; it's owned by the Big Burrito Group—responsible for such local eateries as Casbah, Kaya, Soba, and Eleven—which means that high-quality fare is a given.

AMERICAN
WILSON'S BAR-B-Q $$
700 N. Taylor Ave., 412/322-7427
HOURS: Mon.-Wed. noon-8 P.M., Thurs.-Sat. noon-10 P.M.

Tucked into the deepest recesses of the Mexican War Streets, Wilson's Bar-B-Q has long been lauded as absolutely top-notch Southern pit barbeque. "Genuine" is probably the best word to describe the place: Most everyone takes the award-winning chicken and pork ribs to go, and the shop itself is utilitarian at best. But no matter, as the delectable meat at Wilson's simply falls off the bone and melts in your mouth—the result of a wood-fired grill and a family sauce recipe handed down from ex-slave ancestors, according to employees.

CAFÉS
BUENA VISTA COFFEE
1501 Buena Vista St., 412/224-2778, www.bvcoffee.com
HOURS: Mon.-Fri. 7:30 A.M.-7 P.M., Sat.-Sun. 9 A.M.-7 P.M.

Among Pittsburgh's abundance of coffeehouses, Buena Vista stands out not only for its off-the-beaten-path location—it's in a part of the North Side that lacks a central business district—but also because of its claim to Hollywood-style fame: Buena Vista was a filming location for *Love and Other Drugs,* a 2010 romantic comedy starring Jake Gyllenhaal and Anne Hathaway. Filmed all throughout the city and its suburbs, the Edward Zwick production included a number of scenes shot at Buena Vista, where Hathaway's character worked. The decor here contains many mementos from the film shoot, and the menu consists not only of truly excellent coffee, espresso drinks, and pastries, but also paninis, wraps, and homemade cookies. Most likely though, the major topic of conversation at Buena Vista—at least for the next year or so—will be the film that put the city's Mexican War Streets neighborhood on the big screen.

RESTAURANTS

© MATT STROUD

Hoi Polloi Vegetarian Café and Coffeehouse

HOI POLLOI VEGETARIAN CAFÉ AND COFFEEHOUSE ❸

1100 Galveston Ave., 412/586-4567,
www.hoipolloicafe.com

HOURS: Daily 7 A.M.-5 P.M.

Hoi Polloi—a Greek phrase used sarcastically by hip English-speaking folks to mean something like "the great unwashed masses"—is more of a restaurant than a coffee shop, but the mingling of the two worlds works to this café's distinct advantage: Sweet baked goods are featured, as well as all kinds of organic juices, coffee (of course), and cheap sandwiches and wraps. What's more, it's all vegan- and vegetarian-friendly. In fact, travelers from literally hundreds of miles away drop by this quaint North Side eatery mid-jaunt because of that very reason, and also because Hoi Polloi is in a part of the North Side that's not too posh or stuffy.

GERMAN

PENN BREWERY ❸❸

800 Vinial St., 412/237-9402, www.pennbrew.com

HOURS: Mon.-Sat. 11 A.M.-midnight

The Penn Brewery isn't your average brewpub. The interior is designed to resemble a Deutschland mead hall, and if you time your visit right, you might catch a lederhosen-clad German band entertaining on the outdoor patio. And although it's plenty comfortable to belly up to the bar here and order a Penn Weizen, Penn Brewery is also a fantastic place to dine. Dinners are heavy, authentic, and artery clogging; imagine steak drenched in dark beer sauce or tender beef sirloin rolls stuffed with bacon, and you'll start to get the idea. The lunch menu here is also especially popular and features all manner of *leberwursts* and *burgerneisters*. A small selection of vegetarian entrées and sandwiches are available.

Oakland   Map 2

This is Pittsburgh's university district, which means affordable pub grub, fast food, and wonderful ethnic restaurants can be found almost anywhere. Try to avoid the chains, however, and instead try something new and different that grabs your interest. Oakland is a literal bounty for the food lover, and new spots serving unusual fare open quite frequently.

AMERICAN
FUEL AND FUDDLE $
212 Oakland Ave., 412/682-3473,
www.fuelandfuddle.com
HOURS: Daily 11 A.M.-2 A.M.
A popular college eatery centered around the dual themes of bar food and good beer, Fuel and Fuddle is the perfect place to eat when you can't quite decide what you're in the mood for. The menu consists of large plates of pub grub and finger foods, such as chicken wings, Thai skewers, jack cheese quesadillas, and nacho plates. Beer specials change daily.

HEMINGWAY'S $
3911 Forbes Ave., 412/621-4100,
www.hemingways-cafe.com
HOURS: Mon.-Fri. 11 A.M.-2 A.M., Sat. 6 P.M -2 A.M.
Once a must-see stop on the city's bohemian café circuit, Hemingway's is now more of an epicenter for observing primal meathead behavior. The beer doth flow here, and boy is it cheap. But get here before dark falls, and you might just find the English-pub atmosphere and its attendant pub-grub menu rather charming. What's more, Hemingway's commands an enviable location on the University of Pittsburgh campus, making it a perfect place to meet up for a burger or sandwich before a raging night out. Just make sure you go easy on the $1 Miller Lites, bro.

(THE ORIGINAL HOT DOG SHOP $
3901 Forbes Ave., 412/621-7388,
www.originalhotdogshop.com
HOURS: Sun.-Thurs. 10 A.M.-4 A.M., Fri.-Sat. 10 A.M.-5 A.M.
Much more than just a corner hot dog and pizza shop, "The O," as it's known locally, is

The Original Hot Dog Shop is known locally as "The O."

RESTAURANTS

MARKETS AND GROCERY STORES

Pittsburgh's most popular grocery store chain – by a long shot – is the locally headquartered Giant Eagle. More than 200 stores are located throughout Western Pennsylvania, West Virginia, Ohio, and Maryland, and just about every neighborhood in the city seems to have its own location. Some of the bigger locations even boast in-store cafés, video rental outlets, banks, and daycare centers. Other major area chains include **Shop 'n Save** (various locations, www.shopnsavefood.com, hours vary at each location) and **Foodland** (various locations, www.foodlandstores.com, hours vary at each location). Over the past few years, a number of Foodland stores have been bought out by **Shur Save** (various locations, www.shursavemarkets.com, hours vary at each location).

Wholey's Market

COURTESY OF ROB MATHENY

You'll find the city's solitary **Whole Foods Market** (5880 Centre Ave., 412/441-7960, www.wholefoodsmarket.com, daily 8 A.M.-10 P.M.) in East Liberty, just east of the recently reconstructed Shadyside **Giant Eagle** (5550 Centre Ave., 412/681-1500, www.gianteagle.com, daily 6 A.M.-midnight), which for years now has been going head to head with Whole Foods in the battle for upscale customers. If organic food and healthy eating is your thing but corporations aren't, head to the **East End Food Co-op** (7516 Meade St., 412/242-3598, www.eastendfoodcoop.com, daily 8 A.M.-9 P.M.) in Point Breeze. The co-op has a wonderful in-store café, a fantastic organic produce selection, and probably the best bulk section in town.

The Strip District is home to a number of unique grocery stores. Topping the list is **Wholey's Market** (1501 Penn Ave., 412/391-3737, www.wholey.com, Mon.-Thurs. 8 A.M.-5:30 P.M., Fri. 8 A.M.-6 P.M., Sat. 8 A.M.-5 P.M., Sun. 9 A.M.-4 P.M.), a store so legendary in Pittsburgh that it often does double duty as a tourist attraction. Shoppers come here for the wide selection of fish and meats, while out-of-towners come to gawk at the plush farm animals in the dairy section that play musical instruments at the push of a button. (And by the way, the proper pronunciation isn't "whole-eze," it's "wool-eze.") Don't miss the sushi bar at the store's entrance.

Also check out the **Pennsylvania Macaroni Company** (2010 Penn Ave., 412/471-8330, www.pennmac.com, Mon.-Sat. 6:30 A.M.-4:30 P.M., Sun. 9:30 A.M.-2 P.M.); call it "Penn Mac" if you want to sound like a local. Here you'll find an overwhelming selection of Italian pastas and sauces, and possibly the city's finest cheese counter.

The recently opened **Pittsburgh Public Market** (2100 Smallman St., 412/281-4505, www.pittsburghpublicmarket.org, Fri. 9 A.M.-6 P.M., Sat. 9 A.M.-5 P.M., Sun. 10 A.M.-4 P.M.) can also be found in the Strip, specifically in the Produce Terminal Building. With a diverse collection of more than 40 separate vendors hawking everything from healthy take-away snacks, gifts, beauty products, accessories for pets, and of course, produce and grocery offerings galore, this weekend-only public market is essentially Pittsburgh's answer to the historic Reading Terminal Market in Philadelphia.

Lotus Food Co. (1649 Penn Ave., 412/281-3050, daily 9 A.M.-6 P.M.) is by far the most popular Asian grocery store in the Strip. It carries a multitude of food items imported from North and South Asia, including durian fruit! For hard-to-find and specialty Japanese food stuffs, check out the small but packed **Tokyo Japanese Food Store** (5855 Ellsworth Ave., 412/661-3777, www.tokyostorepgh.com, Tues.-Sat. 10 A.M.-7 P.M., Sun. 10 A.M.-5 P.M.) in Shadyside, which is fun to explore even when you're not planning to buy. You'll find everything from take-away sushi and bento boxes to Japanese bakery foods, Asian periodicals, Asian cookware and snacks, and imported Japanese cigarettes.

And if you're an especially frugal or health-conscious grocery shopper, you'll surely want to wield a cart throughout the aisles of **Trader Joe's** (6343 Penn Ave., East Liberty, 412/363-5748, www.traderjoes.com, daily 9 A.M.-9 P.M.). The store sells organic, vegan, and whole foods at relatively low prices. A bit further afield in the city's suburbs is **Back to Basics** (300 Mt. Lebanon Blvd., Mt. Lebanon, 412/343-8156, www.back2basicsinc.com, Mon. and Thurs. 10 A.M.-8 P.M., Tues., Wed., and Fri. 10 A.M.-6 P.M., Sat. 10 A.M.-5 P.M.) a self-described "nutrition and dietary shop" known for its generous supply of vitamins and supplements. A num-

ber of slightly esoteric wellness services can also be had here, including naturopathy and iridology.

Also located out in the city's northern suburbs – but undoubtedly worth a visit, even if you aren't planning to buy groceries – is the jaw-droppingly enormous **Giant Eagle Market District** (100 Settlers Ridge Center Dr., 412/788-5392, www.marketdistrict.com), located in Robinson Township's relatively new **Settler's Ridge Shopping Center** (www.cbldevelopment.com/settlersridge). Open 24 hours a day, seven days a week, a *Pittsburgh Post-Gazette* reporter referred to the 150,000-square-foot supermarket – quite accurately, in fact – as a "foodie fun park," and even half-seriously suggested that visitors bring along a pair of roller skates with which to traverse the many aisles here. A few of the store's impressive features – to say nothing of the overwhelming selection of both standard and gourmet groceries – include a huge food court, an olive oil station, a pizza bar, a sushi bar, an Asian street food bar, and even a cooking school.

COURTESY OF ROB MAT-HENY

Pennsylvania Macaroni Company, known as "Penn Mac"

nothing less than a Pittsburgh institution. Opened in 1960, it's probably safe to say that anyone who's ever spent time in the nearby Pitt dorms has a story to tell about "The O." The all-natural dogs are world class, but most come here for the ridiculously large baskets of cheese fries, or the cheap pizzas, or at least a six-pack. "The O" is always at its best after dark, when things are crowded and chaotic.

UNION GRILL ⑤⑤
413 S. Craig St., 412/681-8620
HOURS: Mon.-Thurs. 11:30 A.M.-10 P.M., Fri.-Sat., 11:30 A.M.-11 P.M., Sun. noon-9 P.M.

If it's simple, hearty American fare you're after, you won't do much better in this stretch of town than the Union Grill. Burgers are the really big item here, clocking in at around a half pound after cooking. Just about every entrée includes more food than the average person can consume in one sitting, though, from the sandwiches and veggie wraps to the chicken entrées and crab cakes. If you've managed to save room for dessert, make it a slice of the homemade pie, and when the weather's warm, request a sidewalk table for optimum Craig Street people-watching.

ASIAN
LULU'S NOODLES ⑤
400 S. Craig St., 412/687-7777
HOURS: Daily 11 A.M.-10 P.M.

Living somewhere in between cafeteria-style casual dining and chic urban café, Lulu's Noodles is a favorite destination for budget-conscious Pitt and CMU undergrads looking for good value in a stylish setting. Portion sizes are generous, too: Order a noodle dish—the Singapore rice noodles are a good bet—and you'll have a tough time cleaning your plate. Noodle soups are also recommended, and since Lulu's shares a counter and a kitchen with its sister restaurant, Yum Wok Pan Asian Diner, you're practically guaranteed to find something on one of the two menus that appeals—even if it's just a take-away bubble tea.

OISHII BENTO ⑤⑤
119 Oakland Ave., 412/687-3335, www.oishiibento.com
HOURS: Mon.-Fri. 10:30 A.M.-9 P.M., Sat. 11 A.M.-9 P.M.

What a concept: A traditional Japanese *bento* restaurant right in the heart of the university district, featuring a mini-sushi counter, Japanese-style floor seating, and even a selection of Korean dishes. No wonder Oishii Bento—the name means "Yummy Lunchbox"—is such a raging success. Prices are reasonable, the menu is completely unique, and each order of food is its very own work of art. For a truly filling lunch, go with one of the meat or veggie rice bowls. For pure fun, though, simply pick and choose at random; aside from sleeping in and skipping class, Oishii Bento is certainly one of Oakland's most amusing midday distractions.

SPICE ISLAND TEA HOUSE ⑤⑤
253 Atwood St., 412/687-8821, www.spiceislandteahouse.com
HOURS: Mon.-Thurs. 11:30 A.M.-9 P.M., Fri.-Sat. 11:30 A.M.-10 P.M.

A pan-Asian legend that for eons now has been introducing Oakland's college community to Indonesian, Burmese, Thai, Cambodian, and Filipino food, Spice Island Tea House is one of the area's few can't-miss institutions. With its charming mismatched furniture and thatched-roof vibe, even a bad meal here would still be fun—but nearly every Spice Island entrée is a crowd pleaser, especially the Indonesian and Thai rice dishes. (Some of the Burmese soups can be a bit scary.) Along with the restaurant's impressive selection of exotic loose-leaf teas, beer and wine are available.

SUSHI BOAT ⑤⑤
128 Oakland Ave., 412/681-1818
HOURS: Mon.-Fri. 10:30 A.M.-9 P.M., Sat. 11 A.M.-9 P.M., closed Sun.

Slightly cheaper than Oishii Bento across the street (and with a bit more of a low-rent cafeteria vibe), Sushi Boat tends to fill up fast during peak lunch hours, especially as Pitt students arrive to grab a bite between classes. Both Chinese and Japanese dishes are served here, although maki, nigiri, and sashimi sushi are the big draw; expect to pay around $1.50 per piece. For the biggest bang for your buck, go with the vegetarian rice bowl or the seafood fried rice platter.

CAFÉS
KIVA HAN §
420 S. Craig St., 412/687-6355, www.kivahan.com
HOURS: Mon.-Thurs. 7 A.M.-11 P.M., Fri. 7 A.M.-midnight, Sun. 8 A.M.-11 P.M.

A long-time favorite of nearby Pitt and CMU students who tend to use it as something of an extended living room, Kiva Han is probably best known today for its impressive longevity in a part of town that is nearly overflowing with coffee shops—not to mention the corporate café behemoth located directly across the street. So it's a good thing, then, that the shop's espresso, sandwiches, and pastries are so good. Being right on the corner of Forbes and South Craig Streets, the café is also a prime people-watching location, and what's more, folk or electronic musicians occasionally perform here in the evenings.

INDIAN
INDIA GARDEN §§
328 Atwood St., 412/682-3000, www.indiagarden.net
HOURS: Mon.-Fri. 11:30 A.M.-2:30 P.M. and 5-11 P.M., Sat.-Sun. 12:30-11 P.M.

Expect a somewhat chaotic atmosphere at India Garden, one of Oakland's most popular Indian joints (and most authentic, according to some). Every year, it seems, the food here wins some sort of award from a Pittsburgh publication (including the *Pittsburgh City Paper*'s Best Indian award), and you'll certainly understand the hype after trying any of the savory curries, chicken tandooris, or *tikka masalas*. Vegetarians also have cause to rejoice, as the meat-free dishes are absolutely celestial. (Try the eggplant.) Dinners are 50 percent off daily 4–6 P.M. and 10 P.M.–1 A.M.

STAR OF INDIA §§
412 S. Craig St., 412/681-5700
HOURS: Daily 11:30 A.M.-2:30 P.M., Sun.-Thurs. 5-10 P.M., Fri.-Sat. 5-10:30 P.M.

Northern Indian fare is served almost exclusively here, meaning curries and tandooris are the specialty. But unlike at Atwood Street's slightly more jubilant India Garden, the scene can be a bit staid. That said, Star of India is a decent place to bring your parents, or a date that you're trying to impress. Definitely order appetizers of samosas and *nan* (flatbread); both are particularly toasty and crispy, but with a nice softness on the inside. The lamb and vegetarian entrées here are also popular, and when dinner's done, take a stroll through the Indian grocery store across the street for imported soft drinks.

ITALIAN
LUCCA §§§
317 S. Craig St., 412/682-3310, www.luccaristorante.com
HOURS: Mon.-Fri. 11:30 A.M.-2 P.M. and 5-10 P.M., Sat. 5-11 P.M., Sun. 4:30-9 P.M.

Assuming you aren't bothered by the chants of the animal-liberation activists out front, who frequently enjoy protesting the restaurant's use of foie gras, you'll likely fall in love with Lucca, one of the city's more luxurious Italian cuisine establishments. Young movers and shakers and swooning couples on dates flock here for the fettuccine, couscous, and caramelized onions and also for the quaint decor and the staff's impeccable attention to detail. If money's not an issue and you've got a discriminating palate to impress, Lucca's your place.

MEXICAN
MAD MEX §§
370 Atwood St., 412/681-5656, www.madmex.com
HOURS: Daily 11 A.M.-1 A.M.

For lovers of quality Tex-Mex and massive food portions, it doesn't get much better than Mad Mex, a locally based restaurant-and-bar chain. The menu here is an inventive collection of burritos, enchiladas, or

RESTAURANTS

quesadillas with a twist: portobello mush-rooms inside, say, or tofu or chickpea chili. If it's the truly sublime you're after, go with the Dance Marathon Burrito (spinach, por-tobellos, and marinated chicken) or the Kristy's Big Sister's Red Velvet Burrito, complete with *pico de gallo* and zucchini in-side. Graciously, food is half-off every night 11 P.M.–1 A.M.; expect long lines. Other loca-tions are in Monroeville (4100 William Pen Hwy., 412/349-6767), Robinson (Robinson Township, 2 Robinson Plaza, Park Manor Dr., 412/494-5656), Cranberry (20510 Perry Hwy, 724/741-5656), the South Hills (2010 Greentree Rd., 412/279-0200), and the North Hills (7905 McKnight Rd., 412/366-5656).

MIDDLE EASTERN
ALI BABA ⑤⑤
404 S. Craig St., 412/682-2829,
www.alibabapittsburgh.com

HOURS: Mon.-Fri. 11:30 A.M.-2:30 P.M. and 4:30-9:45 P.M.

A longtime Craig Street favorite, Ali Baba is the Steel City's preeminent Middle Eastern deal. ("The best Middle Eastern restaurant in Pittsburgh," according to *Pittsburgh* mag-azine.) And while prices may indeed be fit for a college-style budget, it's easy to pretend you're living large here, what with the de-cidedly classy decor and ambience. In other words, a student dive this most definitely is not, although Pitt and CMU types (and their parents and professors) are almost always in attendance. Food-wise, it's tough to go wrong, although the Shish Kebab Dinner is partic-ularly inviting, as is the Shiek El-Mahshi (roasted eggplant with seasoned lamb). The baklava is an especially agreeable dessert; be aware that the BYO policy extends to wine only.

Dave & Andy's still makes its ice cream with wooden churns and rock salt.

SNACKS AND DESSERTS
DAVE & ANDY'S ⑤
207 Atwood St., 412/681-9906
HOURS: Mon.-Fri. 11:30 A.M.-10 P.M.,
Sat.-Sun. noon-10 P.M.

Without a doubt, this non-chain store is the finest purveyor of ice cream in Pittsburgh. The confections at Dave & Andy's are good for a reason: Ice cream is made the old-fashioned way, with wooden churns and rock salt. The re-sult? Fresh, perfectly creamy ice cream offered in a regularly rotating selection of flavors. Ask for yours in a homemade waffle cone, which includes a handful of M&Ms that plug up the hole at the bottom.

South Side   Map 3

The South Side is widely known as party central to most Pittsburghers, who fill the pubs and taverns here on weekends. East Carson is where you'll find most of the action, including the majority of good places to eat. You'll find some ethnic options here, including a wonderful French restaurant, a good number of Italian places, and two decent Japanese locales. Naturally, pizza shops abound.

AMERICAN
DOUBLE WIDE GRILL 💲💲

2339 E. Carson St., 412/390-1111,
www.doublewidegrill.com
HOURS: Daily 11 A.M.-2 A.M.

Something of a themed restaurant that exists inside a heavily retrofitted old gas station, the Double Wide Grill does a beautiful job of paying homage to mid-century American car culture. Aside from an actual pickup truck suspended above the bar, a wonderful collection of auto-industry detritus hangs from nearly every surface here. The menu features

barbecue, pub-grub style food, and plenty of vegetarian and vegan options, with items such as the Hubcap Fries, Death Row Delmonico, and Build Your Own TV Dinner. The food, while certainly not Pittsburgh's finest, is generally of above-average quality.

🅒 FAT HEAD'S SALOON 💲💲

1805 E. Carson St., 412/431-7433, www.fatheads.com
HOURS: Mon.-Thurs. 11 A.M.-midnight, Fri.-Sat.
11 A.M.-1 A.M., Sun. 11 A.M.-11 P.M.

Fat Head's is easily one of the South Side's best bar and grill joints, although it's more popularly known as a premiere East Carson locale in which to get good and tanked. Clearly, that has much to do with the three dozen or so imports and craft brews on tap, but pick up a menu between pints and you'll find that Fat Heads has much more than just alcohol on offer: in short, a pub-grub-on-steroids menu featuring mostly burgers, sandwiches, and the massive (and massively popular) "headwiches." Diners watching their waistlines, in others

RESTAURANTS

COURTESY OF ROB MATHEN™

The Double Wide Grill serves pub grub in a retrofitted vintage gas station.

words, will want to proceed to Fat Head's with extreme prejudice.

GRAND CONCOURSE $$$

100 W. Station Square Dr., 412/261-1717, www.muer.com
HOURS: Mon.-Thurs. 11 A.M.-10 P.M., Fri. 11 A.M.-11 P.M., Sat. 11:30 A.M.-11 P.M., Sun. 10 A.M.-10 P.M.

Located in the concourse of the old P&LE Railway station, and with seating for 500, the Grand Concourse is quite accurately known as one of Pittsburgh's most elegant and stately places in which to dine, complete with fully refurbished Edwardian-era architectural trimmings. It's also the largest restaurant in the city. The somewhat timid menu is largely seafood based; typical entrées include lobster ravioli, coconut shrimp, and Maryland crab cakes. For a slightly more informal experience, ask to be seated in the Gandy Dancer Bar, where oysters and clams can be ordered alongside olde-style cocktails.

THE ZENITH $$

86 S. 26th St., 412/481-4833, www.zenithpgh.com
HOURS: Thurs.-Sat. 11 A.M.-9 P.M., Sun. brunch 11 A.M.-3 P.M.

A vegetarian café, an art gallery, and an antique shop, all underneath the same roof? Believe it. The Zenith—formerly known as The Zenith Tea Room—is renowned locally for its $10 prix fixe Sunday brunch, where diners help themselves to an astounding spread of pastas, cakes, and breakfast-style entrées. But the weekly menu is equally interesting, consisting of creatively prepared casseroles, stews, and meat-free sandwiches. After your meal, stroll through Zenith's eclectic collection of collectibles and vintage clothing. And definitely don't miss the restrooms, which are some of the most amusingly decorated in the city.

ASIAN
CAMBOD-ICAN KITCHEN $

1701 E. Carson St., 412/381-6199,
www.cambodicankitchen.com
HOURS: Tues.-Sat. 5 P.M.-5 A.M.

Originally a legendary street food cart that fed the hungry barhopping masses of East Carson Street until the wee hours of most mornings, Cambod-ican Kitchen—now reinvented as a sit-down restaurant—has returned to Pittsburgh after a nearly three-year hiatus. Cambod-ican purists need not fret, however—the original "Cat on a Stick" (chicken shish kabob) is still for sale. So too is a wonderfully adventurous menu of fried noodles and wontons, curry rolls and fresh spring rolls, and a sampler platter big enough to share with one or two friends.

NAKAMA JAPANESE STEAK HOUSE $$$

1611 E. Carson St., 412/381-6000,
www.eatatnakama.com
HOURS: Mon.-Sat. 11 A.M.-1 A.M., Sun. 1 P.M.-9 P.M.

Depending on where you sit and what you order at the 200-seat, über-trendy Nakama, a culinary experience here can become just about anything you'd like. Large groups and parties, for instance, flock to the smokeless hibachi tables for filet mignon and hibachi scallops, while late-night arrivals and the happy hour

COURTESY OF ROB MATHENY

Nakama Japanese Steak House

crowd gather around the massive island bar for carafes of sake and pints of Japanese beer. Arriving solo? Try straddling up to the sushi bar, which features a comprehensive menu of sashimi and veggie-based rolls alongside the usual standards.

THAI ME UP 💲💲

1925 E. Carson St., 412/488-8893
HOURS: Mon.-Thurs. 11 A.M.-10 P.M., Fri. 11 A.M.-10:30 P.M., Sat. noon-10:30 P.M.

A fairly recent addition to the city's trendy Thai restaurant scene, Thai Me Up is primarily a take-out joint with a reputation for moan-inducing pad thai, curries, and rice dishes. And while the menu offers a wide range of fusionesque items for both vegetarians and meat-eaters alike, even ravenous carnivores should try the tofu with peanut sauce, not to mention the spicy basil noodles. Eating in is certainly allowed here—there's seating for about 20—and the atmosphere is clean, contemporary, and even a bit sexy. Looking for a particularly sensual experience? Try dipping into the lemongrass soup, but please, try to keep the discernible outbursts to a minimum.

RESTAURANTS

VEGAN AND VEGGIE-FRIENDLY OPTIONS

Just as the average Pittsburgher much prefers the taste of a cold Iron City Light over, say, that of a late vintage California Chardonnay, so too does the Steel City prefer meat over, well, no meat. But vegetarians, and even vegans, need not despair: Pittsburgh is also home to a reasonable number of quality vegan and veggie-friendly eateries.

The Zenith on Pittsburgh's South Side is not only a vegetarian restaurant but also an antique shop and art gallery. Definitely try the hugely popular Tofishy tofu sandwich, and don't miss the always-packed Sunday brunch (11 A.M.-3 P.M.), with its ever-rotating menu.

On the North Side, try **Hoi Polloi Vegetarian Café and Coffeehouse,** a sort of counter-culture gathering spot with a wide array of meat-free soups, salads, and wonderful breakfast foods. Other area cafés with decent selections of veggie-friendly options include **Make Your Mark Artspace & Coffeehouse** in Point Breeze, where you can enjoy the all-veggie lunch menu on the covered back patio, and the much-loved **The Quiet Storm** in Garfield, which almost always offers a fantastic selection of vegan desserts and snacks along with its standard lunch, brunch, and dinner menus. Also try the café at the **East End Food Co-Op** (7516 Meade St., 412/242-3598, www.eastendfoodcoop.com) in Point Breeze for great soups.

Any of the area's six **Mad Mex** (www.mad-mex.com) locations are happy to veg-o-fy practically anything on the menu; the truly hardcore can even request soy cheese and soy sour cream! In fact, the entire family of eateries owned by the Big Burrito Restaurant Group – which includes **Kaya** in the Strip District and **Casbah, Umi,** and **Soba** in Shadyside – are quite good about catering to non-meat and non-dairy eaters.

While meat is in plentiful distribution at Pittsburgh's two Ethiopian restaurants, **Abay Ethiopian Cuisine** and **Tana Ethiopian Cuisine,** both in East Liberty, vegetarians will find more than enough options on either menu to keep their jaws busy as well. Both restaurants are also great group-dining destinations.

Fortunately for vegetarian diners with an affinity for sweets, the new-to-Pittsburgh chain of **Dozen Bake Shops** (www.dozenbakeshop.com, with locations in Lawrenceville, Oakland, Downtown, and inside the Warhol Museum) offer a decent variety of vegan baked goods alongside its regular menu of too-good-to-be-true cupcakes.

For something a bit different, check out the veggie-dog offerings at **Franktuary,** a New York-style gourmet hot dog shop located in the basement of a Downtown church.

For the full scoop on the city's vegetarian and vegan dining scene, log onto the endlessly useful **www.vegguide.org,** which documents such eateries nationwide. Also worth a look are the similar websites **www.happycow.net** and **www.vegetarian-restaurants.net.**

CAFÉS

BEEHIVE $

1327 E. Carson St., 412/488-4483,
www.beehivebuzz.com

HOURS: Mon.-Thurs. 9 A.M.-1 A.M., Fri.-Sun. 9 A.M.-2 A.M.

One of Pittsburgh's most iconoclastic locales in which to sip organic coffee and legally suck down Camel Lights indoors while discussing Sartre, the Beehive has been many different things to many different angst-ridden teens since its opening in 1991. What it remains, however, is a pleasantly comfortable place to immerse one's self into the city's bohemian subculture. The Beehive's interior decor vibe is strictly thrift store—think mismatched furniture and kitschy wall murals—more recent additions have included a nonsmoking room and an outdoor patio perfect for warm-weather days. What else? There's also pinball, wireless access, used paperbacks in the vending machine, and the best-pierced baristas in Pittsburgh. In other words, the spirit of the South Side under one roof.

BIG DOG COFFEE $

2717 Sarah St., 412/586-7306, www.bigdogcoffee.net

HOURS: Mon.-Fri. 6 A.M.-10 P.M.,
Sat.-Sun. 7:30 A.M.-10 P.M.

The South Side is "bustling." That term, of course, is a cliché—especially in travel guidebooks—but the South Side defines the word. It embodies it. It's odd. Erratic. It's a place that easily contains more bars per capita than any neighborhood in the region. And perhaps because of that, there are a ton of coffee shops, likely all designed to cure hangovers. This is one of them. However, unlike the others, which are fairly homogenous (as of this writing there were at least six corporate-owned coffee shops in the neighborhood), Big Dog is owned by a Bulgarian violinist and his bassoonist wife. It's also located in a restored, century-old former bakery, and it serves off-the-chart desserts and ridiculously good food including organic oatmeal, soups, and award-winning gelato. If you're looking for something slightly different, this is undoubtedly it.

The Beehive has pinball and wireless access, as well as coffee and desserts.

CONTEMPORARY AND NEW AMERICAN
CAFE DU JOUR $$
1107 E. Carson St., 412/488-9695
HOURS: Tues.-Sat. 11:30 A.M.-10 P.M.

With the ambience of an intimate European bistro, the flavor of Cafe du Jour has lately been tweaked by its two new owners—both of them young chefs who've introduced to the menu an impressive array of inventive Californian cuisine. This may not sound like much, but in a city where contemporary dining always seems to revolve around dishes from the old country, Cafe du Jour stands out in spades. And don't be afraid to let the servers guide your choices here, as some are wont to do; after all, everything from the portobello soup to the cheese plates to the *cassoulet* (French stew) is simply stunning. Credit cards are not accepted, so come prepared with cash.

DISH $$$
128 S. 17th St., 412/390-2012, www.dishosteria.com
HOURS: Mon.-Sat. 5 P.M.-2 A.M.

Popularly known as one of Pittsburgh's best choices for a first date, Dish is actually a bar that just happens to serve some of the best-prepared small plates and soups on the South Side. Pasta, meat, and fresh fish dishes—as well as a long list of wonderfully sinful desserts—are also on offer here. But for many, the real draw at Dish is its ambience: Lights are always turned down low, and the small tables and considerable lack of elbow room tend to make for a rather cozy dining or drinking experience. Fair warning: Reservations are recommended during the always-busy weekends. No credit cards.

FRENCH
LE POMMIER $$$
2104 E. Carson St., 412/431-1901
HOURS: Mon.-Sat. 5:30-10 P.M.

A South Side stronghold for decades, Le Pommier is practically synonymous with fine French dining and quality cuisine among Pittsburghers. But don't expect a particularly intimate experience; the bistro sits inside a rather sizable storefront smack-dab in the bustle of East Carson Street. Do expect white tablecloth service, however, not to mention a truly attentive staff that is often willing to go above and beyond the call of duty for particularly discerning diners. Thanks to chef Mark Collins, organic, locally grown produce and ingredients find their way into most every dish; diners who simply can't decide should try the four-course prix fixe menu, available Monday through Friday. Le Pommier is also well known for its extensive wine list.

GERMAN
【 HOFBRÄUHAUS $$
2705 S. Water St., 412/224-2328, www.hofbrauhauspittsburgh.com
HOURS: Mon.-Wed. and Fri.-Sat. 11 A.M.-2 A.M., Thurs. 11 A.M.-1 A.M., Sun. 10 A.M.-2 A.M.

Designed to resemble a centuries-old Munich beer hall of the very same name, perhaps the most surprising thing about Hofbräuhaus is that, despite its location in the SouthSide

Hofbräuhaus strictly adheres to the Bavarian beer purity law.

© DAN ELDRIDGE

RESTAURANTS

Works shopping center, a sense of authenticity actually does shine through. There are long tables in the main hall where you can dine, European-style, with perfect strangers. Beer brewed on the premises adheres strictly to the Bavarian beer purity law. And there's also an abundance of live music, as well as an incredibly hearty (and seriously caloric) menu of bona fide Bavarian delicacies. A decidedly less adventurous selection of burgers, sandwiches, and salads is also available. And if you show up after dark, don't forget to visit the outdoor *bier* garden, with its fantastic view of the Monongahela River.

ITALIAN
◖ PIZZA SOLA ❸
1417 E. Carson St., 412/481-3888, www.pizzasola.com

HOURS: Mon.-Wed. 11:30 A.M.-midnight, Thurs.-Sat. 11:30 A.M.-3 A.M., Sun. 12:30 P.M.-midnight

Formerly known as Pizza Vesuvio, Pizza Sola has managed to make a serious name for itself in Pittsburgh on the basis of one solitary gimmick that actually works: It approaches its pie-making as an actual craft. New York City–style thin-crust slices—the type you fold in half lengthwise and eat on the go—are what's on offer here. Even better, the young employees behind the counter take their tradition seriously, tossing every pizza by hand with dough that's made fresh daily. More recently, the shop, which also has locations in Oakland (114 Atwood St., 412/681-7652) and in East Liberty (6004 Penn Circle S., 412/363-7652), has added sandwiches, wings, salads, and desserts to its once-limited menu.

MEDITERRANEAN
GYPSY CAFÉ ❸❸
1330 Bingham St., 412/381-4977, www.gypsycafe.net

HOURS: Tues.-Wed. 5-9 P.M., Thurs.-Sat. 5-11 P.M., Sun. noon-9 P.M.

A cozy neighborhood café tucked safely away from the chaos of East Carson Street, Gypsy Café serves a clever sort of Mediterranean concept cuisine. That means Italy, Greece, and North Africa, but also Eastern Europe,

Gypsy Café serves Mediterranean cuisine.

Ireland, and Spain, to name but a few. Events are a popular draw here; *tamburitza* and jazz musicians occasionally perform, and sometimes tarot card readers offer readings. Because of the occasional private party, hours are somewhat flexible (as is the seasonal menu), so it's always wise to call ahead. Reservations are practically a necessity during nights when nearby City Theatre is in session.

MEXICAN
TAQUERIA MEXICO CITY ❸
2212 E. Carson St., 412/488-8033, www.mex-city.com

HOURS: Mon.-Thurs. 11 A.M.-10 P.M., Fri.-Sat. 11 A.M.-3 A.M., Sun. 11 A.M.-8 P.M.

The pure epitome of the authentic Mexican street taco joint, Taqueria Mexico City started out years ago with one simple and almost unnoticeable location at 111 Smithfield Street, Downtown, before opening a second shop nearby at 409 Wood Street. (Both are still open.) But now that this local chain has expanded to the South Side's much trendier main drag of East Carson Street, its simple and honest burritos, enchiladas plates, and corn-tortilla tacos have practically become the stuff of local legend. That became even truer still once the South Side's only other authentic taqueria—Taco Loco—went out of business. But make no mistake: There's nothing trendy about Taqueria Mexico City; it's simply affordable and well-prepared Mexican cuisine—not much more, and not much less.

🄲 YO RITA ⑤⑤
1120 E. Carson St., 412/904-3557,
www.yoritasouthside.com
HOURS: Sun.-Thurs. 4-10 P.M., Fri.-Sat. 4-11 P.M., Sun. 11 A.M.-2:30 P.M.
Operated by one of the city's most in-demand celebrity chefs, Kevin Sousa, Yo Rita almost instantly became a must-visit destination among local foodies when it opened in the former location of the Iguana Grill. The upscale menu offerings here, which essentially consist of the most inventive and inspired collection of tacos this side of the Alleghenies, might best be thought of as Mexican-American fusion. Think root vegetable with quail egg, pork belly with sour cherries, or flank steak with red onion jam. High-end culinary experimentation is the order of the day here, in other words. So if nachos or bean burritos are what you're after, keep looking.

SNACKS AND DESSERTS
THE PRETZEL SHOP ⑤
2316 E. Carson St., 412/431-2574
HOURS: Mon.-Sat. 7 A.M.-4 P.M.
A veritable Pittsburgh legend, hundreds upon hundreds of soft pretzels are prepared at The Pretzel Shop by hand daily; hang around long enough in the lobby and you're sure to see the master pretzelers and their late 1800s-era

beehive oven in action. Deli-style sandwiches can be ordered on the pretzels as well. And don't forget to request the house special: an absolutely addictive homemade honey mustard sauce.

SPANISH
IBIZA TAPAS AND WINE BAR ⑤⑤
2224 E. Carson St., 412/325-2227,
www.ibizatapasrestaurant.com
HOURS: Mon.-Thurs. 4 P.M.-2 A.M., Fri.-Sat. 4 P.M.-1 A.M.
Owned and operated by local restaurateur Antonio Pereira, who is also responsible for next-door's Spanish-themed restaurant Mallorca, Ibiza boasts 45 small plates—some hot and some cold—from both continental Europe and South America. Style and creativity are in full force here, so be prepared to encounter an exceptional menu. Beef carpaccio, tuna tartar, and stuffed banana peppers with veal are just a few of the many offerings. Particularly obsessive foodies might consider requesting a table with a kitchen view, where the chefs toil on full display.

MALLORCA ⑤⑤⑤
2228 E. Carson St., 412/488-1818,
www.mallorcarestaurant.com
HOURS: Mon.-Thurs. 11:30 A.M.-10:30 P.M., Fri.-Sat. 11:30 A.M.-11:30 P.M., Sun. noon-10 P.M.
A traditional Spanish restaurant in the finest white tablecloth style, Mallorca offers a premiere dining experience that is simply unequaled elsewhere in the city. Families and young couples on dates crowd the gated outdoor terrace or the often-packed dining room here to gorge on Spanish- and Mediterranean-style seafood dishes or the exotic house specialties: roast sucking pig, say, or even goat. And just as they would in an actual Iberian eatery, diners often find themselves lingering to nosh, sample, and sip for hours. Not feeling particularly adventurous? Stick with the paella, for which Mallorca is justly famous.

RESTAURANTS

Mount Washington Map 3

Although it once housed a station on the Underground Railroad, and today houses families of turkey and deer, even to most locals Mount Washington is best known for only three things: The jaw-dropping view afforded from its Grandview Avenue, which stretches the length of its cliffside; the two inclines which traverse the side of the cliff to deliver you there; and Restaurant Row, the small collection of exceedingly romantic cafés and eateries where a plate of veal Lafayette and glass of pinot noir come complete with one of North America's most gorgeous urban views.

Technically, Restaurant Row is located in the small neighborhood of Duquesne Heights, and if you reach Grandview Avenue by way of the Monongahela Incline, which sits directly across the street from Station Square, you'll have quite a hike if you intend to walk to a restaurant—it's approximately one mile. The Duquesne Incline, on the other hand, sits adjacent to the restaurants, but to reach it on foot from Station Square you'll need to walk past the Gateway Clipper Fleet, continue on through the parking lot, and then follow the footpath along the Monongahela River until you see the incline on your left. If you're not sure exactly where you're going, taking a taxi from your hotel would probably be your wisest choice.

It's important to note, however, that as Pittsburgh's fine-dining scene has slowly grown and improved over the years, the reputation of Mount Washington's eateries has declined. Which isn't to say that the food offered here is necessarily poor, but rather, that it's significantly overpriced given its quality. In other words, if extraordinary food is what you're after, you can do much better elsewhere. Yet if it's the view and the experience you want, by all means, come and enjoy yourself. But don't come expecting anything modern: The vibe and the decor along the row are both solidly stuck in the 1970s and '80s.

AMERICAN

GEORGETOWNE INN ⑤⑤⑤
1230 Grandview Ave., 412/481-4424, www.georgetowneinn.com
HOURS: Tues.-Sat. 11 A.M.-3 P.M., Mon.-Thurs. 5-11 P.M., Fri.-Sat. 5 P.M.-midnight, Sun. 4-10 P.M.

Georgetowne Inn is consistently popular, and for good reason. Because while the menu essentially mirrors that of Mount Washington's other food-with-a-view spots (fairly standard beef, seafood, and pasta dishes), the ambience, at least, has been raised a notch or two in the creativity department. Wooden crossbeams stretched between white stucco walls make for a somewhat cozy but still upscale rural experience. And if you plan to arrive with a relatively large party, consider calling ahead to reserve space in the upstairs loft, where the city view is even mightier. Light eaters should try the crab cakes or club-style sandwiches.

GRANDVIEW SALOON ⑤⑤
1212 Grandview Ave., 412/431-1400, www.thegrandviewsaloon.com
HOURS: Mon.-Thurs. 11:30 A.M.-11 P.M., Fri.-Sat. 11:30 A.M.-12:30 A.M., Sun. 11:30 A.M.-9 P.M.

It's easy to understand why the Grandview Saloon's two dining levels—as well as its two outdoor patios—are consistently packed with in-the-know tourists and locals alike: The view afforded from either deck is just as stunning and romantic as any other you'll find along Restaurant Row, and yet the prices are much lower because the atmosphere is more casual. The Saloon, in fact, is much more of a bistro than a fine-dining spot, a fact that the menu clearly reflects. Sandwiches, wraps, chicken salads, burgers, and hoagies are all available, although USDA prime steaks are as well. And if you're primarily interested in drinking, head to the restaurant's lower level, where you'll find a small horseshoe-shaped bar.

LEMONT RESTAURANT $$$
1114 Grandview Ave., 412/431-3100,
www.lemontpittsburgh.com
HOURS: Mon.-Sat. 5 P.M., Sun. 4 P.M., last reservation
Sun.-Thurs. 9 P.M. and Fri.-Sat. 9:30 P.M.

As equally popular as the Cliffside Restaurant is LeMont Restaurant, a five-star locale offering essentially the same amenities as its down-the-street neighbor: traditional American cuisine including seafood and old-school meat entrées. (The two house specialties, for instance, are steak Diane and chateaubriand.) And despite its hopelessly out-of-date decor, LeMont also continues to be something of a hit for wedding receptions and business meetings. Dessert selections are appropriately filling and rich, and, for men, a coat and tie are required. This is a reservation-only venue.

MONTEREY BAY FISH GROTTO $$$
1411 Grandview Ave., 412/481-4414,
www.montereybayfishgrotto.com
HOURS: Mon.-Thurs. 11 A.M.-3 P.M. and 5-10 P.M., Fri.
11 A.M.-3 P.M. and 5-11 P.M., Sat. 5-11 P.M., Sun. 5-9 P.M.

Located inside a high-rise building at the far western end of Grandview Avenue, the Monterey Bay Fish Grotto offers an award-winning selection of fresh fish, flown in daily and served in a visually striking glass-enclosed dining room. The setting is truly remarkable; every table has a phenomenal view of The Point. The steaks and seafood will definitely set you back here, and many a diner has complained that the elevated prices slightly outweigh the quality of the food. But there's simply no debating the fact that your experience here is certain to be unique and memorable. Various private banquet spaces can accommodate parties as small as 20 or as large as 100. And for a gathering that truly impresses, a private wine room with a 24-person capacity and a four-course prix fixe fish dinner can be reserved.

TIN ANGEL $$$
1200 Grandview Ave., 412/381-1919,
www.tinangelpittsburgh.com
HOURS: Mon.-Sat. 5:30-10 P.M.

Tin Angel has long been a hit with tourists and

COURTESY OF ROB MATHENY

Tin Angel

RESTAURANTS

locals alike, and it certainly didn't hurt business when President Bill Clinton and Prime Minister John Major dined here in 1994. On the menu is a bevy of American and Greek cuisine, including Black Forest filet mignon and stuffed grape leaves. You can expect the food quality and the Downtown city view here to be on essentially the same level as at the row's other restaurants: Gazing out the window is almost guaranteed to be awe-inspiring, while your meal will likely be decent enough, but far too expensive.

Shadyside   Map 4

This upscale shopping neighborhood has two main drags—Walnut Street and Ellsworth Avenue—and both are home to a wonderful mixture of pubs, cafés, high-end eateries, and ethnic restaurants. Strolling the length of either street doesn't take long, although we've saved you some of the trouble by listing some of the better options here.

Nearby, East Liberty is a predominantly African American neighborhood that is slowly but surely becoming gentrified, although very few recommendable restaurants exist. There is a Caribbean fast food market, although soul food and Jamaican eateries seem to be found only in Garfield.

AMERICAN
BUFFALO BLUES $$
216 S. Highland Ave., 412/362-5837,
www.buffalobluespittsburgh.com
HOURS: Mon.-Thurs. 11 A.M.-11 P.M., Fri. 11 A.M.-midnight,
Sat. noon-midnight, Sun. noon-10 P.M.
Buffalo Blues is the best sort of sports bar: It isn't too terribly aggro, but it has enough oversized television sets to keep even the most voracious ESPN junkie transfixed. This is also where you'll find one of the most creative selections of chicken wings in town; order yours with mustard sauce, garlic, or any combination of hot and spicy sauces. Not feeling the wings? Burgers are also big here, not to mention jambalaya and ribs, and the chicken salads are stupendous. Make sure you do like the locals and order yours with something unhealthy on top, like barbeque sauce.

HARRIS GRILL $$
5747 Ellsworth Ave., 412/362-5273,
www.harrisgrill.com
HOURS: Daily 4 P.M.-1 A.M.
Something of a contemporary American lounge with a sense of humor, Harris Grill manages to play different roles for different diners. The first floor has a standard pub feel, while the second floor is elegant, and even romantic, with dim lighting and a subtle Mediterranean theme. But take a look at the menu: Goat in a Boat (feta with pita wedges), Chicks with Sticks (marinated chicken breasts), and the infamous Wrongest Dessert Ever, which comes with a deep-fried Twinkie. A great icebreaker atmosphere for first dates, but it's also fun with a big group of friends.

JUICE BOX CAFE $
735 Copeland St., 412/802-7070, www.juiceboxpitt.com
HOURS: Mon.-Sat. 10 A.M.-9 P.M., Sun. 11 A.M.-7 P.M.
An intimately-sized restaurant and juice bar focusing on light and heart-healthy foods, Juice Box Cafe is one of the city's few eateries offering a predominantly raw-food menu. Expect to find all the healthy lifestyle standards here, including sandwiches, wraps, garden salads, fruit smoothies, and freshly-squeezed juices. Both vegetarian and non-veggie options are available, and brunch menu items such as waffles and breakfast burritos are served daily. Juice Box's second location can be found inside the Strip District's Pittsburgh Public Market (2100 Smallman St., 412/281-4505).

© DAN ELDRIDGE

Grab a healthy lunch at Juice Box Cafe.

RESTAURANTS

PITTSBURGH DELI COMPANY $

728 Copeland St., 412/682-3354, www.pghdeli.com
HOURS: Mon.-Wed. 11 A.M.-8 P.M., Thurs.-Sat.
11 A.M.-2 A.M., Sun. 11 A.M.-6 P.M.

Definitely more interesting than the name suggests, the 16 specialty sandwiches at Pittsburgh Deli Company are among the most carefully crafted in town. Four are built specifically for vegetarians; the rest combine a selection of quality meats and cheeses, such as the Tally Ho (spicy ham and buffalo mozzarella on focaccia bread), or the That's Amore! (chicken breast and marinara on a kaiser roll). Don't miss the barrel of free pickles, and if you're around at night, visit the second-floor bar, which often hosts hip-hop and electronic music events.

ASIAN
SOBA $$$

5847 Ellsworth Ave., 412/362-5656,
www.bigburrito.com/soba
HOURS: Sun.-Thurs. 5 P.M.-10 P.M., Fri.-Sat. 5 P.M.-11 P.M.

For exquisitely crafted pan-Asian cuisine and a moderately formal ambience, look no further. Soba consists of two full floors, with a dining room and a well-tended bar on each; half of Soba's patrons on any given night are there for the dry martinis and the schmoozing. Starry-eyed lovers and local pseudo-celebrities can be seen digging into Chef Jamie Achmoody's vegetable samosas and lemongrass strip steak. Wander up to the third floor and you'll find Umi, a Japanese restaurant also affiliated with the Big Burrito Group.

SUSHI TOO $$

5432 Walnut St., 412/687-8744, www.sushitoo.net
HOURS: Mon.-Thurs. 11:30 A.M.-3 P.M. and 5-10 P.M.,
Fri. 11:30 A.M.-3 P.M. and 5-11 P.M., Sat. 11:30 A.M.-11 P.M.,
Sun. 1-9 P.M.

Not to be confused with its sister restaurant, Sushi Two, which is located on the South Side, it seems as if Sushi Too has been serving up Japanese delicacies in Pittsburgh for ages. A fair warning, however: This isn't the place to come if you're looking to impress a date or business associate; the decor is dated and the aesthetic presentation is minimal. But for a night out with friends, it can't be beat. Prices are reasonable, non-fish options abound, and the menu is a blast for adventurous eaters. In other words, this is a sushi restaurant for those interested only in the food itself.

THAI PLACE CAFÉ 🅢🅢
5528 Walnut St., 412/687-8586,
www.thaiplacepgh.com
HOURS: Mon.-Thurs. 11 A.M.-10 P.M.,
Fri.-Sat. 11 A.M.-11 P.M., Sun. noon-9:30 P.M.

Lauded as one of the country's top Thai restaurants, Thai Place is conveniently situated in the heart of Shadyside's shopping district. That isn't to suggest that its ambience is anything special, which it most definitely is not. But for a flawless meal after a Saturday or Sunday of serious pavement pounding, it hits the spot perfectly. Pad thai, of course, is popular here, but the more adventurous should consider the deep-fried squid, or even the boneless crispy duck. Thai curries are also especially mouthwatering. Thai Place's Oakland location is at 311 South Craig Street (412/622-0133). Other locations can be found in Wexford (12009 Perry Hwy., 724/935-8866) and Fox Chapel (1034 Freeport Rd., 412/784-8980).

TYPHOON 🅢🅢
242 S. Highland Ave., 412/362-2005,
www.typhoonpgh.com
HOURS: Mon.-Thurs. 5-10 P.M., Fri.-Sat. 5-11 P.M.

Pittsburgh's most recent addition to the pan-Asian scene, Typhoon refers to itself as "new-style Thai," an adage that'll make perfect sense once you walk in the front door. Opened by the former proprietor of a popular Squirrel Hill Thai restaurant and a locally based filmmaker, the entrées and small dishes here are a far stretch from those you'd find on the streets of Bangkok. Instead, expect inventive veggie and seafood dishes with a twist—ginger calamari with avocado sauce, say, or grilled halibut with

salsa. The decor is equally inviting: Mahogany and bamboo paneling, earth tones, and contemporary art and sculpture complete the experience smartly.

UMI 🅢🅢🅢
5849 Ellsworth Ave., 412/362-6198,
www.bigburrito.com/umi
HOURS: Tues.-Thurs. 5-9:30 P.M., Fri.-Sat. 5-10:30 P.M.

Located on Soba's top floor but with its own separate entrance, Umi is probably Pittsburgh's most style-conscious Japanese eatery. Sushi and sashimi here, prepared with high precision by a true *shokunin* (a master sushi chef), will set you back around $3 a piece. Not a terrible price to pay, considering that executive chef Mr. Shu is one of the city's top sushi celebrities. (Another is Chaya's Fumio Yasuzawa.) Fish-free dishes include teriyaki, miso soups, and even an octopus salad.

CAFÉS
COFFEE TREE ROASTERS 🅢
5524 Walnut St., 412/621-6880, www.coffeetree.com
HOURS: Sun.-Thurs. 6 A.M.-midnight, Fri.-Sat. 6 A.M.-1 A.M.

A caffeinating force in Pittsburgh for more than a decade now, the baristas at Coffee Tree Roasters are so serious about fresh beans that anything older than eight days gets tossed. It's no wonder the Arabica brewed here is so rich and flavorful; it's also no wonder Coffee Tree was the first United States roaster named a Cup of Excellence lifetime member. Grad students in particular seem to appreciate the wide-open space at Coffee Tree; you'll see an abundance of laptops and textbooks on any given afternoon. A quiet room in the back is reserved for particularly studious types. Coffee Tree also has locations in Squirrel Hill (5840 Forbes Ave., 412/422-4427) and in East Liberty's Bakery Square (151 Bakery Square Blvd., 412/362-0966), as well as in the suburban communities of Fox Chapel (48 Fox Chapel Rd., 412/782-5622) and Mt. Lebanon (299 Beverly Rd., 412/344-4780).

CRAZY MOCHA $

5830 Ellsworth Ave., 412/441-9344,
www.crazymocha.com
HOURS: Mon.-Thurs. 7:30 A.M.-midnight, Fri.
7:30 A.M.-1 A.M., Sat. 8 A.M.-1 A.M., Sun. 9 A.M.-midnight
Another branch of the quickly growing Crazy
Mocha chain, now with 26 separate locations,
this café retains a slightly rarified air, and something of a neighborhood feel as well, due to its
choice location on Ellsworth Avenue. Menu
items are just what you'd expect: A full range
of coffee and espresso drinks, with sandwiches
and cheesecakes behind the counter. But even
regular ol' coffee drinkers get their orders delivered straight to the table here—an interesting
concept in the too-often discourteous world of
independent cafés.

CONTEMPORARY AND
NEW AMERICAN

AVENUE B $$

5501 Centre Ave., 412/683-3663,
www.avenueb-pgh.com
HOURS: Tues.-Thurs. 11 A.M.-3 P.M. and 5-10 P.M.,
Fri. 11 A.M.-3 P.M. and 5-11 P.M., Sat. 5-11 P.M.
Featuring the creative culinary artistry of chef
(and co-owner) Chris Bonfili, formerly of East
Liberty's Red Room, who seems to have amassed
a fairly impressive local following, Avenue B is
almost exactly what you'd expect from a contemporary chef-owned operation. The daily-
changing menu features wonderfully executed
interpretations of veggie, meat, and comfort food
dishes, such as roasted beet risotto, Kobe beef
meatloaf, and even a grilled cheese sandwich.
And perhaps not surprisingly, the café's exposed-
brick, BYOB atmosphere appeals to fairly wide
social stratum of diners. In other words, along
with Avenue B's stellar waitstaff and its consistently strong desserts, there isn't much *not* to like.

CAFE ZINHO $$

238 Spahr St., 412/363-1500
HOURS: Mon.-Thurs. 5:30-10 P.M., Fri.-Sat. 5:30-11 P.M.,
Sun. 5:30-9 P.M.
The same crew responsible for the legendary

but now shuttered Baum Vivant (as well as the
Cultural District's recently closed Café Zao)
operates this bistro-style eatery—an actual garage in a residential neighborhood that's been
transformed into something of a culinary hipster's haven. The decor at Cafe Zinho is strictly
thrift-store chic, complete with mismatched furniture and ironically bad art. But entrées and
even desserts are strictly first-class, and artfully
built: Think gourmet dishes complete with
lamb, mussels, and even wild game. The veggie rice bowls and remarkably constructed salads
regularly earn approving clucks from discriminating foodies as well.

ITALIAN

GIRASOLE $$

733 Copeland St., 412/682-2130,
www.733copeland.com
HOURS: Tues.-Thurs. 11:30 A.M.-10 P.M.,
Fri.-Sat. 11:30 A.M.-11 P.M., Sun. 4-9 P.M.
What was previously one of Pittsburgh's very
first independent coffee shops is now Girasole,
a much-loved Italian spot where simple but
lovingly prepared homemade pasta dishes are
drawing customers—the young and moneyed
especially—away from the aging Italian standbys
of Bloomfield. The very welcoming atmosphere
includes a shaded outdoor patio. Especially popular here are the ravioli and light lunch items like
panini and wonderfully airy tiramisu.

MEDITERRANEAN

CASBAH $$$

229 S. Highland Ave., 412/661-5656,
www.bigburrito.com/casbah
HOURS: Mon.-Fri. 11:30 A.M.-2:30 P.M., Sun. 11 A.M.-2 P.M.,
Mon.-Thurs. 5-10 P.M., Fri.-Sat. 5-11 P.M., Sun. 5-9 P.M.
Offering certainly one of the city's most satisfying culinary adventures, Casbah is tough
to miss: It's the tan stucco block built to resemble a Moroccan mosque. Expect a wide
spread of Mediterranean and North African
cuisine that's simply unmatched elsewhere in
Pittsburgh, and be prepared to expand your
version of the exotic while dining; a typical

RESTAURANTS

RESTAURANTS

© DAN ELDRIDGE

Girasole

menu might offer Elysian Fields lamb with red wine jus, roasted duck broth soup, and Prince Edward Island mussels. The menu, which changes daily, is seasonally based and features fresh food from area farms. Wine lovers as well will find themselves pleased; the cellar here is considered one of Shadyside's most selective.

PERUVIAN
LA FERIA ⑤⑤⑤
5527 Walnut St., 2nd Fl., 412/682-4501,
www.laferia.net
HOURS: Mon.-Sat. 11 A.M.-10 P.M.

As befits its fairly obscure culinary status (a Peruvian restaurant in *Pittsburgh?*), La Feria isn't the easiest eatery to find. First, walk into the lobby of Pamela's Diner; then head up the stairs. You'll find yourself in a Latin craft shop, but an interesting selection of Peruvian sandwiches, salads, and entrées can be ordered at the counter; a small number of tables are available for in-house dining. Specials change daily;

regular standbys include empanadas (stuffed pastries), *pudin de pan* (traditional bread pudding dessert), and Peruvian coffee.

SNACKS AND DESSERTS
OH YEAH! ICE CREAM & COFFEE CO. ⑤
232 S. Highland Ave., 412/253-0955,
www.customswirl.com
HOURS: Mon.-Fri. 7 A.M.-11 P.M., Sat.-Sun. 8 A.M.-11 P.M.

Although probably best known for its so-called "ice cream breakfasts," which feature breakfast cereals or buckwheat waffles topped with organic ice cream scoops, Oh Yeah! is also a place where hardcore ice cream fiends can experiment with a menu of mix-ins and flavor combinations that literally puts other scoop shops to shame. Both vegan and sugar-free ice creams are available, as are more than 100 seriously unusual add-ins, including hemp protein, fresh ginger, and habanero pepper powder. The fact that the organic cream comes from Amish grass-fed cows takes some of the guilt out of this guilty pleasure.

Squirrel Hill and Point Breeze — Map 5

One of the largest Jewish neighborhoods on the East Coast, Squirrel Hill is home to a number of kosher eateries. But walk the length of the neighborhood's perpendicular main drags, Murray and Forbes Avenues, and you'll discover just about everything else, from a Korean bubble tea shop to one of the best bagel bakeries in Pittsburgh.

Point Breeze is largely a residential area where few restaurants are located. Self-caterers interested in healthy eating—but looking for a change of pace from Whole Foods—should check out the neighborhood's **East End Food Co-op** (7516 Meade St., 412/242-3598, www.eastendfoodcoop.com).

Located on the opposite side of Frick Park from Squirrel Hill, Regent Square's main drag exists along South Braddock Avenue, which can be covered from one end to the other on foot in about five minutes.

AMERICAN
D'S SIX-PAX AND DOGS ❸❸
1118 S. Braddock Ave., 412/241-4666, www.ds6pax.com
HOURS: Sun.-Wed. 11 A.M.-11 P.M., Thurs.-Sat. 11 A.M.-midnight
A perennial Regent Square favorite, D's Six-Pax and Dogs has possibly the biggest and most diverse selection of imported and microbrewed beer for sale in the city (more than 1,000 options). Particularly amusing is the walk-in cooler, where customers can browse the selection and pick their very own out-of-town six-pack. Hot dogs are exceedingly delicious here as well—they aren't quite gourmet but they're close, and the list of free toppings is seemingly endless. It's a perfect choice when you're not up for greasy bar food, but not hungry enough for a full meal. Veggie dogs are available.

GULLIFTY'S ❸❸
1922 Murray Ave., 412/521-8222, www.gulliftys.us
HOURS: Mon.-Thurs. 11 A.M.-midnight, Fri.-Sat. 11 A.M.-1 A.M., Sun. 10 A.M.-midnight
Gullifty's is something of a local anomaly:

With its massive dining room lit by sunlight and accentuated with high ceilings and balcony seating, just relaxing with a cup of coffee and one of the restaurant's legendary desserts (voted the best in Pittsburgh for more than 20 years) is an experience worth seeking out. The American bistro-style menu, however, is filled to overflowing with all the regulars: sandwiches, entrées, pizza, pasta, burgers, Tex-Mex dishes, and generously portioned salads. Stopping by before catching a movie down the street? Take care to give yourself ample time, as service can sometimes be slow.

THE MAP ROOM ❸❸
1126 S. Braddock Ave., 412/371-1955, www.beesharp.com/MAPROOM
HOURS: Sun.-Sat. 3 P.M.-2 A.M.
Operated by a British expat who has chosen to cover the walls of her cozy and smallish tavern with antique maps of the Old World, The Map Room is essentially an upscale pub where bar food is decidedly more adventurous and of a slightly higher quality than you're likely to come across in most Pittsburgh pubs. Grilled chicken entrées, chowder soup, mussels, and bread pudding are the sorts of delights you'll find here. In other words, comfort food of a sort that perfectly accompanies a pint or two of Guinness, or maybe a cup of hot tea during yet another drizzly Steel City day.

THE SQUARE CAFÉ ❸
1137 S. Braddock Ave., 412/244-8002, www.square-cafe.com
HOURS: Mon.-Sat. 7 A.M.-3 P.M., Sun. 8 A.M.-3 P.M.
One of the neighborhood's most popular early-morning eateries, The Square Café acts as a fairly standard neighborhood diner during its daily breakfast and lunch service. Breakfast fare is of the standard "nuevo diner" variety—tofu scrambles, breakfast quesadillas, french toast with challah bread, and granola—while lunch service is standard American fare (meat and pasta dishes mostly) with a light fusion

RESTAURANTS

twist. Soups, salads, sandwiches, and wraps are also served, as is a fairly standard kids menu featuring PB&J, macaroni and cheese, and chicken fingers.

ASIAN

CHAYA JAPANESE CUISINE $$
2104 Murray Ave., 412/422-2082, www.chayausa.com
HOURS: Mon.-Thurs. 5-9:30 P.M., Fri.-Sat. 5-9:45 P.M.

As a general culinary rule of thumb, a Japanese restaurant filled with actual Japanese diners is usually a sign that you've found the real deal. Chaya, which boasts one of Pittsburgh's two best sushi chefs (Fumio Yasuzawa), operates under a similar assumption: Apparently, this is where the city's Japanese community congregates when they're feeling homesick. So what's all the fuss about? For starters, no one else in town makes their own wasabi in-house. And what's more, fresh fish for sushi and sashimi is flown in chilled—not frozen—from Japan or New York. The remainder of the menu is worth writing home about as well and features a baffling assortment of traditional seafood goodies that aren't easily found on American shores.

CAFÉS

MAKE YOUR MARK ARTSPACE & COFFEEHOUSE $
6736 Reynolds St., 412/365-2117, www.myspace.com/makeyourmarkartspace
HOURS: Mon., Wed., and Thurs. 7 A.M.-7 P.M.; Tues., Fri., and Sat. 7 A.M.-10 P.M.

Just as popular for its vegetarian-friendly light lunches (paninis, quesadillas, and soups) as for its artistically prepared selection of fair trade and organic La Prima coffees, Make Your Mark has done just that in the formerly unremarkable Point Breeze business district, which is slowly becoming something of an actual dining and leisure destination. As the café's name suggests, patrons can leave their own mark here on a wall covered in stainless steel sheets and magnets; other amenities include free Wi-Fi, a leafy backyard patio, and a truly tempting selection of cookies and desserts.

61C CAFÉ $
1839 Murray Ave., 412/521-6161, www.61ccafe.com
HOURS: Mon.-Thurs. 8 A.M.-11 P.M., Fri. 7 A.M.-midnight, Sat. 8 A.M.-midnight, Sun. 8 A.M.-11 P.M.

Looking for Squirrel Hill's hipster contingent?

The 61C Café is named after the 61C bus line.

© DAN ELDRIDGE

Chances are good that at least half of them are lounging at the 61C Café this very moment, hunched over laptops or people-watching on the outdoor patio. To reach the café from Oakland or Downtown, just hop on the 61C, its namesake bus. And once you're here, feel free to indulge your most obscure espresso drink desire; the majority of the 61C baristas are proud professionals. A large selection of pastries and teas is also on offer, and the wireless access is free to all.

TANGO CAFÉ $

5806 Forward Ave., 412/421-1390,
www.tangocafepgh.com
HOURS: Tues.-Thurs. 10 A.M.-10 P.M., Fri. 10 A.M.-11 P.M.,
Sat. 10:30 A.M.-11 P.M., Sun. 10:30 A.M.-9 P.M.

Certainly Squirrel Hill's most exotic coffee shop, Tango Café is tucked into one of the furthest reaches of the neighborhood, just down the street from the Squirrel Hill Theatre. To truly get into the swing of things, order the Tango Submarino (steamed milk with a chocolate bar dropped in), or a Mate Cocido, which is a stress-reducing herbal beverage that's particularly popular in Buenos Aires. Pastries, light sandwiches, and empanadas are also available here, and all are comparable to the offerings you'd come across in an actual Argentine café. Tango Café can be full of surprises, too: Argentine folk musicians can sometimes be found strumming away in a corner, and lessons in both tango and the Spanish language are occasionally offered as well.

CONTEMPORARY AND NEW AMERICAN
POINT BRUGGE CAFÉ $$

101 Hastings St. at Reynolds St., 412/441-3334,
www.pointbrugge.com
HOURS: Tues.-Thurs. 11 A.M.-10 P.M., Fri.-Sat.
11 A.M.-11 P.M., Sun. 11 A.M.-9 P.M.

Located in the same spot as the city's historic Point Restaurant, Point Brugge Café was designed to specifically feel and operate like a familiar neighborhood gathering spot. The atmosphere itself is something of a pleasant cross between traditional European sophistication and the laid back vibe of the West Coast, while the dishes—Asian fusion and contemporary American, mostly—strike a balance between comfort food and modern decadence. As an added bonus, Belgian beers can often be found on tap. Reservations are recommended.

ITALIAN
MINEO'S $

2128 Murray Ave., 412/521-9864,
www.mineospizza.com
HOURS: Sun.-Thurs. 11 A.M.-1 A.M., Fri.-Sat. 11 A.M.-2 A.M.

Claiming to be any city's best pizza joint can be a controversial undertaking, but the family-owned Mineo's has the awards to prove it—dozens of them, from nearly every Pittsburgh publication—lining the walls of their no-frills cafeteria-style shop. It's tough to put a finger on exactly why the pies and slices are so delectable. It could be the generous piling on of cheese. Or maybe be the always-fresh ingredients. Might be the sauces and toppings, both of which Mineo's steadfastly refuses to skimp on. And if you absolutely can't stop by during your time here, they'll happily overnight a pie anywhere in the United States.

MEDITERRANEAN
ALADDIN'S EATERY $$

5878 Forbes Ave., 412/421-5100,
www.aladdinseatery.com
HOURS: Mon.-Fri. 11 A.M.-10:30 P.M.,
Sat.-Sun. 11 A.M.-11:30 P.M.

Yet another ethnic restaurant in Squirrel Hill with a focus on healthy, natural foods, Aladdin's Eatery is now a chain with more than a dozen locations throughout Pennsylvania, Ohio, and Illinois. The vibe couldn't possibly be more independent and homegrown, however: The waitstaff is consistently friendly and helpful, the dining room is strictly smoke-free, and the owners even donate a bit of the profits to local charities. So, how about the food? Even better. The Middle Eastern and Mediterranean dishes here can be made vegetarian or with meat; house specialties include a phenomenal Hummus Shawarma Plate with pita and a Mujadara Plate (steamed lentils and rice with toasted onions).

SNACKS AND DESSERTS
ROSE TEA CAFÉ ❸
5874½ Forbes Ave., 412/421-2238
HOURS: Daily noon-midnight
One of the few places in Pittsburgh serving

bubble tea, which is a flavored green or black tea drink with gummy tapioca balls inside (also try Lulu's Noodles on Craig Street in North Oakland), Rose Tea Café began life strictly as a snack shop, but now serves meals as well. Regulars claim that the food is strikingly similar to authentic Taiwanese cooking; dishes are mostly meat-based concoctions, such as pork and beef stew, ladled over a bed of rice.

Bloomfield and Lawrenceville   Map 6

Mention to a local that you're going out for a bite in Bloomfield, and they'll probably assume you're going to an Italian restaurant (or going to Tessaro's). But the neighborhood known as Pittsburgh's "Little Italy," in fact, is plentiful with many ethnic eateries, including Indian, Thai, and Polish. Which isn't to suggest that decades-old Italian restaurants don't abound. Bloomfield is full of them, and every Pittsburgher seems to have his or her favorite.

Formerly something of a run-down industrial wasteland, Lawrenceville has in the past few years seen an influx of creative and artistic new residents. Here you'll find two good coffee shops, a good number of fairly high-quality restaurants, and even a good ethnic eatery or two.

AMERICAN
TESSARO'S ❸❸
4601 Liberty Ave., 412/682-6809
HOURS: Mon.-Sat. 11 A.M.-midnight
Red meat fanatics—burger lovers especially—should by no means miss out on a trip to one of the city's most mouth-watering eateries. Tessaro's regularly wins awards locally for serving the 'Burgh's best burgers, which weigh in as heavy as a half pound. The secret, some say, are the bits of steak and filet mixed with the meat. If the idea of a gourmet burger isn't grabbing you, try a char-grilled steak or chop instead, or just kick back at the bar and watch the cooks work their magic through the kitchen's viewing window.

ASIAN
THAI CUISINE ❸❸
4625 Liberty Ave., 412/688-9661, www.thaicuisine.com/r/1633.html
HOURS: Mon.-Thurs. 11 A.M.-2:30 P.M. and 5-10 P.M., Fri. 11 A.M.-2:30 P.M. and 5-11 P.M., Sat. noon-11 P.M., Sun. noon-9 P.M.
Of the two Thai restaurants to choose from in Bloomfield, Thai Cuisine is by far the more popular, and for good reason: The pad thai is some of the best in the city, the waitstaff are extremely good-natured and attentive, and the lunch menu is an absolute bargain. This is also a perfect choice for a first date, and with more than 100 items on the menu, even the most timid diners stand a decent chance of finding something to like. (More than two-dozen meatless dishes are also offered.) Particularly popular is the *tom ka gai* (chicken coconut soup), which goes wonderfully with any entrée.

TRAM'S KITCHEN ❸❸
4050 Penn Ave., 412/682-2688
HOURS: Tues.-Sun. 10 A.M.-10 P.M.
Easily one of Pittsburgh's most popular Vietnamese restaurants, even Tram's most loyal customers often feel compelled to describe the ambience with a qualifier, which I'll second here: It's a hole in the wall. But sit down with a steaming bowl of *pho* (Vietnamese soup) and order a round of spring rolls, and you likely won't care; the food at Tram's is always fresh and bursting with flavor, especially

the vermicelli topped with meat or vegetables. Tram's is also a great choice for vegetarian diners.

CAFÉS

☕ COCA CAFÉ $$

3811 Butler St., 412/621-3171, www.cocacafe.net
HOURS: Tues.-Fri. 7 A.M.-3 P.M., Sat. 9 A.M.-3 P.M., Sun. 10 A.M.-3 P.M.

Easily one of Pittsburgh's best coffeehouses in both food and drink quality as well as interior design, the arty COCA Café displays a regularly rotating display of locally produced sculptures and multimedia work on the shelves and walls of its front room. In its back room, retro diner booths have been chopped up and refitted into attractive works of art, and even on roasting summer days the small back patio is shaded and pleasant. Grilled sandwiches and other finger foods are available, La Prima coffee is served, and Sunday

© DAN ELDRIDGE

COCA Café

RESTAURANTS

PITTSBURGH, MEET PARIS!

A somewhat downtrodden, post-industrial village that sits across the Allegheny River from Lawrenceville in Pittsburgh's East End, Millvale is one of the last neighborhoods in town where you might expect to encounter anything approaching artistry or divine inspiration in food. But lo and behold, right there in the middle of North Avenue is the locally worshiped **Jean-Marc Chatellier,** a French bakery so delectable and authentic that some Pittsburghers have claimed its offerings to be superior even to bakeries they've patronized in France itself.

The key ingredient, of course, is owner Jean-Marc, a third-generation baker from Brittany who apprenticed for four years with a master pastry chef in France before finding work in Cape Cod and Los Angeles. His hugely popular Millvale store, where specialties include wedding cakes, Hungarian nut rolls, and classic French pastries, has been open for almost 20 years. During a recent U.S. tour, musician David Byrne even stopped by for a bite; you can read his testimonial, as well as the glowing testimonials of dozens of other customers, at Jean-Marc's website.

Those of you who can't quite seem to make the requisite trip across the 40th Street Bridge will surely be pleased to learn that the Lawrenceville neighborhood now has a highly-regarded French bakery of its own, **La Gourmandine,** which has lately been enjoying rave reviews from area food critics and customers alike. The French expatriate owners, who serve up a delightfully fresh menu of desserts, breads, cakes, and pastries, lived in both Paris and Toulouse before relocating to Pittsburgh.

And finally, it shouldn't come as a huge surprise to learn that Pittsburgh's other new-to-the-neighborhood French eatery is located in the heart of East Liberty, which has been enjoying something of a dining renaissance lately. **Paris 66 Bistro,** which is almost entirely staffed by French employees, is probably best known in the city for its crepes. And while the bistro is just that – a bistro, and not a bakery – one quick peek through the front window will reveal a delectable selection of French breads, pastries, and desserts, all of which can be ordered to go.

brunch here (smoked salmon omelets, vanilla-orange yogurt with granola) is of the particularly pleasing and high-end variety.

CRAZY MOCHA ⑤
4525 Liberty Ave., 412/681-5225,
www.crazymocha.com
HOURS: Mon.-Thurs. 7 A.M.-11 P.M., Fri. 7 A.M.-midnight, Sat. 8 A.M.-midnight, Sun. 8 A.M.-11 P.M.

Still the only independent coffee shop on Bloomfield's Liberty Avenue, Crazy Mocha sets itself apart from the competition with a simple strategy: It serves truly fantastic coffee and espresso drinks. (In other words, no burned beans here.) And while Crazy Mocha is now a rapidly growing chain in the Pittsburgh area with more than 25 separate locations (see www.crazymocha.com), the Bloomfield shop still feels something like a neighborhood secret. Generally filled with an even mixture of laptop-toting grad students and area hipsters, there's even a DVD rental shop inside (Dreaming Ant, 412/683-7326, www.dreamingant.com) with a well-edited library

of independent and foreign features. And as is the case at nearly every Crazy Mocha location, Wi-Fi access here is free.

CONTEMPORARY AND NEW AMERICAN

J'EET ⑤⑤
4200 Penn Ave., 412/682-5338, www.jeetcafe.com
HOURS: Mon.-Sat. 7 A.M.-9 P.M., Sat.-Sun. 10 A.M.-3 P.M.

Owned and operated by a recently transplanted Californian whose brother owns the neighboring Brillobox, the J'eet culinary equation begins with three simplistic food staples—the crepe, the wrap, and the burrito—and then transforms them each into something at once artistic and delicious. French-inspired California cuisine, which is the main offering here, may not seem too unusual. But with its truly unique twists on a number of classic favorites—diners can try Moroccan, Tunisian, or Indian-themed crepes, for instance—J'eet does a decent job of turning the old into something delightfully new. (Insider tip: If you're dining alone, or just coming for coffee, try to grab one of the outdoor stools near the curbside takeaway window.)

RIVER MOON CAFÉ ⑤⑤⑤
108 43rd St., 412/683-4004, www.rivermooncafe.com
HOURS: Wed.-Sat. 5-9:30 P.M.

It's no wonder that a dining experience at River Moon Café, one of Lawrenceville's most creative eateries, is both pleasingly diverse and artistically explosive. After all, Josephine LaRussa-Impola, the owner and head chef, has an astounding 42 years of restaurant experience. All those decades of food preparation seem to come together quite successfully at River Moon, where all manner of Asian, Mexican, and Mediterranean dishes are served, everything is fresh and made from scratch, and literally dozens of teas you've never heard of available. And while most entrées here are of the pasta or chicken variety, there's always more than enough—think pineapple pepper shrimp or pork loin coated in raspberry chipotle sauce—to satisfy even the most eclectic of contemporary foodies.

© DAN ELDRIDGE

Crazy Mocha

INDIAN

TASTE OF INDIA $

4320 Penn Ave., 412/681-7700,
www.tasteofindiapittsburgh.com
HOURS: Mon.-Thurs. 11:30 A.M.-2:30 P.M. and 5-10 P.M.,
Fri.-Sat. 11:30 A.M.-2:30 P.M. and 5-10:30 P.M.,
Sun. 5-10 P.M.

Don't be put off if you visit Taste of India around dinnertime and find the dining room nearly deserted—the crowd tends to thin here after the midday all-you-can-eat buffet, a Pittsburgh trend that's repeated in nearly every area Indian restaurant. Nonetheless, the offerings at Taste of India unquestionably represent North Indian food at its finest, and the affordable portions are surprisingly generous to boot. It's tough to go wrong with any of the entrée choices here, but do consider ordering one of the fantastic *lassis* (a yogurt shake) with your meal.

ITALIAN

DEL'S BAR & RISTORANTE DELPIZZO $$

4428 Liberty Ave., 412/683-1448, www.delsrest.com
HOURS: Mon.-Thurs. 11 A.M.-11 P.M.,
Fri.-Sat. 11:30 A.M.-midnight, Sun. 1-10 P.M.

An always-packed and much-loved local standby, Del's is the place to go in Bloomfield if you want your Italian done *really* right. Hip and picturesque, however, it most certainly is not—the vibe here is definitely much more along the lines of grandma's kitchen than, say, chic eatery. That probably has much to do with the fact that Del's has long been a family-owned and -operated business; the main emphasis here is clearly on classic Italian cooking, not to mention good value. Bring your visiting parents or out-of-town guests to Del's, and try something standard, like lasagna or a Parmesan dish.

PIZZA ITALIA $

4512 Liberty Ave., 412/621-8960
HOURS: Mon.-Thurs. 11 A.M.-10:30 P.M.,
Fri.-Sat. 11 A.M.-11:30 P.M., Sun. 1-8:30 P.M.

If you've ever heard Pittsburgh referred to as "The College City," you likely won't be surprised to learn that the town's East End, where most of its ivory towers are located, is also filled-to-overflowing with pizza shops. So, how to choose? If you're anywhere near Bloomfield, it's Pizza Italia—no question about it. Not only are the pies made here manage to be chewy on a perfectly crispy crust, and not only is the cheese piled high whether the pie is ordered plain or with toppings, but it's also particularly easy on the purse strings—expect to pay around $10 for a large, although prices to seem to slowly creep higher every few months.

LATIN AMERICAN

◖ TAMARI RESTAURANT AND LOUNGE $$$

3519 Butler St., 412/325-3435, www.tamaripgh.com
HOURS: Mon.-Thurs. 11:30 A.M.-10 P.M., Fri.
11:30 A.M.-11 P.M., Sat. 4-11 P.M., Sun. 4-9 P.M.

Allen Chen, whose father owns some of Pittsburgh's most successful Chinese and Thai restaurants, shied away from the food service industry during his childhood. But he eventually took a strong interest in cooking, and became a chef. He also discovered similarities in Asian and Latin food that he simply couldn't shake. He partnered with a friend to create the city's first Latin-Asian fusion bistro. The result is something like a tapas bar—where small dishes are served and generally shared among friends—that features not only Spanish dishes like *ceviche* and *robata* but also flavors from Mexico, China, Thailand, and Japan. The result is simply one of the best and most unique culinary options in Pittsburgh.

POLISH

BLOOMFIELD BRIDGE TAVERN $

4412 Liberty Ave., 412/682-8611,
www.bloomfieldbridgetavern.com
HOURS: Tues.-Sat. 5 P.M.-2 A.M.

Although its days as one of the city's most progressive live-music venues are now little more than a memory, the BBT is still Pittsburgh's premiere locale for Polish food. To truly get into the spirit, order the massive

Polish Platter, which includes *haluski* and *golumpski* (different varieties of cabbage) along with the requisite pierogi (fried dumplings) and kielbasa (sausage). Those expecting particularly attentive service or even a particularly ethnic experience might walk away disappointed, but come for the food and you'll leave with a very satisfied stomach every time. Showing up early is also a good idea, as the BBT's bar crowd generally convenes by early evening.

SNACKS AND DESSERTS

DOZEN BAKE SHOP $

3511 Butler St., 412/621-4740,
www.dozenbakeshop.com

HOURS: Mon.-Thurs. 8 A.M.–8 P.M., Fri. 8 A.M.–9 P.M.,
Sat. 9 A.M.–9 P.M., Sun. 9 A.M.–2 P.M.

It may have taken awhile for the gourmet cupcake trend to fully infiltrate our fair city, but the hugely successful Dozen Bake Shop chain is nothing if not proof-positive that in Pittsburgh, at least, these meticulously designed treats are here to stay. Aside from Dozen's relatively affordable pricing and its commitment to using organic and locally-sourced ingredients, for

instance, customers are encouraged to linger over a cup of Intelligentsia coffee while taking advantage of the free Wi-Fi and watching the magic happen in the wide-open kitchen. Dozen's three other locations can be found in Oakland (417 S. Craig St., 412/420-5135), in Downtown's Cultural District (807 Liberty Ave., 412/281-4800), and inside The Andy Warhol Museum (117 Sandusky St., 412/237-8310).

LA GOURMANDINE $

4605 Butler St., 412/682-2201,
www.lagourmandinebakery.com

HOURS: Tues.-Fri. 7:30 A.M.–4:30 P.M.,
Sat. 9:30 A.M.–4:30 P.M.

Owned and operated by a French couple who previously lived and worked in Paris, this traditional French bakery quickly became a darling of the Pittsburgh foodie community when it opened in the summer of 2010. And while the hand-crafted pastries and other French sweets are certainly big draws here, La Gourmandine is probably best known for its breads, baguettes, and baguette sandwiches. Combination specials for breakfast or lunch, usually involving some grouping of croissant, sandwich, and made-from-

Dozen Bake Shop

scratch quiche, are offered daily. And since the menu of fresh-baked goods changes on a daily basis, you're quite likely to discover something new and unusual during each and every visit.

GRASSO ROBERTO ⑤

4709 Liberty Ave., 412/687-2014,
www.grassoroberto.com
HOURS: Mon.-Sat. 8 A.M.-8 P.M.

Slick, modern, and with a slight air of exclusivity, Grasso Roberto is a welcome neighborhood addition, especially for the sort of Bloomfielder who might otherwise be more inclined to seek out a café in, say, Shadyside. Along with its authentic Italian ambience, all the expected café fare can be had here, such as panini, salads, and espresso drinks. During the summer months, the shop fills with teenagers and window shoppers in search of mouthwatering gelato and sorbetto—frozen confections similar to ice cream.

TURKISH
ISTANBUL GRILLE ⑤⑤

4130 Butler St., 412/683-1623,
http://istanbulgrille.wordpress.com
HOURS: Tues.-Sat. 5-10 P.M., Sun. noon-3 P.M.

True Turkish cuisine has always been exceedingly rare in Pittsburgh, which almost certainly has something to do with the now long-running popularity of Istanbul Grill. Here, diners can find not only certified halal meat but also a full menu of the very same chicken and lamb kebabs found on nearly every urban street corner in Turkey itself. Decidedly more commonplace Middle Eastern and Mediterranean dishes are also on offer (baba ghanush and baklava, for instance), but for a genuine Turkish experience, order a plate of the phenomenal lamb adana and wash it down with a glass of yogurt-y *ayran*. Cubicle dwellers might consider visiting Istanbul's Downtown location (643 Liberty Ave., 412/325-3347, Mon.–Fri. 11 A.M.–3 P.M.).

East Liberty and Garfield — Map 6

The culinary scenes in the up-and-coming and quickly-gentrifying East Liberty and Garfield neighborhoods are arguably the city's most exciting—at least for the time being. Many of Pittsburgh's most progressive chefs have chosen to work in the area, where everything from traditional Ethiopian to Pan-Asian to comfort foods and independent coffee shops can be found. To explore the areas on foot, start just east of Children's Hospital on Penn Avenue before continuing east into the heart of East Liberty, where the Penn Circle area and North Highland Avenue both have quite a lot to offer.

AMERICAN
THE WAFFLE SHOP ⑤

124 S. Highland Ave., 724/681-3886,
www.waffleshop.org
HOURS: Fri. 11 P.M.-3 A.M., Sat. 10 A.M.-2 P.M. and
11 P.M.-3 A.M., Sun. 10 A.M.-2 P.M.

Something of a cross between a conceptual art project, a live-on-stage talk show, and an actual neighborhood restaurant where breakfast foods are served, the Waffle Shop is the brainchild of CMU art instructor Jon Rubin and his students. The online-streaming talk show that's produced here is the Waffle Shop's biggest draw; patrons can choose to be interviewed onstage, or they can become actual interviewers themselves, and archived interviews can always be seen on the restaurant's website. The waffles, incidentally, are said to be quite tasty. Also worth a visit is the Waffle Shop's next door-neighbor sister project, the **Conflict Kitchen** (124 S. Highland Ave., www.conflictkitchen.com, Sun.–Thurs. 11 A.M.–2 P.M., Fri.–Sat. 11 A.M.–2 P.M. and 11 P.M.–3 A.M.), which is a take-away food booth serving cuisine from countries with whom the United States is currently in conflict. The featured countries change roughly every four months.

WOULD YOU LIKE CONCEPTUAL ART WITH THAT?

It's probably fair enough to say that Pittsburgh's culinary scene is just as adventurous and forward-thinking as those of other Mid-Atlantic or Midwestern cities of similar size. In some cases, maybe even more so. But if there's one solitary feature that has always been lacking, it's most likely the outrageous gimmickry that can often be found, say, in the trendy Lower Manhattan dining scene. Recently, however, two students of an accomplished multi-disciplinary artist and Carnegie Mellon University professor changed all that by opening a conceptual art project/restaurant in East Liberty known as **The Waffle Shop.**

So, what exactly *is* the Waffle Shop? Well, for starters, you actually *can* get waffles there. The shop operates on Friday and Saturday nights from 11 P.M. until 3 A.M. (closing time is roughly an hour after the nearby bars close). It also opens on Saturday and Sunday mornings, from 10 A.M. until 2 P.M., and it stays closed for the remainder of the week.

The Waffle Shop

COURTESY OF THE WAFFLE SHOP

The catch here is that when you purchase your waffles, you're also agreeing to take part in a live-streaming talk show broadcast on the shop's website, and also on monitors that play in a continuous loop for passersby while the restaurant is closed. A mock, 1970s-style talk show stage has been erected inside the shop, intended to breed clever interaction; both the interviewers and the interviewees change with some frequency throughout the day.

So yes, you may very well be interviewed on camera here. Or you might be tempted to interview another Waffle Shop patron. As for the general topics of conversation, anything goes, for the most part. Spend some time with the archived videos online, and you'll see what we mean. Inevitably, awkwardness and sex talk seem to be omnipresent, although occasionally, the stream-of-consciousness chatting can become downright fascinating.

And just in case you're curious, the edibles here actually are quite good. After all, it's tough to go wrong with syrup-drenched waffles covered in chocolate sauce and whipped cream ($4–6.50). The decidedly limited menu also offers omelets ($5.50), as well as waffle add-ons like fried chicken ($3.50) and vanilla-bean ice cream ($1.50).

Where you *can* go wrong, however, is by heading to this place after you've had a few too many drinks at the nearby Shadow Lounge, or Kelly's Bar. Your accompanying lack of inhibition, of course, might very well be captured for all the world to see, after which you'll have to hang your weary head in shame. At least, that is, until someone else upstages your performance. Which, when you think about it, is essentially the point.

The overall objective, however, seems even broader than that. The art students who conceived the Waffle Shop studied with Jon Rubin, a Carnegie Mellon professor whose work "explores the social dynamics of public places and the idiosyncrasies of individual and group behavior," according to his website, www.jonrubin.net.

After constructing and executing the Waffle Shop, Rubin and his students embarked on their sophomore effort, **Conflict Kitchen** (www.conflictkitchen.com), a different food-themed project that sits directly next door to the Waffle Shop. Essentially, Conflict Kitchen is a walk-up food stand that serves exactly one carryout dish, and that particular dish originates from a country that is currently involved in a conflict with the United States.

Throughout much of this guide's reporting process, Conflict Kitchen frequently served *kubideh,* a wrap sandwich traditionally served on the streets of Tehran, Iran. It's made of homemade *barbari* bread and filled with mint, onion, black sesame seeds, fresh basil, and spiced ground beef. Following that is cuisine from Afghanistan, and since the featured country changes roughly every four months, it's quite likely that a North Korean goulash of some sort may be on the menu by the time you read this. A Venezuelan stint, not surprisingly, is also in the works.

Events at Conflict Kitchen tend to involve interactive web-video broadcasts similar to those at the Waffle Shop. During once such event, a video documenting a number of stereotypical Pittsburgh institutions (Steelers football, Primanti Brothers sandwiches) was shown via satellite to folks in Tehran, who replied with videos of similar – but distinctly Iranian – staple institutions (a famous sandwich shop, an infamous soccer team). The idea, of course, was to create feelings of connection and brotherhood between two supposedly dissimilar cultures.

"We're artists," Rubin offered during an interview with *Pittsburgh* magazine, "not business people, so we tend to think of things a little backwards."

(Contributed by Matt Stroud, a Pittsburgh-based freelance journalist.)

COURTESY OF THE WAFFLE SHOP

Conflict Kitchen

RESTAURANTS

ASIAN
PLUM PAN-ASIAN KITCHEN ⑤⑤
5996 Penn Circle S., 412/363-7586,
www.plumpanasiankitchen.com
HOURS: Mon.-Thurs. 11:30 A.M.-3 P.M. and 5-10 P.M.,
Fri.-Sat. 11:30 A.M.-3 P.M. and 5-11 P.M., Sun. 4-9 P.M.

Opened in the same space (and largely by the same team) as the sorely missed and seriously expensive gourmet Chinese restaurant known as Richard Chen, the formula of the significantly more down-to-earth Plum seems to involve offering simpler fare at much easier-to-digest prices. Long-time Pittsburgh-area diners might like to think of Plum as something of an upscale Spice Island Tea House, a Pan-Asian eatery in Oakland appealing to the university set. And yet the Thai, Indonesian, Vietnamese, Malaysian, and Chinese offerings at Plum manage to be appropriately sophisticated while still maintaining a semblance of affordability. The space itself is aesthetically gorgeous—not surprising, given the building's former tenant—and the newly installed sushi bar is said to be among Pittsburgh's very best.

SMILING BANANA LEAF ⑤
5901 Bryant St., 412/362-3200,
www.smilingbananaleaf.com
HOURS: Mon.-Thurs. 11 A.M.-9 P.M., Fri.-Sat. 11 A.M.-3 P.M. and 4-10 P.M.

Pittsburgh isn't exactly lacking in Thai restaurants, but as for *quality* Thai restaurants? That's another story altogether. Which is exactly why this recent addition to Highland Park's growing culinary scene was greeted with so much anticipation. And aside from the restaurant's exceedingly small size and its understandably slow service during the busy dinner rush, there's not much to complain about here. The curry and noodle dishes seem to be the biggest hits, although considering SBL's very reasonable rates (lunch entrées can be had for $7–8), a little experimentation may well be in order.

CAFÉS
THE QUIET STORM ⑤
5430 Penn Ave., 412/661-9355,
www.quietstormcoffee.com

HOURS: Mon.-Thurs. 8 A.M.-7 P.M., Fri. 8 A.M.-10 P.M., Sat. 10 A.M.-10 P.M., Sun. 10 A.M.-4 P.M.

This vegetarian- and vegan-friendly café has ambience that might best be described as thrift-store chic. Think mismatched furniture, five-year-old copies of *Maximumrocknroll*, and baristas who pretend not to notice anyone not sporting dreadlocks or a septum piercing. Snotty attitudes aside, however, enjoying an unusual entreé at the Quiet Storm can be a rather pleasant way to pass an evening. Most tables are far enough from each other to allow for private conversations, and the BYOB policy tends to keep the social interactions sufficiently lubricated.

VOLUTO COFFEE ⑤
5467 Penn Ave., 412/661-3000, www.volutocoffee.com
HOURS: Mon.-Fri. 7 A.M.-6 P.M., Sat.-Sun. 9 A.M.-5 P.M.

This is a genuine coffee connoisseur's shop, not unlike something you'd expect to find in the Pacific Northwest, with an emphasis on excellent locally-brewed coffee, unpretentious homemade cookies, and baked-fresh-daily pastries that are delivered from a shop in Pittsburgh's

The Quiet Storm

© DAN ELDRIDGE

northern suburbs. Voluto is located in a relatively new mixed-use housing development on the border of three neighborhoods quickly moving beyond their previous—if not necessarily unwarranted—reputations as hotbeds for petty crime. Voluto, as the unofficial caffeine supplier of that structure, stands to gain quite a bit by making sure your coffee and your experience are as uplifting as possible. Take advantage of the comfy furniture and free Wi-Fi, too.

CARIBBEAN
ROYAL CARIBBEAN ◐⑤
128 S. Highland Ave., 412/362-1861
HOURS: Tues.-Thurs. 11 A.M.-10 P.M., Fri.-Sat. 11 A.M.-11 P.M., Sun. 1-8 P.M.
Located next door to Pittsburgh's first Ethiopian restaurant, Royal Caribbean was one of the first international eateries involved in what might now be thought of as the culinary pioneering of East Liberty. Today, the area is chock-a-block with inventive restaurants, a fact that's at least partly attributed to the presence of this honestly authentic, BYOB Caribbean café. The most recommended menu items include the legendary spicy jerk chicken, the goat curry, and the fresh fruit juices, but do be forewarned: Because Royal Caribbean tends to stir up just a few daily batches of its regular dishes, the entrée you're looking forward to may be unavailable if you arrive too late in the day.

CONTEMPORARY AND NEW AMERICAN
DINETTE ◐⑤
5996 Penn Circle S., 2nd level, 412/362-0202, www.dinette-pgh.com
HOURS: Tues.-Thurs. 5-10 P.M., Fri.-Sat. 5-11 P.M.
Yet another entrant into Pittsburgh's swiftly growing family of restaurants that proudly fly the locally-sourced-and-organic flag, Dinette is a brilliantly-designed minimalist bistro offering gourmet flat-bread pizzas along with what is easily one of the city's most sophisticated wine lists. And aside from its daily-changing menu, Dinette has quite a lot to brag about: *Pittsburgh* magazine named it one of the city's 25 best restaurants in 2010, while during the

same year, owner and chef Sonja Finn ranked as a semi-finalist for a prestigious James Beard Foundation award. For those with the money to spend, Dinette offers a culinary experience unique to just about any other you're likely to find within the city's limits.

E² ◐⑤
5904 Bryant St., 412/441-1200, http://e2pittsburgh.com
HOURS: Tues.-Fri. 11 A.M.-4 P.M. and 5-10 P.M., Sat. 9 A.M.-2 P.M. and 6-10 P.M., Sun. 9 A.M.-2 P.M.
Located on a quiet but expanding block near the picturesque Highland Park Reservoir, E² (pronounced "E-squared") is an absolute must for the high-end breakfast connoisseur. The menu provides some of the best—and most unique—brunch fair in the region. The menu changes from week to week, although standard fare runs the gamut from sugar-dusted beignets and perfectly poached eggs to some of the best doughnuts you've ever dreamed of. Late risers need not despair, daily lunch and dinner menus are now available. Since the restaurant does not have a liquor license, they encourage diners to BYOB.

◖ SALT OF THE EARTH ⑤⑤⑤
5523 Penn Ave., 412/414-9088, www.saltpgh.com
HOURS: Mon.-Sat. 5 P.M.-1 A.M.
Two years of planning culminated in the opening of Salt of the Earth, easily the city's most anticipated restaurant in years. Much of that had to do with Salt's co-owner and chef, the venerable and avant-garde Kevin Sousa, who has lately become something of local—and even national—culinary legend. Sousa is a proponent of a culinary movement known as molecular gastronomy, in which the principals of science are brought into the kitchen. What's more, SOTE is the first restaurant at which Sousa has had the luxury of calling literally all the shots, and his genius truly shines through here, with contemporary interpretations of everything from pork belly to lamb shoulder to a seriously forward-thinking cocktail menu. If you try one high-end eatery during your time in Pittsburgh, definitely make it this one.

SPOON $$$
134 S. Highland Ave., 412/362-6001,
www.spoonpgh.com
HOURS: Mon.-Thurs. 11:30 A.M.-2 P.M. and 5-10 P.M.,
Fri.-Sat. 11:30 A.M.-2 P.M. and 5-11 P.M., Sun. 5-9 P.M.

Fawning articles and positive reviews can't say enough about Spoon, one of the East End's newest avant-garde eateries, where seasonal and locally-sourced ingredients are combined with unparalleled creativity. The brilliant menu is the result of executive chef Brian Pekarcik's intimate knowledge of food and its many possibilities: how to match seemingly dissimilar foods, for instance. Consider a dish known as Ahi Tuna Two Ways, which pairs a sushi crab roll with a noodle salad. And yet, if an unusually inventive twist on classic American cuisine isn't exactly what you're after, consider stopping by Spoon's sister restaurant, **BRGR,** located right around the corner at 5997 Penn Circle South. Gourmet hamburgers and milkshakes are served from noon until late evening, daily.

ETHIOPIAN
ABAY ETHIOPIAN CUISINE $$
130 S. Highland Ave., 412/661-9736,
www.abayrestaurant.com
HOURS: Tues.-Sat. 11:30 A.M.-2:30 P.M. and 5-10 P.M.,
Sun. 11:30 A.M.-2:30 P.M. and 5-9 P.M., closed Mon.

It's often said by fans of fine dining that a major American city simply doesn't rank on the sophistication scale unless it can claim at least one Ethiopian restaurant. So imagine the joy of Pittsburgh's foodie community when Abay Ethiopian Cuisine appeared not long ago in the quickly gentrifying East Liberty district. Thankfully, the food here has more than lived up to everyone's expectations: The menu is an exotic combination of spices, oils, and vegetables. And as is the custom when eating Ethiopian-style, no utensils are used. Instead, the beans, rice, and vegetables—served communally on one large plate—are dutifully sopped up with a piece of tortilla-like bread known as *injera*. In other words, Abay provides adventure and education mixed with sustenance and satisfaction.

TANA ETHIOPIAN CUISINE $$
5929 Baum Blvd., 412/665-2770,
www.tanaethiopiancuisine.com
HOURS: Mon. 5-11 P.M., Tues.-Sun. 11 A.M.-2:30 P.M. and 5-11 P.M.

Ethiopian cuisine, famous for its spicy vegetable and meat dishes that are eaten without utensils, is represented by two East End establishments, and there's been a fair amount of enthusiastic local debate over which is more authentic. The dispute hinges over whether Abay—an award-winning Ethiopian eatery mere blocks away at 130 South Highland Avenue—offers superior fare to Tana, the newer and least advertised of the two. But at least two indisputable facts are clear: Both of these restaurants have inspired a faithful following, and both will give you a taste of crafted Ethiopian cooking from actual expats who have chosen to bring their culinary skills to one of Pittsburgh's fastest-growing neighborhoods.

FRENCH
PARIS 66 BISTRO $$
6018 Centre Ave., 412/404-8166,
www.paris66bistro.com
HOURS: Tues.-Sat. 11 A.M.-2:30 P.M. and 5-9:30 P.M.,
Sun. 10 A.M.-2:30 P.M.

As a self-described purveyor of "everyday French cuisine," this crepe hub prides itself on being the exact opposite of the stereotypical French restaurant in America: It's both affordable and non-exclusionary. At the same time, it manages to retain an entirely authentic vibe, thanks no doubt to the owner and head chef, both of whom were trained as master crepe makers in France. Designed to look, smell, and feel like a Parisian sidewalk café, Paris 66 also serves up French pizza, Parisian pastries, and daily-made French desserts.

INDIAN
PEOPLE'S INDIAN RESTAURANT $
5147 Penn Ave., 412/661-3160
HOURS: Mon.-Sat. 11:30 A.M.-10 P.M.

Its exterior may not be the most welcoming, but show up for the weekday all-you-can-eat lunch buffet and you'll immediately understand why

© DAN ELDRIDGE

Paris 66 Bistro

Garfield's best-kept culinary secret probably won't be a secret for long. Featuring spicy cuisine from the northern Indian state of Punjab, People's Indian Restaurant has a menu extensive enough for vegetarians and meat-eaters alike. Smoky tandoor dishes are especially smart picks, as is the chewy and puffy Punjabi *nan* (Indian bread). Ten dollars will buy you the buffet plus tip with a bit left over. Evening entrées (chicken korma, vindaloo) are equally affordable.

ITALIAN
SPAK BROTHERS PIZZA ⑤
5107 Penn Ave., 412/362-7725, www.spakbrothers.com
HOURS: Mon.-Thurs. 11 A.M.-10 P.M., Fri. 11 A.M.-11 P.M., Sat. 1-11 P.M.
Owned and operated by ambitious siblings who grew up in the city's suburbs, this Garfield-area pizzeria serves truly delectable versions of typical pizza shop fare. The Spaks, however, have also carved out a unique niche as purveyors of vegetarian and vegan offerings not available anywhere else in the region, the vast majority of which are so surprisingly flavorful that even meat-loving omnivores have become regular

customers. Meat-free wings, tacos, cheese steaks, and even meatless sausage and pepperoni are all available here. And what's more, the shop largely sources local and sustainable ingredients.

SNACKS AND DESSERTS
VANILLA PASTRY STUDIO ⑤
6014 Penn Circle S., 412/361-2306, www.vanillapastry.com
HOURS: Tues.-Fri. 9 A.M.-6 P.M., Sat. 9 A.M.-4 P.M., Sun. 10 A.M.-2 P.M.
Owned and operated by a former Pennsylvania Culinary Academy instructor of the Pastry Arts (seriously!), Vanilla Pastry Studio is something of a fantasy land for grown-ups with a serious sweet tooth. Offerings include everything from artistic wedding cakes to muffins, loaf breads, gourmet cookies, and cupcakes that more than a few locals claim are superior to those sold by the much-loved Dozen Bake Shop chain. This clean and modern shop also handles unique requests for weddings and special events; if there's an unusual sugary creation you'd like to commission, there's a good chance Vanilla Pastry can bring it to life.

RESTAURANTS

© DAN ELDRIDGE

Vanilla Pastry Studio

Greater Pittsburgh   Map 7

CONTEMPORARY AND NEW AMERICAN

TIN FRONT CAFÉ $$

216 E. Eighth Ave., Homestead, 412/461-4615, www.tinfrontcafe.com

HOURS: Tues.-Thurs. 8 A.M.-8 P.M., Fri. 8 A.M.-9 P.M., Sat. 10 A.M.-9 P.M.

Self-described by its owner as a vegetarian restaurant in what was once a strictly meat-and-potatoes market, the seriously quaint and rustic Tin Front Café is also a picture-perfect metaphor for what seems to be a revival of the Homestead area's former greatness. The wooden bar, for instance, was brought over from the area's sorely missed Chiodo's Tavern. And even avowed omnivores have conceded that the Tin Front's award-winning vegetarian chili is perhaps the city's very best. There are also alcoholic coffee beverages on offer, and a cozy back patio where (gasp!) all-meat barbeques may soon be taking place.

EUROPEAN

SOUP SEGA $

449-451 W. Eighth Ave., Homestead, 412/461-6188, www.bmnecc.org

HOURS: Sat. 9 A.M.-noon

Pittsburghers love to brag about the four distinct seasons the city experiences each year, regardless of the fact that two of them—winter and fall—tend to be bone-chillingly cold. Thankfully, this is also the time of year when Soup Sega awakens from its warm-season slumber. This West Homestead gem features volunteer cooks who work out of a Bulgarian-Macedonian cultural center, and who serve up numerous varieties of soup based on traditional Bulgarian recipes. Available only on Saturdays from 9 A.M. to noon, the take-away selections here are nevertheless worth the trip: Think Balkan bean, feta-filled strudel, and dill dumplings. Soup Sega provides a homemade warmth you're unlikely

to find anywhere else in Pittsburgh—whether it's freezing outside or not.

SNACKS AND DESSERTS

JEAN-MARC CHATELLIER $

213 North Ave., Millvale, 412/821-8533, www.jeanmarcchatellier.com

HOURS: Tues.-Fri. 7 A.M.-5 P.M., Sat. 7 A.M.-2 P.M.

Selling both European and American pastries, cakes, breads, pies, and more, this tiny and unassuming Millvale bakery has long been considered one of the city's best-kept secrets. The French-trained owner, Jean-Marc, is a third-generation baker who worked as a pastry chef in a number of American and European pastry shops and restaurants before eventually settling in Pittsburgh, where he's now been based for almost two decades. Wedding cakes and all manner of unusual holiday breads and pastries can also be procured here, although the house favorite seems to be Jean-Marc's flaky, buttery croissants, which are absolutely not to be missed.

NANCY B'S BAKERY $

415 W. Seventh Ave., Homestead, 412/462-6222, www.nancybsbakery.com

HOURS: Mon.-Fri. 9 A.M.-5 P.M.

Occasionally referred to by its regular customers as the city's best-kept secret, Nancy B's is a two-decades-old Homestead tradition that has only recently begun to experience its fair share of mainstream media love. That's partially thanks to the readers of *Pittsburgh* magazine, who awarded it with a "Best Chocolate Chip Cookie" award in 2010. And how right they were: More than 1,000 of the oversized and astonishingly toothsome cookies come out of Nancy B's oven on a daily basis. And that's to say nothing of this homegrown shop's other fare, which includes brownies, cakes, pies, and a version of nearly every classic homemade cookie one could possibly imagine.

NIGHTLIFE

It can be easy enough at times to holler and moan about Pittsburgh's distinctive lack of serious nightlife options, but remember: This is a small town, and although the city's nightlife scene almost certainly has a little something to offer almost everyone, chances are good that you may have to dig deep in order to truly find what you're looking for.

For instance, where bigger urban areas may have dozens of gay clubs, or ten different jazz bars, Pittsburgh may be home to only five or six. Maybe less. Maybe more. The major difference you're likely to discover here, however, lies in the sense of community that's ever-present in the neighborhood bars, and in the tiny East End art galleries that transform into cutting-edge live music venues on weekend nights.

To a large degree, nightlife in Pittsburgh in synonymous with two separate South Side destinations: There's the main drag of East Carson Street, which has been described as the longest uninterrupted stretch of bars in the country. There's also the shopping and tourist-friendly destination known as Station Square, which is home to a complex of hard-partying dance clubs. If you're looking for a scene that's slightly grittier and significantly more authentic, check out the hipster bars dotting the East End neighborhoods of Lawrenceville, Bloomfield, and East Liberty; a good number of them also double as art galleries and intimate concert venues.

Making nice with the locals and the regulars, though, is probably the best way to learn about Pittsburgh's entertaining and often hidden nightlife secrets. For instance, while local

HIGHLIGHTS

LOOK FOR ◖ TO FIND RECOMMENDED NIGHTLIFE.

◖ **Most Creative Cocktails:** With its pre-Prohibition vibe, its highly-skilled mixologists, and an incredibly complicated menu of old-school cocktails, **Embury** is the city's premiere 1920's pseudo-speakeasy (page 121).

◖ **Best Dive Bar:** Hipsters and locals adore its cheap swill with equal fervor: It's **Gooski's,** of course, Pittsburgh's most authentic house of late-night debauchery (page 121).

◖ **Best Theme Bar:** Nearly every surface of the South Side's truly unique **Over the Bar Bicycle Café** is plastered with bike memorabilia, and the city's most fervent cyclists can almost always be spotted bellying up to the bar, or grabbing a smoke by the bike racks outside (page 123).

◖ **Best Bar for a First Date:** It's hip, it's laid-back, and it has a fantastic outdoor patio. Chatting over tacos and Coronas at the **Round Corner Cantina,** in fact, may be the perfect way to vet that potential significant other you've been eyeing (page 125).

◖ **Best Neighborhood Bar:** The **Squirrel Hill Café,** known to locals as "The Cage," has been around forever, and it welcomes all comers with open arms. In Squirrel Hill, at least, this is the bar where everybody knows your name (page 126).

◖ **Best Dance Club:** The dance clubs at Station Square seem to open and close with alarming frequency, but the current top dog is certainly **Whim,** with its high-end laser-light system and its always creative theme nights (page 128).

◖ **Best Mixed Gay-and-Straight Bar:** Shadyside's upscale **Spin Bartini & Ultra Lounge** is just as popular with heteros as it is with the East End's growing gay community, making it the perfect place for a little late-

night cruising, no matter what your sexual predilection (page 130).

◖ **Best Live-Music Venue:** Easily the most intimate live-music experience in the city, **Club Café** is the place to catch up-and-coming singer-songwriters just before they break into the mainstream. A host of jazz, blues, and folk legends perform here regularly as well (page 132).

◖ **Best Lounge:** Operated by the same team responsible for the nearby Shadow Lounge, the endlessly stylish **AVA** is an absolute bounty of wild dance parties, unexpected jazz sessions, and deliciously healthy food (page 135).

Over the Bar Bicycle Café

pubs generally close for the night at 2 A.M., there are after-hours bars and unusually creative nightlife events here that even many Pittsburgh natives don't know about. So belly up to the bar, get to know your neighbor, and start exploring the Steel City like the locals do: with an always open-minded attitude, and with good friends in tow.

Bars

BAR 11
1101 Bradish St., 412/381-0899
HOURS: Mon.-Fri. 10:30 A.M.-2 A.M., Sat. noon-2 A.M.
COST: No Cover
Map 3

With an atmosphere that much more closely resembles a house party than an actual bar, it's perhaps surprising that the unmarked Bar 11 has stayed such a well-kept secret for so long. No need to mince words, however: Bar 11 is a tried-and-true dive; it's the even-tempered waitstaff and the creative party-favor shtick that keeps things exciting. The room is perpetually lit by black lights and covered in aluminum foil, and patrons are encouraged to draw on each other with highlighter pens.

BELVEDERE'S
4016 Butler St., 412/687-2555,
www.myspace.com/belvederesbar
HOURS: Mon.-Sat. 7 A.M.-2 A.M., Sun. 11 A.M.-2 A.M.
COST: $2-4
Map 6

Essentially a dive bar of the decidedly hip variety, Belvedere's also frequently doubles as a live music venue, hosting classic punk bands and newer indie acts alike. The city's all-female roller derby league, the Steel City Derby Demons, often holds its after-parties here following bouts. And while a wide array of themed parties takes place here regularly, including a popular '80s night and a punk-rock karaoke night, the real draw at Belvedere's is the truly unique energy and ambiance of the place: gritty, honest, dirty, and downright fun.

BLOOMFIELD BRIDGE TAVERN
4412 Liberty Ave., 412/682-8611
HOURS: Mon.-Sat. 11 A.M.-1 A.M.
COST: No Cover
Map 6

Although popularly known as Pittsburgh's best choice for authentic Polish dining, the BBT, as it's known locally, is also a popular neighborhood bar and live-music destination. There isn't anything too terribly exciting on tap here, although the bar's parking lot and its front porch always fill with bike messengers and activist types during the weekly Thursday Dollar Night, when import and craft-brewed bottles past their expiration date are hawked for a buck each. Drum and bass events, which often feature legendary deejays, are staged here once or twice a month, and the Calliope folk music society holds its open mike nights here.

CHURCH BREW WORKS
3525 Liberty Ave., 412/688-8200,
www.churchbrew.com
HOURS: Mon.-Sat. 11:30 A.M.-12:45 A.M.,
Sun. noon-9:45 P.M.
COST: No Cover
Map 6

Located in a lovingly restored Catholic church where actual pews are used for seating, and massive beer tanks sit atop the altar, this Lawrenceville brewpub and restaurant offers one of the city's most unusual drinking and dining experiences. The award-winning beers brewed here include a light and a dark lager, an English pale ale, a stout, and a specialty brew that changes on a monthly basis. And yet Church Brew Works is probably just as well

NIGHTLIFE

NIGHTLIFE

COURTESY OF VISITPITTSBURGH

Church Brew Works

known for its gourmet pub grub menu, featuring high-end interpretations of pasta, seafood, salads, sandwiches, and the ever-popular brick oven pizza. The church itself, by the way—formerly known as St. John the Baptist—is fairly stunning; its collection of stained glass windows alone is worth the trip.

DEE'S CAFÉ
1316 E. Carson St., 412/431-1314, www.deescafe.com
HOURS: First floor Mon.-Sat. noon-2 A.M., Sun. 2 P.M.-2 A.M.; second floor Thurs.-Sun. 9 P.M.-2 A.M.
COST: No Cover
Map 3

Less of a dive bar than a home away from home for some of the South Side's most ambitious imbibers, Dee's is dirty, dank, and perpetually clouded in smoke since it is one of the bars in the city that is exempt from the smoking ban. Best of all, it's cheap and probably the most fun you'll have in any of Pittsburgh's shot-and-a-beer bars, especially if you hang around long enough to get to know the locals. What does the crowd look like? Picture a Nine Inch

Nails concert, circa 1994: combat boots, trench coats, Manic Panic hair, etc. The crowd at the upstairs bar, where pint glasses are strictly verboten, is a touch older and more upscale. Action around the billiards tables on both levels is always in full effect.

DOC'S PLACE
5442 Walnut St., 412/681-3713, www.docsplacepittsburgh.com
HOURS: Mon.-Thurs. 4 P.M.-2 A.M., Fri.-Sat. noon-2 A.M., Sun. 3 P.M.-2 A.M.
COST: No Cover
Map 4

After 20 straight years at the corner of Walnut and Bellefonte Streets in Shadyside, it's easy to understand how Doc's Place has become an East End institution: It's got a great location, a nonsmoking martini bar, and satellite TV screening almost nonstop sports. But even draught-only drinkers who couldn't care less about the playoffs have another perfectly good reason to show up—namely, the massive rooftop patio, which, incidentally, is one of the city's most pleasant places to doff a pitcher of Yuengling when the weather's balmy. Generally, the crowd here is college-aged and of the fraternity and sorority persuasions. (In other words, a great choice for well-dressed singles on the prowl.)

EMBURY
2216 Penn Ave., 1st Fl., 412/434-1230,
www.firehouse-lounge.com
HOURS: Mon.-Sat. 5 P.M.-2 A.M.
COST: No Cover
Map 1

A 1920s pre-Prohibition cocktail bar where classic drinks like the Sazerac and the Dark 'n' Stormy are painstakingly crafted by bartenders who actually care about the art of alcohol, Embury is an absolute one-of-a-kind in Pittsburgh. The so-called mixologists behind the bar, for instance, are all attired in period-appropriate costume, right down to the suit vest and the waxed handlebar mustache. And although you'll pay a princely sum for the experience of enjoying a drink here, it's more than worth it just to soak in the detail-rich speakeasy atmosphere. If you're looking for something a bit more sophisticated than a cheap lager or a house red, in other words, you simply won't find a more unique choice in town.

GOOSKI'S
3117 Brereton St., 412/681-1658
HOURS: Mon.-Sat. 3 P.M.-2 A.M.
COST: $4-5 live music shows
Map 6

Call it a dive, call it a hipster hangout, or call it Pittsburgh's most legendary neighborhood watering hole—just make sure that before leaving town you spend at least one weekend night at Gooski's, preferably with a pitcher of cheap beer in front of you. Long known as one of the hardscrabble Steel City's most representative hangouts, the true beauty of Gooski's lies in its diametrically opposed clientele: Saddle up to the bar, and you'll soon find yourself in conversation with an unemployed steel miner, or maybe a tough-talking motorcycle maven. Area hipsters—many who aren't from the area

at all, but who've driven for miles just to make the scene—fill the bar's booths and the billiards room. On Saturday nights, local garage rock bands perform.

JACK ROSE BAR
1121 E. Carson St., 412/431-3644,
www.jacksbarpittsburgh.com
HOURS: Mon.-Sun. 7 A.M.-2 A.M.
COST: No Cover
Map 3

Take our word for it: No one goes to Jack Rose Bar, which probably has greater name recognition than any other watering hole along the South Side strip, for its beverage selection. Nor do they go for the atmosphere, the ambience, or the music. That's because Jack's is the city's meat market *par excellence,* plain and simple. Being that this is Pittsburgh, that generally means an overabundance of thick-necked men in white ball caps and coeds with teased hair and high heels. It also means an almost nightly procession of fistfights, so do hang on tight to your Iron City should you find yourself packed into a far corner. In true Steel City style, Jack's never closes its doors, except when forced by Pennsylvania law.

KELLY'S BAR
6012 Penn Circle S., 412/363-6012
HOURS: Mon.-Thurs. 5 P.M.-midnight,
Fri.-Sat. 5 P.M.-2 A.M.
COST: No Cover
Map 6

One of Pittsburgh's newest nightlife successes, the lovingly refurbished Kelly's is practically synonymous with style and sophistication, but in a slightly retro and ironic sort of sense. With its art deco design, Wurlitzer jukebox, and Tiki-themed back deck, it's no surprise that Kelly's has played such an important role in the recent revitalization of East Liberty. The bad news is the too-cool-for-school waitstaff, some of who are infamous for their inattentiveness. You'll soon forget about all that, however, after getting your hands on one of the bar's expertly mixed cocktails or a jerk-chicken burger from the surprisingly competent kitchen.

NIGHTLIFE

LAVA LOUNGE

2204 E. Carson St., 412/431-5282,
www.lavaloungepgh.com
HOURS: Mon.-Sun. 4 P.M.–4 A.M.
COST: Sun.-Thurs. no cover, Fri. and Sat. $3
Map 3

One of two South Side bars operated by the owners of the Beehive coffee shop, Lava Lounge looks a lot like it sounds. Picture a tavern where, say, the Flintstones might pass an evening, and you'll start to get the idea: Tables, booths, and high-backed chairs are all designed to resemble a liquid molten lava flow. Even the interior design is creatively cave-like. Do be aware that draft beer isn't available; wine, pricey imports, and cocktails are what you'll be drinking here. Unknown rock bands—some from out of town, but mostly local—play in the back room periodically. Deejays spin retro '80s records and other hipster miscellanea most nights.

MULLANEY'S HARP & FIDDLE

2329 Penn Ave., 412/642-6622,
www.harpandfiddle.com
HOURS: Tues.-Sat. 11:30 A.M.–2 A.M.
COST: No Cover
Map 1

Mullaney's certainly isn't the only Irish pub in the city, although it is unquestionably one of the best designed and most inviting. And because it sits relatively far from the majority of the Strip's meat-market bar district (but still within walking distance), Mullaney's doesn't get a ton of walk-in traffic. Revelers here are generally well-intentioned regulars, or maybe folk music fans who've come for the live music and jig dancing. Traditional Irish entrées (shepherd's pie, corned beef and cabbage) can be ordered in between rounds of Guinness.

NEW AMSTERDAM

4421 Butler St., 412/904-2915,
www.myspace.com/newamsterdam412
HOURS: Sun.-Fri. 4 P.M.–2 A.M., Sat. noon-2 A.M.
COST: $5-10 for special events
Map 6

It's certainly no coincidence that one of Pittsburgh's newest bastions of hipster cool, the bar and café known as New Amsterdam, is located smack-dab in the heart of Lawrenceville's main drag, which is quickly transforming into one of Pittsburgh's most exciting destination neighborhoods for the creative set. As for the bar itself, which is a squat brick square of a building with a garage door entrance opening onto the sidewalk, it's

New Amsterdam

quite unlike anything else in the area. The exterior, for instance, is plastered with a gorgeous skull-motif mural by the local artist Matt Spahr, and the food and drinks—wings, mac and cheese, fish tacos—pay appropriate homage to the neighborhood's blue-collar traditions. Whether you're looking to refuel or simply do a bit of people-watching, this new Lawrenceville tradition is an absolutely solid choice.

OVER THE BAR BICYCLE CAFÉ
2518 E. Carson St., 412/381-3698,
www.otbbicyclecafe.com
HOURS: Mon.-Fri. 11 A.M.-2 A.M., Sat. and Sun. noon-2 A.M.
COST: No Cover
Map 3

Although Pittsburgh has steadily grown into something of a seriously enthusiastic bicycling city over the past few years, the recent arrival of this bike-themed bar and café has felt, to some degree, like an honest-to-goodness confirmation that the cycling scene in Bridge City has become an important and lucrative big business. At OTB, you'll find bicycling tchotchkes and memorabilia hanging from—and nailed onto—nearly every available surface. All manner of cyclists eat and drink here regularly, and even the delightfully toothsome pub-grub menu pays homage to the sport. Vegetarian-friendly seitan wings are just 25 cents each on Thursdays, group rides are occasionally scheduled, and the microbrew list is comparable to those at most other East Carson Street watering holes. Naturally, arriving on two wheels is strongly encouraged.

PETER'S PUB
116 Oakland Ave., 412/681-7465
HOURS: Mon.-Sat. 11 A.M.-2 A.M., Sun. noon-2 A.M.
COST: $1-5 Thurs.-Sat after 9 P.M. on DJ or live music nights
Map 2

Only at Peter's Pub can one experience all the raucousness and debauchery of a Pitt frat party without actually having been invited. University athletes and the type of undergrads

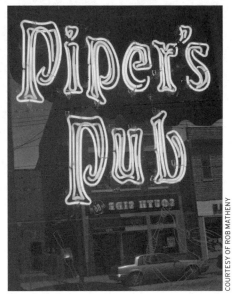
COURTESY OF ROB MATHENY
Piper's Pub

NIGHTLIFE

who obsessively follow the NCAA playoffs are whom you can expect here; also count on ridiculously affordable daily beer specials ($1 Miller Light drafts aren't uncommon). On the second floor is a separate bar, as well as a dance floor that quickly grows sweaty and crowded on weekend nights.

PIPER'S PUB
1828 E. Carson St., 412/381-3977, www.piperspub.com
HOURS: Mon.-Sat. 11 A.M.-2 A.M., Sun. noon-2 A.M.
COST: $1-5 Thurs.-Sat after 9 P.M. on deejay or live music nights
Map 3

A drinking and dining mecca for the city's British expat community, Piper's Pub has all the charm of an authentic English pub. At the bar, selections on draft include Strongbow, Old Speckled Hen, Smithwick's, and Boddingtons; the single-malt scotch menu is literally dozens of names long, and bottled beers are available from all across the British Isles and beyond. A large dining room fills the majority of the bar, which is perfectly fitting, considering how tasteful the pub grub is; try the Ploughman's platter (a cheese plate with apple slices and gherkins) or the Guinness stew. Traditional Irish bands perform most weekend nights, and live footie matches are even beamed in via satellite.

REDBEARD'S
201 Shiloh St., 412/431-3730, www.redbeardspgh.com
HOURS: Mon.-Sun. 11 A.M.-2 A.M.
COST: No Cover
Map 3

Located just steps from the lobby of the Monongahela Incline and the overlook decks of Grandview Avenue, Redbeard's is probably the only Mount Washington bar that doesn't come complete with an intimidating, locals-only feel. Of course, the majority of the folks who line the bar here and fill the back booths *are* locals, but Duquesne University students in particular flock here for Redbeard's many discount beer and wing nights. Because of its generous size, Redbeard's can accommodate quite a crowd on warm summer evenings, which is also when the umbrella-covered patio seating fills up especially fast.

REMEDY
5121 Butler St., 412/781-6771, www.remedypgh.com
HOURS: Mon. and Sat. 4 P.M.-2 A.M., Tues.-Fri. 3 P.M.-2 A.M., Sun. 5 P.M.-2 A.M.
COST: No Cover
Map 6

Formerly home to the Floridian-themed Ray's Marlin Beach Bar & Grill, where seafood was served and ironic dance parties took place on the top floor, Remedy has thankfully managed to retain much of what made Ray's such a well-loved spot. At its core, Remedy is still a quirky neighborhood hotspot with obscure microbrews on tap and old-school hip-hop on the jukebox. The bar's best feature, though, may be its large size and unusual layout; with three floors and an outdoor deck, Remedy can sometimes feel like a few different bars packed into one building. Art shows are a regular feature here, as are the deejay-hosted weekend dance parties. And appropriately enough, the

© MATT STROUD

Remedy

menu is filled with both vegetarian and comfort food options.

◖ ROUND CORNER CANTINA

3720 Butler St., 412/904-2279,
www.roundcronercantina.com
HOURS: Mon.-Tues. 5 P.M.-midnight, Wed.-Sat.
5 P.M.-2 A.M., Sun. noon-5 P.M.
COST: $10 for deejays, special events,
and holiday parties only
Map 6

Easily of one the Lower Lawrenceville area's hottest and most-talked-about new drinking and dining destinations, Round Corner Cantina is a gorgeously decorated Mexican-style bar and eatery catering to the same sort of young and artsy crowds that frequent Brillobox and the nearby New Amsterdam. Formerly a neighborhood dive, the Cantina has been thoroughly refurbished with a sort of old-timey wagon-wheel theme, complete with retro hand-painted signage and rickety wooden seating. The menu features a surprisingly authentic selection of Mexican street food and imported Mexican beer; deejay nights and dance parties occasionally take place on the weekend.

THE SHARP EDGE

302 S. St. Clair St., 412/661-3537,
www.sharpedgebeer.com
HOURS: Mon.-Thurs. 11 A.M.-midnight, Fri.-Sat.
11 A.M.-1 A.M., Sun. 11 A.M.-9 P.M.
COST: No cover
Map 6

Respected by beer snobs locally, and even countrywide, the Sharp Edge is perhaps best known for its extensive selection of obscure Belgian drafts. With more than 300 internationally crafted and brewed beers available, there's something for everyone here, no matter which European or developing nation you'd like to explore in pint or bottle form. Few of the imported selections come cheap, of course; try the $3 mystery brew if you're drinking on a budget. Burgers, sandwiches, pizzas, and other assorted American finger foods are also a big draw. If you'd prefer your dinner party quiet, grab a table in the back room.

SILKY'S SPORTS BAR & GRILL

1731 Murray Ave., 412/421-9222
HOURS: Mon.-Fri. 3 P.M.-2 A.M., Sat. and Sun. 11 A.M.-2 A.M.
COST: No Cover
Map 5

If Squirrel Hill's venerable hipster havens aren't exactly your idea of a good time, consider Silky's, a welcoming sports bar with a friendly, nonexclusionary vibe. During particularly important sporting contests—or any time the Steelers are playing—Silky's can get a bit overrun with rowdy and often overzealous fans. But any other day of the week, it's a perfectly anonymous place to unwind with an Iron City, a burger, and a side of fries. And although it appears small from the outside, Silky's two floors and upper balcony are actually quite roomy, making it a smart choice for large groups.

THE SMILING MOOSE

1306 E. Carson St., 412/431-4668,
www.smiling-moose.com
HOURS: Mon. 2 P.M.-2 A.M., Tues.-Sat. 11 A.M.-2 A.M.,
Sun. noon-2 A.M.
COST: $5-10 Sat.
Map 3

Something of an unofficial headquarters for the city's tattooed contingent, Goth girls, old-school punk rockers, and Vespa-driving mods. Perhaps not surprisingly, fistfights aren't uncommon here. Obscure speed metal and punk bands play free shows in the back of the bar most weekends; if the noise gets to be a bit much, simply slip up to the new second-floor bar, where conversation and a game of billiards can be more easily accomplished.

SMOKIN' JOE'S

2001 E. Carson St., 412/431-6757,
www.smokinjoessaloon.com
HOURS: Mon.-Sat. 10 A.M.-2 A.M., Sun. 11 A.M.-2 A.M.
COST: No Cover
Map 3

The success of Smokin' Joe's, which from the outside appears to be simply yet another in an endless procession of bars, is based on a relatively simple philosophy: Stock a larger variety

COURTESY OF ROB MATHENY

The Smiling Moose

of beer than the guy next door. *Way* larger. We're talking hundreds and hundreds, some on draft, some in the massive cooler just inside the front door. In a nutshell, that's why serious drinkers come to Joe's. The interior is rather cramped and plain, and although budget wing nights are a draw for some, the pub grub here really isn't much to write home about (try Fat Heads next door if you're really hungry). Insider's tip: Don't pass up Joe's just because the bar is packed to overflowing; there's often ample seating on the second floor balcony.

☾ SQUIRREL HILL CAFÉ
5802 Forbes Ave., 412/521-3327
HOURS: Mon.-Sat. 10 A.M.-2 A.M., Sun. 11 A.M.-2 A.M.
COST: No Cover
Map 5

Don't bother calling it the Squirrel Hill Café, as it's fairly unlikely that anyone will know what you're talking about. It's known locally as "The Cage," a relatively unimposing room filled only with cafeteria-style booths, two TV sets tuned to sports, and a small balcony that opens only on busy nights. But don't be fooled: The Cage

has long been one of the city's most popular scenester bars, largely because of Squirrel Hill's former popularity with musicians and artists. But even though rents have risen here, the vibe at The Cage remains. Grad students from CMU and Pitt have long populated the bar's booths as well; show up during the afternoon to spot English teachers grading term papers while sipping pints of Guinness or Penn pilsner.

THUNDERBIRD CAFÉ
4023 Butler St., 412/682-0177,
www.thunderbirdcafe.net
HOURS: Mon.-Sat. 7 A.M.-2 A.M., Sun. 11 A.M.-2 A.M.
COST: $3-15 during live music shows
Map 6

If you're looking for an authentic dive bar in the East End—in other words, one that hasn't long ago been gentrified by college students—the Thunderbird Café might just be your place. And what's more, although the Thunderbird was previously known as little more than a cheap spot to get good and sloshed, it's now known as a cheap spot to get good and sloshed while taking in live music, often of the indie-

© MATT STROUD

Thunderbird Café

COURTESY OF ROB MATHENY

Tiki Lounge

rock or alt-country variety. It's also not a bad place in which to wind down after knocking down the bowling pins at Arsenal Lanes, which is located just down the street on the corner of Butler and 44th Streets.

TIKI LOUNGE

2004 E. Carson St., 412/381-8454, www.tikilounge.biz
HOURS: Mon.-Sat. 4 P.M.-1 A.M., Sun. 8 P.M.-2 A.M.
COST: No cover downstairs, $5-10 upstairs
Map 3

It ain't Trader Vic's, but it comes mighty close. Tiki Lounge is the city's solitary Polynesian-themed bar, a fact that's made all too clear even to the casual passerby—just keep your eyes peeled for the massive Tiki god in the front window. (You'll have to pass through his massive mouth before gaining entry to the lounge.) Inside, it's something of a South Pacific paradise, with wooden masks, bamboo stalks, and all manner of Hawaiian island paraphernalia lining the walls, including an indoor waterfall. The cocktail menu is equally exotic: Choose from such wonders as a Headhunter, a Fu Manchu, and a Coconut Kiss. Deejays light

up the relatively small dance floor with pop and house music on weekends.

TOWN TAVERN

2009 E. Carson St., 412/325-8696,
www.towntavernpittsburgh.com
HOURS: Mon. 5 P.M.-2 A.M., Tues.-Sun. 11:30 A.M.-2 A.M.
COST: No Cover
Map 3

If there was ever a watering hole model just waiting to be cloned and replicated in college towns throughout the nation, it was the frat-boy bar. And the Town Tavern, a chain of college-kid pubs operating nearly identical locations around the country, has apparently done just that. The relatively simple set-up, though, does seem to work: The first floor resembles a turn of the century pub, with faux antiques and mahogany woodwork, while the second floor offers a dance floor with deejays. As long as you can get past the meathead atmosphere, Town Tavern can be good fun; themed parties are a regular fixture, and the generally convivial staff does a decent job of interacting with the crowd.

Dance Clubs

BAR ROOM PITTSBURGH

7 E. Carson St., 412/434-4850, www.barroompgh.com

HOURS: Thurs.-Sat. 8 P.M.-2 A.M.

COST: $5-10 includes entrance to all three clubs, $20 and up for special events and parties

Map 3

Over the years, Station Square has most certainly seen more than its fair share of trendy, over-the-top dance clubs, and Bar Room appears to be one of the latest contenders. College students in particular seem to be taking the bait—Bar Room even dispatches its own school bus every Thursday night to area campuses. And aside from the club's seriously strict dress code, which frowns on hoodies, baggy jeans, hats, and athletic jerseys, pure wild abandon on the dance floor seems to be the name of the game here. You can also expect VIP bottle service ($99 and up) and hip-thrusting, radio-ready dance music, as well as an impressive slew of special-event nights, which are generally advertised online. The club offers complimentary limo pickup on Fridays (call for reservations and details).

SADDLE RIDGE

7 E. Carson St., 412/434-8100, www.saddleridgepittsburgh.com

HOURS: Thurs.-Sat. 7 P.M.-2 A.M.

COST: $5

Map 3

Pittsburgh's first (and indeed, its only) country-and-western saloon, Saddle Ridge isn't exactly tops in the authenticity department. No sawdust floors, for instance, or well-worn swinging doors leading to the men's room. But as a slightly Disney-fied theme bar, Saddle Ridge serves today's country-and-western set with aplomb. Only the newest and most popular C&W hits are spun by top-of-their-game deejays, mechanical bull rides keep the alpha males occupied, and the female servers get into the act with dangerously tailored Wild West wear. Line-dancing instruction even takes place on occasional weekends; call for updated schedules.

WHIM

7 E. Carson St., 412/281-9888, www.whimpitt.com

HOURS: Thurs.-Sat. 9 P.M.-2 A.M.

COST: $5-10, $20 and up special events and parties

Map 3

Perhaps the city's swankest and most architecturally impressive dance club, Whim more or less manages to eschew the cheeseball aesthetic of the standard Station Square meat market. The vibe here is actually somewhat European, what with the club's minimalist, brushed-metal furniture and the dance floor's multihued laser lights. Outside the VIP areas, the seating offers a great view of the often-packed dance floor. And naturally, special event nights ('80s, hip-hop, Top 40) with discounted drink specials abound; check the website or for details.

Whim

© MATT STROUD

ZEN SOCIAL CLUB

125 W. Station Square Dr., 412/528-4847, www.myspace.com/zenpgh

HOURS: Mon. midnight-3 A.M., Thurs. 12:30 A.M.-3 A.M., Fri.-Sat. 10 P.M.-3 A.M.

COST: $6-12

Map 3

A self-described "two room, multilevel Asian-inspired nightclub," Zen seems to attract a slightly older and more mature crowd than most of the city's other nightclubs, the vast majority of which host college nights at least once a week. Zen, on the other hand, has something of a sinfully luxurious opium den ambiance about it, and better still, it stays open well past 3 A.M. most nights. But because Zen is now a private, members-only club, the general public can only celebrate here during the days and times listed above.

Gay and Lesbian

BLUE MOON

5115 Butler St., 412/781-1119, www.thenewbluemoon.com

HOURS: Mon. 4 P.M.-midnight, Tues.-Sun. 4 P.M.-2 A.M.

COST: No Cover

Map 6

A seriously low-key neighborhood pub—basically a dive bar for Lawrenceville's GLBT crowd—the Blue Moon is not exactly the city's classiest queer joint. Far from it, in fact. But if it's a truly judgment-free zone you're looking for, look no further. Because while a night out here can be equal parts rude and rambunctious, it can also be a wildly good time, assuming you're willing to let loose just a bit, and to let go of your inhibitions. The frequently scheduled events (drag and fashion shows, for instance) are just as fun, and equally goofy. And don't miss the back-room bar, known as Pub 51, with its vintage bar and back patio.

CATTIVO

146 44th St., 412/687-2157, www.cattivo.biz

HOURS: Wed.-Sun. 4 P.M.-2 A.M.

COST: $5-10 after 9 P.M.

Map 6

A surprisingly massive gay bar and dance club tucked away in a somewhat sketchy area of Lawrenceville, Cattivo is especially popular with Pittsburgh's lesbian crowd. But make no mistake: Cattivo isn't a high-end lounge, and the interiors are certainly nothing to shout about. The crowd, however, is said to be exceptionally friendly and accepting, Steelers games are shown on a big screen, and a pub-grub-style kitchen serving pizza, hoagies, and wings stays open until 1 A.M. Every Friday and Saturday night, deejays get the crowd moving in Cattivo Sotto, the bar's lower level dance floor.

PEGASUS

1740 Eckert St., 412/766-7222, www.pittpegasus.com

HOURS: Fri.-Sat. 10 P.M.-2 A.M.

COST: $5-10

Map 7

Although the infamous Liberty Avenue Pegasus location spent untold years as the undisputed granddaddy of Pittsburgh's queer nightclub scene, it sadly closed its doors in 2009 before reopening inside the Pittsburgh Eagle, a much more obscure gay club located on the far reaches of the North Side. Today, Pegasus still attracts a decidedly young crowd, and as a result, cruising, flirting, and anonymous hookups tend to be the main attraction here. A club-ready mix of house and pop music can always be heard screaming from the deejay booth, and on Fridays, the 18-plus set shows up in full force.

PITTSBURGH EAGLE

1740 Eckert St., 412/766-7222, www.pitteagle.com

HOURS: Mon.-Sat. 7 P.M.-2 A.M.

COST: $3

Map 7

Although not located in one of the city's safest neighborhoods (you absolutely need a car

NIGHTLIFE

to get here, and even some cabbies might have trouble finding the place), the Pittsburgh Eagle consistently draws swarms of loyal club goers every weekend night. Without a doubt, the Eagle exists within Pittsburgh's hidden-gem category; the deejays do an outstanding job of getting the crowd on the dance floor, and at the club's top level, drag queens often perform with willing accompaniment from the crowd. The Eagle's first two floors are now home to the recently relocated Pegasus, a gay club that attracts a much younger crowd.

▌ SPIN BARTINI & ULTRA LOUNGE
5744 Ellsworth Ave., 412/362-7746,
www.spinbartini.com
HOURS: Daily 4 P.M.-2 A.M.

COST: No cover Mon.-Fri., $5 an up Sat. and Sun. and special events
Map 4

Located in the former home of the Cuban-themed Club Havana, this stylish and fashion-forward lounge doesn't specifically market itself as a gay club. Still, Shadyside's GLBT crowd does seem to have claimed Spin as yet another boast-worthy attraction in what is quickly becoming known as a gay neighborhood. As for the interiors here and the experience itself, both are very much what you'd expect from a club referring to itself as an ultra lounge: The liberal and open-minded patrons here are generally stylish and upscale, as is the club itself. Dressing to impress is strongly encouraged.

Live Music

ALTAR BAR
1620 Penn Ave., 412/263-2877, www.altarbar.com
HOURS: Thurs. and Sun. 6 P.M.-midnight, Fri. and Sat. 9 P.M.-2 A.M.
COST: $5-15
Map 1

Although it had a fairly impressive run as a nightclub where cocktail waitresses often dressed up in Catholic schoolgirl uniforms, the Strip District's Altar Bar, which is located inside one of the city's many churches-turned-businesses, is now a live music venue featuring pop and rock bands. And while the experience of catching a show here isn't entirely unlike the experience you might have at Mr. Small's, the city's other concert venue located inside a disused church, bands performing at Altar Bar tend to be of the slightly less impressive variety: tribute acts and cover bands, for instance, make frequent appearances.

BRILLOBOX
4104 Penn Ave., 412/621-4900, www.brillobox.net
HOURS: Mon.-Sat. 7 P.M.-2 A.M.
COST: No cover downstairs, $6-12 upstairs
Map 6

Pittsburgh's newest see-and-be-seen spot for the bedhead crowd, Brillobox is run by a husband-and-wife team who relocated here after establishing themselves in New York City's contemporary art world. The ground floor is strictly a drinking establishment where Cat Power and M.I.A. records serenade the city's hipster glitterati; the owners' tastefully displayed paintings and sculptures decorate the walls and shelves. Live music takes place on the second floor, which conveniently has its own bar tucked into the back corner. Local pop and indie-rock bands perform here about as often as do national touring acts; other popular happenings include deejay nights and the occasional multimedia art show or literary event.

PITTSBURGH'S HOLIEST HOUSES OF SIN

Consider for a moment one of Pittsburgh's oddest development trends: Over the past 15 years or so, plucky entrepreneurs have been transforming old and abandoned churches into bars, cafés, and nightclubs. Is it a testament to the industrious nature of the Steel City, or just plain ol' blasphemy? You be the judge.

A restaurant and brewpub that serves some of the tastiest gourmet pizzas in town, **Church Brew Works** (3525 Liberty Ave., Lawrenceville, 412/688-8200) opened about 15 years ago in the shuttered St. John the Baptist chapel. Sure to be especially offensive to the ultra-devout are the brewpub's steel and copper tanks, which occupy the place of honor upon the altar. Mother Mary, pray for us.

Located in the industrial burgh of Millvale, St. Ann's became the site of Pittsburgh's most radical church transformation when a recording studio by the name of **Mr. Smalls** (400 Lincoln Ave., Millvale, 412/821-4447) moved in. Small's has since grown to become one of the city's most popular concert halls, and now serves up an almost nightly mix of punk, reggae, and hip-hop.

Once a Presbyterian church servicing Ukrainian immigrants, **Charlie Murdoch's Dueling Piano Bar** (1005 E. Carson St., South Side, 412/431-7476, www.murdochsrocks.com) is now one of the only two dueling piano bars in the city. Even better than the elegant double staircase and the massive rectangle bar are the stained-glass windows, which feature classic Catholic imagery. Makes you feel a bit guilty by your fourth or fifth Yuengling, but what the hell?

One of Pittsburgh's most sinful transformations has taken place in (where else?) the Strip District, where **Altar Bar** (1620 Penn Ave., 412/263-2877, www.altarbar.com) can now be found. Formerly a naughty nightclub featuring cocktail waitresses in Catholic schoolgirl uniforms, Altar Bar is now primarily a live music venue, where pop and rock acts perform regularly. We're not entirely convinced that the Father, the Son, or the Holy Ghost would green-light this particular project. Then again, it doesn't look like anyone's asking.

There's also **The Union Project** (801 N. Negley Ave., Highland Park, 412/363-4550, www.unionproject.org), a multipurpose space located inside the former Union Baptist Church. Quite unlike the aforementioned locales, the Union Project is the sort of place where good deeds are done on a regular basis; visual artists create here, community organizers organize here, and inner-city youth gain valuable life skills and work experience here. The Union Project also has its very own café, the Union Station, so feel free to stop by if you're interested in simply poking around. To make a financial donation to the Union Project, call or visit the organization's website.

And, by the way, if you're planning on patronizing some of the aforementioned businesses but still haven't settled on accommodations, consider bunking down for a night at **The Priory** (614 Pressley St., 412/231-3338 or 866/377-4679, www.thepriory.com), a charming and recently upgraded bed-and-breakfast on the North Side that was once a Benedictine monastery. It's within easy walking distance of Downtown, breakfast is served inside the old refectory, and wireless Internet access is available in all rooms and throughout the premises.

And for those of you who can't seem to tear yourselves away from the beautiful city of Pittsburgh, bunking down permanently in a former church is a realistic option here as well. The architecturally unique condos and lofts of the **Angel's Arms Condominiums** (1 Pius St., 412/363-4000, www.angelsarms.net), located in the South Side Slopes, were built upon the structure of the former St. Michael the Archangel church. Prices currently start at $281,100.

CARNEGIE MUSIC HALL OF HOMESTEAD

510 E. 10th Ave., 412/368-5225, www.librarymusichall.com

HOURS: Doors open half hour before scheduled performance; phone ticketing Mon.-Fri. noon-5 P.M.

COST: $20 and up

Map 7

Although the Music Hall at the Carnegie Library's Homestead branch has been hosting musicians and performers of all stripes for decades now, it was only recently transformed into the sort of midsized concert venue that hosts national rock, pop, and indie bands. Touring jam bands and reunited classic acts are also a big draw here; comedy shows and the occasional play are sometimes booked as well. And while local fans have been known to kvetch about the venue's uncomfortable seating and its strict no-alcohol policy, the good news is that shows here are all-ages. Designed in the tradition of the grand American music hall, this is an ideal antidote to the significantly grungier rock venues in the city.

CHARLIE MURDOCH'S DUELING PIANO BAR

1005 E. Carson St., 412/431-7476, www.murdochsrocks.com

HOURS: Fri. and Sat. shows start at 8 P.M.

COST: $4

Map 3

Known to regulars as the home of the city's only dueling piano rock show, Charlie Murdoch's is located inside a beautifully restored Presbyterian church on the South Side Flats. The live onstage show, which also includes band sets and comedy bits, happens every Friday and Saturday night at 8 P.M. on the main floor of the church. A separate and significantly more laid-back experience takes place in the basement, where deejays spin and a second, smaller bar can be found. Patrons can also hop onstage and perform, karaoke-style, while the professional house band backs them up, usually with classic rock standards.

◖ CLUB CAFÉ

56 S. 12th St., 412/431-4950, www.clubcafelive.com

HOURS: Bar daily until 2 A.M.; first show daily 7 P.M., door opens at 6 P.M.; second show daily 9 P.M., door opens at 8 P.M.; hours subject to change based on performance schedule (see website for up-to-date details)

COST: $5-15

Map 3

No other live music experience in Pittsburgh comes anywhere near to that at Club Café, which likes to call itself the city's premiere "wired" nightclub. (Most shows are filmed live; an *Austin City Limits*–style TV program and a DVD series have already been produced.) The room here is so small, and the seating so close to the stage, it's practically possible to reach out and touch the performers mid-song. Music is generally of the singer-songwriter variety; past artists include Jill Sobule and Citizen Cope. Blues and indie-pop bands also show up with some regularity; the crowd generally consists of well-behaved young professionals.

CLUB ZOO

1630 Smallman St., 412/201-1100, www.clubzoo.net

HOURS: Fri.-Sat. 7:30 P.M.-1 A.M.

COST: $10 Fri., $12 Sat.; live music tickets start at $20

Map 1

After a long and successful run as Metropol, an industrial music dance club that doubled as one of the most popular live music venues in the city, the converted warehouse at 1700 Penn Avenue in the Strip has been reborn as Club Zoo. Technically, Club Zoo is an under-21 spot where high schoolers can congregate in an alcohol-free environment. But much like Metropol, live music is also a big seller; marquee-level alternative and hip-hop acts can easily draw thousands of fans here. With its post-apocalyptic warehouse vibe, Club Zoo is a particularly amenable place to catch guitar-heavy rock.

DIESEL

1601 E. Carson St., 412/431-8800, www.dieselpgh.com
HOURS: Wed.-Sun. 9 P.M.-2 A.M.
COST: $5-15
Map 3

Located in the same space that once housed the legendary Nick's Fat City, Diesel is a sort of a glossy, two-venues-in-one nightlife establishment. Comprised of two levels and featuring dance floors and multiple bars, the overall vibe here is much more "trendy nightclub" than "live music venue." And in fact, Diesel does spend much of its week as a throbbing nightclub, complete with big-name deejays, high-tech lighting, and overpriced VIP bottle service. But rock, pop, and metal shows are a huge draw here; two of the city's biggest concert producers—Elko and Joker—host countless bands at Diesel. Discerning live music fans frequently complain about the club's sound quality, but for those focused on atmosphere, Diesel is a standby for live entertainment.

GARFIELD ARTWORKS

4931 Penn Ave., 412/361-2262,
www.garfieldartworks.com
HOURS: See website for concert dates and times.
COST: $10 cover, show prices vary
Map 6

Although technically a visual arts gallery, Garfield Artworks is also one of the most prolific live-music venues in town, booking an almost nightly schedule of underground rock bands, avant-jazz artists, goth and industrial outfits, and the occasional electroclash spectacle. This is thanks in no small part to the locally infamous Manny Theiner, a longtime music promoter who has been bringing indie bands to Pittsburgh for two decades. The digs here aren't much to look at—Garfart is nothing more than a big open box, sometimes with a plastic tub of free beer stashed in a far corner. No matter, though—the disaffected and mostly teenage indie-rockers tend to provide more than enough visual stimulation.

LITTLE E'S

949 Liberty Ave., 2nd floor, 412/392-2217,
www.littleesjazz.com
HOURS: Wed.-Sun. 5:30 P.M.-12:30 A.M., see website for specific performance dates and times
COST: $5-10
Map 1

Considering that the opening of Little E's put an end to a lengthy recent stretch during which Pittsburgh essentially had no full-time jazz clubs, it's little surprise that the live music performances here been so overwhelmingly successful. Warm, relaxing, and truly intimate, Little E's feels something like an undiscovered secret or a hidden downtown bar, complete with exposed brick walls, a decent cocktail list, and a menu featuring soups, salads, sandwiches, and Cajun-influenced entrées. Blues musicians perform here regularly as well.

MODERNFORMATIONS GALLERY

4919 Penn Ave., 412/362-0274,
www.modernformations.com
HOURS: Gallery Thurs. 7-9 P.M., Sat. 1-4 P.M., closed last Sat. and first Thurs. each month to prepare for next art opening; see website for details on performances and other special events
COST: $5-10 live music
Map 6

Much like its down-the-street neighbor Garfield Artworks, ModernFormations is also first and foremost an art venue, yet it hosts a wonderfully cutting-edge calendar of indie- and art-rock groups. When particularly popular acts pass through, MoFo can find itself packed from wall to wall, so take care to arrive early when the next Skin Graft or Dischord band stops by. Insider's tip: If you're feeling hunger pains between bands, grab an order of fresh spring rolls from Pho Minh, the Vietnamese place next door.

MOONDOG'S

378 Freeport Rd., 412/828-2040
HOURS: See website for show times and dates.
COST: $15 and up performances
Map 7

Moondog's isn't particularly easy to get to

NIGHTLIFE

without your own method of transportation—it sits way north of the city in a blue-collar burgh along the Allegheny River—but if authentic local and national blues music is your bag, it's more than worth the trip. When live music isn't happening, Moondog's acts as a cozy neighborhood pub. But on most weekends, local R&B acts and singer-songwriters like Norm Nardini take the stage. Sometimes true blues legends show up; over the past decade and a half, Moondog's has hosted the likes of Keb Mo, Koko Taylor, and A. J. Croce.

MR. SMALL'S THEATRE

400 Lincoln Ave., 412/821-4447, www.mrsmalls.com

HOURS: See website for show times and dates, skate park schedule, and recording studio availability.

COST: $10–50 performances, VIP balcony seating available at additional cost

Map 6

Cleverly located inside the nave of the former St. Ann's Catholic church, Mr. Small's is a midsize venue with near-perfect acoustics. Performers here run the gamut, although hip-hop, indie rock, and metal acts make up the vast majority of the club's schedule. What's more, a professional-grade recording studio is located onsite, and the company also maintains its own low-key record label. An affiliated skatepark is located nearby, and for aspiring rock stars, Small's offers occasional workshops and music camps.

REX THEATRE

1602 E. Carson St., 412/381-6811, www.rextheatre.com

HOURS: See website for show times and dates.

COST: $10–30 performances

Map 3

Formerly a movie theater with a fantastic art deco facade, the Rex has since transformed itself into a midsize concert venue without actually, well, transforming much. The reclining theater seats were never removed, for instance, so even during big-name punk shows, the energy level can feel rather lackluster. The popcorn and candy counter in the front lobby remains as well; it's now a bar. The occasional alternative burlesque performance

Rex Theatre

or independent film screening also takes place here. Better still, the theater's original art deco signage can still be seen.

31ST STREET PUB

3101 Penn Ave., 412/391-8334, www.31stpub.com

HOURS: Pub hours Wed. 3–9 P.M., Thurs.-Fri. 3 P.M.-2 A.M., Sat. 9 P.M.-2 A.M.; Thurs.-Sat. shows start at 10 P.M., Mon.-Wed. shows start at 9 P.M.

COST: $10 in advance, $12 at the door

Map 6

Owned and operated by a heavily tattooed Harley-Davidson enthusiast, the 31st Street Pub is the Steel City's official headquarters for gritty garage rock, punk, and all other subgenres generally associated with black leather and power chords. The crowd here tends to be equally underworldly; depending on which band is on the bill you might spot aging junkie punks, skinheads, heavy metal fans, or smartly coifed hipsters. If you're looking to get soused, you've come to the right place. Domestic beer, served in plastic cups, is exceedingly cheap, and Jägermeister is available on tap.

Lounges

ALTO LOUNGE

728 Copeland St., 412/682-1074, www.altolounge.com

HOURS: Wed.-Sun. 5 P.M.-2 A.M.

COST: No Cover

Map 4

A relatively sophisticated lounge that is literally awash in a collection of calming blue lights, Alto's success has much to do with the fact that there's nothing else quite like it in the immediate vicinity. And although it largely caters to Shadyside's grad student and young professional population, this is also the perfect choice for a first date—the minimalist furniture and decor seems a bit futuristic and a touch romantic, at all once. The cocktail menu, of course, is decidedly high end. You'll also find bottle service, an impressive wine list, and a modest offering of appetizers.

◖ AVA

126 S. Highland Ave., 412/363-8277, www.avapgh.net

HOURS: Mon.-Sat. 6 P.M.-2 A.M.

COST: No cover, $5-10 events

Map 6

Co-owned and operated by Justin Strong of the legendary Shadow Lounge, which sits right next door, AVA seems to offer a dozen good reasons to visit for nearly every night of the week: live hip-hop and jazz shows, networking events for creative professionals, cutting-edge dance nights, and a stellar sandwich-and-burrito menu. And that's to say nothing of the fact that AVA is simply a laid-back and fashionable lounge at which to enjoy a beer or a specialty martini. If nothing else, don't miss the legendary live jazz nights, Mondays at 9 P.M.

FIREHOUSE LOUNGE

2216 Penn Ave., 412/434-1230,

www.firehouse-lounge.com

HOURS: Mon.-Thurs. and Sat.-Sun. 5 P.M.-2 A.M.,

Fri. 4 P.M.-2 A.M.

COST: No cover

Map 1

Although something of an overambitious meat market on the weekends, middle-of-the-week evenings find the Firehouse Lounge at its relaxing and intimate best. The vibe is casual but eclectically upscale; a smallish dance floor sits at one end of the room, a spacious bar in the center, and a conversation and mingling area—complete with boudoir-style couches—on the other. The Firehouse is indeed a perfect place to meet friends for an after-work wind-down.

S BAR

1713 E. Carson St., 412/418-7227, www.sbarpgh.com

HOURS: Mon.-Sun. 6 P.M.-2 A.M.

COST: No cover

Map 3

Something of a cross between a martini bar, a meat market, and a minimalist, chilled-out lounge where Pittsburgh's beautiful people come to play, S Bar manages to remain upscale and decidedly hip at the very same time. Deejay nights in particular are a big draw here—Mega Man, Sean Perry, and Jazzy Jeff have all previously graced the decks. And although the atmosphere at S Bar is certainly more slick and glossy than at your average East Carson Street watering hole, the dance floor, at least, is fairly democratic—you'll generally find a decent mix of college kids, B-boys, hipster types, and young professionals mixing it up.

SHADOW LOUNGE

5972 Baum Blvd., 412/363-8277,

www.shadowlounge.net

HOURS: See website for events calendar;

some showstake place at AVA

COST: $5-10 shows

Map 6

Hip-hop dance parties, spoken-word battles, and live music are what you'll generally find on the calendar at the community-oriented Shadow Lounge, although both the vibe and the crowd seem to morph considerably as the day stretches on. Show up during early afternoon and you'll find yourself in an East Village–esque tea and coffee shop, complete with thrift-store furniture and jazz on the sound system. The party goes off almost every night, and that may mean a deep-house deejay, a documentary film screening, a live-rock show, or drinks and conversation in the newly constructed back room.

VILLA SOUTHSIDE

1831 E. Carson St., 412/431-3535, www.villasouthside.com

HOURS: Wed.-Fri. 5 P.M.-2 A.M., Sat. 7 P.M.-2 A.M.

COST: No cover

Map 3

A clean and minimalist bar and nightclub that also offers a fairly extensive tapas and appetizer menu, the two-story Villa Southside is owned and operated by the same family who ran Bruschetta's, the Italian eatery that formerly occupied this very space. Villa, however, is certainly a departure, considering that the dance floor, the modernist stone deejay booth and the high-end lounge furniture topped with

candles are the major draws here. There's also a large outdoor patio, which is perfect on warm nights, and a plethora of plasma TVs screening—you guessed it—pro sports.

Z LOUNGE

2108 E. Carson St., 412/716-3920

HOURS: Mon.-Thurs. 6 P.M.-2 A.M., Fri.-Sat. 5 P.M.-2 A.M.

COST: Downstairs no cover, upstairs $5-10 for events

Map 3

Formerly known as Zythos Lounge, the newly christened Z Lounge still retains its former glory as a hotspot for flavor-of-the-month deejays and the electronic music crowd. Which isn't to say that this isn't also a decent place for simply sitting and enjoying a beer; the lounge is small, dark, and intimate enough to create a fairly successful romantic atmosphere. Two or three small tables are often set up on the sidewalk outside during the summer, and live bands occasionally perform in the bar's second lounge on the top floor.

COURTESY OF ROB MATHENY

Enjoy an intimate evening at Z Lounge's ground-floor bar or take in its club scene upstairs.

ARTS AND LEISURE

Here's an idea for a potentially explosive experiment: Once you arrive in Pittsburgh, ask a local musician, and then a visual artist, a journalist, a photographer, a dancer, and an actor what each one has to say about the state of the arts here. If history is anything to go by, you'll want to duck soon to avoid the flying hyperbole.

Which isn't to say that the members of Pittsburgh's creative class have particularly bad attitudes, or that they don't approve of the music and art being created here. On the contrary, the general consensus among the town's right-brained types seems to be that when it comes to competing in the arts on an international scale, our community simply isn't living up to its potential. And because Pittsburgh is a sizeable city that feels so much like a small town, and because the living is so cheap and easy in Southwestern Pennsylvania, potential is probably the one word you'll keep humming to yourself if you spend enough time here.

Naturally though, more than a few creative types have taken full advantage of the town's growing opportunities. In years past, for instance, the East End neighborhoods of Garfield and East Liberty have seen the once-bedraggled Penn Avenue corridor transformed into a collection of contemporary galleries. And recently, scores of locally grown conferences and lecture series have continued to draw impressively large crowds.

Of course, as is to be expected in any midsize urban area with limited resources, Pittsburgh artists tend to pick up and leave with alarming frequency; the city's economic and cultural

HIGHLIGHTS

LOOK FOR ◖ TO FIND RECOMMENDED ARTS AND ACTIVITIES.

◖ **Best Gallery for Pop-Culture Enthusiasts:** Dig on the retro artwork at Lawrenceville's **Zombo Gallery,** which also sells novelty toys and has a screen printing shop and a massage studio on the premises (page 143).

◖ **Best Theater:** Popularly known as Pittsburgh's most forward-thinking theater, the South Side's adventurous **City Theatre** stages new works, spoken word, and the occasional world premiere (page 145).

◖ **Best Art-House Cinema:** Take a journey back to the Golden Age of cinema at **Oaks Theater,** a recently restored art deco theater built in 1941 (page 150).

◖ **Most Interactive Festival:** Explore the width and breadth of the Steel City on two wheels during Bike Pittsburgh's annual **BikeFest,** a ten-day celebration of cycling culture at its very finest (page 152).

◖ **Best City Park for Serious Mountain Bikers:** The challenging trails that crisscross **Frick Park** are some of the most pulse-pounding in the entire state (page 158).

◖ **Best Way to Explore Allegheny River:** Cruising the length of the Allegheny River in one of **Kayak Pittsburgh**'s canoes or kayaks is a wonderfully relaxing way to experience the Steel City (page 169).

◖ **Best Public Swimming Pool:** Built by the wealthy industrialist Henry W. Oliver, the South Side's **Oliver Bath House** is a gorgeous spot for an afternoon dip. The pool is heated, it's located indoors, and it even boasts a splendid cathedral ceiling (page 181).

◖ **Sickest No-Charge Skatepark:** With endless concrete bowls and a wealth of street skating accoutrements, it's no wonder **Boyce Park Skatepark** is considered one of the Greater Pittsburgh area's best spots to push wood (page 183).

◖ **Best Yoga Studio for Beginners:** Friendly, welcoming, and never stuck-up: That's the in-house attitude at the city's four **Amazing Yoga** studios, making it the smart choice for nervous yoga newbies (page 184).

Check out the retro artwork at Zombo Gallery.

© MATT STROUD

gatekeepers have long been scratching their heads and hoping for a solution to the apparent brain-drain. Grassroots arts organizations and community groups like the Sprout Fund have been doing their part, spending copious amounts of time and money in an attempt to make Pittsburgh a more attractive and a more exciting place to live and play.

So what exactly does the future of creative expression look like in the Steel City? Certainly, some things are expected to improve: The August Wilson Center for African American Culture finally opened to the public after years of planning and fundraising, for instance. Pittsburgh is also now home to one of only three cartoon art museums in the country. And the Lawrenceville neighborhood is becoming nationally known for its DIY arts and crafts scene. In the meantime, the city's creative population—potentially explosive as it may well be—will no doubt continue to soldier on.

The Arts

GALLERIES

All galleries offer viewings by appointment in addition to their stated hours.

BOX HEART

4523 Liberty Ave., 412/687-8858, www.boxheart.org
HOURS: Tues. 11 A.M.–6 P.M., Wed.–Sat. 10 A.M.–6 P.M., Sun. 1–5 P.M.
Map 6

Much like the emerging artists who live in the neighborhood, Box Heart gallery is a grassroots sort of place where handmade jewelry, handmade soaps, and other crafts can be found among paintings and other items of visual art by local up-and-comers.

FUTURE TENANT

819 Penn Ave., www.futuretenant.org
HOURS: Wed.–Sat. 1–5 P.M.
Map 1

The Pittsburgh Cultural Trust hosts this project of Carnegie Mellon University, an ever-changing art space where exhibitions might take the place of amateur installations, literary events, video art presentations, or pretty much anything else the creative mind can conceive. Given the truly experimental nature of Future Tenant, shows can understandably be somewhat hit or miss. And although use of the space isn't technically limited to artists from the CMU community, the work of the school's students and faculty are certainly represented with frequency. MFA exhibitions take place at the end of each school semester.

THE IRMA FREEMAN CENTER FOR IMAGINATION

5006 Penn Ave., 412/924-0634, www.irmafreeman.com
HOURS: Gallery Sat. 2–5 P.M., see website for dates and times for workshops, classes, and other educational programs
Map 6

Essentially a cross between a community outreach center, an arts school, and a gallery, the seriously ambitious mission of Garfield's Irma Freeman Center for Imagination involves "enrich[ing] and diversify[ing] the local community by building positive experiences in a multicultural progressive setting." Quite a mouthful, to be sure. But the center's cofounder, Sheila Ali, has already developed a fairly extensive schedule of classes including yoga, mosaic-making, and green technology workshops designed to be taken by parents and their children. The center also showcases visual arts exhibits, including a rotating selection of paintings by the late Irma Freeman herself—an incredibly prolific Pittsburgh artist, who also happened to be Ali's grandmother.

ARTS AND LEISURE

JAMES GALLERY

413 S. Main St., 412/922-9800, www.jamesgallery.net
HOURS: Mon.-Sat. 9 A.M.-5 P.M.
`Map 7`

One of the city's most respected houses of contemporary, modern, and older works, James Gallery exhibits work not only by Pittsburgh's top artists, but also by national and international artists of note. Work displayed here represents all manner of media, including sculpture, photography, and fiber arts, and many of the artists represented by the gallery are available for site-specific commissions.

MANCHESTER CRAFTSMEN'S GUILD

1815 Metropolitan St., 412/322-1773,
www.manchesterguild.org
HOURS: Gallery Mon.-Fri. 10 A.M.-5 P.M.; see website for MCG's jazz performance schedule, workshops, and classes
COST: Jazz performance tickets $25-50
`Map 7`

Something of a cross between an educational music and arts facility, a gallery, and a concert space with an on-site recording studio, Manchester Craftsmen's Guild is one of the local scene's most intriguing and culturally philanthropic arts institutions. Located in out-of-the-way Manchester, not far from some of the city's roughest North Side neighborhoods, it's appropriate that the guild offers arts and photography classes to disadvantaged high schoolers. Grown-ups can take courses as well, although many folks who flock here do so for the notable jazz concert series. Anyone is free to wander into the main lobby, however, which doubles as the guild's ever-changing, multimedia art gallery.

MENDELSON GALLERY

5874 Ellsworth Ave., 412/361-8664,
www.mendelsongallery.net
HOURS: Tues.-Sat. noon-6 P.M.
`Map 4`

Particularly interesting and worth a visit not only for its extensive collection of impressive modern selections (work by Keith Haring and Robert Mapplethorpe has been featured in the

GALLERY CRAWLS

There are currently two neighborhood-wide art gallery crawls that occur in Pittsburgh on a regular basis, and both events make for loads of good fun, even if contemporary art isn't necessarily your thing. The Pittsburgh Cultural Trust sponsors the **Gallery Crawl in the Cultural District,** a free quarterly event that tends to take on something of a party atmosphere as the night wears on. As many as two dozen Downtown galleries, museums, and other venues are generally involved, and aside from simply showcasing new visual art, live music and theater are also featured. Visit www.pgharts.org for specific dates and times, as well as a complete schedule of events and exhibits, all of which are free.

The significantly edgier **Unblurred Gallery Crawl** happens during the first Friday of each month. The vast majority of its exhibitions and performances take place inside the galleries and cafés of the Penn Avenue Arts Corridor in Garfield and East Liberty. And as with the Cultural District's crawl, live performances are a big part of the Unblurred experience; expect to witness anything from spoken word to live music, and from modern dance to glass blowing. Visit http://friendship-pgh.org/paai/unblurred for monthly schedules.

past), but also for the fact this East End gallery doubles as the home of its owner, Steve Mendelson.

MILLER GALLERY AT CARNEGIE MELLON UNIVERSITY

Purnell Center for the Arts, 5000 Forbes Ave.,
412/268-3618, http://millergallery.cfa.cmu.edu
HOURS: Tues.-Sun. noon-6 P.M.
`Map 2`

Founded in 2000 by Regina Gouger Miller, an artist and alumna of CMU's School of Art, the 9,000-square-foot, three-story Miller Gallery is one of the city's most surprising and accessible venues of contemporary art, where exhibitions are always free to the public. As a division of the school's College of Fine Arts, it's also a place where members from the greater Pittsburgh community—including those who don't normally travel in artistic circles—are encouraged to widen their interpretation and understanding of contemporary art. Arts-related lectures and special events are occasionally scheduled.

MOST WANTED FINE ART

5015 Penn Ave., 412/328-4737,
www.most-wantedfineart.com
HOURS: By appointment only.
Map 6

Owned and operated by the artist Jason Sauer, a transplant from Texas, whose work generally consists of large-scale installations and even demolition derby cars, Most Wanted is yet another Garfield-based contemporary art gallery featuring occasional live performances by punk, indie, and wildly experimental bands. Community outreach events happen here on an occasional basis, as do events featuring poets and other performing artists. Openings are held during monthly First Fridays. Additional hours are by appointment only. See website for information on the gallery's music/performance schedule.

PITTSBURGH CENTER FOR THE ARTS

6300 5th Ave., 412/361-0873, www.pittsburgharts.org
HOURS: Mon.-Wed. 10 A.M.-5 P.M., Thurs. 10 A.M.-9 P.M., Fri.-Sat. 10 A.M.-7 P.M., Sun. noon-5 P.M.
Map 4

A self-described "non-profit community arts campus," the Pittsburgh Center for the Arts is one of the region's most unique resource centers for visual artists. Artists-in-training can sign up for one of the center's ever-popular studio classes, while working professionals can apply to the residency program that takes place at various sites throughout the city. The work displayed in the gallery here is produced largely by southwestern Pennsylvanians with various skill levels. You'll find works by well-established artists displayed alongside pieces by newcomers.

© MATT STROUD

Most Wanted Fine Art

DR. SKETCHY'S ANTI-ART SCHOOL

Founded over five years ago in Brooklyn by the New York-based artist Molly Crabapple, Dr. Sketchy's Anti-Art School (www.drsketchy.com) is essentially a cross between a burlesque performance and a college-level life drawing class. Underground performers dressed like pin-up girls pose for amateur artists, the cocktails flow freely, and the results are often masterpieces of "alt drawing" (or at least cool new tattoo sketches).

Today, Dr. Sketchy's is literally a worldwide phenomenon, with branches spread all throughout North and South America, Europe, Asia, and Australia. Appropriately enough, the Pittsburgh branch of Dr. Sketchy's is headed by Joe Wos of Downtown's ToonSeum, and classes take place on a somewhat irregular basis at the South Side's **Gypsy Café** (1330 Bingham St., 412/381-4977, www.gypsycafe.net). Admission is $10; visit http://drsketchy.blogspot.com for more information and an updated schedule of gatherings.

PITTSBURGH GLASS CENTER

5472 Penn Ave., 412/365-2145, www.pittsburghglasscenter.org
HOURS: Tues.-Thurs. 10 A.M.-7 P.M., Fri.-Sun. 10 A.M.-4 P.M.
Map 6

Not content to exist simply as a static gallery, the nonprofit and architecturally stunning Pittsburgh Glass Center is also an education hub. Aspiring glass blowers can attend a slew of classes here, including flameworking, casting, and hot glass workshops. Show up during an evening exhibition and you'll find staff members and student glass blowers alike demonstrating their skills and often selling their wares; glass jewelry is an especially popular item. Or simply peruse the current exhibition at the Hodge Gallery—stunning creative glass art and mixed-media shows happen here

regularly. The gallery is open late during First Fridays. See the website for current dates and times for classes and workshops.

THE SHOP

4314 Main St., 412/951-0622, www.myspace.com/onartandperformancevenue
HOURS: By appointment only.
Map 6

As the sixth DIY-style visual and performing arts space launched by enterprising Pittsburgh curator Lauri Mancuso, who formerly ran similar spaces in Garfield, East Liberty, Wilkinsburg, and Braddock, there's no telling how long The Shop will survive before inevitably picking up, moving on, and changing its name. But for the time being, everything from live performance to film and video to local and international contemporary art can be enjoyed at this modest Bloomfield space, which also acts as a working artist's studio. Indie bands perform regularly as well.

SILVER EYE CENTER FOR PHOTOGRAPHY

1015 E. Carson St., 412/431-1810, www.silvereye.org
HOURS: Wed. and Fri. noon-6 P.M., Thurs. noon-8 P.M., Sat. 11 A.M.-5 P.M., Mon.-Tues. reserved for educational programming
Map 3

Aside from the occasional student shows that take place at Pittsburgh Filmmakers' Melwood Photography Gallery, the Silver Eye Center is the city's solitary locale dedicated exclusively to the photographic arts. The gallery has two small but inviting rooms that showcase Pittsburgh-based artists and artists from around the world. Independent films are occasionally screened at Silver Eye as well.

SOCIETY FOR CONTEMPORARY CRAFT

2100 Smallman St., 412/261-7003, www.contemporarycraft.org
HOURS: Mon., Wed., and Sat. 10 A.M.-5 P.M.; Tues. 10 A.M.-7 P.M.; Sun. 10 A.M.-2 P.M.
Map 1

Located in an industrial warehouse space, the Society for Contemporary Craft has been presenting exhibitions both duly conservative and wildly eccentric for more than 30 years. The permanent collection includes blown glass by Dale Chihuly and rare chairs by the likes Frank Gehry and Mr. Imagination; clay, metal, and fiber crafts are also on display. Temporary exhibitions might feature anything from decoupage collages by inner-city high school kids to outsider art from the Deep South to utilitarian Native American crafts. Should you find yourself at the Steel Plaza "T" station Downtown, be sure to check out the society's satellite gallery, located inside the One Mellon Bank Center building.

SPACE
812 Liberty Ave., 412/325-7723,
www.spacepittsburgh.org
HOURS: Wed.-Thurs. 11 A.M.-6 P.M., Fri.-Sat. 11 A.M.-8 P.M.,
Sun. 11 A.M.-5 P.M.
Map 1

Curated by a former *Pittsburgh City Paper* arts editor, SPACE is perhaps the city's most contemporary-minded arts emporium. And with deejays, live music, and hordes of the city's prettiest young things showing up *en masse* for nearly every event, openings tend to more closely resemble house parties than the stale wine-and-cheese happenings found at your average gallery. Special attention is paid to local artists whose work may be otherwise ignored or overlooked, especially those photographers, visual artists, or installation builders who consistently push the envelope.

UNSMOKE SYSTEMS
1137 Braddock Ave., Braddock,
www.unsmokeartspace.com
HOURS: Vary depending on show
Map 7

Something of a multipurpose art gallery and events venue housed in a former Catholic school, UnSmoke Systems is one of the many "urban reuse" projects that is helping to transform the dilapidated town of Braddock into a nationally-known community of cutting-edge creative types. Currently, UnSmoke hosts a number of artists-in-residence who work in the building's converted studio spaces. But just like the town of Braddock itself, its doors are open to just about anyone in need of space for a creative project or event.

WOOD STREET GALLERIES
601 Wood St., 412/471-5605,
www.woodstreetgalleries.org
HOURS: Tues.-Thurs. 11 A.M.-6 P.M., Fri.-Sat. 11 A.M.-8 P.M.
Map 1

Certainly one of Pittsburgh's most ambitious contemporary galleries, Wood Street, which is publicly funded by the Pittsburgh Cultural Trust, is so named because of its location above the Downtown Wood Street "T" station. Exhibitions here are decidedly hit or miss but almost always worth at least a cursory look. Multidisciplinary artists from Pittsburgh and, indeed, around the world, have shown here; the curators seem to have especially weak spots for industrial-themed installation art and wildly contemporary video art. Conceptual photography projects show up occasionally, as do local arts experts who participate in the galleries' eye-opening noontime lecture series.

◖ ZOMBO GALLERY
4900 Hatfield St., 412/904-3703,
www.zomboworld.com
HOURS: Wed.-Sat. 1-7 P.M., Sun. 1-5 P.M.
Map 6

Helmed by the local artist, musician, deejay, and midcentury Americana pop-culture enthusiast Michael "Zombo" Devine (better known by Pittsburgh barflies as DJ Zombo) Lawrenceville's Zombo Gallery is easily one of the most exciting and multifaceted new additions to the city's swiftly growing creative arts scene. And yet as the gallery's website address attests, this business is much more than just a simple collection of visual art. The gallery—which generally presents the sort of contemporary art made popular by *Juxtapoz* and *Hi-Fructose* magazines, as well as galleries like L.A.'s La Luz de Jesus—also encompasses a screen printing shop and a novelty toy shop, as well as a massage studio, **The Devine Touch Therapeutic Massage** (503/970-8696,

Zombo Gallery

the Opera) can be found. And as for the simply stunning $43 million restoration? Let's just say that it's no wonder the Benedum is now on the National Register of Historic Places.

BYHAM THEATER

101 6th St., 412/456-1350,
www.pgharts.org/venues/byham.aspx
Map 1

At just over 200 years old, the Byham Theater (originally known as the Gayety Theater, and then as the Fulton) remains one of the most important cornerstones of the city's Cultural District theater scene. And although the Gayety was largely a vaudeville house and the Fulton a movie theater, today the main stage presents a mixture of dance, ballet, theater, and even live music. The fully restored, 1,500-seat interior is nothing but classic American music hall; apparently no detail was spared. Imagine a luxurious lobby, a full balcony, and friendly ushers who escort latecomers to their seats with a flashlight. The Byham is a true American classic.

CABARET AT THEATER SQUARE

665 Penn Ave., 412/325-6766, www.clocabaret.com
Map 1

The Civic Light Opera most certainly has a long and storied history in Pittsburgh. It premiered back in 1946 with a production on the Pitt campus before moving into the Civic Arena, and then Heinz Hall, before finally settling in at the Benedum Center. The 265-seat Cabaret at Theater Square, however, is less than ten years old, and it's there that the CLO's cheery and accessible brand of musical theater is performed year-round. And although the majority of the Cabaret's guests enjoy musical revues and family-friendly shows like *Nunsense* from within the comfort of a traditional theater seating, the dinner-and-a-show option is available here as well. Late-night cabaret entertainment also takes place at the adjacent **Backstage Bar** (655 Penn Ave., 412/325-6769, www.pgharts.org/venues/backstagebar.aspx), which features outdoor dining and always-free entertainment.

www.devinetouchmassage.com), owned by Devine's wife, Julie. Rock bands occasionally perform here as well, and unusually creative arts-related events happen frequently; visit the website to stay up-to-date.

PERFORMING ARTS

BENEDUM CENTER FOR THE PERFORMING ARTS

719 Liberty Ave., 412/456-6666,
www.pgharts.org/venues/benedum.aspx
Map 1

Formerly known as the Stanley Theater, the Benedum Center is another of Pittsburgh's Downtown Cultural District cornerstones. The Pittsburgh Opera, the Civic Light Opera, and the Pittsburgh Ballet Theater all use the building as a home base, so patrons here are often seasonal subscribers of the fur-draped and jewel-encrusted variety. This is also where mainstream Broadway fare (*Cats, Phantom of*

CHARITY RANDALL THEATRE

Forbes Ave. at Bigelow Blvd., 412/624-7529,
www.play.pitt.edu

`Map 2`

One of the three performance spaces used by the University of Pittsburgh's Theatre Department (the other two are the Henry Heymann Theatre, located just downstairs, and the Cathedral of Learning's Studio Theatre), the Charity Randall Theatre is an intimate, 478-seat auditorium. This is where the vast majority of student-run performances take place; Shakespeare is particularly popular, and years past have seen a similar glut of student-friendly fare (George Bernard Shaw, Andrew Lloyd Webber). Artists-In-residence working at Pitt can often be seen performing alongside the student actors.

SHAKING UP THE BOARDS

Looking for theater that's a touch more progressive than the standard Cultural District fare? Consider tracking down a performance by one of the following progressive companies.

Already legendary in Pittsburgh for its Midnight Radio series – which is something of an ultra-modern version of Garrison Keillor's *A Prairie Home Companion* – **Bricolage** (www.webbricolage.org) is quite possibly the hottest theater company in Pittsburgh today. It produces a wide range of original work and adaptations, as well as truly unique interactive experiences.

Also pushing the live entertainment envelope is **The Microscopic Opera Company** (www.microscopicopera.org), which offers short and ultra-modern chamber operas in seriously intimate spaces.

On the contemporary dance front, **The Pillow Project** (www.pillowproject.org) is certainly worth paying attention to. Something of a cross between a multimedia dance company and an experimental performance art collective, this group has already created a fascinating body of free-form dance work, including flash mob-like public performances.

Decidedly lower-brow but still good fun are the performances of the **Bridge City Bombshells**, an alterna-burlesque troupe of tattooed and buxom beauties who stage occasional shows at clubs and arts-related events around town. Visit them online at facebook.com/bridgecitybombshells.

(CITY THEATRE

1300 Bingham St., 412/431-2489,
www.citytheatrecompany.org

`Map 3`

Known as one of the city's most experimental and adventurous companies, City Theatre is tucked away in a cozy, red-brick building just a block from the corner of East Carson and 13th Streets. The 270-seat main studio has something of an industrial warehouse feel, a vibe that works especially well when the performance is particularly edgy. Artistic Director Tracy Brigden has been leading the company since 2001 and has since produced monologues, a number of world premieres, and even an oddly avant-garde live music experience with Pittsburgh's own Squonk Opera.

HEINZ HALL

600 Penn Ave., 412/392-4900,
www.pittsburghsymphony.org

`Map 1`

Anyone interested in taking in a performance by the Pittsburgh Symphony Orchestra will need to settle in at Heinz Hall, which is the ensemble's Downtown home base. And although not currently at the very top of its game—as it was during conductor Lorin Maazel's tenure—the PSO has consistently been recognized by experts around the world as one of the country's greatest orchestras. The hall itself is a splendidly restored former hotel and boasts such features as an adjustable orchestra pit and an outdoor garden plaza with a waterfall. Guided tours are available to groups of eight or more.

ARTS AND LEISURE

KELLY-STRAYHORN COMMUNITY PERFORMING ARTS CENTER

5941 Penn Ave., 412/363-3000,
www.kelly-strayhorn.org

Map 6

As its name implies, the Kelly-Strayhorn doesn't support a home theater company, but rather opens its doors to a widely diverse range of events and performances. Located in the heart of East Liberty's quickly gentrifying business district, the center is named in honor of two East Libbers who made it big: Stage man Gene Kelly and jazz great Billy Strayhorn. Past events have included area high school dance companies, traditional dancers from India and Brazil, and even film screenings.

NEW HAZLETT THEATER

Allegheny Square E., 412/320-4610,
www.newhazletttheater.org

Map 1

Located smack-dab in the middle of the Central North Side, the non-profit New Hazlett is something of an anything-goes, all-purpose arts facility. Plays are staged here on

a regular basis, but so too are live music and spoken word performances, as well as various literary and artistic community gatherings. Performing arts organizations of all sorts, in fact, pop up regularly at the New Hazlett, although new work by both the contemporary Dance Alloy troupe and the decidedly quirky Barebones productions theater company can be seen here with some regularity.

PITTSBURGH PLAYHOUSE

22 Craft Ave., 412/621-4445,
www.pittsburghplayhouse.com

Map 2

Situated in a somewhat obscure stretch of South Oakland (if you can find Magee-Women's Hospital, you're close), the Pittsburgh Playhouse is home to a professional company known as The Rep, as well as three student companies based at the nearby Point Park University: A children's theater company, a dance company, and a standard theater company. In other words, there's a *lot* going on at the playhouse during any given month—indeed, there are 235 performances annually—so

the O'Reilly Theater

COURTESY OF ROB MATHENY

there's a good chance that no matter your specific arts preference, you'll be able to find something here that grabs your attention.

PITTSBURGH PUBLIC THEATER (AT THE O'REILLY THEATER)

621 Penn Ave., 412/316-1600, www.ppt.org

Map 1

Unbeknownst to even most locals, the O'Reilly Theater was designed by superstar architect Michael Graves, a name you might recognize if you've lately perused the kitchenware aisle at Target (Graves is also a product designer). The 650-seat theater opened in late 1999, and it was built specifically with acoustic excellence in mind. It's also the only theater space Downtown featuring a "thrust" stage, meaning that the audience surrounds the stage floor on three sides in a "U" shape. Performances here are suitably eccentric while still maintaining mainstream appeal; successful Off-Broadway and comedy shows seem to do well.

CONCERT VENUES
A. J. PALUMBO CENTER

600 Forbes Ave., 412/396-5140, www.duq.edu/palumbo-center

Map 1

Although technically the home of the Duquesne University Dukes and Lady Dukes basketball teams, the A. J. Palumbo Center frequently transforms into a pop and rock concert hall after dark. Only the biggest artists at the top of their game perform here; years past have seen Public Enemy, Jane's Addiction, Green Day, and Counting Crows take the stage. Other entertainment and sporting events happen occasionally, such as wrestling and boxing. Insider's tip: To avoid being crushed on the floor during a rock show, arrive early and grab a seat in the general admission bleachers nearest the stage.

CARNEGIE MUSIC HALL

4400 Forbes Ave., 412/323-1919, www.pittsburghchambermusic.org

Map 2

Tucked into the same building as the Carnegie Museums of Art and Natural History, the

beautifully restored and antique Carnegie Music Hall is a 1,928-seat venue often described as "acoustically perfect." That's good news for the patrons of the Pittsburgh Chamber Music Society, a group that performs here regularly; folk concerts organized by Calliope, a local folk music society, take place here as well. And the Carnegie Lecture Series brings to the music hall an always-impressive rotation of literary celebs.

CONSOL ENERGY CENTER

1001 Fifth Ave., 412/642-1800, www.consolenergycenter.com

Map 1

It's true that plenty of Pittsburghers still mourn the loss of our city's architecturally stunning Civic Arena, the former home of the Stanley Cup–winning Pittsburgh Penguins. However, it turns out that the replacement—located almost directly across the street—isn't half bad. The LEED Gold–certified CONSOL Energy Center is packed with amenities: A brewpub; a 12,000-square-foot Penguins team store; a dozen escalators; a fine dining restaurant, and according to the Center's website, the widest seats of any NHL stadium, at 24 inches. Big name pop acts and rock bands perform here regularly as well, as will the Pittsburgh Power, the city's new Arena Football League pro team.

FIRST NIAGARA PAVILION

665 Rte. 18, Burgettstown, 724/947-7400, www.firstniagarapavilion.com

Map 7

As Western Pennsylvania's largest concert venue, First Niagara Pavilion is essentially Pittsburgh's version of Denver's Red Rocks Amphitheater, or the Gorge Amphitheater in the Pacific Northwest. Formerly known as the Post-Gazette Pavilion, and before that the Coca-Cola Star Lake Amphitheater, this is where the touring summer festivals stop on their way through the tri-state area; Lilith Fair, Phish, and the Grateful Dead have all taken the stage in years past. Tickets can be purchased for the seating area near the stage, which is in fact covered by a pavilion. Most show-goers prefer the cheaper general admission tickets, however, with which you'll stake out a spot on the grass. Keep in mind that the Pavilion is roughly a 45-minute drive from Downtown Pittsburgh.

PEPSI-COLA ROADHOUSE

565 Rte. 18, 724/947-1900, www.pepsiroadhouse.com

Map 7

Imagine going to a dinner theater way out in the sticks, but instead of a murder-mystery taking place on stage, you're being entertained by a country-and-western act from a bygone era. That's the scene at the Pepsi-Cola Roadhouse, where hundreds of show-goers squeeze in around tables to nosh on barbeque ribs and nod their heads to Kenny Rogers or Dwight Yoakam. A number of video projection screens and a state-of-the-art sound system fill the roadhouse, so even if you don't happen to be right up against the stage, it's practically guaranteed to be an unequivocally intimate experience.

PETERSEN EVENTS CENTER

3719 Terrace St., 412/323-1919, http://web-smg.athletics.pitt.edu

Map 2

Constructed by the University of Pittsburgh in 2002 as a home for the Pitt Panthers basketball team, the main stadium at Petersen Events Center can seat roughly 10,000 fans, and that's not including club and luxury seats. Sports and fitness isn't the only game here, however; top-selling pop and hip-hop acts like Counting Crows and Outkast perform frequently. In fact, Downtown's Mellon Arena is the only large-capacity venue in town with more seating. Alcohol isn't available at this venue.

STAGE AE

400 North Shore Dr., www.promowestlive.com/pittsburgh

Map 1

Located near the site of the old Three Rivers Stadium, this North Shore concert hall is the newest addition to Pittsburgh's live music scene, hosting cutting-edge rock and pop acts that have yet to develop household-name status. It was designed to look, sound, and feel like the popular LC Pavilion in Columbus, Ohio. And that's a good thing, since Pittsburgh has long been lacking a venue that's larger than a club, but smaller than an amphitheater.

TRIB TOTAL MEDIA AMPHITHEATRE

1 W. Station Square Dr., 412/642-1100, www.tribtotalmediaamp.com

Map 3

Located just across the Monongahela River from Downtown, the Trib Total Media Amphitheatre is simply the most recent name for the outdoor concert stadium that has occupied spot over the years; the venue has also been known as the Melody Amphitheatre, the IC Amphitheatre, and the Chevrolet Amphitheatre. And although the venue itself doesn't consist of much more than an open-ended tarp with a stage on one end, summer concerts can be especially pleasant here when the sun begins to set, and when the lights of Downtown Pittsburgh's skyline begin to illuminate. Bands performing here are generally of the Top 40 variety; pop-punk, country, and jam bands are particularly popular. The venue closes during the snowy winter months.

CINEMA

CARNEGIE SCIENCE CENTER
RANGOS OMNIMAX THEATER

1 Allegheny Ave., 412/237-3400, www.carnegiesciencecenter.org

COST: $8 adult, $6 senior and child

Map 1

Leave it to the smart folks at the Carnegie Science Center to improve ever so slightly on the already fascinating IMAX theater experience, a high-quality, large-screen film format where the picture is usually three stories high, or roughly 50 feet. The Carnegie's screen, however, is four stories high. It's also concave, so that the on-screen action takes place not just in front of you, but also on both sides. Thankfully, the seats recline, so there's no need to worry about painful neck strain.

HARRIS THEATER

809 Liberty Ave., 412/682-4111,
www.pghfilmmakers.org
COST: Ticket prices vary depending on film or
programming.
Map 1

As a member of the Pittsburgh Filmmakers
family of art house cinemas, Harris Theater
is one of the most progressive places to watch
movies in town. And aside from a few adult
bookstore video booths, it's the only theater in
the Downtown area. Independent and foreign
films are what you'll find here, although since
many movies screen only for a limited time,
you'll want to move quickly if something grabs
your interest. If you're in town specifically for
the annual Three Rivers Film Festival, you'll
be spending a lot of time at the Harris, which
will quite likely be the closest theater to your
Downtown hotel.

MANOR THEATER

1729 Murray Ave., 412/422-7729,
www.cinemagicpgh.com
COST: $9.25 adult, $6.50 matinee before 6 P.M.,
$6.50 senior and child

Map 5

Following the recent closure of Forward
Avenue's Squirrel Hill Theatre, the Manor
Theater is now the neighborhood's solitary cinema house. Still, it continues to screen a decent
number of so-called big-budget indie films—
movies that have a somewhat limited release, in
other words, but that generally aren't too terribly left of center. Family fare and children's pictures also screen regularly here, which makes
good sense given the abundance of youngsters
in this family-friendly neighborhood. With a
total of four screens, there's bound to be something that appeals to you. Insider's tip: The
nearby **Gullifty's** (1922 Murray Ave.) is a perfect spot for post-movie coffee and dessert.

MELWOOD SCREENING ROOM

477 Melwood Ave., 412/681-5449,
www.pghfilmmakers.org
COST: Ticket prices vary depending on film or
programming.
Map 6

Located on the second floor of Pittsburgh
Filmmakers (a film, video, and photography
production center and training facility in

TOM SAVINI, AUTEUR OF MONSTER MAKEUP AND SPECIAL EFFECTS

With the exception of horror film director
George Romero, who in 1968 directed the genre-
defining *Night of the Living Dead* in Pittsburgh's
northern suburbs, Tom Savini is far and away
the most famous and respected Pittsburgher
working in the scary-movie business today.

Unlike Romero, however, Savini made his
name not as a director, but rather as an unusually skilled and precise auteur of monster
makeup and special effects. In fact, chances
are good that you've recoiled in terror yourself
after encountering a Savini-built creature on
the silver screen; his ghosts, ghouls, goblins,
and fiends have raised hell in films including
*Dawn of the Dead, Friday the 13th, Monkey
Shines,* and *Creepshow 2.*

And yet curiously enough, Savini's latest

endeavor is playing out within the education
sector. **Tom Savini's Special Make-Up Effects Program,** as the four-semester-long associate's degree program is known, operates
out of the **Douglas Education Center** (130
Seventh St., 724/684-3684, www.dec.edu) in
Monessen, about 30 miles due south of Pittsburgh in Washington County.

Students are taught special effects basics
like sculpture, mold making, and cosmetic
makeup before exploring more advanced
ground, such as animatronics and airbrush
illustration techniques. The program's instructors are all accomplished industry vets
themselves, and at the end of the fourth semester, Savini himself often reviews and cri-
tiques student portfolios.

North Oakland), Melwood Screening Room is the city's premiere locale for ultra-unusual indie films. When Matthew Barney's Cremaster Cycle came to town, for instance, the Melwood was the no-brainer choice to host. Student films play in this 130-seat venue as well, as does the local phenomenon known as Film Kitchen, a monthly independent film and video series featuring a selection of mostly local-made shorts.

◖ OAKS THEATER

310 Allegheny River Blvd., Oakmont, 412/828-6311, www.theoakstheater.com
COST: $8 adult, $6 matinee before 6 P.M., $6 senior and child; $10-20 films and features part of a special programming series
Map 7

It's no wonder the Oaks Theater was named Best Independent Movie Theater by the readers of *Pittsburgh City Paper;* as a 70-year-old institution, it's one of the very few movie houses in town that genuinely evokes the Golden Age of cinema. Even better, seating is most definitely not limited—430 film fanatics can gather together at the Oaks, which, yes, is still a one-screen operation. And while independent and foreign films are shown throughout the week, a regular series of midnight cult classics (*Rocky Horror,* plus films by David Lynch, George Romero, et al.) takes place regularly as well. A popular event known as Cine Brunch, during which a light brunch is served prior to the screening of a film classic, happens at 10 A.M. on the second Saturday of each month.

REGENT SQUARE THEATER

1035 S. Braddock Ave., 412/681-5449, www.pghfilmmakers.org
COST: Ticket prices vary depending on film or programming.
Map 7

A 300-seat, single-screen art-house cinema, Regent Square Theater is located on the opposite side of Frick Park from Squirrel Hill. Regent Square, like Oakland's Melwood Screening Room and Downtown's Harris Theater, is also a member of the Pittsburgh Filmmakers family; that means that eclectic films both domestic and foreign are the order of the day.

Festivals and Events

Perhaps because so many pockets of Pittsburgh still preserve a proud small-town vibe, it's not unusual to see even the most plebian of neighborhood parades, block parties, and ethnic-themed gatherings packed full of families, teenagers, or anyone else who happens to wander by. And should you choose to show up at one of Pittsburgh's annual citywide fests, you might wonder if maybe the entire town hasn't arrived. In particular, the Three Rivers Arts Festival, First Night Pittsburgh, and Light Up Night are absolute can't-miss events for any true local, or for that matter, any visitor interested in understanding what it means to live in the Steel City in the 21st century.

In other words, most festivals here are true community events, and not just excuses to swill cheap beer out of plastic cups (although if that's what you're looking for, you won't likely be disappointed).

The weeks between Memorial Day and Labor Day are a particularly active time for outdoor gatherings and organized events.

WINTER
FIRST NIGHT PITTSBURGH
Pittsburgh Cultural Trust, 803 Liberty Ave., 412/471-6070, www.firstnightpgh.com
COST: Free
Map 1

Yeah, we know: December 31 is actually the *last* night of the year, not the first. But hey, this is Pittsburgh; we're not exactly known for sweating the small stuff. Not that First Night is ever anything small. On the contrary, this is one of the most popular and packed events of

BOATS FOR SAIL

You can probably guess the main motive of most folks who flock *en masse* each year to the ever-popular **Pittsburgh Boat Show** (www.pittsburghboatshow.com, 412/798-8858), which takes place in late January or early February at the Monroeville Convention Center. With literally acres of new and used vessels on offer, there's really no better selection of seaworthy craft anywhere else in the tri-state area. But the boat show isn't all about buying and selling. There are also boating and fishing seminars, displays of classic and antique boats, safe boating education classes, and more. Tickets are $8; children under 12 are admitted free with an adult.

the entire year, regardless of the fact that it's usually freezing cold outside. The party takes place in and around the Market Square and Cultural District areas of Downtown, and the celebration, naturally, is all about ringing in the New Year. The twist is that this party is family-friendly and alcohol-free. Entertainment changes a bit from year to year, but generally involves onstage music and dance, a street parade, copious food booths, and, at the end of the night, a spectacular fireworks display.

LIGHT UP NIGHT
Pittsburgh Downtown Partnership, 412/566-4190, www.downtownpittsburgh.com
COST: Free
Map 1

For Pittsburghers, Light Up Night signals the official start of the holiday season each November. Tens of thousands of people stream into Downtown for the occasion, which literally consists of lighting up the night; major department stores and small businesses alike line their facades with blinking holiday lights, and the city suddenly becomes a mini–Winter Wonderland. A few special exhibits are erected as well, including a massive Christmas tree near

the Market Square fountain; the fountain becomes an outdoor ice skating rink during this time of year. Also festively lit up and worth a look is Station Square, which can easily be reached on foot by traversing the Smithfield Street Bridge.

PITT NATIONALITY ROOMS HOLIDAY TOURS
Cathedral of Learning, University of Pittsburgh, corner of 5th Ave. and Bigelow Blvd., 412/624-6000, www.pitt.edu/~natrooms
COST: Self-guided tours free; guided tours $3 adult, $1 child
Map 2

What better time to tour the Nationality Rooms at Pitt's Cathedral of Learning than the holiday season (November–January), when every room is fully decked out in each country's respective holiday style? Even if you've already toured the rooms, which are a series of fully functional classrooms designed and decorated to resemble classrooms from 26 separate nations, the holiday tour is still worth considering, especially if you're traveling with youngsters who might benefit from learning something about the international traditions of Christmas.

SPRING
PEDAL PITTSBURGH
Station Square at Carson St. at the Smithfield Street Bridge, 412/232-3545, www.pedalpittsburgh.org
COST: $25
Map 3

Pittsburgh may not be well known as a popular city for cyclists, but what with its hills, valleys, bridges, waterways, and, yes, miles of bike trails, it's a simple fact that one of the best ways to experience the unique sights and landscape of the city is atop two wheels. And that's exactly why Pedal Pittsburgh, which, by the way, is a recreational ride and not a race, is so popular. More than 2,000 cyclists show up every year in May at the Chevy Amphitheatre in Station Square, where the ride begins and ends; the six separate courses range from 6 miles to 60 miles, so whether you're a hardcore cyclist or

ARTS AND LEISURE

you're leading a family of small children, you'll be able to fully participate at a comfortable pace. Departures take place in the early morning; lunch and live entertainment is scheduled during the middle of the day.

PITTSBURGH FOLK FESTIVAL

1000 Fort Duquesne Blvd., David L. Lawrence Convention Center, 412/565-6000 (center), 412/278-1267 (office), www.pghfolkfest.org
COST: $10 adult, $9 adult over 55, $2 child 2-12, free kids under 2
Map 1

Now in its fifth decade, the Pittsburgh Folk Festival, which takes place in May, presents an ideal opportunity to explore the cultural intricacies of more than two dozen nationalities, all without leaving Downtown. Ethnic food and entertainment is offered throughout the day, and visitors have the chance to practice ethnic dances or to simply shop for souvenirs in the international bazaar. Participating nationalities vary from year to year; participants in 2006 included nationals from Pakistan, Germany, India, Ireland, Poland, Scandinavia, Croatia, and many more.

PITTSBURGH INTERNATIONAL CHILDREN'S FESTIVAL

West Park, 412/321-5520, www.pghkids.org/festival.htm
COST: One show $8 pp, two shows $14 pp, three shows $18 pp
Map 1

For parents who aim to be educationally responsible, but who can't possibly bear to suffer through another brain-numbing performance of *Barney on Ice,* the Pittsburgh International Children's Festival may be just the thing. Each May, a weeklong showcase of professional theater companies from around the world is held, much to the delight of kids of all ages. England, Germany, China, West Africa, and even Pittsburgh were represented in last year's festival; performances run the gamut from acrobatics to music and dance to comedy and drama.

ST. PATRICK'S DAY PARADE

Begins at Liberty Ave. and 11th St., www.pittsburghirish.org/parade
COST: Free
Map 1

Get this: Pittsburghers are so nuts about St. Paddy's Day that, depending on which day the holiday actually falls on, it's sometimes celebrated *twice.* It works like this: The St. Patrick's Day Parade always takes place on a Saturday in March, so if St. Paddy's Day falls on a weekday, the parade will happen the Saturday *before* the actual holiday. Confused yet? Just remember this: In Pittsburgh, that means two excuses to party. And what a party it is. The parade, which begins as early as 10 A.M. and snakes through Downtown, is a fête of almost unbelievable proportions. Think floats, marching bands, and a very inebriated crowd. And no, you don't have to be Irish (or a connoisseur of green beer) to join in.

SUMMER

◖ BIKEFEST

3410 Penn Ave., 412/325-4334, www.bike-pgh.org/events/bikefest
COST: Varies; most daytime events are free
Map 6

Organized annually by the politically active and nonprofit Bike Pittsburgh organization, which for years now has been working to transform Pittsburgh into a safe, friendly, and accessible place for cyclists, BikeFest is a phenomenal ten-day-long celebration of bicycle culture at its very best, with an emphasis on education and inclusiveness. Everything from bike races to leisurely rides to bike scavenger hunts, bike polo games, bike workshops and even bike-themed movie screenings and readings take place throughout the festival. And although the fest's specific events change slightly with each passing year, the city's ever-growing cycling community can always count on a phenomenal opening day kickoff party, featuring deejays, raffles, and a silent auction.

CINEMA IN THE PARK

Various city parks, 412/422-6426, www.city.pittsburgh.pa.us/parks/cinema_in_the_park.htm

COST: Free

When it comes to wholesome and affordable summer entertainment that's appropriate for the entire family, it's tough to beat the city's Cinema in the Park program, which offers an entire season's worth of free movies screened out-of-doors at seven different public parks. The films start as soon as the sun sets, and each park has a different screening schedule, making it theoretically possible to see a free movie each day of the week from June through August. Most locals enjoy the movies picnic-style, complete with blankets and coolers full of food. Alcohol, however, is strictly forbidden. Oakland's Schenely Park is probably the event's most popular location. Call or visit the website for park locations and detailed schedules.

FOURTH OF JULY

Point State Park

COST: Free

Map 1

Pittsburgh's celebration of Independence Day probably won't come across as anything outside the norm to those born and raised between sea and shining sea. Pittsburgh's celebration takes place at Point State Park; arrive early to secure a seat near the rivers. Blankets or portable chairs are suggested if you'll be staying awhile, and entertainment is generally provided by massive public address–style speakers blasting patriotic rock 'n' roll.

HOTHOUSE

Various locations, www.sproutfund.org/hothouse

COST: $60 general admission

Organized annually in June to benefit the Sprout Fund, an organization working to keep Pittsburgh a fun and artistic place to live and play, Hothouse is one of the most important events of the year for the city's see-and-be-seen crowd. The location tends to change each year, as do the performers and art installations, but if you'd like to know who is on the roster

before laying out cash for a ticket, simply log onto the Sprout Fund's website and look for the list of artists who've won cash grants over the past year. Past award recipients include an artist who makes puppets out of drier lint and a Pittsburgh-affiliated group that organized a sidewalk-chalk mural competition. However, the majority of Hothouse exhibits are relatively sophisticated and meant to be taken seriously. Dress to impress.

PENNSYLVANIA MICROBREWERS FEST

800 Vinial St., 412/237-9402, www.pennbrew.com

COST: $32

Map 1

Craft brewers from all across Pennsylvania and beyond gather annually in June for this celebration of obscure and creatively brewed beer. The event, which has been going strong since 1995, conveniently takes place at the North Side's Penn Brewery. Attendees are welcome to sample nearly unlimited quantities of roughly 100 different beers, from Belgian Ales to India Pale Ales to organic beers. A meal is included with the price of admission.

PITTSBURGH BLUES FESTIVAL

412/460-2583, www.pghblues.com

COST: $20-25

Map 7

Not content to simply celebrate the blues, the Pittsburgh Blues Festival, which takes place in July, is also a highly successful food drive that has also raised $600,000 for the Greater Pittsburgh Community Food Bank during its 12 years of existence. Of course, most folks do come primarily for the music and no wonder: Nationally and internationally acclaimed artists perform throughout the weekend, and especially big-name acts take the stage every evening. The location of the festival changes every year, so be sure to call or visit the festival's website well in advance. The setup is always the same, however: Food vendors offer Southern-themed eats, a Kids' Zone tent keeps the little ones amused, and hours upon hours of good ol' American blues fill the ears.

ARTS AND LEISURE

PITTSBURGH MARATHON

Starts in Downtown Pittsburgh, 412/586-7785,
www.pittsburghmarathon.com
Map 1

After its much-publicized five-year hiatus, during which the city lacked the funds to keep it operational, the hugely popular Pittsburgh Marathon was finally brought back to life in 2009, thanks in large part to its new corporate sponsor, Dick's Sporting Goods. The city's especially hilly terrain, of course, makes the marathon a visual delight for those used to running races in much flatter cities; the course covers portions of the North Shore, the South Side, Oakland, Shadyside, and Bloomfield, and it also crosses each one of the city's three rivers. Less advanced runners also have the option of competing in a half-marathon; relay teams are also an option. There's also a kid's marathon for runners ages 5–14. The registration fees are $80–120 for the full marathon, $70–110 for the half marathon, and $230–320 for the relay marathon. The lowest price listed is for early-bird registration. Registration prices increase as the marathon date approaches.

PITTSBURGH THREE RIVERS REGATTA

Point State Park, 412/875-4841,
www.threeriversregatta.net
COST: Free
Map 1

One of the city's most beloved summer events, the four-day-long Three Rivers Regatta pays tribute to one of Pittsburgh's most valuable resources: its winding waterways. The festival takes place in July inside Downtown's Point State Park, and, naturally, many of the best events take place in the drink. Families can enjoy Grand Prix Powerboat races, personal watercraft stunt shows, bass fishing, and even a boat demonstration by the U.S. Navy from the stadium-style seating that lines the Allegheny River. But fun stuff happens on land and in the air, too: hot air balloon rides, a dog Frisbee show, a U.S. Navy parachute team exhibition. There's even a concert series featuring marquee-level acts.

PITTSBURGH TRIATHLON AND ADVENTURE RACE

33 Terminal Way, Friends of the Riverfront,
412/488-0212, www.friendsoftheriverfront.org,
www.pittsburghtriathlon.com
Map 1

The Pittsburgh Triathlon, a serious physical endurance test involving water, cycle, and foot races, will undoubtedly be your only opportunity to swim in the fairly polluted Allegheny River without being considered completely out of your mind. But this isn't a contest to be taken lightly; the event, which takes place in August, begins with a 1.5K swim from the North Shore to the Roberto Clemente Bridge and back, and then a rigorous 40K bike ride along I-279, and finally a 10K run along the Allegheny River. In other words, don't bother entering unless you're in absolutely top physical shape. Observing the race is an event in itself, however, and there's always the Adventure Race—a light two-mile canoe paddle followed by a 3.2-mile run that takes place at the same time as the Pittsburgh Triathlon. This is a good option for people who are not physically fit enough to participate in the triathlon, but are looking for a challenge nonetheless. The registration fees are $60–80 for the Adventure Race, $120–170 for the Adventure Race Relay, $95–120 for the International Triathalon, $190–240 for the International Triathalon Relay, $80–10 for the 5Sprint Thiathalon, and $160–210 for the Sprint Triathalon Relay. An additional $10 USA Triathalon fee is required for each athlete. The lowest price listed is for early-bird registration. Registration prices increase as the marathon date approaches.

PITTSBURGH VINTAGE GRAND PRIX

Schenley Park, 412/687-1800,
www.pittsburghvintagegrandprix.com
Map 2

A 10-day festival of races, car shows, and motorsports events, the Pittsburgh Vintage Grand Prix features one of the finest vintage car shows of its kind in the country. A bevy of classic car enthusiasts—all amateur drivers—motor throughout the streets of leafy Schenley Park for 10 days each July. Motorists arrive in what will almost certainly be the most unusual assortment of vehicles you've ever seen in one setting; expect mint-condition antique and specialty vehicles from all over the world. Proceeds benefit Pittsburghers with disabilities, although all events are free for spectators.

PRIDEFEST AND PRIDE IN THE STREET

Liberty Ave., Downtown, 412/246-4451,
www.pittsburghpride.org
COST: Pride in the Street $25, PrideFest Free
Map 1

Organized by the Delta Foundation of Pittsburgh and taking place in the heart of the Golden Triangle, PrideFest and Pride in the Street are two separate but related celebrations of gay life and culture that happen during the same weekend in June; the events culminate with the ever-popular **Pride Awareness March.** Both events are day-long affairs that happen out-of-doors on Liberty Ave., where various deejays and gay-culture icons perform on stage. Other festival events range from spoken word performances to drag shows to carnival games. Food and drink vendors are also plentiful, and PrideFest features a beer garden that requires a separate $25 entrance fee.

THREE RIVERS ARTS FESTIVAL

Point State Park and other Downtown locations,
412/281-8723, www.artsfestival.net
COST: Free
Map 1

Pittsburgh simply wouldn't be the same without the much-loved Three Rivers Arts Festival, a two-week-long June celebration of live music, crafts, dance, performance, visual and contemporary art, and even a touch of carnival culture. Founded more than 35 years ago by a committee affiliated with the Carnegie Museum of Art, portions of the festival take place at various locations throughout Downtown, although the bulk of the activity happens in and around Point State Park. Keep your eyes peeled for festival schedules, which include maps and free concert listings. You'll need to stroll the length of Downtown's Penn and Liberty Avenues to explore all the participating galleries, while vendors who arrive from around the country to hawk handicrafts cluster near the Hilton, just across the street from Point State Park and the never-ending row of food carts. Installations and a performance art shows can be found just inside the park.

FALL

A FAIR IN THE PARK

Mellon Park, 412/370-0695, www.afairinthepark.org
COST: Free
Map 4

A contemporary arts and crafts festival that has been organized by the Craftsmen's Guild of Pittsburgh for over four decades now, the three-day A Fair in the Park has long been one of the Pittsburgh art community's most anticipated annual celebrations. More than 20,000 craft obsessives from Pittsburgh and beyond arrive each year to shop for handmade works of jewelry, glass, metal, clay, and much more. A packed-full schedule of activities and entertainment is also a big part of the fun: Glassblowers, metalsmiths, and sculptors can be observed in the act of creation, and a wide variety of musicians and performing artists set up shop as well. The Children's Museum of Pittsburgh also sponsors a popular family and children's area, where the little ones can get their craft on, free of charge.

MEXICAN WAR STREETS HOUSE AND GARDEN TOUR

412/323-9030, www.mexicanwarstreets.com
COST: $50 in advance, $60 at the door
Map 1

Neighborhood renovation is the theme of the decidedly upscale Mexican War Streets House Tour during September, when owners of gorgeously restored homes in Pittsburgh's Victorian-era district open their doors and allow complete strangers to tramp through their living rooms. Many homes you'll see along the tour are listed on the National Register of Historic Places; even swankier is the black-tie pre-tour gala; it takes place in a different location each year. The tour is given

ARTS AND LEISURE

in the Mexican War Streets neighborhood of the North Side. You will need to visit the website or call 412/323-9030 for ticket and location information.

OKTOBERFEST
412/237-9400, www.pennbrew.com
COST: Free
Map 1

Although smaller and less popular Oktoberfest celebrations take place at a handful of brewpubs throughout Southwestern Pennsylvania every September, Pittsburghers on the hunt for the biggest and best party always head to the outdoor patio at **Penn Brewery** (www.pennbrew .com). The event takes place over the length of two weekends, and the festivities follow the same schedule as Oktoberfest in Munich. And just like in Germany, the party is all about food, drink, music, and dance. Traditional German bands perform in both the outdoor tent and the restaurant. All manner of schnitzels and wursts are available, as is the brewery's special-edition Oktoberfest brew. Within the city limits, Oktoberfest is also celebrated at **Hofbräuhaus Pittsburgh** (www.hofbrauhaus-pittsburgh.com) at SouthSide Works, where a portion of the event involves the crowing of Miss Oktoberfest. For *serious* Oktoberfest fans willing to take a bit of a drive, the free-to-the-public **Pennsylvania Bavarian Oktoberfest** in Canonsburg (about a 30-minute drive from Downtown) is known as one of the biggest celebrations of its type in the country. Call 724/745-1812 for more information.

PITTSBURGH DRAGON BOAT FESTIVAL
Riverfront Park, 724/348-4836, www.pdbf.org
COST: Free
Map 3

Something of a cross between a rowing competition and a celebration of pan-Asian culture, the Pittsburgh Dragon Boat Festival has been growing in popularity for years now. For the uninitiated, a dragon boat is a long canoe-like vessel constructed to resemble (what else?) a dragon; the boats and races are a 2,400-year-old Chinese phenomenon. In Pittsburgh, the

festivities commence near the boat launch at the South Side's Riverfront Park. Each boat fits 20 paddlers as well as one captain, known as a steersperson, and a drummer who pounds from the back of the boat. Non-racers will have more than enough to keep them busy as well; activities include martial arts, tai chi, and origami demonstrations.

PITTSBURGH IRISH FESTIVAL
1000 Sandcastle Dr., Riverplex at Sandcastle, Homestead, 412/422-1113, www.pghirishfest.org
COST: Sat. and Sun. $10 adult in advance or $12 adult at the gate, $8 student and senior, $5 military and police officers; Fri. $3–5; ID card required for student, senior, military, and police discounts
Map 3

Sandcastle's Riverplex waterpark is the site of the city's annual weekend celebration of the Emerald Isle, the Pittsburgh Irish Festival. Taking place in September, many activities revolve around the main stage, where both traditional and contemporary Irish musicians perform daily. Celtic dancing, traditional musical instrument demonstrations, traditional Irish eats, and activities aimed specifically at children round out the long weekend. But do be aware that although the festival is advertised as family friendly, a good number of attendees here tend to get pretty inebriated. So if you're sensitive about exposing your kids to this kind of behavior, you might consider hiring a sitter.

PITTSBURGH NEW WORKS FESTIVAL
111 9th St., CAPA, 412/881-6888, www.pittsburghnewworks.org
COST: $10 per performance, $25 festival pass
Map 1

For thespians and theater buffs in the Steel City, no event compares with the New Works Festival, an annual showcase of one-act plays that stretches over a four-week period in September and October. As is the case with most new-works festivals, an even mixture of comedy, drama, and highly experimental work is presented, and although a number of performances are the work of Southwestern

Pennsylvania–based playwrights, playwrights from across the country are represented as well. Shows take place at a variety of locations around town. The main location of the festival is at Pittsburgh's Creative and Performing Arts High School in Downtown, although many events are held at various other locations.

RICHARD S. CALIGUIRI CITY OF PITTSBURGH GREAT RACE

Starts at Frick Park, 412/255-2493, www.rungreatrace.com

COST: Registration fees $18 pp in advance, $25 during month of race; prices for additional race weekend events vary

`Map 5`

When the Pittsburgh Marathon was temporarily cancelled several years ago due to citywide financial troubles, the annual Great Race, held each September, was the city's sole opportunity for competitive foot racing. Now that the marathon is back and stronger than ever, the Great Race has once again taken something of a back seat, although it remains a decidedly serious sporting event that attracts pro athletes from all around the world. The contest consists of a 5K run and walk (about 8 miles), as well as a 10K run (about 16 miles). The run, which begins at Squirrel Hill's Frick Park and ends at Point State Park, Downtown, generally draws as many as 10,000 participants. But unless

you're at the absolute height of your competitive game, don't count on coming home with a prize; Kenyan athletes almost always take top honors. Teams consisting of three to five runners are also welcome to compete.

THREE RIVERS FILM FESTIVAL

Various locations, 412/681-5449, www.3rff.com

COST: Opening and closing night tickets $15, single tickets $9, Six-Pack Pass $45 (includes admission to six films), Silver Screenie Pass $110-125 (good for admission to all films, events, and director receptions), Symposium tickets $15 adult and $8 student and Pittsburgh Filmmakers members

An annual presentation of the Pittsburgh Filmmakers family, the Three Rivers Film Festival is now a quarter of a century old. Documentaries, foreign films, locally produced shorts, and a wide and varied schedule of films that would otherwise never be screened in a market as small as Pittsburgh's are shown at three separate locations: the **Regent Square Theater** (1035 S. Braddock Ave., Edgewood), **Harris Theater** (809 Liberty Ave., Downtown), and **Melwood Screening Room** (477 Melwood Ave., Oakland). The festival takes place in November and special events vary from year to year. Past festivals have featured music ensemble Pere Ubu's live accompaniment to a Roger Corman film, and a screening of nickelodeon films from the early 1900s.

Recreation

Due to the city's ongoing success of its professional sports teams—the Steelers, the Pirates, and the Penguins—Pittsburgh has been known as "The City of Champions" since the 1970s. It's only fitting, then, that the recreational opportunities in the city and its outlying areas should provide ample opportunities for training, competing, and playing hard.

Joggers and walkers, for instance, can enjoy the miles of trails inside Schenley Park, while the mountain biking paths that run through

Frick Park are said to be some of the best in the country.

Naturally, Pittsburgh's three rivers (Allegheny, Monongahela, Ohio) offer ample opportunities for water activities, such as boating, canoeing, rowing, and yachting, all of which take place throughout the warmer months. And in the winter season, skiing and snowboarding excursions aren't more than an hour away in the Laurel Highlands.

For those who lack the competitive spirit, but still enjoy a bit of healthy exercise, recreational opportunities abound. Caves not far from the city can be explored with experienced spelunkers who act as guides. The state's only official lawn bowling court is located in Frick Park, and the city itself provides a plethora of tennis courts and swimming pools. Venture deep into Schenley Park during the year's coldest season, and you'll find families ice skating inside the park's ever-popular rink.

No matter what the season, you won't need to dig deep during your time in Pittsburgh to discover just about any sort of outdoor fun.

PARKS

Thanks in large part to the tireless work of a group of Pittsburgh civic and business leaders who in 1999 created an organization known as the Riverlife Task Force (now known simply as Riverlife), Pittsburgh is finally in the midst of creating what will surely be known as one of the country's most gorgeous and inspiring riverfront parks. Currently being referred to as **Three Rivers Park,** and still very much in the construction phase, the project is brilliantly utilizing the city's huge amount of urban waterfront property, which includes both banks of the Ohio, Allegheny, and Monongahela Rivers.

A riverfront park along the South Shore and a massive restoration of Point State Park and its legendary fountain are currently underway, while other projects—including a West End pedestrian bridge and a riverfront park in Lawrenceville—are still being planned. And while the entirety of Riverlife's construction plans aren't scheduled to be complete until 2020, it will no doubt be a genuine thrill to watch as Pittsburghers slowly develop more intimate and meaningful connections with their native waterways—a goal that has unfortunately not been realistic for city dwellers here, until now. Visit www.riverlifepgh.org for updates and more information.

Meanwhile, the city's most popular long-standing leafy escapes, namely Schenley Park and Frick Park, continue to provide both recreation and respite for Pittsburghers; entering their gates is something akin to entering an entirely different world, while still remaining right within the center of town. And unlike the reception you may receive in bigger towns, locals here are generally amenable to welcoming an out-of-towner into their game of Ultimate Frisbee or pickup basketball.

Interested in schmoozing with the college crowd? Head to Schenley Park's Flagstaff Hill (it's across the road from Phipps Conservatory), where CMU students play, sunbathe, and flirt whenever the weather's warm.

◖ FRICK PARK

Corner of Forbes Ave. and S. Braddock Ave., 412/422-6550, www.pittsburghparks.org
Map 5

The largest of the city's parks, Frick Park practically begs walkers, joggers, and bikers to get lost among its many trails and forested areas. But strolling the valleys and hills is hardly the only recreational option. Frick also has a number of playgrounds that are perfect for families with small children, as well as a wide-open field where dogs are allowed to run leash-free. You'll also find red clay tennis courts here and a lawn bowling green (the only public court in Pennsylvania), where competitive seniors can be found whiling away the afternoon.

HIGHLAND PARK

Highland Ave., 412/422-6550, www.pittsburghparks.org
Map 6

Located in an East End neighborhood of the same name, Highland Park sits on an overlook atop the Allegheny River, close to the Pittsburgh Zoo. Because of its enviable vista, the park is especially popular with joggers but also with walkers who enjoy circling the 0.75-mile path around the reservoir, a historic city site officially known as Reservoir No. 1. The sand volleyball courts are a popular destination in the summer, as is the swimming pool, which is the only long-course pool in Pittsburgh.

MELLON PARK

Corner of 5th Ave. and Shady Ave., 412/255-2676
Map 4

Unlike the majority of Pittsburgh's other

© DAVID FULMER

spring in Mellon Park

public parks, Mellon Park is relatively tiny. If you've ever visited the Pittsburgh Center for the Arts, you've also been in Mellon Park—it's the green space that surrounds the center. The area directly behind the center is a gorgeously restful and hilly expanse—it's also one of the city's quaintest locales for an afternoon or evening picnic. On the opposite side of bustling Fifth Avenue you'll find Mellon Park's Tennis Bubble, a court with a bubble-like covering that protects players from the biting cold throughout the winter and early spring.

SCHENLEY PARK
Boundary St. at Schenley Dr., 412/422-6523, www.pittsburghparks.org
Map 2
Donated to the city by Mary Schenley in the late 1800s and designed by William Falconer, Schenley Park is home to 456 green acres of inner-city paradise. From the Carnegie Library in Oakland, simply stroll over the Panther Hollow Bridge and toward the expanse of hills

and trees; you'll likely forget you're smack-dab in the center of a city in no time.

Recreation opportunities are many and varied on the fields and greens of Schenley, which is one of the largest city-operated parks in the eastern region of the country. Along with its 13 tennis courts, swimming pool, soccer field, running track, ice skating rink, and hiking trails, there's an 18-hole golf course and a relaxing, somewhat secluded lake.

BICYCLING
In 1990, Pittsburgh's cycling community received a mighty blow when *Bicycling* magazine named it one of the 10 worst biking cities in the United States. More than two decades later, a lot of the bad news remains. Pittsburgh motorists, for instance, still show little respect for roadside cyclists. And in the vast majority of the city's neighborhoods, bike lanes remain all but nonexistent.

Yet the biking scene here is slowly improving, thanks largely to the efforts of the nonprofit Bike Pittsburgh organization (www.bike-pgh.org),

ARTS AND LEISURE

CRITICAL MASS

Yes, the infamous bicycle revolution has a monthly ride in Pittsburgh. Established in San Francisco, Critical Mass is an activist-led event that takes place in dozens of cities worldwide once a month. The cyclists always time their ride with the onset of rush hour; the idea is to fill busy urban streets with bikes, thus encouraging motorists to at least contemplate the notion of cheap, nonpolluting forms of alternative transportation. Many of the cyclists at any given Critical Mass claim their ride to be a celebration of biking and not a protest, but do be aware that rides are often monitored by police. Arrests are not unusual. To join Pittsburgh's event, which takes place at 5:30 P.M. on the final Friday of every month, simply show up with a bicycle at the giant dinosaur outside the Carnegie Museum, located on Forbes Avenue in Oakland. Visit www.pghcriticalmass.org for more information.

a grassroots bicycle advocacy group that curates untold numbers of bike-related events in the city, and which holds considerable sway with the powers-that-be in Harrisburg.

Bike shops have lately been opening at a surprisingly rapid clip here as well, while Free Ride (www.freeridepgh.org), a DIY-style society that recycles and reuses old bikes, continues to supply Pittsburghers of all income levels with affordable wheels. There are even two new bicycle magazines being published in Pittsburgh: *Urban Velo* (www.urbanvelo.org) and *Bicycle Times* (www.bicycletimesmag.com). Clearly, some things are beginning to change for the better.

Trails

ELIZA FURNACE TRAIL
Trailhead starts in Downtown and ends in Oakland, north of Schenley Park, www.city.pittsburgh.pa.us/trails
Map 1

Also known as the **Jail Trail** because of the route it takes behind the Downtown Allegheny

County Jail, the Eliza Furnace Trail is a 3.5-mile-long path that is technically an extension of the Three Rivers Heritage Trail. Much of the route runs right alongside a major expressway, and it would be misleading to pretend that more than a small stretch or two of the Eliza Furnace is a peaceful pathway. Its beauty, however, lies in its location; the trail starts smack-dab in the center of Downtown, and it has a convenient exit point in North Oakland, right in between the Pitt and CMU campuses. This is an obvious boon to any of the thousands of East Enders who work Downtown, as any other route into the city is fraught with unruly traffic and undue stress.

To enter the trail from Downtown, travel south on Grant Street, away from the Strip District and toward the Monongahela River. The trail literally abuts the river, so keep going and you'll eventually run into it.

THREE RIVERS HERITAGE TRAIL
Heinz Field to the 40th Street Bridge, alongside the Allegheny River, www.friendsoftheriverfront.org
Map 1

Stretching for nearly 40 miles along both sides of the Allegheny, Monongahela, and Ohio Rivers, the well-maintained Three Rivers Heritage Trail begins as a concrete path on the North Shore, where it runs right alongside the Allegheny River. The trail is an absolute treat for urban cyclists, joggers, and walkers. The length of the trail running through the North Shore is also where you'll find the **Vietnam Veterans Monument,** the **Korean Veterans Memorial,** and the gigantic, striking, and somewhat controversial (because of its lumpy appearance) **Mister Rogers Statue.**

The Vietnam memorial, which features life-size statues of soldiers returning home from war to greet their families, stands mere feet from the Allegheny shoreline and almost exactly between Heinz Field and PNC Park. It's capped by an egg-shaped canopy meant to symbolize a hibiscus flower, which represents rebirth and regeneration and is native to tropical regions throughout the world, including Southeast Asia. The Korean War memorial is a bit farther east; it represents the 2,401 Pennsylvanians who died during the war. (California is the only state in the country that suffered more losses.) The memorial features a number of tall but thin blocks, fanned into a semicircle design. During certain times of the day, columns of sunlight, which the memorial's designer hoped would represent aspects of both shared and individual experiences, stream through the blocks. There are also commemorative plaques on the site documenting the war's chronology and a memorial wall engraved with names of the fallen soldiers. You'll find the Mister Rodgers statue atop the Manchester Bridge Pier, which sits just outside the south entrance to Heinz Field.

THE GREAT ALLEGHENY PASSAGE: BICYCLING FROM PITTSBURGH TO WASHINGTON, D.C.

If you live in Pittsburgh, driving to Washington, D.C., is a bore. The turnpike is long and lugubrious, and the dwarfish hills roll on forever. At five hours, the drive is *just* too long – and once you hit the beltway traffic, Pittsburghers regret ever leaving home.

But thanks to the Great Allegheny Passage (www.gaptrail.org), biking to the nation's capital is an overland adventure. After years of construction, cyclists can now pedal from southern Pittsburgh to Cumberland, Maryland, and from there take the **C&O Canal Towpath** (www.bikewashington.org/canal) straight into Washington. Based on a retired railroad line, the Passage winds along the **Youghiogheny River,** bisects **Ohiopyle State Park,** passes over the **Laurel Highlands,** and slices through a number of quirky Pennsylvania towns.

Now nearly complete, the Passage is among the longest, most scenic **Rails-To-Trails** projects in North America. And with the right preparation, almost anybody can ride it.

The path is mostly even gravel, and although cyclists have to pump the entire way (there's not much coasting), the level ground makes for easy progress. Travelers will relish the views of hills and water, and every few hours a freight train huffs its way across the river, its whistle echoing down the valley. You'll cross truss bridges and pass hidden factories, and – most titillating of all – you'll pass through **Big Savage Tunnel,** a 3,295-foot-long tunnel that cuts clean through **Big Savage Mountain.** Don't worry, though – the inside is lit.

The Passage is still a work in progress, and you'll find some patchy spots right away. For instance, the trail does not yet link between Pittsburgh's South Side and the official trailhead in Boston (Pennsylvania), a major flaw that engineers hope to correct in the near future. For now, cyclists are encouraged to bike through Squirrel Hill and descend the Homestead Grays Bridge, then take riverside roads until reaching the town of Duquesne. It's a little convoluted, but a good map will set you straight.

Most bikers only ride parts of the Passage – from Pittsburgh to Ohiopyle, where they meet friends for whitewater rafting ventures, or from Pittsburgh to Cumberland, thus completing the 150-mile tour. The full mega-transect to D.C. takes about a week; more and more riders complete the C&O section each year. Sensible people will prefer the late spring or early fall, as the region gets hot and humid in summer. Keep in mind that lodging is often seasonal, and the towns are pretty spread out (if you're leaving West Newton, for instance, Connellsville lies a full 26 miles down the way).

Cyclists can ride the Passage on their own, or they can call any number of touring companies. Whatever your level, the Passage doesn't require a lot of cross-country training, only a good road bike, ample supplies, and some maintenance skills. Whether you try an afternoon excursion or a seven-day odyssey, the Passage will almost certainly take *you* for a ride.

(Contributed by Robert Isenberg, a writer and stage performer based in Pittsburgh. His book about traveling in post-war Yugoslavia, The Archipelago, *is available from Autumn House Press.)*

ARTS AND LEISURE

Continue east along the path, with the river on your right, and soon the walkway will turn to dirt. Eventually the massive Heinz factory will appear on your left; much of it was recently converted into loft apartments.

The dirt trail turns to rock and begins to peter out around the 40th Street Bridge, at which point you'll have to turn around and head back to the city. Another option would be to explore the 13-acre **Millvale Riverfront Park,** which sits underneath the bridge. The park is home to a gazebo, a covered picnic pavilion, and the training facility of the Three Rivers Rowing Association.

To discover the route's other stretches, take note of the map-covered plaques that line the trail. An interactive online map and downloadable PDF maps of the Three Rivers Heritage Trail can be found online at www.friendsoftheriverfront.org.

Resources
DASANI BLUE BIKES PROGRAM
33 Terminal Way, off E. Carson St., 412/488-0212
`Map 3`

Organized by Friends of the Riverfront, the corporate-sponsored Dasani Blue Bikes Program offers the use of an absolutely free bike—a sky-blue beach cruiser—for anyone wishing to explore the length of the city's Three Rivers Heritage Trail. The bikes are stored in a locker at the start of the trail near Terminal Way on the South Side, but it's necessary to first visit the Friends of the Riverfront office, where riders will be issued a swipe card after showing a state-issued driver's license or passport. The cards are then validated for one year, and only two rules apply: Bikes must be returned before dark, and they're to be used on the Heritage Trail only. (Although we seriously doubt you'd be taken away in handcuffs if you veered off the path here and there.)

FREE RIDE
214 N. Lexington Ave., inside Construction Junction, 412/254-3774, www.freeridepgh.org
`Map 5`

Staffed by the sort of cycling enthusiasts you'd expect to find leading a Critical Mass rally, Free Ride is a recycle-a-bike shop where old and discarded rides are given a new lease on life. The program works like this: Bikes are donated to Free Ride in a generally sorry state of disrepair. Volunteers spend hours in the shop bringing the bikes up to code. The resulting mountain bikes, road bikes, and BMX bikes are then sold at affordable rates.

The deal is even better if you already own a beat-up ride: The mechanics at Free Ride will help out with repairs at no charge, and will even educate riders about bike maintenance along the way. But here's the rub: Anyone who receives free assistance is asked to give back by volunteering a bit of his or her time at the shop. Marxism on two wheels and a saddle seat, you might say.

SPECTATOR SPORTS
Thanks to the Steelers' two recent Super Bowl victories, in 2006 and 2009, local sports fanatics have once again had good reason to think of Pittsburgh as the City of Champions. And although the Pirates continue to be ranked toward the bottom of the National League, as they have been for seemingly countless seasons now, the Penguins have scored something of a recent victory with the opening of a brand-new arena known as the CONSOL Energy Center.

To be certain, interest in pro sports never really seems to wane in Pittsburgh, regardless of the current standing of the town's teams. Also popular are the exceptionally talented University of Pittsburgh squads; the men's football and basketball teams especially are followed with something approaching religious fervor.

Baseball
PITTSBURGH PIRATES
PNC Park box office, corner of Federal and General Robinson Sts., 800/289-2827 (tickets), http://pittsburgh.pirates.mlb.com
COST: $9 general admission (bleacher seats)
`Map 1`

There certainly aren't many Major League

COURTESY OF ROB MATHENY

PNC Park, home of the Pittsburgh Pirates

Baseball teams in existence today with re-cords as disappointingly poor as that of the Pittsburgh Pirates. Following a 2009 de-feat by the Chicago Cubs, for instance, the Pirates earned the unfortunate distinction of having the longest consecutive run of losing seasons not just in baseball, but in any North American professional sport. What's more, the club's 2010 season was its 18th losing season in a row. Ouch.

Still, a small but dedicated core of diehard fans continues to follow the team on televi-sion and, to a slightly lesser degree, at the ballpark.

What's more, Buccos game tickets are af-fordable and exceedingly easy to come by, even on game day. Seats can be found for as low as $17 at www.stubhub.com, while general ad-mission bleacher tickets (purchased at the PNC Park box office) go for just $9.

Basketball

The hardcore B-movie fanatics among you may be able to recall *The Fish that Saved Pittsburgh*, a 1979 film that portrayed a pro basketball team with skills so poor that an astrologer (Stockard Channing) was brought in to assist. But alas, the Pittsburgh Pythons were nothing more than a fictional crew, and to this day the Steel City lacks an NBA team.

DUQUESNE DUKES

1302 Forbes Ave., A. J. Palumbo Center, 412/232-3853 (tickets), www.goduquesne.com

COST: $9 pp; group and student discounts available

Map 1

College basketball fans who can't score tickets to a Panthers match might instead check out the Duquesne Dukes, a much-lauded Atlantic 10 Conference crew that calls Duquesne University home. According to *U.S. News & World Report,* the Dukes have nearly as much prowess in the classroom as they do on the court: The magazine recently ranked the school's athletic program 15th in terms of grad-uation rates.

ARTS AND LEISURE

COURTESY OF ROB MATHENY

panther statue outside Heinz Field

PITT PANTHERS

3719 Terrace St., Petersen Events Center,
412/648-8076, www.petersenevents center.com
COST: Free
Map 2

Probably the most popular b-ball squad in the city, the University of Pittsburgh's Pitt Panthers are a Big East crew frequently ranked near the top of the league. Home games are played at the recently built Petersen Events Center—it's generally favored by sports journalists as one of the county's finest college basketball arenas. Also of interest at Petersen is the **McCall Panthers Hall of Champions.** Located in the center's lobby, it displays decades worth of Pitt athletics achievements. The hall is open Monday–Friday, 9 A.M.–5 P.M., as well as during all men's basketball games.

Football
PITT PANTHERS

100 Art Rooney Ave., Heinz Field, 800/643-7488 or 412/648-7488 (tickets), www.pittsburghpanthers.com
COST: $50 general admission; $25 student with

University of Pittsburgh Student ID; $85-285 sideline, endzone, box, and club seats
Map 1

The University of Pittsburgh's Pitt Panthers football squad has a particularly impressive history, with possibly an even more impressive list of famous alumni. Dan Marino, Tony Dorsett, Mike Ditka, Pop Warner, and scores of NFL players have all spent time as Panthers. Perhaps fittingly, the team now plays its home games at Heinz Field, which is also the home base of the Pittsburgh Steelers. The Panthers' most intense rivalry is with the West Virginia University Mountaineers; the two teams meet every Thanksgiving for a game known as the Backyard Brawl. The Brawl is an experience not to be missed, although tickets are hard to come by. Pitt and the Penn State Nittany Lions also maintain a healthy rivalry.

To purchase game tickets, visit the team's website or www.petersenevents center.com. You can also purchase tickets at the Petersen Events Center Ticket Office (corner of Desoto and Terrace Streets in Oakland). The office is open Monday–Friday 8:30 A.M.–5 P.M.

ARTS AND LEISURE

CATCHING STEELERMANIA

No matter how long or short your visit to Pittsburgh, and no matter the time of year or the purpose of your stay, and regardless of your interest in professional sports, you're nearly guaranteed at some point to find yourself in the midst of a conversation about the Pittsburgh Steelers, our town's six-time Super Bowl–winning NFL superstars. It's been said, in fact, that Pittsburgh's popular culture and Steelers culture are essentially one and the same. And if you're lucky, you may even run into a local fan afflicted with a full-fledged case of Steelermania; believe me when I tell you there are more than a few of them about.

In the summer of 2010, in fact, the Carnegie Mellon art professor Jon Rubin beautifully documented Steelermania by curating "Whatever It Takes" at the school's Miller Gallery; it was a simply awe-inspiring exhibition of Steelers fan collections both passionate and bizarre. It introduced the city to a wide variety of Steelers superfans, including Ron Vergerio, better known as "Steeler Ron" (www.steeler-

ron.com), who has spent the past seven years covering nearly every inch of his body with Steelers-themed tattoos.

So-called "Steelers rooms," residential spaces packed floor-to-ceiling with all manner of Steelers memorabilia, are also popular throughout Western Pennsylvania. The overwhelmingly cluttered Steelers man-cave of Carnegie resident Denny DeLuca was featured in the Miller Gallery exhibition and can still be seen on the gallery's website. But a simple Google search will turn up dozens of similar rooms, from the embarrassingly garish to the truly astonishing.

To experience a taste of Steelermania without even leaving your own hometown, pay a visit to one of the hundreds of Steelers bars around the country; these are pubs where displaced Pittsburghers gather during game days to cheer on the black-and-gold. A directory of national and even international Steelers bars can be found online at www.steelersbars.com, www.steeleraddicts.com, and www.post-gazette.com/steelernation.

© DAN ELDRIDGE

a van transformed by a Steeler fan

PITTSBURGH PASSION

930 E. Carson St., George Cupples Stadium,
724/452-9395, www.pittsburghpasssion.com
COST: $14 adult, $7 child and student, $10 senior and
military
Map 3

Formed in 2002, the Pittsburgh Passion is a professional, all-women's contact football team and a member of the National Women's Football Association (NWFA). Oddly, the majority of the players had very little football experience before joining the Passion. Some had barely played the game at all, and instead came from softball, volleyball, soccer, basketball, lacrosse, or hockey backgrounds. In other words, you'll want to pack your sense of humor along with the beer coolers and binoculars. The Passion plays home games from late April through mid-June at George Cupples Stadium.

PITTSBURGH POWER

1001 Fifth Ave., CONSOL Energy Center, 888/769-2011,
www.consolenergycenter.com,
www.pittsburghpowerfootball.com
COST: $15-180; season tickets are also available
Map 1

This banner at Heinz Field celebrates the Pittsburgh Steelers, six-time Super Bowl champions.

Slated to begin its first eight-game season in April 2011, and co-owned by the legendary Steelers Hall of Fame receiver Lynn Swann, the Pittsburgh Power is a team new to the Arena Football League—it was added during a recent four-team league expansion. Chris Siegfried, most recently of the Arkansas Twisters, will act as the Power's head coach, while Bernard Morris, who spent one year each with the Arkansas Twisters and the Jacksonville Sharks, will be the team's first starting quarterback. And as for the team's color scheme? You guessed it: black and gold.

PITTSBURGH STEELERS

100 Art Rooney Ave., Heinz Field, 412/323-1200,
www.steelers.com
COST: $100-900
Map 1

As the fifth-oldest team in the NFL, and the franchise with perhaps the most widespread fan base of any professional football club, it's no exaggeration whatsoever to think of the Pittsburgh Steelers as a way of life—or even a religion—for many locals here. Indeed, Steelermania and Pittsburgh culture can easily be thought of as one and the same. And although the Steelers in 2008–2009 managed to claim an unprecedented sixth Super Bowl victory—the first and only team in the history of the NFL to do so—it's probably fair to say that the so-called "Super Steelers" of the 1970s still stand out in most fans' minds as the crew to permanently define the organization.

Steelers tickets are notoriously hard to come by. Your best bet is the scalpers who troll outside all home games, but be forewarned that scalping is technically illegal; purchase tickets (none of which are guaranteed to be authentic) at your own risk. Fans can also try calling the Steelers ticket office at 412/323-1200.

ARTS AND LEISURE

COURTESY OF ROB MATHENY

Hockey
PITTSBURGH PENGUINS

1001 Fifth Ave., CONSOL Energy Center, 412/642-1800, www.consolenergycenter.com, http://penguins.nhl.com

COST: $45-215

`Map 1`

Less popular than the Steelers but followed with much more seriousness and intensity than the Pirates, the Penguins arrived in Pittsburgh in 1967 when the NHL expanded by adding six clubs. And although the team's first two decades were fairly unremarkable, the tables began to turn significantly when the legendary Mario Lemieux was added to the roster in the mid-1980s. Indeed, in 1992 the Penguins took home the Stanley Cup for the second time in a row.

Today, "Super Mario" Lemieux is the Penguins' owner, and following a fairly bitter dispute concerning the club's future, the

REMEMBER THE IGLOO

You might say it all started back in 2004, when Pittsburgh Penguins owner Mario Lemieux presented the city with something of an unfortunate ultimatum: Build my team a new hockey arena, he threatened, or I'll take them to another town. Back then, the Penguins had been playing home games at Mellon Arena — formerly known as the Civic Arena, and lovingly referred to by fans as the Igloo — since 1967, and Lemieux's gripes about the stadium were certainly warranted. It was old, beat-up, and dusty. And its famous retractable dome roof barely worked; it hadn't been opened or closed in ages.

These days, the Penguins play hockey inside the brand-new CONSOL Energy Center, which sits just across the street from the old arena. But now, the city has another controversy on its hands: Although original plans called for razing Mellon Arena and building a mixed-use retail and housing development in its place, a group of historic preservationists known as Save the Igloo has since voiced its own dissenting opinion. The group wants the arena preserved as a historic monument. And thanks to the dome's retractable roof, it's apparently a contender to be placed on the National Register of Historic Places.

Nearly everyone in the city, it seems, has an opinion about whether or not the Igloo should be preserved. A recent economic feasibility study concluded that it would make more financial sense to demolish the arena. The preservationists, on the other hand, contend that turning the Igloo into a town square, complete with restaurants and a hotel, could bring untold tourism dollars into the city.

But regardless of anyone's grand plan for the Mellon Arena and its surrounding 28-acre plot, the decision ultimately rests with the arena's owner, the Sports and Exhibition Authority. And in mid-September 2010, the SEA voted unanimously to have it demolished.

Technically speaking, however, the story isn't over just yet. If the preservationists can somehow prove the arena's historic status, the demolition may be stalled. But for all intents and purposes, it looks as if one more part of Pittsburgh's 20th-century experience is near to entering the history books, and disappearing from the present altogether.

the Mellon Arena, also known as the Igloo

COURTESY OF ROB MATHENY

Pens have since relocated to the brand-new CONSOL Energy Center.

For information about purchasing individual game tickets or season tickets, visit http://penguins.nhl.com or visit the CONSOL Energy Center box office. Tickets are also available for sale by season ticket holders at www.ticketmaster.com/ticketexchange.

Horse Racing

LADBROKE AT THE MEADOWS

210 Racetrack Rd., Washington, 724/225-9300, www.themeadowsracing.com

`Map 7`

About a half hour's drive south of Pittsburgh is Ladbroke at the Meadows, a harness facility with a year-round racing schedule; its website proclaims it as "Greater Pittsburgh's best-kept secret." That may be something of a stretch, but because of its somewhat secluded location near the town of Canonsburg, it is true that the Meadows doesn't see the sort of traffic it probably deserves. Admission and parking are both free at the Meadows, which offers both casual and fine-dining options. Check out the facility online for live racing schedules and wagering information, or call any one of the Meadows's off-track betting locations if you'd rather not visit the track: New Castle (2004 W. State St., 724/654-2221), Harmarville (1 Anchor Dr., 412/828-0610), Coraopolis (7700 University Blvd., 412/262-3100), or West Mifflin (7025 Clairton Rd., 412/650-9000).

Rugby

Although the combative sport of rugby is still a relative novelty in North America, its popularity in Pittsburgh seems to be growing. The **Pittsburgh Rugby Club,** for instance, claims more than 300 members of all ages and both sexes. Aside from simply playing, the club is also a do-good nonprofit organization that occasionally does its bit to help out with various community service projects.

If you'd simply like to see the teams rumble, however, head over to www.pghrugby.com and view the upcoming schedules; most matches take place in Boyce Park.

PITTSBURGH HARLEQUINS RUGBY FOOTBALL CLUB

Eisele Rd. at Cove Run Rd., Founders Field, Indianola, www.pittsburghharlequins.org

COST: Free

`Map 7`

Especially serious are the players of the Pittsburgh Harlequins Rugby Football Club. The club was founded in 1973 and today is a member of the USA Rugby Football Union, the Mid-Atlantic Rugby Football Union, and the Potomac Rugby Union. The team plays on a green known as Founders Field, which is located about 16 miles from Downtown Pittsburgh in Indianola. Visit the team's website for an updated game schedule.

RUGGERS PUB

40 S. 22nd St., 412/381-1330, www.ruggerspub.com

HOURS: Daily 11 A.M.-2 A.M.

COST: Free

`Map 3`

To get a feel for the size and intensity of Pittsburgh's rugby scene yourself, show up at

Ruggers Pub

Ruggers Pub, which also serves as the local headquarters of the Pittsburgh Rugby Club. The players congregate and refuel here after local matches. The experience of seeing a team fill the pub after a win can be quite eye-opening, especially for Americans who know little about the, uh, ruggedness of the sport. Naturally, matches are shown on the telly here, but if you'd rather hit the field yourself, contact the area club at www.pghrugby.com. For information about joining the **South Pittsburgh Hooligans Men's Rugby Club,** call 412/734-8998 or visit www.southpittrugby.com.

WATER ACTIVITIES

For a city with a geographical nucleus surrounded on three sides by waterways, it's surprising that Pittsburgh's captains of industry haven't devised more ways to take advantage of perhaps the town's loveliest natural resource. But dive deep enough, and you'll find more than a thing or two to keep you busy off dry land. The local nonprofit organization **Venture Outdoors** (304 Forbes Ave., 2nd Fl., Downtown, 412/2555-0564, www.ventureoutdoors.org) is responsible for a surprisingly large percentage of the activities that take place on Pittsburgh's rivers; check its website or newsletter for a bevy of outdoorsy activities, both water- and land-related.

Rowing and Kayaking
◖ KAYAK PITTSBURGH
412/969-9090, www.kayakpittsburgh.org
HOURS: Mon.-Fri. 11 A.M.-dusk, Sat.-Sun. 10 A.M.-dusk
COST: Free Mon.-Fri., $5 Sat.-Sun.
Map 1

Kayak Pittsburgh offers what may very well be the most enjoyable and affordable way to explore Pittsburgh's waterways. The company rents flat-water kayaks that even the completely non-experienced can easily navigate. Canoes and hydrobikes are also available. To reach the rental shack, cross the Sixth Street Bridge (also known as the Roberto Clemente Bridge) from Downtown and head toward the North Side; the shack sits underneath the staircase, adjacent to PNC Park. Rental prices for solo

YACHTING AND BOATING FACILITIES

We know what you're thinking: Yachts, marinas, and pleasure craft in working-class *Pittsburgh?* Believe it. In fact, locals self-conscious of the town's rough-and-tumble image have long boasted of the fact that Allegheny County has more registered boats – more than 25,000 – than any other county in the state. Maybe there's more blue blood than blue collar in Pittsburgh these days, after all.

Understandably, rising fuel costs have lately cleared the channels of the rivers to some degree. But for boaters to whom $3 a gallon isn't an issue, the local waterways remain indisputably picturesque locales in which to take to the drink. The Downtown skyline and city parks take on an almost majestic presence when viewed from a floating vessel. And words can barely describe the extraordinary experience of moving on water past the industrial detritus and shuttered steel mills that line the river's outer reaches.

Newcomers to the area might want to start their exploration of the yachting scene online at the website of **National Safe Boating Council** (www.safeboatingcouncil.org), which maintains a Pittsburgh chapter.

Particularly popular with the area's biggest-spending boaters, **Fox Chapel Marine Sales & Service** (1366 Old Freeport Rd., 412/967-1500, www.foxchapelmarine.com) claims to have the largest selection of both new and used craft in the tri-state area. Financing is available here, and the dealership often runs specials on pre-owned boats and new boats alike.

Once it's time to start laying out cash, a trip to **P&L Boat Sales** (1401 Preble Ave., Manchester, 412/323-1010, www.pandlboatsales.com) might be in order. The pleasure craft retailer is located right next to the West End Bridge in Manchester on the North Side, and has not only a knowledgeable staff but also a wide selection of boats on display in its showroom.

kayaks are $15 for the first hour and $8 for every additional half-hour. Kayak Pittsburgh also does business in the three-foot-deep Lake Elizabeth, located in the North Side's Allegheny Commons (near the National Aviary). A perfect location for kayaking with kids, rentals are free at Lake Elizabeth on weekdays, and just $5 per boat on weekends. North Park Lake is the company's other kayaking locale, although at the time of writing it was closed for dredging. Kayak Pittsburgh Downtown is open from May to October 31.

THREE RIVERS ROWING ASSOCIATION
412/231-8772, www.threeriversrowing.org
COST: Annual membership dues $385 adult, $720 families, $215 student; membership rates include full facility usage, kayak, scull, sweep, and dragon boat usage, and program discounts
Map 1

Pittsburgh's Three Rivers Rowing Association is a nonprofessional group that organizes rowing and kayaking activities and events on the Allegheny River. Anyone is welcome to join in or become a member, regardless of age or experience. The TRRA has two facilities, one on Washington's Landing under the 31st Street Bridge, and another in the Millvale Waterfront Park, underneath the 40th Street Bridge. But exploring the association's website before stopping by would be prudent; there you'll find detailed information about kayak tours, rowing classes and events, listings for sweep and sculling classes, information about joining a Dragon Boat team, and quite a bit more. Call for information about purchasing an annual membership, which provides access to all TRRA facilities and equipment. Activities generally take place between April and November.

Fishing
DOWNTOWN TRIANGLERS/ VENTURE OUTDOORS
304 Forbes Ave., 2nd Fl., 412/255-0564, www.ventureoutdoors.org
Map 1

Pittsburgh's ubiquitous Venture Outdoors group is also responsible for creating what may indeed be the city's strangest waterway activity: **Urban Fishing,** hosted by the Downtown TriAnglers. Every Wednesday 11:30 A.M.–1:30 P.M. during the summer season (May 5–Sept. 29), Downtown office workers and all would-be fishers are invited to cast a reel into the drink; fishing takes place at the North Shore Riverfront Park, which is easily accessed on foot by crossing any of the bridges spanning the Allegheny River. (Call in advance to inquire about the TriAnglers' specific location, as fishing spots tend to change from week to week.) Rods, reels, and bait are provided for a flat $20 season fee ($5 day passes are also available), although fishers will need to show a Pennsylvania fish license ($21), which can be purchased at sporting goods stores such as Dick's (350 E. Waterfront Dr., 412/446-9940, www.dickssportinggoods.com) or online at www.fish.state.pa.us. Thanks to ongoing efforts to keep the rivers clean, you can expect to snag a variety of smallmouth bass, catfish, and carp.

KEYSTONE BASS BUDDIES
www.kbass.com

The largest fishing tournament club in the state of Pennsylvania, the Keystone Bass Buddies is something of a cross between a social club and a competitive team. Members gather often to practice their respective angling techniques in a number of Western Pennsylvania's rivers. For more information about the group, or to download a membership application, visit the not-for-profit organization's website or email steve@kbass.com.

Water Park
SANDCASTLE
1000 Sandcastle Dr., Homestead, 412/462-6666, www.sandcastlewaterpark.com
HOURS: Mid-June-late-Aug. daily 11 A.M.-6 P.M.
COST: $29.99 adult, $23.99 adult after 3 P.M., $19.99 senior and child under 48 inches
Map 7

Sandcastle is one of the Pittsburgh area's premiere amusement parks, second in popularity only to Kennywood. The park is located in Homestead next to the Waterfront shopping complex and boasts 14 water slides, a wave pool, hot tubs, and a children's area. Special events include "Dive in Movies," during which family-friendly films are projected above a pool, and the "Waves Under 18 Party," a dance party that, yes, takes place in a wave pool. After dark, the over-21s head to Sandbar, an on-site outdoor nightclub.

WINTER RECREATION
Ice Skating
If you've never before had the pleasure of skating on ice, be aware that it's a much more difficult endeavor than inline skating. In Pittsburgh, a good place to learn the basics is the **Airport Ice Arena** (330 Hookstown Grade Rd., Parkway West, Moon Township, 412/264-2222, www.airporticearena.com), where future hockey players and figure skaters also train.

ICE CASTLE ARENA
990 Castle Shannon Blvd., Castle Shannon, 412/561-9090, www.icecastlearena.com
HOURS: Call for hours of operation
COST: $7 general admission, child 5 and under free
Map 7

The indoor Ice Castle Arena in Castle Shannon is open year-round; public skating takes places on two NHL regulation-size rinks. Beginning adult skaters and children can take lessons at the Ice Castle, which is also a perfect location to host a child's birthday party.

THE RINK AT PPG PLACE
PPG Place, 412/394-3641, www.ppgplace.com/rink
HOURS: Mon.-Thurs. 11 A.M.-10 P.M., Fri.-Sat. 11 A.M.-midnight, Sun. noon-8 P.M.
COST: $7 adult, $6 child and senior; skate rental $3
Map 1

The Rink at PPG Place is Downtown Pittsburgh's version of the winter skating experience at Manhattan's Rockefeller Center (although PPG is actually 2,000 square feet larger). Located directly south of Market Square in the shadow of Philip Johnson's dramatic PPG Place building, the rink opens for business every year on Light Up Night in November and closes in early March. The experience of circling the rink's lighted

Christmas tree, especially after dark, is absolutely unforgettable.

SCHENLEY PARK SKATING RINK
1 Overlook Dr., 412/422-6523
HOURS: Call for hours of operation
COST: $4 adult, $3 senior and child (17 and under); skate rental $2.50
Map 2

The Schenley Park Skating Rink, located near the park's tennis courts and baseball fields, is open from November through March. Inline skaters and roller hockey players often fill the rink during the summer months. And since students from nearby Pitt and CMU flock here on weekend nights, the rink can be a decent place to take a first date—or to find a first date. Should your coupling turn into something more serious, consider returning on February 14 for the annual "Valentine's on Ice" event.

Skiing, Snowboarding, and Snowmobiling
The ski and snowboarding season in Western Pennsylvania generally runs from mid-December through mid-March, weather conditions permitting. But even when the powder isn't falling, it's usually still possible to hit the slopes, as the area's better resorts cover their mountains in artificial snow when Mother Nature fails to provide.

Snowmobile hobbyists might want to visit the website of the **Pennsylvania State Snowmobile Association** (www.pasnow.org, 888/411-7772), which works to maintain trails and a high level of snowmobiling safety throughout the state.

For more information about ski areas and resorts statewide, consult the Pennsylvania Ski Area Association at www.skipa.com.

BOYCE PARK
675 Old Frankstown Rd., Monroeville, 724/733-4665, 724/733-4656, www.alleghenycounty.us/parks/bpfac.aspx
Map 7

The ski slopes at Boyce Park won't be of much

interest to the advanced skier, but they're ideal for beginners and the generally timid. And because Boyce Park is located in nearby Monroeville, this is the perfect choice for a day trip. Snowboarders here have access to two quarter pipes and one of the longest half pipes in Pennsylvania. Adult slope fees are a reasonable $10 a day.

HIDDEN VALLEY
FOUR SEASON RESORT
1 Craighead Dr., Hidden Valley, 814/443-8000,
www.hiddenvalleyresort.com
Map 7

Hidden Valley Four Season Resort is located in the picturesque Laurel Highlands, about 60 miles east of the city. Although it started life more than 50 years ago as a family-run bed-and-breakfast, it now offers a year-round schedule of activities, including downhill and cross-country skiing, hiking, biking, and golfing. The ever-popular Seven Springs Resort is nearby, as is the white-water rafting destination of Ohiopyle. The 28 different trails and slopes at Hidden Valley are open roughly 9 A.M.–9 P.M.; call 866/443-7544 for snow reports. Adult lift tickets are $30–54 on weekends, $25–30 on weekdays. Adult season passes are $545.

NEMACOLIN WOODLANDS RESORT
1001 LaFayette Dr., Farmington, 800/422-2736,
www.nemacolin.com
Map 7

This is a truly luxurious vacation spot offering all manner of recreation possibilities, including adventure sports (off-road driving, fly-fishing), culinary classes, and the occasional wine tasting. Skiers and snowboarders can take advantage of 10 separate slopes and a half pipe atop the 2,030-foot Mystic Mountain. Snow tubing is also big here. Nemacolin is located in Fayette County, about 60 miles southeast of the city. Daily adult passes are $38 ($20 for cross-country skiing or snowshoeing); adult season passes are $129. A 30-minute dog sledding ride, by the way, will set you back $125, or $150 for two riders.

SEVEN SPRINGS MOUNTAIN RESORT
777 Waterwheel Dr., Champion, 800/452-2223,
www.7springs.com
Map 7

The peak at Seven Springs Mountain Resort has an elevation of nearly 3,000 feet with a vertical drop of 750 feet; it boasts 14 slopes and 17 trails. Its longest trail is 1.25 miles long. No wonder Seven Springs is one of the area's most popular ski resorts. (*Ski Magazine* rated it the number-one resort in the mid-Atlantic.) The expert-level snowboard park is 400 feet wide and 500 feet long. Daily lift ticket rates range from $38 to $68, while season pass rates vary; call for detailed information. To call the snow report, dial 800/523-7777.

SNOZONE
1530 Hamilton Rd., Bethel Park, 412/831-5080,
www.snozone.net
Map 7

Not up for a ski trip, but still want to have fun in the snow? Check out the tubing scene at SnoZone, which recently moved to a new location on the grounds of the Cool Springs Golf and Family Recreation Center (www.coolspringsgolfcenter.com) in Bethel Park. Tubers can zoom down what is certainly one of the longest runs in the region, which gets covered in piles of fluffy faux-snow whenever the weather fails to comply. Rates range between $12 and $16 for adults and children; season passes are $125.

GYMS AND HEALTH CLUBS
If you're looking to get in a good workout while in Pittsburgh, you're in luck, no matter what your income level or, for that matter, your current physical condition. Because just like fitness fanatics themselves, exercise facilities here come in nearly every shape and size. There are state-of-the-art clubs filled with steam rooms and beautiful people. There are no-frills iron pumping gyms that might befit a Rocky Balboa in training. And thankfully, there's just about everything else in between.

CLUB ONE

6325 Penn Ave., 412/362-4608
HOURS: Mon.-Thurs. 5:30 A.M.-10 P.M., Fri.
5:30 A.M.-9 P.M., Sat.-Sun. 8 A.M.-6 P.M.
Map 6

With memberships currently running at about $80 per month, this is certainly one of the pricier fitness facilities in town. But Club One isn't just a gym, it's a full-fledged health club complete with a heated swimming pool overseen by a lifeguard, a basketball court, a complete schedule of yoga and aerobics classes that take place in an upstairs studio, and a racquetball court. And the clean and spacious locker rooms, complete with complimentary toiletries, are a thing of true beauty.

FITNESS FACTORY

212 S. Highland Ave., 412/362-6306,
www.fitnessfactorypgh.com
HOURS: Daily 24 hours
Map 4

There's much to recommend about Shadyside's Fitness Factory, which sits right on the border of Shadyside and the recently gentrified corner of East Liberty. For starters, the membership rates are seriously competitive. In fact, with the exception of Edgewood's new Planet Fitness location, you're not likely to find a better deal anywhere in town.

The equipment is relatively run-of-the-mill, and some of it is slightly outdated, but there seems to be more than enough of almost everything, and lines rarely form around even the most popular pieces of equipment. And while you won't find a pool or sauna, there is a tanning bed and a steady stream of eardrum-shattering house music blasting from the sound system. The clientele is generally friendly, accommodating, and college-aged.

PLANET FITNESS

1635 S. Braddock Ave., 412/244-3440,
www.planetfitness.com
HOURS: Mon.-Fri. 24 hours, Sat.-Sun. 7 A.M.-7 P.M.
Map 7

Conveniently located in the Edgewood Town Centre plaza, this is the only Planet Fitness franchise found within Pittsburgh proper—the other area club is in West Mifflin's Century Square shopping center, at 3505 Mountain View Drive. Planet Fitness, of course, is the purple and gold–hued chain that has locations popping up in strip malls and suburban areas across the country with alarming speed. For anyone not in the know, the company's two main claims to fame are its "no judgments" attitude and its unbelievably low membership rates—generally around $10 per month.

Serious weightlifters should keep in mind that Planet Fitness isn't necessarily a place to get pumped; free weights are relatively scarce, whereas cardio equipment fills nearly 50 percent of the room. Still, the equipment here is always new and in top-working order. If it's a budget-minded workout you're after, Planet Fitness is seriously tough to beat.

PNC YMCA

236 Fifth Ave., 412/471-9622,
www.ymcaofpittsburgh.org, www.newyintown.org
HOURS: Mon.-Fri. 5 A.M.-9 P.M., Sat. 7 A.M.-5 P.M., Sun.
10 A.M.-3 P.M.
Map 1

If you're searching for a gym in Downtown, consider skipping Bally's and take a tour of the city's newest YMCA location instead, which sits right in Market Square. The $4.2 million location is truly a sight to behold; among numerous other amenities it features 42,000 square feet of space, a 25-meter indoor pool, and a wellness center stocked with cardio and weight-training equipment. There are also step aerobics and stress-management classes, yoga programs, and personal nutrition counseling. Membership fees are $60–85 per month, as well as a one-time initiation fee of $100.

SOUTH SIDE ATHLETIC CLUB

2026 E. Carson St., 412/488-1120
HOURS: Mon.-Fri. 5 A.M.-9 P.M., Sat.-Sun. 8 A.M.-4 P.M.
Map 3

A fairly cut-and-dried exercise room with a convenient location, the facilities at the South

ARTS AND LEISURE

Side Athletic Club are about as simple as they come: One cardio room and one free-weight and Nautilus room, with a reception desk separating the two. It might not sound like much, but the gym pickins' are exceedingly slim on the South Side; your only other option here is the somewhat daunting Southside Ironworks, which is located in an out-of-the-way spot near the Birmingham Bridge.

URBAN ACTIVE FITNESS CLUB
19 Bakery Square Blvd., 412/204-0055, www.urbanactive.com
HOURS: Mon.-Thurs. 5 A.M.-11 P.M., Fri. 5 A.M.-9 P.M., Sat. 8 A.M.-7 P.M., Sun. 9 A.M.-7 P.M.
Map 6

The city's newest fitness club can be found in East Liberty's still-growing Bakery Square development, and boy is it a doozy: With its ultra-

---

FITNESS AND RECREATION FOR THE ANTI-JOCK

In a town where the act of consuming a 16-ounce can of Iron City Beer is often spoken of as a metaphor for exercise (locals like to talk of "pumping a pint of Iron"), it's only fitting that sundry sports and recreational activities should abound for the beer-bellied, the uncoordinated, the unathletic, and the otherwise altogether out-of-shape. Which isn't to say that Pittsburgh's myriad and offbeat outdoor pursuits aren't physically demanding. Consider the local chapter of the Hash House Harriers, for instance: a motley crew of men and women who jog for miles upon miles throughout the city's back streets, stopping only occasionally to raise their spirits, you might say, at a neighborhood tavern.

But whatever your current level of physical vigor, you're almost certain to find some sport or activity of interest in Pittsburgh. In other words, welcome to the City of Champions, where even a 255-pound running back named after a mass-transit vehicle (the Pittsburgh Steelers' Jerome Bettis, a.k.a. "The Bus") can become an honest-to-goodness American hero.

HASH HOUSE HARRIERS
A self-described "drinking club with a running problem," the Hash House Harriers were formed in the 1930s by a group of British soldiers stationed in Malaysia. Looking for a creative way to combine exercise with social activity, they modified the English game of hares and hounds into something of a drinking contest. Today, Hash House Harriers clubs, known as kennels, exist in just about every major city

on Earth – Pittsburgh included. To put it simply, a hash is a combination of a long-distance jog, a scavenger hunt, and a keg party. Anyone is welcome to join in; call the **Pittsburgh Hash Hotline** for details at 412/381-6709, or go online at www.pgh-h3.com.

LAWN BOWLING
Lawn bowling, an ancient Roman game that was first introduced to America by the British, is perfect for players young and old, and regardless of physical fitness. Unlike the variety of bowling that takes place along a wood-paneled lane, part of the strategy involves knocking an opponent's ball out of play. The bowling green in Point Breeze's Frick Park – not far from the Henry Clay Frick estate – is the only such court in the region. Open bowling takes place on Saturdays and Sundays at 1 P.M. For more information, call 412/782-0848, or visit the website of the **Frick Park Lawn Bowls Club** at www.lawnbowlingpittsburgh.org.

LAWNMOWER RACING
Oddball sporting doesn't get much more bizarre than during the lawnmower racing events that take place at the **Shadetree Center in Butler County.** The suburban cowboys who saddle up at the Shadetree generally do so during the weekends (events happen twice a month), and because their lawnmowers are usually jacked up and seriously modified, races can actually be quite thrilling. Visit www.shadetreespeedway.com for schedules, rules, and more. Also useful is www.heymow.com, an Internet message board for lawnmower

modern interior design and slightly space-age lobby, that's simply no other gym like it in the city. Cardio addicts can actually enjoy movies on a big screen in the gym's Cardio Cinema. There are racquetball and basketball courts on-site, as well as a pool, a smoothie bar, a sprint track, and a wonderful collection of new free weights and machines. Guests staying at the adjacent Marriott Springhill Suites can use the facility free of charge.

X SHADYSIDE
5608 Walnut St., 412/363-9999, www.xshadyside.com
HOURS: Mon.-Fri. 24 hours from 6 A.M. Mon. to 9 P.M. on Fri., Sat. 8 A.M.-6 P.M., Sun. 9 A.M.-6 P.M.
Map 4

Although X Shadyside claims to be the city's only 24-hour health and fitness club, it's actually not—the gym closes at 6 P.M. on Saturday and Sunday nights. Still, it is one of two gyms

racers, and www.letsmow.com, the website maintained by – get this – the United States Lawnmower Racing Association.

PINBALL
If you know much at all about pinball, you'll no doubt be impressed to learn that Pittsburgh is home to the **World Pinball Championships,** an annual series organized by PAPA (www.papa.org), the Professional Amateur Pinball Association. The championship games take place in suburban Scott Township. Do be aware, however, that the majority of the flipper fanatics here will be adults, not children. More than $33,000 in prize money changes hands during the tournament; the winner takes home $10,000. For more information about the local pinball scene, visit www.pinburgh.com.

ROCK & BOWL
Looking for an unusual way to spend a Monday evening that involves ugly shoes, indie rock, and cheap beer in plastic cups? You might try paying a visit to **Rock & Bowl at Arsenal Lanes** (212 44th St., 412/683-5992, www.arsenalbowl.com) in Lawrenceville. It's a once-a-week event where hipster types and college kids bowl to the accompaniment of a local rock band. The night will set you back $8, which includes all the frames you can squeeze in between 9 P.M. and the stroke of midnight. And no need to feel self-conscious about your nonexistent bowling skills; while some of Pittsburgh's best bowlers frequently congregate at Arsenal Lanes, they tend to steer clear of this event.

SOAPBOX RACING
Technically illegal and seriously underground, the **Pittsburgh Illegal Soapbox Society** (raunchily taking the acronym "PISS") is a local group of daredevil adrenaline junkies who gather secretly to race homemade soapbox cars down dangerously winding streets. According to the Society's website, "fresh blood" is more than welcome, but you'll need to carefully abide the society's understandably strict rules if you plan on being permanently accepted into the club. And although the soapbox racing season technically runs year-round, the vast majority of rides take place during the warmer months. To learn more, visit http://pissburgh.weebly.com.

ULTIMATE FRISBEE
A noncontact team sport that combines elements of soccer, basketball, and American football, Ultimate Frisbee was created in 1960 by college students who originally tossed around pie dishes. Today the sport is played internationally, and more than 50 countries hold tournaments. Contrary to popular belief, however, UF players must be in top physical shape to perform well. The local organization known as **Pittsburgh Ultimate** (www.pittsburgh-ultimate.org) is home to a number of seasonal leagues, as well as college teams, a women's league, and a junior league. Visit the organization's website to find contact information for the various team representatives.

© DAN ELDRIDGE

Urban Active Fitness Club

in the city where you can get 'round-the-clock workout access, and the facilities, by the way, are top-notch. Free weights are plentiful and seemingly brand new, but the machines, which work the body's muscles with an almost uncanny precision, are even better; you simply won't find a better (or newer) selection in town.

X Shadyside has no swimming pool or steam room, but it does boast its own room of cardio equipment and a spacious studio where yoga and aerobics classes take place (all classes are included in the price of a gym membership, which is roughly $50 a month, not including an initiation fee).

The average exerciser here tends to be the same sort of person you'd see shopping along Shadyside's streets: gorgeously styled young women and men. Need more convincing? X Shadyside was recently voted the "Best Gym for Spotting Hotties" by the readers of *Pittsburgh City Paper.*

GUIDED AND WALKING TOURS

Much like San Francisco, a town to which Pittsburgh is occasionally compared, you'll find that a good number of neighborhoods here are hilly, rough-hewn, and generally best explored on foot (or at the very least, atop a bicycle). The guided walking tours organized by the Pittsburgh History and Landmarks Foundation are a good place to start—they're packed with intriguing historical and architectural trivia, and most are only an hour long. But once you get your footing, try striking out on your own—dig through a neighborhood you haven't passed through before, or maybe even one you've never heard of before.

The Greater Pittsburgh area is filled with rarely visited but historically curious pockets; to enjoy the city's more obscure reaches on your own, head to the Pennsylvania section of the Carnegie Library or any local bookstore and look for locally published guides and maps, many of which aren't widely distributed outside the area. *Seeing Pittsburgh* by Barringer Fifield (University of Pittsburgh Press) includes both walking and driving architectural tours; *60 Hikes Within 60 Miles: Pittsburgh* by Donna Ruff (Menasha Ridge Press) offers diverse hiking suggestions in the city and beyond; *The Steps of Pittsburgh* by Bob Regan (Local History Co.) is a fascinating guide to the city's 712 sets of outdoor steps; *The Bridges of Pittsburgh,* also by Bob Regan (Local History Co.) is considered the definitive guide to the city's hundreds of cross-river spans. And when you're ready to get out of town, pick up *Quick Escapes Pittsburgh* by Michelle Pilecki (Globe Pequot), which offers a rundown of 25 mini-vacations in mostly tranquil settings.

JUST DUCKY TOURS

125 W. Station Square Dr., 412/402-3825, www.justduckytours.com

COST: Adults $19, child 3-12 $15, child 3 and under $5

Map 3

Nearly every decent-sized American town with river real estate now has an amphibious vehicle city tour. Pittsburgh's version, headquartered at Station Square, is Just Ducky Tours. The tour, which passes through Downtown, parts of the North Shore, and the Monongahela and Ohio Rivers, takes place in a vintage World War II amphibious vehicle, able to traverse both land and sea. Tours are roughly an hour long; expect to be pelted with miscellaneous Pittsburgh trivia and bad jokes. Just Ducky operates April 1 through October 31, and on weekends only in November.

PITTSBURGH HISTORY AND LANDMARKS FOUNDATION TOURS

100 W. Station Square Dr., Ste. 450, 412/471-5808, www.phlf.org

COST: Free

Map 3

The Pittsburgh History and Landmarks Foundation is a nonprofit preservation group whose members work to save the city's most important structures from demolition or misuse. In an effort to educate the public about certain buildings and parts of the city they may have otherwise passed by without so much as a single thought, the group has organized a number of wonderfully educational guided walking tours.

The tours are a smart place to start for anyone interested in learning about the historical relevance of the city, packed as they are with intriguing well-researched trivia. Most tours are roughly an hour long, and although donations are encouraged, all tours are free. Some of the more popular excursions include an architectural tour of the South Side, a look at the Old Allegheny County Jail, and a stroll through Downtown's historical 5th and Forbes Corridor.

PITTSBURGH NEIGHBORHOOD TOURS

412/481-0561, ext. 17, www.pittsburghneighborhoodtours.com

COST: Free

Partly conceived and created by the city's own tourism bureau, the wonderfully educational Pittsburgh Neighborhood Tours were designed not only for tourists and other out-of-towners, but also for longtime locals who may not have taken the time to explore some of the city's most unique and culture-rich areas.

To participate, simply point your Internet browser to the Neighborhood Tours website and start clicking. You'll find reams of insider information about neighborhoods like Bloomfield, Mount Washington, the Strip District, and the South Side. A handful of detailed and self-guided tour suggestions are available for each of the featured neighborhoods.

THE PITTSBURGH TOUR COMPANY DOUBLE DECKER TOURS

445 S. 27th St., SouthSide Works, 412/381-8687, www.pghtours.com

COST: All-day passes $20 adult, $10 child

Map 3

As the city's solitary hop-on, hop-off bus tour, the Pittsburgh Tour Company offers one of the most convenient and thrilling ways to explore the city. Tours take place aboard a genuine mid-century double-decker bus from London.

ARTS AND LEISURE

© DAN ELDRIDGE

The Pittsburgh Tour Company Double Decker Tours

The bus travels from the SouthSide Works plaza to Station Square before heading to the Rivers Casino on the North Shore, the Heinz History Center and Wholey's Fish Market in the Strip District, and then to Downtown before returning again to the SouthSide Works.

PITTSBURGH WALKING

412/362-8451, www.pittsburghwalking.com

COST: $50 minimum for one hour, $100 minimum for three hours

You might call it a walking tour for the sort of person who doesn't normally enjoy taking tours: Pittsburgh Walking is a solitary organization led by Steel City history buff Donald Gibbon, who leads highly personalized tours of Downtown and its environs. But unlike the experience you'd probably have inside, say, a double-decker Redline tour bus, the Pittsburgh Walking experience is whatever you choose to make it. In other words, if

given a bit of advance warning, Gibbon will research and plan tours in other city neighborhoods tailored to an individual or group's specific interest.

Gibbon is also happy to meet tour-goers at their Downtown hotel, or in Oakland, or on the North Side…or pretty much wherever. And as Gibbon's website says, his tours, which differ slightly each time he gives them, can be as long or short as the customer desires.

PNC PARK TOURS

115 Federal St., 412/325-4700, http://pittsburgh.pirates .mlb.com/NASApp/mlb/pit/ballpark/tours.jsp

HOURS: Tours March-Sept. Mon-Fri. and one Sat. per month at 10 A.M., noon, and 2 P.M.

COST: $7 pp

Map 1

You don't necessarily need to be a Pirates fan to enjoy a tour of the ball club's newest North Side stadium. In fact, given that PNC Park is

PITTSBURGH'S QUIRKIEST TOURS

As Pittsburgh's popularity as a tourism destination continues to slowly grow, so too does its selection of sightseeing tours. Over the last few years, a good number of exceptionally quirky and unique Pittsburgh tours have entered the marketplace, and while some proved unpopular with visitors and ultimately disappeared, others have gone on to become local mainstays. The following is a selection of can't-miss tours for anyone genuinely interested in digging deep into the city's history and culture.

'BURGH BITS AND BITES FOOD TOUR

During these unique culinary walking tours of various Pittsburgh neighborhoods, tour-goers wander through the Strip District, Bloomfield, Mount Washington, or Lawrenceville, sampling regional foods and learning about local culinary history along the way. Tours are generally 2.5 hours long and cost $35 per person (www.burghfoodtour.com, 800/979-3370).

GREEN GEARS PEDICABS

Pittsburgh's only bicycle-powered pedicab service, the drivers of Green Gears (so-named because of the cabs' non-polluting eco-friendliness) pedal along the streets of the South Side, the North Shore (on game days), Downtown, and the Strip District. The charge is roughly $1 per block; the pedicabs can also be rented for special events (www.greengearspedicabs.com, 412/343-7334).

HAUNTED PITTSBURGH GHOST TOURS

As the self-described "archivists of Pittsburgh's nightmares," the guides of Haunted Pittsburgh (www.hauntedpittsburghtours.com, 412/302-5223) host walking tours and

pub crawls in Oakland, the South Side, and Mount Washington on Saturday nights from May through Halloween. Tours are $15 per person. For something a little less scary, try the company's **Pittsburgh Baseball Tours** (www.pittsburghbaseballtours.com), which take place near PNC Park and around the North Shore and also cost $15.

MIKE'S CARRIAGE SERVICE

Featuring romantic horse-drawn carriage tours throughout Downtown and Station Square, Mike's refers to itself as "Pittsburgh's premier source for horse-drawn entertainment." Downtown tours are $28; Station Square carriage rides are $20-50, depending on the length of the ride (www.caustelotfarms.com, 412/913-0664).

RIVERQUEST

Formerly known as Pittsburgh Voyager, the RiverQuest (www.riverquest.org, 412/231-2712) organization offers a wide range of river-based educational programs for both children and adults. Tours take place aboard the *Explorer*, an eco-friendly triple-decker boat; passengers use the city's rivers as something of a living classroom, where they learn about science, sustainability, and more. Visit the website for more information, as tour times and program schedules vary widely.

YOUR ACTIVE CITY

Can't find a Pittsburgh tour that properly suits your fancy? Not a problem: Simply ring up the good folks at Your Active City (www.youractivecity.com, 412/303-0566), who specialize in custom walking and biking city tours, as well as pedicab-powered tours. Most of the company's standard tours involve the city's uniquely hidden spaces and unknown historical facts.

considered by many baseball insiders to be one of the country's finest parks, this is an experience that even a non-sports fan might find worthwhile.

Naturally, tour participants will have a chance to view sections of the park not open to fans during game time. Some of the experiences include a trip down to the field itself and an up-close-and-personal view of the batting cages and even the press box, which is generally considered the best seat in the house.

RIVERS OF STEEL HERITAGE TOURS
338 E. 9th Ave., Homestead, 412/464-4020,
www.riversofsteel.com
COST: About $20
Map 7

Comprising 3,000 square miles throughout seven counties of Southwestern Pennsylvania, the Rivers of Steel Heritage Area was created by U.S. Congress in 1996. The purpose was to honor the culture and the American way of life that existed hand-in-hand with the industry of Big Steel—an industry that no longer exists in this part of the county.

In Pittsburgh's Homestead neighborhood, however, it's now possible to tour the areas where steel production took place. Tours and their themes occasionally change, so it's best to call or check the organization's website before planning a trip. Past tours, however, have explored the infamous site of the Homestead Steel Strike of 1892 and the remains of the Carrie Furnace. Visitors can also take narrated, self-guided tours of the immediate area by renting audio devices with headphones.

SEGWAY IN PARADISE
724/625-3521, www.segwayinparadise.com
COST: $49

It's a fairly safe bet to assume that the majority of the people reading this book don't own a Segway and have never ridden one but have always wanted to try. If that's you, and if you're in Pittsburgh, you're in luck. A local sightseeing organization now offers two-hour tours aboard the battery-powered, self-propelled scooters. Appropriately enough, Segway in

Paradise pioneers begin their exploration at the Carnegie Science Center on the North Side before heading over the Allegheny River to Point State Park, through Downtown, and then over the Monongahela River to Station Square before looping back.

ADVENTURE SPORTS
THE CLIMBING WALL
7501 Penn Ave., 412/247-7334,
www.theclimbingwall.net
COST: $30 introductory class (includes equipment rental)
Map 5

An intense full-body workout, a sometimes terrifying experience, a serious mental test, and an absolute blast: That pretty much sums up the sport of indoor rock climbing, which can be practiced safely and affordably at The Climbing Wall at The Factory in Point Breeze. Beyond the basic introductory class, private advanced lessons and kids' lessons are also available. Can't make it to Point Breeze? Make the scene instead at the SouthSide Works' REI (412 S. 27th St., 412/488-9410, www.rei.com), where shoppers who are REI members can ramble up an indoor wall before picking up a new pair of discounted Merrells.

PUBLIC SWIMMING POOLS
Because of the area's troubling financial woes, the city has had a tough time over the past few summers paying the employees of its 31 outdoor public pools. One recent season even saw every single pool close early—well before the cool weather of fall had set in. But things are apparently looking up: After receiving more than $600,000 in donations from corporations and foundations, the city reopened more than half its pools in 2006. During the 2010 summer season, meanwhile, a total of 18 outdoor swimming pools were opened to the public.

Pool tags are required for season-long admission; a family of four pays $60; adults 16 years and older pay $30 each; passes for children 3–15 years old are $15. Not a city resident? Not a problem, although you'll be expected to hand over a whopping $45 for the season. Daily admission is available for those not interested in purchasing a season pass. The cost is $4 for adults 16 years and up and $3 for children 3–15. For info about pool locations or tag purchases, call 412/323-7928, or visit www.city.pittsburgh.pa.us/parks/swimming.htm.

Pittsburghers are rather fond of the city's three **wave pools,** all of which are wheelchair accessible and open every day from June through September (with some exceptions). Adult admission is $4; kids 6–12 and adults over 60 pay $3; kids 5 and under pay $1. The pool in **Boyce Park** (675 Frankstown Rd., 724/325-4677) is the most conveniently located if you're staying in the city; there's a snack bar and plenty of sunbathing space on the premises. **Settler's Cabin Park** in Oakdale (1225 Greer Rd., 412/787-2667) boasts trails, log cabins, a diving pool, and a wave pool. **South Park** (Buffalo Dr., 412/831-0810) also has a wave pool, as well as 9- and 18-hole golf courses, an ice skating rink, 33 lighted tennis courts, and a model airplane field.

Some of the most convenient and popular city pool locations include Schenley Park Pool and Ormsby Pool.

❿ OLIVER BATH HOUSE
38 S. 10th St., 412/488-8380
HOURS: Mon.-Fri. 9 A.M.-9 P.M., Sat.-Sun. noon-9 P.M.
Map 3

Possibly the most interesting of all the public pools is also the only one located indoors, and it's open year-round. The Oliver Bath House was built by Oliver Iron and Steel in 1910. The corporation's owner, a successful industrialist by the name of Henry W. Oliver, had it constructed specifically for his employees who had nowhere else to bathe. Five years later, Oliver presented the structure as a gift to the city. With its cathedral ceiling and blue-tiled, well-heated pool (the water is usually around 80°F), the bathhouse is the absolute picture of peace and serenity (especially during adult swim). It's especially popular with area seniors.

ORMSBY POOL
79 S. 22nd St., 412/488-8377
HOURS: June 17–Sept. 6 Mon.-Fri. 1-7:45 P.M. and Sat.-Sun. and holidays 1-5:45 P.M.
COST: Daily admission fee $4 adult 16 and older, $3 child 3-15
Map 3

If there were a competition for the most conspicuous and oddly located public pool, Ormsby would win it, hands down. Yet on the flip side, you won't have any trouble finding the place: Simply drive or walk across the Birmingham Bridge toward the South Side, and once you reach East Carson Street, there it is, right on the corner of one of the city's busiest intersections. Which isn't necessarily a bad thing, although if you don't like the idea of the world at large being able to see you in your bathing suit, you'd probably be better off swimming elsewhere. Then again, its convenience is exactly what makes Ormsby such a popular place: Where else can you perform a cannonball splash one minute, and then be gulping down a cold pint of Iron City Light the next? And aside from the many pubs on the Carson Street Strip, the pool also sits right next door to a public library, just down the street from the SouthSide Works shopping center, and an easy walk to dozens of popular neighborhood cafés and boutiques.

SCHENLEY PARK POOL
1 Overlook Dr., Schenley Park, 412/422-4266
HOURS: June 17–Sept. 6 Mon.-Fri. 1-7:45 P.M. and Sat.-Sun. and holidays 1-5:45 P.M.
COST: Daily admission fee $4 adult 16 and older, $3 child 3-15
Map 2

As one of the most popular public swimming spots in the city, the Schenley pool on scorching summer days can feel just as crowded as a Florida beach during Spring Break. Undoubtedly, that has much to do with its convenient location near Central and South Oakland, neighborhoods with a lot of concrete, a lot of young people, and very few private swimming pools.

The facility itself is fair, but not outstanding.

ARTS AND LEISURE

There isn't much shade to speak of, although the pool is appropriately large. Young children (as well as the young at heart) will appreciate the fact that Schenley Park's ubiquitous ice cream truck passes by dozens of times a day.

TENNIS

Tennis players in Pittsburgh are rather, uh, well served when it comes to choosing a court, whether public or private. An indispensable website is **Court Matters** (www.johnlaplante.com/tennis), which attempts to describe and map every court in Allegheny County. So far 224 courts have been documented, including indoor courts, courts with unusual surfaces, and even apartment complexes with courts.

For practical information about area news and events, including info about clinics, tournaments and leagues, visit the **Tennis in Pittsburgh** website (www.tennisinpittsburgh.com).

Citiparks maintains regional tennis courts in Frick Park, Highland Park, McKinley Park, Mellon Park, Schenley Park, and West Park, as well as in 50 smaller neighborhood parks. For locations and addresses, call 412/244-4188. The **Citiparks Tennis Program** offers lessons for children, adults, and seniors. Tennis camps sponsored by Citiparks for children 5–17 years old take place every June and July. Call 412/665-4017 for information, or visit Citiparks online at www.city.pittsburgh.pa.us/parks.

One of the city's best racquet sports specialty shops is **Tennis Village** (5419 Walnut St., 412/621-2399). Located in Shadyside for well over two decades now, it stocks shoes, clothing, accessories and supplies for tennis, racquetball, and squash players.

MELLON PARK TENNIS CENTER
6425 5th Ave. at Beechwood Blvd., 412/665-4017
Map 4

Ever driven past a structure on 5th Avenue near Penn Avenue that resembles a giant inflatable dome and wondered what went on there? Now you know: It's nothing less than an indoor, year-round tennis court. Known locally as the Tennis Bubble, the dome itself measures an impressive 118 feet wide by 265 feet long. Most enthusiasts will be pleased to learn that the playing surface is a Premiere Court (a slightly cushioned hard court), and that when the dome is removed during the summer months, use of the courts are free to the public. (Inexplicably, the bubble isn't removed every summer.) Players should call ahead to reserve one of the bubble's five courts which cost between $20–30 per hour, depending on the time of the day and the day of the week. The bubble, which maintains a pleasant temperature of 65°F, is open 7 A.M.–11 P.M. every day of the week.

SCHENLEY PARK TENNIS COURTS
Overlook Rd., Schenley Park,, 412/244-4188, www.pittsburghparks.org
Map 2

It's easy to understand why the courts in Oakland's Schenley Park are so popular with Pittsburgh's racket enthusiasts. For starters, the park features an impressive 13 courts that sport hard, Plexipave surfaces. And with so many courts to choose from, players are almost certain to find at least a few spaces open on any given day of the week, even though the area quite often hums with activity. What's more, the area is well lit, and all courts are in wonderful condition—which is saying something, given that the city-sponsored facilities are free and open to the public. Do be aware that the courts, which sit next to Schenley Park's soccer and softball fields, are often in use Saturday mornings and weekday evenings by city-sponsored tennis clinics or tournaments.

WASHINGTON'S LANDING TENNIS COURTS
Washington's Landing
Map 7

A 42-acre island formerly known as Herr's Island, and located about two miles east of Downtown on the Allegheny River, the formerly blighted area referred to as Washington's Landing is today a collection of expensive townhomes, a marina, a rowing center, and one of the most gorgeously situated public tennis courts in all of Pittsburgh. With an unbelievably beautiful riverside setting, it almost wouldn't matter if the courts here were uneven and cracked. And while three of the five courts are in fact in poor condition, two are perfectly usable. That less-than-perfect situation doesn't often create a problem, because due to its somewhat obscure location, the courts usually see very little action, even on perfect weather days.

The playing surface here is hard, and there are no lighting or restroom facilities. To find the courts, drive north along the 31st Street Bridge (from the Strip District toward Route 28), then take a left onto the downward-sloping ramp, which sits mere feet from the end of the bridge. Take a left at the bottom of the ramp and follow that road until it dead-ends into the tennis courts' parking lot.

SKATEBOARDING

As is the case in most cities, skateboarding parks in Pittsburgh come in two distinct classes: There are city-sponsored public parks, which are free, and there are private parks, all of which require skaters to cough up an admission fee.

For more info about area parks, visit www .skateboardpark.com. For specific information about the three city-operated parks (McKinley, Polish Hill, and Sheraden), call 412/255-2539. A nearly-complete list of all skateboarding parks in the Greater Pittsburgh region can be found on the website of the **Three Rivers Inline Club**, at www.skatepittsburgh.com. Also useful is the local **Skate Soup** blog, at www .skatesoup.com.

AE RIDE SKATEPARK

2525 Rochester Rd., Cranberry, 724/776-4806, www.twp.cranberry.pa.us
Map 7

Located behind the Cranberry Municipal Center and constructed over the course of just one day (with help from the Pittsburgh-based American Eagle Outfitters corporation), AE Ride is a free park featuring a veritable bevy of ramps, rails, stairs, platforms and benches—a street skater's dream come to life. There are also a number of quarter-pipes, launch ramps, and small half-pipe ramps.

(BOYCE PARK SKATEPARK

675 Old Frankstown Rd., Monroeville,
www.alleghenycounty.us/parks/bpfac.aspx
HOURS: Daily dawn-dusk
Map 7

One of the city's newest public skate parks, and generally considered by locals to be one of the very best, the medium- and large-sized concrete bowls and the street skating areas here are conveniently located near the Boyce Park wave pool. Aside from the park's wealth of rolling concrete real estate, skaters also appreciate the fact that Boyce is free-of-charge to all comers. No quite so popular with the locals, though, is the over-enthusiastic pad and helmet rule; you'll need to be covered in something approaching plastic armor if you hope to spend any serious time here.

IMPERIAL SKATEPARK

810 Rte. 30, Findlay Township's Clinton Community Park, www.findlay.pa.us
HOURS: Daily dawn-dusk
Map 7

Generally agreed upon as the best and most challenging skate park in the Greater Pittsburgh area, Imperial Skatepark is nothing less than a concrete dream. Here you'll find a beautifully constructed concrete snake run, a kidney-shaped pool, and small ramps scattered throughout. There's also a standard street area with rails, as well as a half pipe. The park is well lit and open late, and BMX riders are welcome.

MCKINLEY SKATEPARK

Bausman St., Beltzhoover
HOURS: Daily dawn-dusk
Map 7

Located in Beltzhoover's McKinley Park, this skate park is often empty during the day. Offering a four-foot metal half pipe and a decent collection of street obstacles, the park can be accessed by taking the Liberty Tunnel out of the city and then turning left onto Route 51 South. From there, hang another left onto Bausman Street; you'll soon see the park on your left. Thrift store connoisseurs should take care not to miss the nearby **Red White & Blue Thrift Store** (935 Ohio River Blvd., 412/766-6098).

MR. SMALLS SKATEPARK
40 Riverfront Dr., 412/821-8188, www.mrsmalls.com
HOURS: Call for seasonal hours.
COST: Two-hour clinic $20, one-on-one instruction $25/hr
`Map 6`

Situated not far from the East End is the extremely popular Mr. Smalls Skatepark, which you'll find underneath the 40th Street Bridge on the Millvale side of the Allegheny River. Along with a large street course and a huge vert ramp that was used in the 2001 X Games, Mr. Smalls offers private and group lessons for beginning skaters and has an on-site skate shop.

PENN HILLS EXTREME SPORTS PARK
102 Duff Rd., Penn Hills, 412/795-3500, www.pennhills.org
HOURS: Daily dawn-dusk
`Map 7`

Located in Duff Park and not far from the Penn Hills Shopping Center on Rodi Road, the Penn Hills Extreme Sports Park is free to the public, and open to skateboarders, in-line skaters and BMX riders. And because area teens actually contributed ideas when it came time to design the park's layout, the end result was fairly impressive; obstacles include a mini-ramp, a quarter pipe, a pyramid, stairs, ledges, and a number of movable boxes.

SHERADEN SKATE PARK
Tuxedo St., Sheraden, 412/255-2539
HOURS: Daily dawn-dusk
`Map 7`

A decent enough park which was unfortunately constructed with pre-fabricated parts, the West End's Sheraden Park features quarter pipes, a

so-called fun box with a ledge, and a number of rails for sliding and grinding.

WEST PENN SKATE PARK (POLISH HILL BOWL)
450 30th St., 412/622-7353
HOURS: Daily dawn-dusk
`Map 6`

The Polish Hill Bowl, as it's known to locals, is the easiest to reach if you don't have a car. It's also not far from Gooski's—convenient should you care to do a bit of pre- or post-session drinking. The 77A and 77B buses pass by the park, as does just about every other 54C, but be sure to ask the driver if his or her route passes through Polish Hill. True to its name, the park doesn't offer much more than a bowl, albeit a relatively nice one. Some street skating facilities are also on-site.

BOWLING
ARSENAL LANES
212 44th St., 412/683-5992, www.arsenalbowl.com
`Map 6`

With much more to offer than your standard neighborhood bowling alley, it's no surprise that Lawrenceville's Arsenal Lanes has become such a popular hang-out spot for the East End's artiest inhabitants. The Wednesday night Rock & Bowl event—where live rock acts perform directly on the lanes—draws an especially large crowd, although so too do the many other special nights here, including Friday's ever-popular karaoke night. Probably the alley's best feature, however, is its Upstairs Saloon, which overlooks the smaller and somewhat hidden Hollywood Bowl room, an intimate bowling space filled with bright-shining lights.

YOGA, MEDITATION, AND MARTIAL ARTS
☾ AMAZING YOGA
5823 Ellsworth Ave., 412/661-1525, www.amazingyoga.net
`Map 4`

One of the city's most popular and progressive yoga studios, Amazing Yoga now has four separate locations, including a new Shadyside studio (730 Copeland St.) and one each in Wexford (2606 Brandt School Rd.) and on the South Side (1506 E. Carson St.) Taking an introductory class at Amazing Yoga is the perfect choice for anyone who still considers the practice a bit mystical or odd, largely because the reigning philosophy here is one of acceptance, community and all-inclusiveness. Snotty attitudes are a big no-no, in other words, which may explain why Amazing has won the *Pittsburgh City Paper*'s "Best Yoga Studio" and "Best Yoga Teachers" awards for four years running. Baptiste power yoga is the predominant style practiced at Amazing, where single drop-in classes are $15, or $11 for students. A 30-day unlimited pass, good at any Amazing location, is $125.

BREATHE YOGA STUDIO

1113 E. Carson St., 3rd Fl., 412/481-9642,
www.pittsburghyoga.com
Map 3

Located in a 1,400-square-foot studio in the heart of the South Side Flats, Breathe Yoga offers beginning and intermediate Hatha classes, including Iyengar classes, and a Yoga Basics class, which focuses on simple breathing and posture techniques. That doesn't begin to describe the school's full schedule, however. Breathe also squeezes in the occasional Middle Eastern dance class, as well as capoeira and modern dance instruction. There's also have a full schedule of workshops focused on specific aspects of yoga and spirituality. Drop-in yoga classes are $13, or $9 for students and seniors. First-time classes are just $5.

KEARNS SPIRITUALITY CENTER

9000 Babcock Blvd., Allison Park, 412/366-1124,
www.falundafa-pgh.org
Map 7

Falun Gong, also known as **Falun Dafa,** is an ancient Chinese meditation technique closely related to *qigong,* in which the mind and body are refined and improved through various low-impact exercises and meditative techniques.

What makes Falun Gong slightly different is that its practitioners also focus on the improvement of moral character. Despite (or maybe because of) the persecution and numerous arrests of Falun Gong groups in China, English-speaking organizations have popped up in cities all over the world during the past decade or so. A free Falun Gong informational class takes place every Monday 10–11:30 A.M. at the Kearns Spirituality Center in Allison Park.

SCHOOLHOUSE YOGA

2401 Smallman St., 412/401-4444,
www.schoolhouseyoga.com
Map 1

Yoga studios in Pittsburgh seem to arrive and then disappear with frequency, which makes it all the more heartening to witness the success of Schoolhouse Yoga, an organization that did, in fact, start out in a disused Lawrenceville schoolhouse. Today, Schoolhouse operates four increasing popular locations, and all shops offer a wide variety of classes at all skill levels. Ashtanga, Hatha, and Kundalini yoga classes are all available. Other varieties include Gentle Yoga, for students recovering from an injury or illness, Prenatal Yoga, and even Plus-Size Yoga for Men & Women, which is specially designed to fit the needs of overweight students. Schoolhouse's other three locations can be found at 2010 Murray Avenue in Squirrel Hill, at 5417 Walnut Street (on the second floor) in Shadyside, and at 2737 East Carson Street in the SouthSide Works. Drop-in classes are $15; a four-class pass is $50; an eight-class pass is $80; and a 12-class pass is $100.

STILL MOUNTAIN TAI CHI AND CHI KUNG

Mount Lebanon, 412/480-9177,
www.stillmountaintaichi.com
Map 7

Because Pittsburgh doesn't have much of an immigrant Chinese community to speak of, you won't find the martial art of tai chi practiced in public parks here as it is in, say, San Francisco's Washington Square. But the ancient form of

ARTS AND LEISURE

Schoolhouse Yoga

Chinese exercise is taught at a number of Kung Fu and martial arts studios around town, including Still Mountain Tai Chi and Chi Kung. The practice at Still Mountain leans toward Chinese Buddhism and involves a combination of martial arts, spiritual development, and health. A wide variety of classes and workshops take place at the Still Mountain studio, including classes that involve weapons, self-defense, and meditation workshops. Tuition per month for group classes is $100; private sessions are $60 per hour or $30 per half-hour; one-hour taped sessions with instruction and critique is $75; and private group sessions are $60 for the first person and $15 for each additional person.

SHOPS

While Pittsburgh hasn't really been thought of as a premiere shopping destination since its midcentury heyday as a booming steel town, an eclectic and thriving new boutique scene has created quite a buzz of late, thanks in large part to a number of highly visible, much adored, and locally-based online shopping ventures, namely ModCloth (www.modcloth.com), the indie clothing purveyor, and Moop (www.moopshop.com), which sells unique designer bags.

Yet as Pittsburgh continues to rapidly shed its outdated Rust Belt image, beloved local shops and hipster boutiques alike still pride themselves on quality, value, and friendly home-town service. Throw in unparalleled seasonal sales that allow shoppers of almost every budget an opportunity to scoop up some of their favorite brands and hand-made goodies, and it's easy to see why Pittsburgh has become a modern shopper's paradise—not to mention many a savvy fashionista's best-kept secret.

Inside the city itself, especially in the shopping havens of Shadyside, Oakland, Squirrel Hill, and most recently in Lawrenceville and East Liberty, you'll find a plethora of establishments to please even the pickiest of shoppers. And because Pittsburgh is still home to a significantly large senior citizen population, its antique shops, thrift stores, and vintage and consignment stores tend to offer incredible selections at very reasonable prices.

What's more, Pittsburgh has lately become something of a haven for the arts and crafts scene, thanks in large part to the city's

COURTESY OF ROB MATHENY

SHOPS

HIGHLIGHTS

LOOK FOR  TO FIND RECOMMENDED SHOPS.

 **Best Place to Shop When You've Got Nothing to Wear:** It's tough to go wrong at Shadyside's **Little Black Dress,** an upscale women's boutique specializing is classic clothing that's always in style (page 198).

 **Best Place to Shop Like a Celeb:** Pick up an oversized bag and sunglasses at Lawrenceville's hip **Sugar Boutique,** and you'll be gossip-rag ready in no time (page 199).

 **Best Gift Shop:** A cross between a novelty store, a gag shop, and a classy gift boutique, **Kards Unlimited** is a perfect one-stop shop when you need to pick up a present for Grandma, your kid brother, or, of course, yourself (page 201).

 **Best Retail Shop for the Etsy Set:** With everything from handmade T-shirts and housewares to gift cards and jewelry, **Wild Card** is ground zero for the city's crafting scene (page 203).

 **Best Way to Naturally Beautify:** When it comes time to rejuvenate your skin, consider the all-natural and age-defying methods offered at **Bloom Organic Skincare Parlor** (page 204).

 **Most Ethical Place to Shop:** Featuring eco-friendly and sweatshop-free clothing, handbags, and more, **Equita** is the last word in guilt-free consumerism (page 206).

 **Best Place to Score Rare European Shoes:** The classically stylish men's and women's shoes at **Bondstreet Shoes** may be imported from old-world craftsmen abroad, but the prices are surprisingly reasonable (page 210).

 **Easiest Way to Keep Your Mountain Bike in Tip-Top Shape:** Pay a visit to the friendly folks at **Thick Bikes,** a fantastic neighborhood spot for bike repairs, used and new cycles, and all manner of biking paraphernalia (page 217).

© DAN ELDRIDGE

Wild Card

affordable housing and studio costs. Shoppers can expect to find one-of-a-kind, handcrafted goods by local artisans in boutiques throughout the city. Be sure to inquire about open studio hours and clean-out sales for a chance to see these talented Pittsburghers at work, and to pick up one-of-a-kind pieces at a fraction of their regular retail prices.

Arts and Crafts

ARTISTS IMAGE RESOURCE
518 Foreland St., 412/321-8664,
www.artistsimageresource.org
HOURS: Vary; see website for the gallery's current calendar
Map 1

While it currently has no official "shop" per se, Pittsburgh's Artist Image Resource, known locally as AIR, features an Open House initiative that provides print lovers a rare opportunity to discover and take home one-of-a-kind prints by unknown and well-known artists alike. The perfect excuse to throw away your old dorm room posters forever, AIR is also home to monthly exhibits in addition to other special events, such as its annual October Benefit, where prints by regional and national artists are made available for purchase. Many of AIR's events also offer visitors a chance to see master printers at work, or even to experiment with printing techniques like letterpress or lithography themselves. Tuesday and Thursday nights from 6 to 10 P.M. are especially busy times at AIR; that's when locals are allowed to use the gallery's screen printing studio to create their own T-shirts, tote bags, and more for a small fee.

FIREBORN STUDIOS
2338 Sarah St., 412/488-6835, www.fireborn.com
HOURS: Tues.-Thurs. noon-6 P.M., Fri.-Sat. noon-4 P.M.
Map 3

Every piece of functional pottery sold in this South Side studio and shop is created on the premises by Fireborn's founders, the master potters Dan Vito and Donna Hetrick. They also stock experimental works, one-of-a-kind objects, and discontinued items, often at deeply discounted prices. Heavily inspired by the 19th-century arts and crafts movement, the gallery is as warm, accessible, and inviting as the work found inside it, and Fireborn's "fat" mugs are the best thing to happen to coffee since the home grinder. Fireborn also provides classes for aspiring potters of all skill levels, and their kiln openings offer a rare chance to observe freshly glazed pots and other creations as they transform into beautiful works of art.

THE GALLERY 4
206 S. Highland Ave., 412/363-5050,
www.thegallery4.us
HOURS: Tues.-Sat. 2-8 P.M.
Map 6

Though something of a newcomer to the Pittsburgh art scene, this understated gallery and boutique created quite a buzz with its March 2010 grand opening exhibit, which featured work from the legendary street artist Shepard Fairey. Since then, Gallery 4 has continued to bring notable artists from around the country into Pittsburgh, many of them from street art, pop art, and graffiti backgrounds. And since Gallery 4 opened with the intent of being much more than a just traditional space for art, it also offers limited-edition vinyl toys, street wear, prints, and other collectible and uniquely manufactured objects d'arte.

GALLERY ON 43RD STREET
187 43rd St., 412/683-6488,
www.galleryon43rdstreet.com
HOURS: Tues.-Sat. 11 A.M.-6 P.M.
Map 6

Lifelong weaver Mary Coleman's shop is located just off of the hustle and bustle of Lawrenceville's Butler Street, and features one-of-a-kind arts and crafts from throughout the

Western Pennsylvania region. Coleman's impressive rugs, runners, and placemats can be seen throughout the gallery shop, and while you won't find the latest cutting-edge or controversial exhibit here, you can always expect to find beautifully crafted and tasteful work in a number of more traditional mediums, such as ceramics, pottery, and porcelain. In other words, Gallery on 43rd Street is the perfect place to find a gift for the parents, or a lovely tea kettle and mugs for Grandma.

IRISH DESIGN CENTER
303 S. Craig St., 412/682-6125,
www.irishdesigncenter.com
HOURS: Mon.-Fri. 10 A.M.-5:30 P.M., Sat. 10 A.M.-5 P.M.
Map 2

An Irish import shop offering all the standard tchotchkes (rings, books, etc.), the real gems at the Irish Design Center are the authentic sweaters and other cozy knits and linens. All are hand-knit, and all are absolutely the real deal (not mass-produced, in other words). What's more, the knits carried here—blankets, throws, pullovers, and shawls—are all very uniquely styled. The shop also offers Celtic travel services and uniquely themed tours of Ireland. But if you can't quite afford a world-class tour of the Emerald Isle, not to worry: Simply pick up a bottle of Inis perfume at the Design Center, which has been described by more than one devotee as "Ireland in a Bottle."

KNIT ONE
2721 Murray Ave., 412/421-6666, www.knitone.biz
HOURS: Sun. noon-4 P.M., Mon. 11 A.M.-4 P.M., Tues. and Thurs. 10 A.M.-8 P.M., Wed., Fri., and Sat. 10 A.M.-5 P.M.
Map 5

Simply put, Knit One is every knitter's paradise. A large and well-lit store decorated with woven area rugs, Knit One also offers the largest amount and widest variety of both yarns and knitting classes in the city. Classes run the gamut from the relatively simplistic (Introduction to Lace Knitting) to the advanced (Modular Knitting; Intarsia Method). Even the inventory itself is artistic here, displayed as it is in modular shelving that is cleverly attached to

the shop's walls. The shop's owner also offers private lessons to help even the most impatient and distracted of aspiring knitters complete their own yarn-spun creations.

PITTSBURGH CENTER FOR THE ARTS
6300 5th Ave., 412/361-0873, www.pittsburgharts.org
HOURS: Tues.-Wed. and Fri.-Sat. 10 A.M.-5 P.M., Thurs. 10 A.M.-7 P.M., Sun. noon-5 P.M.
Map 4

In addition to the gallery here, which displays a rotating schedule of visual art and installations by both emerging and established artists, PCA maintains a wonderful gift shop with a large variety of pieces, all of them created by locals. The shop's collection has grown to include work by over 200 artists from throughout the Western Pennsylvania region, and in just about every medium imaginable, from fiber, ceramic, and glass work to jewelry, photography, and paper arts. Especially popular is the annual YART sale, which runs from Black Friday through the first week of January; it features uniquely gorgeous work at bargain basement prices.

THE STORE AT THE SOCIETY FOR CONTEMPORARY CRAFT
2100 Smallman St., 412/261-7003,
www.contemporarycraft.org
HOURS: Mon.-Sat. 10 A.M.-5 P.M.
Map 1

The relatively small gift shop at this folk art museum generally carries handmade purses, scarves, and stationery, as well as decorative items made of glass and wood. Known simply as The Store, you'll also find a small selection of home furnishings here, such as lamps, tables, and chairs. Jewelry, toys, and other small gift items are popular and generally well stocked. In addition to The Store, the Society for Contemporary Craft also offers cutting-edge exhibitions focused on non-mainstream art, community outreach programs, classes and seminars, and a family-friendly drop-in studio (free to the public) where both grown-ups and the little ones alike can make some of their own brilliant creations.

Books and Music

AWESOME BOOKS
5111 Penn Ave., 412/362-1574
HOURS: Vary; call for current hours
`Map 6`

A relative newcomer to Pittsburgh's eclectic and thriving literary scene, Awesome Books is located in the former space of the Clay Penn gallery, right in the heart of the Penn Avenue arts corridor. The shop got its start—as well as its unusual name—when the current co-owners were offered a collection of more than 10,000 "awesome" books from an out-of-business retailer. Still, Awesome is home to a relatively modest-sized collection of mostly used books, with literature, art, history, and religion among them. Do be aware that the shop doesn't tend to keep regular hours; the proprietors both have other jobs, so call ahead if you're coming from across town.

THE BIG IDEA INFOSHOP
504 S. Millvale Ave., 412/687-4323,
www.thebigideapgh.org
HOURS: Mon.-Sat. 1-9 P.M.
`Map 6`

A volunteer-run bookshop specializing in leftist politics, queer issues, and other radical and alternative cultures, the Big Idea Infoshop originally existed only as a small corner of a small room in the now-defunct Mr. Roboto Project in Wilkinsburg. Along with the standard collection of neo-anarchist lit, the shop also stocks a good selection of zines and other independent publications. Volunteers are always needed, and

© DAN ELDRIDGE

Awesome Books

the store hosts numerous discussion groups on the aforementioned subjects.

CALIBAN BOOKSHOP

410 S. Craig St., 412/681-9111, www.calibanbooks.com
HOURS: Mon.-Sat. 11 A.M.-5:30 P.M., Sun. 1-5:30 P.M.
Map 2

Specializing in rare first editions, leather-bound books, and fine arts and philosophy tomes, Caliban Bookshop carries the sort of printed curiosities you simply aren't going to stumble across at the neighborhood Barnes & Noble. Treasures seem to show up almost daily, and if you're looking to sell something rare and counterculture-esque, Caliban may very well be looking to buy. They even make house calls and provide appraisal services to individuals and institutions. Just about every last item from the *McSweeney's* catalog is stocked here, and a tiny CD store, Desolation Row, can be found in the back corner.

CITY BOOKS

1111 E. Carson St., 412/481-7555
HOURS: Mon.-Sat. 10:30 A.M.-4 P.M., Sun. 1-4 P.M.
Map 3

Probably best known for its extensive philosophy collection, out-of-print reads, and other academic tomes, City Books has been a South Side neighborhood staple for years—not to mention an especially calming respite from the alcohol-fueled antics of East Carson Street. It's nothing to lose an afternoon here, or even an entire day, browsing through the endless stacks of literary goodies. The shop is also known for its schedule of readings and discussions featuring international and local literati alike.

THE COMIC BOOK INK!

116 Smithfield St., 412/263-2002,
www.thecomicbookink.com
HOURS: Mon.-Sat. 11 A.M.-5:30 P.M., Sun. 1-5:30 P.M.
Map 1

Recognizable by its ten-foot-tall plaster replica of the Incredible Hulk, which greets passersby on the corner of Smithfield Street and Liberty Avenue, Downtown, The Comic Book Ink is owned by a bankruptcy attorney (and serious comic geek) whose law offices are located three floors above the shop. You can expect to find all the comic store staples here: a dollar bin, a decent selection of Marvel and DC Comics back issues from the 1980s and '90s, graphic novels and trade publications, and a wall lined with current releases. The shop's discounted subscription service is especially popular.

COPACETIC COMICS

3138 Dobson St., 3rd fl., 412/251-5451,
www.copaceticcomics.com
HOURS: Tues.-Thurs. 11 A.M.-5 P.M., Fri.-Sat. 11 A.M.-7 P.M.,
Sun. noon-4 P.M.
Map 6

Much more than just a run-of-the-mill comic book shop, Copacetic is also home to one of the city's better collections of independent and self-published comics, books, and zines. They also stock a huge library of classic lit (everything from Homer to Whitman), as well as classic and obscure DVDs, and jazz and indie CDs. Regardless of its eclectic and well-edited inventory, though, the truth is that many of Copacetic's best customers stop by just for a chance to shoot the bull with owner Bill Boichel—a veritable encyclopedia of American pop culture, and perhaps Pittsburgh's chattiest boutique owner. Copacetic recently relocated from its shoebox-sized Squirrel Hill location to a Polish Hill building that also houses **Mind Cure Records** (412/621-1715, www.myspace .com/mindcurerecords), an indie shop specializing in vinyl, and **Lili Coffee Shop** (412/682-3600), a friendly neighborhood joint with great treats.

JERRY'S RECORDS

2136 Murray Ave., 412/421-4533,
www.jerrysrecords.com
HOURS: Mon.-Sat. 10 A.M.-6 P.M., Sun. noon-5 P.M.
Map 5

Named by no less an authority than *Rolling Stone* magazine as one of the best record shops in the United States, vinyl enthusiasts have been known to travel from as far away as Japan to dig through the crates of over one million records at this Squirrel Hill institution. The size

© DAN ELDRIDGE

Jerry's Records

of the selection here simply boggles the mind; there seem to be sections devoted to just about every genre of music on earth, including some you probably never knew existed. Turntables and accessories are also sold, and prices on all but the rarest of finds are surprisingly affordable. And while unfounded rumors have long predicted the end of Jerry's legacy, the shop is indeed still growing strong. Jerry's own son, in fact, recently opened a new a mini-shop inside the store known as **Whistlin' Willie's** (412/478-4023, www.whistlinwillies.com); it's an exclusive purveyor of reasonably priced 78 rpm records.

MYSTERY LOVERS BOOKSHOP

514 Allegheny River Blvd., Oakmont, 412/828-1877, www.mysterylovers.com
HOURS: Mon.-Sat. 10 A.M.-5 P.M., Sun. noon-4 P.M.
Map 7

This Raven Award–winning shop located just a few miles east of the city has been an Oakmont community staple since first opening its doors in 1990, and has welcomed countless touring mystery writers over the years. One of the largest specialty mystery book shops in the country, Mystery Lovers is also known for hosting seven separate book clubs, and for regularly offering intimate catered dinners with popular authors. Various readings, lectures, and workshops take place throughout the year.

PAUL'S CDS

4526 Liberty Ave., 412/621-3256,
www.myspace.com/paulscds
HOURS: Mon.-Sat. 10 A.M.-7 P.M., Sun. noon-5 P.M.
Map 6

Often voted "Best Local Record Shop" by *Pittsburgh City Paper* readers, Paul's CDs is something of a local headquarters for indie- and art-rock aficionados. Its Bloomfield location is a tiny little box of a store, and yet its supremely well-edited collection is consistently top-notch. You'll find the best of the best here in terms of traditional blues and jazz, world music, hip-hop, electronic, and all manner of experimental sounds. DVDs and a small music magazine section are also popular, as is the used CD bin in the front of the store. The aloof staffers are nevertheless exceedingly knowledgeable, and can special-order just about anything.

PHANTOM OF THE ATTIC COMICS
411 S. Craig St., 412/621-1210,
www.myspace.com/pota_comics
HOURS: Mon.-Tues. and Fri.-Sat. 10 A.M.-7 P.M.,
Wed. 1-8 P.M., Thurs. 10 A.M.-8 P.M., Sun. 10 A.M.-5 P.M.
Map 2

With a new and much roomier location right above **Top Notch Art Center** (412/355-0444, www.tnartsupply.com) on Oakland's South Craig Street (look for the giant pencil), Phantom of the Attic has long been a Pittsburgh comic book institution. Regulars tend to show up in droves every Wednesday, when upwards of 100 new issues are added to the shelves. The inventory here, in other words, is serious. And because Phantom's new well-lit space is so sprawling and large, you're nearly guaranteed to find what you need. Meanwhile, the shop's old location—directly across the street—is now home to **Phantom of the Attic Games** (406 S. Craig St., 412/682-6290), a favorite hang-out for the Dungeons & Dragons set. The POTA Games location is in a building that also houses **Wicked Discs** (412/682-5007, www.wickeddiscs.com), a punk and metal music shop, and **Black Cat Tattoos** (412/621-1679, www.blackcattattoos.net).

UNIVERSITY OF PITTSBURGH BOOK CENTER
4000 5th Ave., 412/648-1455, www.pitt.edu/~bookctr
HOURS: Mon.-Thurs. 8:30 A.M.-6:30 P.M.,
Fri.-Sat. 9 A.M.-5 P.M.; call for summer hours
Map 2

Not content to exist solely as a locale for new Pitt students to purchase textbooks and school supplies, the massive Pitt Book Center has such a well-stocked selection of fiction and nonfiction, as well as gifts and accessories, that you'll barely need to stop by a Borders or Barnes & Noble during your four years here. Of course, non-students fill the Book Center as well, which boasts a particularly well-stocked regional section. Be prepared to leave all your belongings in a locker at the store's entrance.

Clothing and Accessories for Men

CHARLES SPIEGEL FOR MEN/ THE GARAGE
5841 Forbes Ave., 412/421-9311, www.charlesspiegel.com
HOURS: Mon., Wed., Fri., Sat. 10 A.M.-6 P.M.; Tues. and Thurs. 10 A.M.-9 P.M.; Sun. noon-5 P.M.
Map 5

Certainly one of the best spots in Pittsburgh for unique designer clothing, this location is technically two stores in one. Charles Spiegel for Men claims a wide swath of the space, and it's on these racks that you'll find a great mix of suiting, including pieces by Vestimenta, Etro, and J Keydge. The Garage offers much more casual and trendy gear, perfect whether you're at the club or simply out at the café. And aside the atmosphere here being especially warm and friendly, it's also the best place in town to take your boyfriend if he needs to kick it up a notch in the style department.

LARRIMOR'S
249 Fifth Ave., One PNC Plaza, 412/471-5727,
www.larrimors.com
HOURS: Mon.-Wed. and Fri.-Sat. 9 A.M.-6 P.M.,
Thurs. 9 A.M.-8 P.M.
Map 1

Family-owned and -operated for over 70 years, Larrimor's is the place to visit in Pittsburgh when you're ready to invest in those few key wardrobe pieces that every man should have: a great suit, a proper pair of shoes, a few tailored shirts, and a briefcase or satchel. The shop's business-casual and women's departments are exceptional as well, although there's no doubt that what Larrimor's does best is suiting. The customer service at Larrimor's is exceptional in all departments: Alterations are done onsite by master tailors and seamstresses, the shop offers a concierge service and accepts private appointments for viewings

© DAN ELDRIDGE

Charles Spiegel for Men

and fittings, and designer trunk shows and other promotional gatherings happen often.

MODA

5401 Walnut St., 412/681-8640,
www.modapittsburgh.com
HOURS: Mon.-Fri. 11 A.M.-8 P.M., Sat. 10 A.M.-7 P.M.,
Sun. noon-5 P.M.
Map 4

Carrying a wide variety of designer collections and "it" labels from Marc Jacobs, Lanvin, and Paul Smith to Rag & Bone, Woolrich, James Perse, and Nice Collective, Moda is one of the Pittsburgh area's most fashion-forward clothing stores for men, complete with a decent shoe collection and a somewhat snooty staff. While the store does carry a small but fantastic selection of suiting, its primary focus is largely centered around more casual, ready-to-wear merchandise, like designer denim, casual button-downs, graphic tees, and trendy accessories and watches.

MOOP

406 S. Main St., www.moopshop.com
HOURS: By appointment only, email info@moopshop
.com to schedule an appointment
Map 7

While the handmade unisex bag designer and manufacturer known as Moop doesn't have a standard retail location, its Main Street studio is always abuzz, and the company welcomes appointments for tours and product viewing. Sample designs hang on a rack at the front of the studio, making it simple to have a look for yourself. And the staffers are always happy to explain exactly what goes into making their well-designed and beautifully crafted bags. Available in several styles and solid fashionable colors, the aesthetic of Moop bags is very clean and minimalistic. And while some of the bags are most certainly designed for women, Moop's selection of backpacks, messenger bags, and letter and porter bags make a wonderfully hip and utilitarian alternative to the classic leather briefcase for men.

SHOP 412

420 S. 27th St., SouthSide Works, 412/586-7507,
www.shopfouronetwo.com
HOURS: Mon.-Thurs. 11 A.M.-8 P.M., Fri.-Sat. 11 A.M.-10 P.M.
Map 3

Branded as an urban lifestyle store, Shop 412 offers customers an eclectic and diverse line of unusual street wear, high-end sports wear, outerwear, hats, and limited-edition sneakers and boots from both domestic and European designers. And while other local street wear shops (Sneaker Villa, Time Bomb) tend to primarily carry urban wear of the oversized thug variety, Shop 412 offers a more discerning and grown-up approach to urban fashion.

CDs, DVDs, and mix tapes are also sold, and because Shop 412 blogs about new product arrivals on its website, you can easily shop online or by phone if a trip to the South Side isn't possible.

Clothing and Accessories for Women

BAILEY & BAILEY
425 Walnut St., Sewickley, 412/741-0700
HOURS: Mon.-Tues. and Thurs.-Fri. 10 A.M.-6 P.M., Wed. 10 A.M.-8 P.M., Sat. 10 A.M.-5:30 P.M.
Map 7

At Bailey & Bailey, absolutely one of the area's top spots for tracking down new and unique designer names, customers can always expect to come across recent lines from favorites such as Cynthia Vincent, Parameter, and Anna Sui. Ultimately, this is a great place to find trendy fashions with a classic, ageless appeal. Expect also to find chic T-shirts in the softest of knits, as well as wonderfully silky camisole dresses with perfect detailing. But since the store is a bit outside the city, we recommend calling ahead, assuming you're looking for a specific piece by a specific designer. Employees at Bailey & Bailey are especially kind and honest, and even if what you're looking for isn't in stock, you'll probably find that they're quite talented at steering you toward other appropriate pieces.

CHERYL W
6736 Reynolds St., 412/365-2115, www.cherylw.com
HOURS: Mon., Wed., Fri., and Sat., 10 A.M.-5:30 P.M.; Tues. and Thurs. 10 A.M.-7:30 P.M.
Map 5

Probably because of its amazing selection of both costume jewelry and fine gem jewelry—not to mention its great accessories—Cheryl W seems to attract the thrifty and single college gal just as much as it does the moneyed and middle-aged East End professional. Come for the handbags and the hair clips, or simply while away a few minutes by poking through the decent-sized selection of affordable and unique handmade jewelry. The recently relocated boutique shares an entrance with Make Your Mark Artspace & Coffeehouse in Point Breeze.

CHOICES
5416 Walnut St., 412/687-7600
HOURS: Mon.-Sat. 10 A.M.-5:30 P.M., Wed. 10 A.M.-8 P.M.
Map 4

Long known as one of Pittsburgh's more elite shops, Choices has nevertheless recently started selling more contemporary collections that are a little easier on the wallet. The space is wide open and very minimalist—think hardwood floors and off-white gallery walls. Keep in mind, however, that this is not off-the-rack shopping; the racks contain only one or two of each item for viewing, and if you find something you're fond of, a salesperson will bring the piece to your fitting room. Conveniently enough, everything is tailored in-house and the staff has grown quite friendly in recent years.

EB PEPPER
5411 Walnut St., 412/683-3815, www.ebpepper.net
HOURS: Mon. 9 A.M.-5 P.M., Tues. and Thurs.-Sat. 9:30 A.M.-5:30 P.M., Wed. 9:30 A.M.-8 P.M., Sun. noon-5 P.M.
Map 4

This shop is an absolute must for women who consider themselves among the city's most stylish; the lower level at eb Pepper consists mainly of career and formal attire, while the top floor is not to be missed for its endlessly chic casual wear. You'll find suiting here by the ever popular Milly, casual clothing by Nikka, as well as all the standards in premium denim, such

WEARING PITTSBURGH PRIDE

It's certainly not news that in the fickle world of fashion, trends have a way of coming and going with every last changing direction of the wind. That's true even in Pittsburgh, where being well-dressed often means putting on a pair of pleated Dockers and tucking in your button-down.

Yet, Pittsburgh's latest bout of economic growth seems to have instilled a genuine sense of civic pride among the city's 20- and 30-something sets; as a result, a surprisingly large number of them have been proclaiming their rekindled Steel City love by launching independent, DIY-style T-shirt companies.

The often-ironic Pittsburgh tee has lately become such a local staple, in fact, that area boosters have organized events to celebrate **International T-Shirt Day** (June 21). And as of this writing, a **Pittsburgh T-Shirt Show** (www. pghtee.com) is being organized. Shirts will be on display, available for sale, and even created on-site by local screen printers.

To pick up some wearable Pittsburgh pride of your own, start by visiting **Neighbor Teaze** (www.neighborteaze.com) online, where vin-tage-style shirts touting various Pittsburgh neighborhoods are on offer.

ChampYinz (www.champyinz.com) is another local favorite, with many of its designs referencing local sports culture. ("70 percent of the world is covered in water," reads one such shirt. "The rest is covered by Polamalu.")

Other area T-shirt purveyors of note include **WearPittsburgh** (www.wearpittsburgh.com), whose founder describes his shirts as a "love letter to the City of Pittsburgh;" the decidedly punk-rock **Commonwealth Press** (1931 E. Carson St., 412/431-4207, Mon.-Fri. 9 A.M.-5:30 P.M., www.commonwealthpress.org), which now has a retail store where custom shirts can be ordered; and the **Cotton Factory** (www.cottonfactory.com), which offers a small selection of Pittsburgh-specific shirts in addition to its huge catalog of novelty tees.

(Contributed by Carrie Ann, a designer and lifestylist based in Pittsburgh and Philadelphia.)

---

as Citizens of Humanity and Paper Denim & Cloth. The store is perhaps best known, however, for its mascot: Ms. Pepper's pet pug, Chloe, who practically lives at the store and who incidentally struts her own style with custom fashions by **Spoiled Pets** (412/422-2116), a local hand-tailored dog clothier.

EMPHATICS

301 Grant St., One Oxford Centre, 3rd Fl., 412/471-4773
HOURS: Mon.-Fri. 10 A.M.-6 P.M., Sat. 10 A.M.-5 P.M.
Map 1

Without a doubt, Emphatics is the largest and one of the best high-end designer shopping experiences in Pittsburgh for both men and women. With its sleek and sophisticated atmosphere and sales team, Emphatics carries all of the fashion industry's heavy hitters, including Prada, Jean-Paul Gaultier, Stella McCartney, Alexander McQueen, and more. And despite the sometimes shockingly high price tags, you can expect to be treated like royalty from the moment you walk in the door—the service here is incredibly warm and friendly. You'll be assisted even when trying on garments—for women, the store carries appropriate bras, shoes, and even try-on costume jewelry that enables customers to see exactly how their new clothes will look, fit, and feel. And if your budget is a touch tight, feel free to ask if the store has anything off-season still tucked away in the back. Custom alterations and tailoring are both complimentary.

HIP'TIQUE

5817 Ellsworth Ave., 412/361-5817, www.hiptiquepa.com
HOURS: Tues.-Sat. 10:30 A.M.-6 P.M., Sun. noon-4 P.M.
Map 4

Located in a retrofitted, 126-year-old Victorian home in Shadyside, Hip'tique has been one of the neighborhood's best kept secrets since its opening in 2005. Co-owned by two best friends, this personality-rich boutique offers a wide variety of clothing, accessories, and decor by youthful and up-and-coming designers such as Tracy Reese, Central Park West, Plenty, Akiko, and more. Full of character, a little bit funky, and with relatively affordable prices, Hip'tique is a perfectly eclectic mix of high-end fashions and laid-back attitudes.

JUPE BOUTIQUE
2306 E. Carson St., 412/432-7933,
www.jupeboutique.com
HOURS: Mon.-Sat. 11 A.M.-7 P.M.
Map 3

This fairly new boutique, co-owned by fashion professionals Cara Moody and Amanda Hall, was opened with the aim of bringing fresh, contemporary fashion to area customers at price points they could actually afford. And though Jupe does stock a few higher-end lines, which goes a long way in helping to diversify the store's inventory, most pieces here are from designers like Free People, Mink Pink, and Soda Blue. Appropriately enough, Jupe (French for "skirt") has taken home several "best of" awards from local publications during its first few years of business. Jewelry, shoes and accessories can also be picked up here.

◖ LITTLE BLACK DRESS
5896 Ellsworth Ave., 412/363-6442
HOURS: Tues.-Sat. 10 A.M.-5 P.M.
Map 4

Owned by designer and former Bosnian refugee Diana Misetic, Little Black Dress is a truly incredible boutique that has become something of a local institution among Pittsburgh fashionistas. Effortlessly chic yet relaxed and inviting, LBD primarily sells the designs that Misetic herself creates from a studio located just above the shop. And aside from having an incredible eye for style, and being truly understanding of both fit and function, Misetic is also known for her skill in making recommendations for customers based on their needs, tastes, and body types. While it's true that LBD

does primarily offer little black dresses, the on-site designers can also create custom, one-of-a-kind dresses for clients looking for something a little extra special.

MAXALTO
5426 Walnut St., 412/683-0508,
www.maxaltofashion.com
HOURS: Mon.-Tues. and Thurs.-Sat. 10 A.M.-5 P.M.,
Wed. 10 A.M.-7 P.M.
Map 4

A super funky and fun little boutique where customers sit on plush velvet couches while deciding what to purchase, simply visiting MaxAlto is an experience in and of itself. The shop carries lines by Betsey Johnson, Anna Sui, LAMB, Just Cavalli, and others of similar ilk. The decor here is unique and spunky: antique hatboxes used as shoe displays, fitting rooms with long velvet curtains. The owner is particularly nice, and wonderful sale items can always be found in the back of the shop.

PITTSBURGH JEANS COMPANY
2222 E. Carson St., 412/381-5326,
www.pittsburghjeanscompany.com
HOURS: Mon.-Sat. 11 A.M.-7 P.M., Sun. 11 A.M.-6 P.M.
Map 3

Aside from having the largest collection of premium denim in the city (think Siwy Jeans, Habitual, Paige Premium Denim, and Rock & Republic), PJC also has some of the best tops to go along with them. The store is an absolute haven for denim lovers—it boasts fitting specialists, the best in-house denim tailoring in the city, special-order shipping, and best of all, free alterations.

PURSUITS
740 Filbert St., 412/688-8822
HOURS: Mon.-Sat. 10:30 A.M.-5:30 P.M., Sun. noon-4 P.M.
Map 4

A bit more bohemian and New Age-y than your average women's clothing store in Shadyside, Pursuits is a wonderfully eclectic boutique that carries way too many brands to mention here. Don't expect big-name designer gear but, rather, relaxed fashions, dresses, and more affordable

SHOPS

© DAN ELDRIDGE

Sugar Boutique

indie labels. If you're going for a more effortless, bohemian-chic vibe, you'll find everything you need (and then some) at Pursuits, without breaking the bank. Candles and other various accessories are also available.

🄲 SUGAR BOUTIQUE

3703 Butler St., 412/681-5100,
http://sugarboutique-style.blogspot.com
HOURS: Tues. and Fri.-Sat. 11 A.M.-6 P.M.,
Wed.-Thurs. 11 A.M.-7 P.M., Sun. noon-3 P.M.
Map 6

It's no wonder Paramount Pictures filmed a scene for a romantic-comedy production in this Lawrenceville boutique; pardon the cliché, but Sugar really is sweet. The shop's layout is exceedingly minimalist, but with richly textured details; Think antique tables, potted plants, and curved bamboo garment rods. Perhaps the best thing about Sugar, though, is the clothes themselves, most of which are from independent designers, many of whom are local. At a time when you can purchase nearly everything online with a couple of clicks, it's a rare treat to

stumble upon a place like Sugar Boutique. And with its strong local focus, it does double-duty as a place where visitors and newcomers alike can familiarize themselves with Pittsburgh's many talented designers and craftspeople.

ZIPPER BLUES

5817 Forbes Ave., 412/421-8060,
www.shopzipperblues.com
HOURS: Mon.-Wed. and Fri.-Sat. 10 A.M.-6 P.M.,
Thurs. 10 A.M.-8 P.M.
Map 5

The newest addition to Pittsburgh's premium denim scene, Zipper Blues offers blue jean aficionados a wide array of stylish tops and tees in addition to the usual high-quality denim suspects: Citizens of Humanity, Joe's Jeans, Miss Me, Red Engine, and AG Jeans. The stylishly minimalistic but inviting Squirrel Hill store also sells unique sports T's and jerseys, primarily from Original Retro Brand. If you have to wear a sports jersey to work on game day, Pittsburgh girls, these are without a doubt the only tops to buy.

SHOPS

Gifts and Specialty Shops

CULTURE SHOP

1602 E. Carson St., 412/481-8284

HOURS: Mon.-Wed. noon-9 P.M., Thurs.-Fri. noon-10 P.M., Sat. 11 A.M.-10 P.M., Sun. noon-5 P.M.

Map 3

A wonderfully unique import shop offering clothing, accessories, and gifts from (mostly) India and the Far East, the Culture Shop feels something like a cross between a Haight-Ashbury head shop and a magic store straight out of a *Harry Potter* novel. Bohemian accoutrements abound: incense, peasant dresses, silver rings, and statues bearing the likeness of Ganesha. But many come specifically for the striking jewelry, as should you, assuming you're looking for something expressly unique without the requisite high price tag. Strapped for cash or feeling nostalgic for your college days? There's always Nag Champa!

DIVERTIDO

3701 Butler St., 412/687-3701, www.divertidoshop.com

HOURS Tues.-Wed. and Fri.-Sat. 11 A.M.-6 P.M., Thurs. 11 A.M.-8 P.M., Sun. 11 A.M.-3 P.M.

Map 6

Those looking for fresh and inspired gift ideas would do well to stop by Lawrenceville's Divertido. This hip little shop offers a selection of handmade totes and purses, beautiful silk scarves, affordable jewelry, fun greeting cards, retro-style dinnerware and home decor, and lots of non-traditional gifts for babies and kids (including casual garb, unusual toys, and some really cool children's books). Helpful but not overly pushy staffers make selecting gifts for even your pickiest friends and loved ones a breeze, but be forewarned: All but the most disciplined of shoppers will likely leave with more than a few gifts for themselves, too.

Divertido

© MATT STROUD

YAPPIN' YINZERS

Who says Pittsburghers can't handle a good-natured ribbing every now and again? Certainly not Alex Kozak, a Pittsburgh native and Duquesne University grad known for creating two novelty plush dolls, the Yappin' Yinzers, which were designed to poke fun at the regional Pittsburgh dialect – Pittsburghese – as well as the "yinzers" who speak it.

Currently, the line of dolls consists of just one male, known as Chipped Ham Sam, and one female, known as Nebby Debby. Sam sports a mullet, a Steelers jersey and cut-off denim shorts, while Debby wears a black-and-gold mesh top and a pair of giant hoop earrings. But the real joke comes when you push their bellies: These are talking dolls, complete with hilariously stereotypical Pittsburgh sayings. "Yinz better settle dahn!" says Nebby Debby. "Jeez oh man," says Chipped Ham Sam. "Quit jaggin' ahrand!"

Sam and Debbie dolls sell for $19.95 each; they're available in a number of Pittsburgh-area boutiques, or online at www.yappinyinzers.com.

E HOUSE

1511 E. Carson St., 412/488-7455,
www.ehousecompany.com
HOURS: Mon.-Thurs. 11 A.M.-6 P.M., Fri.-Sat. 11 A.M.-7 P.M., Sun. noon-5 P.M.
Map 3

Self-described as the most eco-friendly store in Western Pennsylvania, E House deals exclusively in products that tread lightly upon the earth. You'll find organic household products, as well as a wide selection of all-natural home decor, clothing, and accessories (many of them handmade). Looking for a journal or a purse made out of an old license plate? Or maybe a belt designed from an actual automobile seat belt, and decorated with bottle caps? This is your spot, then.

KARDS UNLIMITED

5522 Walnut St., 412/622-0500,
http://kardsunlimited.blogspot.com
HOURS: Mon.-Sat. 9:30 A.M.-9 P.M., Sun. noon-5 P.M.
Map 4

Hardly your average card store, this Shadyside favorite is more of a well-edited novelty shop that also carries an impressive stock of books, comics, graphic novels, posters, candles, T-shirts, wrapping papers, and unusual jewelry items, such as jewel encrusted cigarette cases and lighters. Anyone looking for witty gifts from Knock Knock, stylish Blue Q products (for home and body), or yummy-smelling Yankee candles would do well to take a look here, as Kards Unlimited's selection is the largest in town.

MARJIE ALLON FINE STATIONARY

5406 Walnut St., 412/621-1373,
www.marjieallonstationery.com
HOURS: Mon.-Fri. 10 A.M.-5:30 P.M., Sat. 10 A.M.-5 P.M.
Map 4

As Shadyside's premiere fine paper and gift shop for over twenty years now, Marjie Allon has long been the city's go-to source for writing sets, tasteful gift cards, wedding and party invitations, graduation and birth announcements, and both social and business stationary. This largely upscale shop also carries an assortment of sophisticated gifts and tasteful Pittsburgh-themed merchandise and souvenirs—very much unlike the mass produced souvenirs found in shops throughout the Strip District. If you're looking for a tasteful gift for a colleague or the parents, Marjie Allon is truly one of the best that Pittsburgh has to offer—no wonder it regularly attracts fawning attention in wedding publications nationwide.

SNOW LION IMPORTS

201 Craig St., 412/687-5680, www.snowlionimports.com
HOURS: Mon.-Fri. 11 A.M.-5:30 P.M., Sat. 11 A.M.-4 P.M.
Map 2

Snow Lion Imports is Pittsburgh's first and only location for Tibetan and Himalayan arts,

© DAN ELDRIDGE

S.W. Randall Toys & Gifts

artifacts, religious items, and handicrafts, the vast majority of which were acquired by the owners during trips to Nepal, India, and Tibet. The shop's Craig Street location carries items such as silver and turquoise jewelry, books and CDs, statues, Tibetan signing bowls, prayer flags, bags, clothing, prayer wheels, and a truly impressive collection of Tibetan carpets. Located in the shop's far corner is Sherpa Gear (www.sherpaadventuregear.com), a separate store offering a wide variety of trekking and adventure travel clothing; a portion of the Sherpa Gear proceeds are sent to underprivileged Nepalese kids.

store and a huge collection of dolls and unique toys that you simply won't find at a department or discount store, S.W. Randall Toys & Gifts has been one of Shadyside's most treasured gems for years. Located just off of Walnut Street, this truly magical shop is a rare treat for both children and grown-ups alike. Staffers are wonderfully talented at recommending uncommon, age-appropriate gifts, and can place special orders for most items, including collectible dolls. The company also has locations in Squirrel Hill (5856 Forbes Ave., 412/422-7009) and Downtown (630 Smithfield St., 412/562-9252).

S.W. RANDALL TOYS & GIFTS
806 Ivy St., 412/687-2666, www.swrandalltoys.com
HOURS: Mon., Tues., Thurs.-Sat. 10 A.M.-6 P.M.;
Wed. 10 A.M.-8 P.M.; Sun. 11 A.M.-4 P.M.
`Map 4`
With the ambiance of an olde-fashioned toy

TOADFLAX
500 Walnut St., 412/621-2500, www.toadflax.com
HOURS: Mon.-Tues. and Fri. 10 A.M.-6 P.M., Sat.
10 A.M.-5 P.M., Wed.-Thurs. 10 A.M.-8 P.M.
`Map 4`
This gorgeous floral shop and gift boutique

© DAN ELDRIDGE

Wild Card

offers a true feast for the senses, thanks in large part to the bouquets of the fine fresh-cut flowers—displayed in large modern vases—dotting the otherwise minimalist decor. Whether you're selecting a single lily or rose stem, or asking the shop to arrange a bouquet for that special someone, Toadflax does an exquisite job. Arrangements come complete with unobtrusive greens, premium paper, and satin ribbon. Toadflax also stocks a wide variety of gift items at all price points, including fine candies and chocolates, richly scented premium soy-based candles, coffee table books, skin and body care products, crystal goods, and modern ceramic and blown glass vases.

◀ WILD CARD
4029 Butler St., 412/224-2651, www.wildcardpgh.com
HOURS: Tues.-Wed. and Fri.-Sat. 11 A.M.-7 P.M., Thurs.

11 A.M.-7 P.M., Sun. noon-6 P.M.
Map 6

Described by one Yelp.com reviewer as "one of the coolest shops selling handmade goods I've ever been to," this Lawrenceville darling easily lives up to its online reputation. With the store's eye-popping colors and impressive inventory, including greeting cards, stationary, wallets, jewelry, T-shirts, and more (nearly all made by Pittsburgh crafters), Wild Card is part gift shop and part art gallery, all wrapped up in one handsomely designed little package. In addition to showcasing new exhibits from local artists each month, Wild Card is also home to the Pittsburgh Craft Collective, which boasts an array of arts and crafts classes on everything from yarn spinning to polymer clay jewelry making.

Health and Beauty

🄲 BLOOM ORGANIC SKINCARE PARLOR

5220 Butler St., 412/849-1891; www.bloomskincare.net

HOURS: By appointment only; Mon.-Thurs. 9 A.M.-8 P.M., Fri.-Sat. 10 A.M.-5 P.M.

COST: Basic services $50-110

Map 6

Erinn Thompson's serene skincare studio has quickly built a fiercely loyal customer base, and for good reason: Aside from being an expert esthetician and arguably the best waxer in town, Thompson only uses all-natural, organically sourced products in a gorgeous Victorian parlor. What's more, she consistently protects her customers' privacy and peace of mind—you won't bump into your neighbor in the waiting room—and all treatments are customized. Bloom also offers a complete menu of waxing and tinting services in addition to high-quality eyelash extensions, and men will especially enjoy Thompson's facials and back treatments.

DAQUILA HAIR COLOR STUDIO

6006 Penn Circle S., 412/361-0900, www.daquilahair.com

HOURS: Sun. noon-4 P.M., Tues. and Thurs. noon-8 P.M., Wed. 10 A.M.-6 P.M., Fri.-Sat. 10 A.M.-4 P.M.

COST: Basic women's services $25-130, basic men's services $10-30.

Map 6

Daquila's precision cut and expert hair coloring services are among the best you'll find in Pittsburgh, especially if you're looking for a more modern, fashion-forward, or avant-garde style. Staffers at this effortlessly hip yet personable salon are all Parisian trained, and it shows. Daquila offers a wide variety of cut, color, highlight, treatment, and styling options to suit almost every need or occasion. And the salon is popular with the gents due to its complimentary bang and nape touch-ups (for existing customers), not to mention its reasonable rates—men's cuts start at just $25.

© MATT STROUD

Bloom Organic Skincare Parlor

DEAN OF SHADYSIDE

5404 Centre Ave., 412/621-7900,
www.deanofshadyside.com
HOURS: Mon. noon-8 P.M., Tues. 9 A.M.-6 P.M.,
Wed. 10 A.M.-8 P.M., Thurs. 9 A.M.-8 P.M., Fri. 9 A.M.-5 P.M.,
Sat. 8 A.M.-4 P.M.
COST: Haircuts $25-75
Map 4

With locations in the Hillman Cancer Center (5115 Centre Ave., Level 3, 412/647-2811), at UPMC Montefiore (3459 Fifth Ave., Floor 7, 412/692-2969), and the Oxford Athletic Club in Wexford (100 Village Club Dr., 724/933-9777), it's no wonder Dean of Shadyside is such a well-loved Pittsburgh salon. Though not generally thought of as one of the trendier salons in town, Dean of Shadyside was one of first in the area to offer Great Lengths hair extensions. Today, Dean's is the only area salon specializing in hair for cancer patients, including extensions and thickening treatments (wig specialists are on staff). The Wexford location is also a full-service spa and the main locations all offer hair cutting, coloring, and style services, including manicures, pedicures, and waxing.

ESSPA KOZMETIKA ORGANIC SPA

17 Brilliant Ave., Aspinwall, 412/782-3888,
www.esspa.net
HOURS: Mon. 10 A.M.-8 P.M., Tues.-Sat. 9 A.M.-8 P.M.,
Sun. 11 A.M.-5 P.M.
COST: Spa packages $150-600
Map 7

Well worth braving the ten minute drive from town, Aspinwall's ESSpa Kozmetika has been named the city's best day spa for the last five years (and counting) by handfuls of local publications. The usual assortment of facials, treatments, and peels are offered here, but so too are manicures and pedicures, make up and lash extension applications, massages, mud body wraps and salt scrubs, traditional waxing, and the latest pain-free hair removal service. Working on-site is one of Pittsburgh's premiere plastic surgeons, the Harvard-trained Dr. J. Peter Rubin, who provides cosmetic surgery consultations in addition to Botox, collagen, and Restylane injections.

MCN SALON

5932 Penn Circle S., 412/441-5151, www.mcnsalon.com
HOURS: Tues.-Thurs. 9 A.M.-9 P.M., Fri. 8 A.M.-8 P.M.,
Sat. 8 A.M.-5 P.M.
COST: Basic services $25-65
Map 6

Since relocating into brand new digs on East Liberty's increasingly fashionable Penn Circle South, MCN Salon has improved considerably on its classic urban-chic vibe (think rich cherry wood floors, fresh cut flowers, and a killer view). Specializing in color but also offering hair cuts, textures, waxing, manicures, pedicures, and more, MCN consistently gets rave reviews from loyal customers. And definitely don't forget to say hello to Josie—the owner's English bulldog, and the unofficial salon mascot.

PAGEBOY SALON & BOUTIQUE

3613 Butler St., 412/224-2294, www.pageboypgh.com
HOURS: Sun. 10 A.M.-5 P.M., Tues. 11 A.M.-6 P.M., Wed.
11 A.M.-7 P.M., Thurs.-Fri. 11 A.M.-8 P.M., Sat. 10 A.M.-8 P.M.
COST: Basic services $10-65
Map 6

More of an all-around style headquarters than simply a salon and boutique, Pageboy exudes an aesthetic that celebrates individuality, resourcefulness, and beauty. Indeed, the collective Pageboy experience includes a full service salon, personal styling and shopping, mid-century modern furnishings, and both men's and women's apparel and accessories from a range of local and national indie designers. With its exposed brick and duct work and its crafty displays, this Lawrenceville gem is truly is a one-stop shop for both your personal and lifestyle needs.

SEWICKLEY SPA

337 Beaver St., 412/741-4240, www.sewickleyspa.com
HOURS: Daily 8:30 A.M.-6:30 P.M.
COST: Packages and treatments $15-160
Map 7

Very high-end but not the least bit pretentious, Sewickley Spa is the absolute epitome of relaxation and peacefulness. Year after year, in fact, a good number of spa enthusiasts and

Pageboy Salon & Boutique

trade publications claim it to be among the Greater Pittsburgh area's very best spas. The atmosphere is more or less in tune with what you'd expect at any high-quality spa, yet with Victorian-inspired finishing touches and details that complete the picture perfectly: waterfalls, comfy plush chairs, and changing rooms with trays of fruit and pastries. If that's not convincing enough, consider that a total of 112 ultimate spa treatments are offered. There's a good reason women and men both can be spotted here: There's literally something for everyone.

Home Decor and Furnishings

ASIAN INFLUENCES
3513 Butler St., 412/621-3530, www.asianinfluences.com
HOURS: Wed.-Sat. 11 A.M.-6 P.M.
Map 6

Each and every item in this Butler Street homage to the Far East has been personally selected by shop owner and interior designer Susan Fischer. Many of her antique and one-of-a-kind pieces were acquired during years of antique shopping and auction-going, both in the United States and abroad. This is an ideal boutique to visit, then, if you're looking for something a bit exotic with which to beautify your home or office. Unusually unique lamps and lighting fixtures are sold at Asian Influences as well, which is also something of a paradise for those who love containers like baskets, boxes, and tins.

EQUITA
3609 Butler St., 412/353-0109, www.shopequita.com
HOURS: Call for seasonal hours
Map 6

Self-described as a shop that provides "essentials for ethical living," Equita is so beautifully organized—and its products so eye-catching—

© MATT STROUD

Equita sells the essentials for ethical living.

that even the least socially conscious shoppers will find it hard to keep their wallets closed. You'll find a decent selection of home furnishings here as well as dinner and kitchen wares, towels and bedding, and baskets and stationery, all sourced by organic, green, and fair-trade providers. Equita also stocks casual wear for the whole family, and because the staff here is so knowledgeable about ethical living in general, they're a fantastic resource for those who may be new to conscientious shopping.

FRESH HEIRLOOMS
5218 Butler St., 412/512-5098, www.freshheirlooms.com
HOURS: Thurs.-Fri. 1-6 P.M., Sat. noon-4 P.M.
Map 6

Lawrenceville's Fresh Heirlooms is the sort of store you'd expect to discover if *ReadyMade* magazine, say, morphed itself into a retail establishment. In other words, the shop offers handmade items created from reclaimed and repurposed materials. Most products are designed and made in-house by the shop's owner and her family, all of whom are skilled

craftsman, and who are committed to making high-quality products that will stand the test of time. The store also stocks creations by local salvage artists, and offers design consultations; the artisans here will even create custom work from your own furnishings and products.

HOT HAUTE HOT
2124 Penn Ave., 412/338-2323, www.hothautehot.net
HOURS: Mon.-Tues. and Thurs.-Fri. 10 A.M.-4 P.M., Sat. 9 A.M.-5 P.M.
Map 1

Specializing in eclectic and truly one-of-a-kind furniture pieces, the artists at Hot Haute Hot select used, vintage, or antique furniture items and customize each with a truly unique touch of creativity and top-notch craftsmanship. In other words, this is the perfect showroom for anyone on the hunt for a truly singular gem. The shop also creates custom items on commission for interested shoppers and for commercial spaces. To put it plainly, Hot Haute Hot is the polar opposite of your run-of-the-mill, standard contemporary furniture shop.

SHOPS

PERLORA

2220 E. Carson St., 412/431-2220 or 800/611-8590,
www.perlora.com

HOURS: Mon.-Tues. and Thurs.-Sat. 10 A.M.-6 P.M.,
Wed. 10 A.M.-8 P.M., Sun. noon-5 P.M.

Map 3

Offering trendy contemporary furniture, Perlora is located in a retrofitted building that is now a loft-style showroom. Perlora also staffs a few interior designers available to help with projects of all sizes, which makes sense given the ultra-modern and traditional designs for sale, not to mention the ergonomic chairs and mattresses available. And while it's true that Perlora's furniture can be pricey, the originals are quite striking and not easily available elsewhere in the city.

TOURNESOL

808 Ivy St., 412/682-0599 or 866/682-0115,
www.tournesolgifts.com
HOURS: Tues.-Sat. 10 A.M.-5 P.M.

Map 4

Owned and operated by a globe-trotting lover of antiques and fine home furnishings, Tournesol strives to stock items that are difficult—if not nearly impossible—to find elsewhere in the city. (Or anywhere else, for that matter.) Along with offering a diverse selection of fine French table linens, porcelain and recycled glass dinnerware, and fine art and lighting, the shop also stocks a small but well chosen vintage and antique selection. What's more, the boutique itself is simply gorgeous, complete with hardwood floors and three marble fireplaces. If you're in the market for a worldly and sophisticated gift, or even something for the home, a visit to Tournesol is a must.

WEISS HOUSE

324 S. Highland Ave., 412/441-8888,
www.weisshouse.com
HOURS: Mon.-Tues. and Thurs.-Fri. 10 A.M.-6 P.M.,
Wed. 10 A.M.-8 P.M., Sat. 10 A.M.-5 P.M.

Map 4

Carrying high-end furniture lines like B&B Italia, Cassini, and Ligne Roset, Weiss House employs a highly educated crew of interior designers who specialize in custom work, contemporary kitchen design, and residential renovations. The store has a large selection of carpeting, as well as exotic wood flooring materials. Recently added items include Asian antiques—all of them hand-selected and one of a kind. They also have a small offering of home decor items and gifts such as coffee table books and candles.

Kids' Stores

BABYLAND

5542 Penn Ave., 412/362-1222, www.babylandpa.com
HOURS: Mon.-Sat. 10 A.M.-6 P.M., Sun. noon-4 P.M.

Map 6

The largest baby and infant retailer in Western Pennsylvania, Babyland carries just about any accessory you could possibly imagine that an infant or its parents might desire: cribs, strollers, highchairs, breast pumps, toys, diaper bags—even Pittsburgh Steelers apparel for the littlest football fan in your family. Admittedly, Babyland hardly has the world's greatest atmosphere, but the prices are great, the selection is huge (with new designer lines added regularly), gift ideas are everywhere, and there's even a kids' section featuring furniture, bedding, and more, which means you can continue shopping here even after your baby has grown a bit older.

BECOMING MOMMY

5833 Forbes Ave., 412/421-9600,
www.becommingmommy.com
HOURS: Mon., Wed., Fri.-Sat. 10 A.M.-5 P.M.;
Tues. and Thurs. 10 A.M.-7 P.M.; Sun. noon-4 P.M.

Map 5

Located just across the street from Littles Shoes, Becoming Mommy has been consistently called the best maternity shop in the city since its 2008 opening. The staff here is exceedingly

FREE TOYS

If there's one organization in Pittsburgh that truly understands the financial stress inherent in raising children, it's the 35-year-old **Pittsburgh Toy Lending Library** (5401 Centre Ave., 412/682-4430, www.pghtoys.com, Mon.-Wed. and Fri. 9:30 A.M.-2:30 P.M., Thurs. 9:30 A.M.-6 P.M., Sat. 9:30 A.M.-12:30 P.M.), a volunteer-run cooperative based in Shadyside. And although the library features an indoor playspace for kids aged six and under, the real jewel here is the truly rich collection of more than 300 children's toys that can be rented temporarily and brought home. First visits to the library are free; after that, membership levels range from $25-175 per year. Parents willing to volunteer receive the lowest rates.

breast pumps, nursing bras, and everything else you'll need before and after a baby's arrival. Items are designer, high-quality, and relatively well-priced. Becoming Mommy is definitely the place for Pittsburgh's hip and chic mommas to stock up on their growing wardrobes.

TOTS & TWEEDS
809 Ivy St., 412/661-6500, www.totsandtweeds.com
HOURS: Mon.-Sat. 9:30 A.M.-5 P.M.
Map 4

If you're looking for stylish, high-quality clothes for your little ones from top-of-the-line designers, Tots & Tweeds of Shadyside (in business for over 50 years now) may soon become your favorite Pittsburgh store; some of the clothing and accessories carried here simply can't be found anywhere else in town (think Florence Eisenman, Petit Bateau, Geiger of Austria, and Kathleen Haggerty). If you're the sort of discriminating young parent who considers your baby's uniquely upscale look just as important as your own, this is the spot you're looking for. A small collection of girls' dance dresses, children's wedding attire, and both maternity and infant gear are all stocked.

helpful and friendly, and the inventory vast yet carefully selected. Offerings include everything from work and casual wear to formal wear and accessories, as well as baby carriers,

Pet Supplies and Grooming

A DIAMOND IN THE RUFF
155 S 18th St., 412/381-2200, www.diamondinruff.com
HOURS: Mon.-Wed. and Fri. 8 A.M.-6 P.M.,
Thurs. noon-8 P.M., Sat. 8 A.M.-4 P.M.
COST: Grooming $35-65 dogs, $35-45 cats
Map 3

Known as much for its grooming services as for its signature alternatives to harsh pet shampoos and alcohol-containing conditioners, this popular Southside pet spa and boutique truly is a diamond in the rough. You'll be thrilled at your pooch's fresh new scent, though Diamond in the Ruff also stocks a full line of other shampoos and conditioners specially engineered to bring out the best qualities of different fur types and colors. Therapeutic scrubs, mud masks, and facial scrubs for Spot are also available. Spa packages

include a moisturizing paw treatment and complimentary teeth brushing. Be aware that the last bath is given two hours before close here, and appointments are strongly recommended.

THE DOG STOP
1140 Washington Blvd., 412/361-0911,
www.thedogstop.net
HOURS: Daycare Mon.-Fri. 7 A.M.-7 P.M., Sat.
10 A.M.-4 P.M.; boarding daily 24 hours
COST: Boarding $22-36 per night; daycare $22 full day for the first dog, $15 for each additional dog; grooming $28-55; self-wash service $10 small dogs under 25 lbs.; $15 large dogs 25 lbs. and up
Map 6

Offering a wonderful service for busy dog owners who don't like the idea of leaving their pets at home alone, The Dog Stop takes pains to make sure your favorite hound stays happy, healthy, and socialized—with people as well as other dogs—throughout the day. The Dog Stop also offers full-service boarding 365 days a year, but what really sets this one out from the pack is its ingenious Doggie Bus Stops program. For dog owners too harried to make the morning trip to the facility, The Dog Stop has established drop-off and pick-up locations throughout the city where you can see your pampered pooch onto the bus for his own morning commute into daycare. Current stops are located Downtown, on the South Side, and in Strip District, but customers are invited to recommend additional locations as needed.

GOLDEN BONE PET RESORT
6890 5th Ave., 412/661-7001,
www.goldenbonepetresort.com
HOURS: Mon.-Sat. 9 A.M.-5 P.M.
COST: Boarding rates per day $15 cats, $25-38 dogs; grooming $30-40 cats, $18-70 dogs
Map 6

Located just a stone's throw from the East End neighborhoods of Shadyside and East Liberty, Golden Bone Pet Resort seems to be the favored kennel among discerning dog owners in the city. Decent kennels are never cheap, of course, but Golden Bone offers an exceptional value, and it also does double duty as

a grooming spot—you'll find bathing and other grooming rates at much better prices here than at retail chains and other grooming businesses throughout the city. But assuming you're leaving Spot for an overnight stay, you'll be pleased to learn of the in-house amenities, which include air conditioning, in-floor heat, two large outdoor exercise areas, and around-the-clock care and security. Nervous pet owners interested in touring the facilities may do so Monday–Saturday 1–3 P.M.

SMILEY'S PET PAD
215 S. Highland Ave., 412/362-7556,
www.smileyspetpad.com
HOURS: Mon.-Fri. 10 A.M.-7 P.M., Sat. 10 A.M.-5:30 P.M., Sun. noon-5 P.M.
Map 4

Consistently one of the best independently owned pet supply stores in town, Smiley's carries just about everything imaginable for cats, dogs, and other small animals. You'll find nearly every line of pet food on the market here, from all-natural brands to the vet-recommended Eukanuba and Science Diet lines. Smiley's also stocks handmade toys and collars for both dogs and cats, not to mention a great selection of fleece bedding. There are always a few sweaters and T-shirts on hand for the fashionable pup, and if the store doesn't have something in stock, a customer can always request a special order.

Shoes

BEST-MADE SHOES
5143 Liberty Ave., 412/621-9363,
www.bestmadeshoes.com
HOURS: Tues.-Sat. 10 A.M.-4 P.M.
Map 6

Aside from brands like Danska and Alegria, you won't find the most fashion-forward shoes at Bloomfield's Best-Made. What you will find, however, is the city's best selection of comfort footwear, custom shoes, and orthotics, all being sold by board-certified pedorthists and master shoemakers. If you have any foot, leg or

back pain, and have trouble finding shoes that fit properly, you can rest assured that a trip to Best-Made will have you feeling a heck of a lot better in no time. In addition to offering custom shoes, the family-owned Best-Made also provides shoes for diabetics, and both extra-large and extra-wide shoe sizes.

◖ BONDSTREET SHOES
5533 Walnut St., 412/687-3663,
www.bondstreetshoes.com
HOURS: Tues.-Sat. 10 A.M.-6 P.M.

Map 4

If you're in the market for high-quality, moderately priced European shoes (for men or women) or modern but understated accessories, Bondstreet should certainly be your first stop. Voted "Best New Shoe Store" by *Pittsburgh* magazine, Bondstreet is the exclusive U.S. distributor of German-based Lloyd and Tamaris shoes, and also does a decent trade online. If you're unfamiliar with European footwear, though, a visit to the store is recommended for proper sizing. The shop's beautifully minimalistic, Euro-chic decor and the expert service without pretention make for a genuinely pleasant experience. Even better still, Bondstreet provides a complimentary in-house shoe repair service for all store purchases. Most shoes here are in the $150–450 range.

© DAN ELDRIDGE

Little's Shoes

FOOTLOOSE
736 Bellefonte St., 412/687-3663,
www.footlooseshadyside.com
HOURS: Mon.-Tues. and Thurs.-Sat. 10 A.M.-5:30 P.M.,
Wed. 10 A.M.-9 P.M.

Map 4

Footloose is a relatively small boutique specializing almost entirely in high-end women's designer lines from Italy, Spain, and France. You'll find a very well-chosen collection of pumps, platform stilettos, sandals, and boots, and prices accurately reflect their quality. And while anyone with a fascination for sky-high heels or adorable ballet flats will likely find themselves in metaphorical footwear heaven here, there's a second Footloose location in Mount Lebanon's Galleria Mall (1500 Washington Rd., 412/531-9663, www.galleriapgh.com) where a more practical selection of walking and sporting shoes can be found. Most shoes here are priced at $150–500.

LITTLE'S SHOES
5850 Forbes Ave., 412/521-3848 or 800/646-7463,
www.littlesshoes.com
HOURS: Mon.-Sat. 9:30 A.M.-9 P.M., Sun. noon-5 P.M.

Map 5

While Pittsburgh today has more to offer the modern, stylish man than ever before, there was a time when Little's was one of the city's only independently owned shops offering a large collection of well-chosen, casual men's shoes. The shop is quite large and seemingly always overstaffed, and on the many racks and shelves here you'll find everything from sneakers to formal styles. Brands include reliable, standard fare like Kenneth Cole, Clarks, Birkenstock, Diesel, Cole Haan, Puma, and Steve Madden. In the women's section, which is significantly larger than the men's section and offers much trendier choices, you'll also find handbags and accessories. Try to avoid showing up on busy Saturdays.

PAVEMENT
3629 Butler St., 412/631-6400,
www.pavementshoes.com
HOURS: Mon.-Wed. and Fri.-Sat. 11 A.M.-6 P.M.,
Thurs. 11 A.M.-7 P.M., Sun. 11 A.M.-3 P.M.

Map 6

A desperately-needed addition to the city's shoe scene, Pavement boasts a carefully and creatively curated assortment of designer shoes, as well as a smaller selection of clothing and

SHOPS

© DAN ELDRIDGE

Pavement

hand-made accessories from designers and labels such as Miz Mooz, Irregular Choice, Matt & Nat, and Faryl Robin. With its urban rustic-chic vibe (think gallery-white walls and track lighting juxtaposed against antler sculptures and vintage decor), you'll never want to leave. Perhaps not surprisingly, the owners and staff here are exceedingly knowledgeable and stylish, and as an added bonus, Pavement only stocks merchandise from eco-conscious vendors.

Shopping Districts and Centers

BAKERY SQUARE
Corner of Penn Ave. and Bakery Square Blvd., 412/683-3810, www.bakery-square.com
Map 6

Located on a stretch of Penn Avenue in East Liberty that was once home to a bustling Nabisco plant, Bakery Square is Pittsburgh's new "it" place to work, shop, dine, and play. The $130M facility is home to the city's best new gym—Urban Active Fitness Club—as well as retail shops like Anthropologie and West Elm. Even Google's recently relocated Pittsburgh offices are here. And while the new center's architecture certainly could have been a bit more inspired, it is nevertheless one of a growing number of LEED-certified green developments in the city—there's even designated parking available for hybrid cars.

A Trader Joe's supermarket is just a couple blocks west, at 6343 Penn Avenue, and the EastSide shopping center (Whole Foods, Borders) is also nearby.

THE GALLERIA OF MT. LEBANON
1500 Washington Rd., 412/561-4000, www.galleriapgh.com
HOURS: Mon.-Sat. 10 A.M.-9 P.M., Sun. noon-5 P.M.
Map 7

An upscale if slightly small indoor shopping mall located deep in the South Hills, The Galleria is home to a number of treasured retailers that have no other locations in the city. To name just a few, you'll find Larrimor's,

H. Baskin Clothier, A Pea in the Pod, Crabtree & Evelyn, Nicole Miller, and Restoration Hardware here, as well as a movie theater and small food court. As far as malls go, the Galleria is almost never too terribly noisy or crowded—holiday shopping season excluded, of course.

PENN AVENUE

Penn Ave. btwn. 16th and 24th Sts.,
www.neighborsinthestrip.com
Map 1

Although the Strip District is often referred to as Pittsburgh's only 24-hour neighborhood, the heartiest shoppers among you will want to arrive during the daylight hours on Friday, Saturday, or Sunday, when the widest variety of curbside vendors and street performers set up shop along Penn Avenue. And while you'll certainly find a good number of specialty boutiques here—antique stores, for instance, and home decor shops—it's worth keeping in mind that the Strip is very tourist-friendly, and as such it's home to dozens of little shops hawking touristy trinkets of questionable quality. You'll find knockoff Steelers T-shirts here, and Pittsburgh-themed memorabilia of all sorts, including postcards, ball caps and books. The Strip is also something of a public market, and with a bit of poking around it's possible to procure everything from gourmet coffee and cheeses to imported Italian meats and high-end kitchen gadgets. The best fun to be found here, however, can usually be had by simply wandering the streets and exploring at length. And don't forget to check out Smallman Street, which runs parallel to Penn Avenue and is home to a few unusual shopping surprises of its own.

PITTSBURGH PUBLIC MARKET

2100 Smallman St., 412/281-4505,
www.pittsburghpublicmarket.org
HOURS: Fri. 9 A.M.-7 P.M., Sat. 9 A.M.-5 P.M.,
Sun. 10 A.M.-4 P.M.
Map 1

Located in the Produce Terminal Building near the corner of 17th and Smallman Streets,

the 10,000-square-foot Pittsburgh Public Market is not only one of the city's favorite shopping destination sites and its most popular new tourist attraction, it's also the very first public market the city has seen in nearly five decades. Just over 40 different vendors were represented at the market during its grand opening in September 2010, and as it happens, the many businesses represented here offer a lot more than simple foodstuffs. True, you'll find everything from bagels to beer, cookies, candies, barbecue, and even pasta, wine, and a high-end deli at the market. But also on offer are pet treats, beauty products, and boutiques selling Moroccan housewares and Indian handicrafts. Street artists and musicians can sometimes be found here as well. And as the market is only currently open on Fridays, Saturdays, and Sundays, don't forget to plan your trip accordingly.

THE SHOPS OF ONE OXFORD CENTER

Corner of 4th and Grant Sts., 412/391-5300,
www.shopoxford.com
Map 1

The go-to shopping location for Pittsburgh's wealthiest citizens, The Shops of One Oxford Center—located inside a glass atrium within an impressive 45-foot glass tower—are nearly all breathtaking, either for their beauty or their staggering price tags. Surprisingly enough, most all the shop owners and staffers here are quite helpful and friendly, and willing to assist with both corporate sales needs as well as budget-minded customers. Some of the retailers you'll find here include Emphatics, Kountz & Rider, Philip Pelusi, and St. Moritz Chocolatier. The exclusive Three Rivers Club also has a home in the building; there's also a newsstand, a hair salon, and a food court.

16:62 DESIGN ZONE

Btwn. Penn Ave. and Butler St. from 16th to 62nd Sts.,
www.1662designzone.com
Map 6

Officially starting in Pittsburgh's Strip District before reaching the Lawrenceville neighborhood, the 16:62 Design Zone is essentially Pittsburgh's

EAST LIBERTY'S CHANGING FORTUNES

It is an oft-repeated truism – by city planners, or other professionals who take matters of urban renewal seriously – that an influx of artists into a downtrodden neighborhood is one of the very best indicators of that neighborhood's future economic growth. The same thing may well be said about an area's culinary scene: If hip and progressive restaurants are opening up in a part of town not necessarily known for that sort of thing, it's a good guess that an economic stimulus of some sort is on the neighborhood's near-horizon.

And that's exactly why the suddenly-hot dining scene in Pittsburgh's East Liberty neighborhood is such a fascinating new phenomenon. In the first edition of this guidebook, for instance, which was published in June 2007, the culinary scene in East Liberty was so sadly barren and unappealing that it didn't even warrant being included as a category. But this time around, it boasts some two-dozen individual reviews, a number of them covering some of the most inventive eateries this city has seen in years. Which begs a very obvious question: What exactly has been going on in this corner of the city's East End?

The answer, perhaps not surprisingly, is far from obvious. Most long-time locals, however, would probably agree that it all began back in 2000, when **Home Depot** (400 N. Highland Ave., 412/363-9150, www.homedepot.com) invested some $20 million in the opening of a so-called "big-box" store at a failed Sears site in the neighborhood.

At the time, East Liberty was well-known throughout the city as a dangerous area with active street gangs. And that was exactly why Home Depot's sizable investment in the area was seen as such a positive economic indicator. (It was also the store's very first urban location.) The shop flourished to a great degree, and other retail corporations soon followed suit, including **Whole Foods, Borders** (5986 Penn Circle S., 412/441-1080, www.borders .com), and **Trader Joe's.**

A 145,000-square-foot **Target** store is currently being planned, and even **Google** got involved: It traded its offices at Carnegie Mellon University for a 40,000 square-foot space at a new East Liberty retail development known as **Bakery Square** (www.bakery-square.com), which is being partially built on the site of a former Nabisco plant, and where an **Anthropologie** (6425 Penn Ave., 412/441-2302, www .anthropologie.com) store recently opened. Also joining the Bakery Square party is the recently opened **Marriott SpringHill Suites** hotel, which connects via an enclosed walkway to the gorgeously modern **Urban Active Fitness Club.** A branch of the local **Coffee Tree Roasters** chain is located just across the parking lot, and future additions to the square may include a **West Elm,** and possibly a **Neiman-Marcus** location.

But no matter how promising this retail development may in fact appear to outsiders, the city and its developers have not been able to escape the inevitable charges of gentrification that have been lobbed upon it for the better part of ten years now. It is true, after all, that the mostly African-American residents of some 1,400 public housing units were displaced – and saw their high-rise apartment buildings demolished – in order to make way for new construction. But in a hard-luck Rust Belt city like Pittsburgh, it can somehow seem dishonest to cry foul when formerly forlorn areas like East Liberty are genuinely beginning to look up. And the truth is that after five decades of steady decline, this small corner of the city's East End is once again becoming a true destination for Pittsburghers with money to spend.

To learn more about East Liberty's changing fortunes, visit www.eastlibertypost.com and www.bakery-square.com. Also recommended is local filmmaker Chris Ivey's *East of Liberty*, a feature-length documentary about the neighborhood's many changes. Screening times and locations are posted at www.east ofliberty.com.

arts, crafts, and interior design district. As such, it's overflowing with galleries, boutiques, and open studios. And as Lawrenceville has, in recent years, found itself home to some of the best independently owned and operated shops in the city (Wild Card, Sugar, Pavement, Fresh Heirlooms, and Who New? all come to mind), shopping in the 16:62 Design Zone has become a great way to support local artists. Numerous events are organized throughout the year here, including the annual **Joy of Cookies** tour and the hugely popular **Art All Night** party (www .artallnight.com), where guests enjoy a full 24 hours of art and music. For more information about the area, visit www.lawrencevillecorp.com and www.lvpgh.com.

SOUTHSIDE WORKS

445 S. 27th St., 412/481-8800,
www.southsideworks.com
Map 3

An outdoor shopping center complete with exclusive boutiques, big-box chain stores, cafés and restaurants, a movie theater, and even high-end apartment buildings, it didn't take long for SouthSide Works to earn its reputation as one of the city's most successful recent retail projects. Clothiers here include Urban Outfitters, Benetton, BCBG, Kenneth Cole, Puma, Forever 21, REI, American Eagle, and H&M. You'll also find a Sharper Image store, a Joseph-Beth Bookstore, two coffee shops, an Irish bar, a luggage store, and a dentist (whew!). For more information, visit the **Guest Services kiosk** outside the Cheesecake Factory.

THE WATERFRONT

300 Waterfront Dr., Homestead, 800/366-0093,
www.waterfronttowncenter.com
Map 7

Perched along the Monongahela River in between Squirrel Hill and Homestead, The Waterfront is a massive outdoor shopping center located on the former site of the Homestead Steel Mill. Try to arrive at the Waterfront by traveling through Squirrel Hill and then crossing the Homestead High Level Bridge, also known as the Homestead Grays Bridge, as the view of the river and of Homestead beyond is spectacular.

You'll find just about everything you'd expect in a traditional mall here, in addition to a cinema with stadium seating, dozens of eateries, a grocery store, a hardware store, a Target, and much more.

COURTESY OF ROB MATHENY

SouthSide Works

SHOPS

Skateboarding and Bicycle Shops

CHEAP SKATES

1985 Lincoln Way, White Oak, 412/678-0808,
www.pacheapskates.com
HOURS: Mon. and Fri. 1-7 P.M., Tues.-Thurs. 1-8 P.M.,
Sat. noon-6 P.M., Sun. noon-5 P.M.
Map 7

Located just outside McKeesport, Cheap Skates
has been a skateboarding community staple in
Pittsburgh since 1987, and an absolute legend in the nationwide skating community for
nearly as long. Its retail location has the area's
largest collection of boards, shoes, hats, DVDs,
and skate-inspired street wear. And don't forget
to check the shop's website before visiting, as
you'll often find specials and secret sales mentioned only online.

CLANKWORKS

3401 Butler St., 412/567-1419, www.clankworks.com
HOURS: Tues.-Thurs. 10 A.M.-7 P.M.
Map 6

As Pittsburgh continues to become an increasingly bike-friendly city, it's perhaps no surprise
that specialist boutiques like ClankWorks have
finally made the scene. ClankWorks designs
and manufactures all its accessories in-house;
the studio/shop also carries merchandise
from high-quality, style-conscious vendors
like Seattle Bike Supply and Velo Orange.
And because the shop's co-owners both live
and work in the back of the building, visitors are always welcome to stop in and have
a look at the studio's production methods.
The signature item here is a bamboo veneer
fender that sells for $30, or $50 for a pair.
Insider's tip: Directly across the street are the
offices of **Bike Pittsburgh** (3410 Penn Ave.,
412/325-4334, www.bike-pgh.org), where
you can pick up free copies of the always
in-demand **Pittsburgh Bike Map,** as well as
the **Bike Commuting 101** guide.

IRON CITY BIKES

1985 331 S. Bouquet St., 412/681-1310,
www.ironcitybikes.com

HOURS: Mon.-Fri. 11 A.M.-7 P.M., Sat. 11 A.M.-5 P.M.,
Sun. noon-4 P.M.
Map 2

Located in the heart of South Oakland, the
somewhat rough-around-the-edges Iron City
Bikes carries a wide variety of high-quality bicycles, accessories, apparel, and merchandise
from manufacturers including Norco, Surly,
Velocity, ToPeak, and Haro. Iron City also
provides bicycle maintenance services, and
it boasts an amazing collection of used bikes
starting at just $20 each. Do be forewarned,
however, that while staffers here are extremely
knowledgeable, they can tend to seem a bit intimidating to cycling newbies.

ONE UP SKATE

1409 E. Carson St., 412/432-7007, www.oneuppgh.com
HOURS: Mon.-Tues. and Thurs. noon-7 P.M., Wed. and
Fri.-Sat. noon-8 P.M., Sun. noon-5 P.M.
Map 3

Something of a cross between an upscale

One Up Skate

and apparel, with labels like Vans, Addidas, and Dickies all well represented. A dizzying array of beautifully shiny skate decks—neatly stacked floor to ceiling on brackets—is also on offer here. And what's more, the quite knowledgeable and surprisingly friendly staff offer private skate lessons by appointment at Mr. Smalls Funhouse in Millvale.

◖ THICK BIKES

62 S. 15th St., 412/390-3590, www.thickbikes.com
HOURS: Daily 10 A.M.–6 P.M.
Map 3

Originally located in Brooklyn, Thick Bikes is a full-service repair shop that has been fabricating chromoly bicycle frames and other custom parts since 1996. And while the small showroom here is packed tight with some of the best bikes and cycling products on the market, including a wide selection of used cycles and messenger gear, Thick Bikes is probably best known among locals for its honesty and its concern for safety. For those ready to make a serious investment, the shop also deals in made-to-order bicycles—some so stylish they'll even have drivers drooling.

© MATT STROUD

Thick Bikes

boutique and an old-school skate shop, One Up quickly became a South Side institution after first opening its doors in 2003. The store boasts an impressive collection of skate shoes

Vintage and Antiques

AMBIENCE BOUTIQUE

1039 S. Braddock Ave., 412/243-5523,
www.ambianceboutique.org
HOURS: Tues.-Wed. and Fri.-Sat. 11 A.M.–5:30 P.M.,
Thurs. 11 A.M.–8 P.M.
Map 5

A subsidiary of Bethlehem Haven, a non-profit organization established to provide assistance to homeless women in the Pittsburgh area, all three of the city's Ambience Boutiques are lovely little thrift shops stocked full of both new and consigned designer labels, accessories, and home furnishings. Conveniently located in Regent Square, Lawrenceville (4735 Butler St., 412/697-0773), and Oakmont (Allegheny River Blvd., 412/828-1946), the shops even carry formal evening wear and furs and usually

a large collection of shoes, all at very reasonable prices. Ambience also opens its space for private after-hours shopping parties (perfect for birthday girls of all ages).

CONSTRUCTION JUNCTION

214 N. Lexington St., 412/243-5025,
www.constructionjunction.org
HOURS: Mon.-Fri. 8 A.M.–5 P.M., Sat. 9 A.M.–5 P.M.,
Sun. 11 A.M.–4 P.M.
Map 5

Though not technically a vintage or antique shop per se, Construction Junction is actually Pittsburgh's used building-materials supply warehouse, and an excellent place to find anything and everything for that home-improvement project you're working on—everything

Need a sink or toilet? Find one (or several) at Construction Junction.

© DAN ELDRIDGE

from decorative doors and windows to old toilets, filing cabinets and plywood. And because the shop was started with the intention of keeping construction supplies out of landfills, everything here is available for literally a fraction of the price you'd pay at a big-box building supply store. Perhaps not surprisingly, Construction Junction is a favorite among Pittsburgh's DIY community.

DESIGNER DAYS BOUTIQUE

5846 Ellsworth Ave., 412/441-0330,
www.designerdaysboutique.com
HOURS: Tues. and Thurs.-Sat. 10 A.M.-5:30 P.M.,
Wed. 10 A.M.-7 P.M., Sun. 11 A.M.-4 P.M.

Map 4

An upscale consignment shop where only the most exclusive designer labels—Prada, Gucci, and Chanel, to name just a few—are sold at often shockingly low prices, Designer Days is operated by the National Council of Jewish Women, which works to improve the lives of women and children in the Pittsburgh area. Everything from casual, career and eveningwear is carried here, as well as designer accessories, handbags, and women's shoes. Private shopping parties for your club or organization can also be hosted here; visit the shop's website for details.

EONS FASHION ANTIQUE

5850 Ellsworth Ave., 412/361-3368
HOURS: Mon.-Fri. noon-6 P.M., Sat. 11 A.M.-6 P.M.,
Sun. noon-5 P.M.

Map 4

A great spot for both men's and women's fashions from the "1880s through the 1980s," Eons is possibly best known for its sidewalk mannequin that's dressed up daily by the store's eclectic owner. The best finds here are definitely dresses, costume jewelry, and hats, although there are also loads of very feminine pieces and some wonderful pants and shirts for guys. Being that Eons is a tiny store with a ton of clothing and accessories stuffed into its various nooks and crannies, browsing here can sometimes be a slight bit frustrating, but the owner is friendly, helpful, and exceedingly patient.

SPENDING FOR A GOOD CAUSE

Though inspired by Judaic ideals, the Pittsburgh branch of the **National Council of Jewish Women** (www.ncjwpgh.org) is a grassroots, non-sectarian and not-for-profit organization dedicated to improving the quality of life for Pittsburgh-area women, children, and families. The Council runs a wide array of programs including consignment shops, book drives, services for the elderly, and even a campaign to raise community awareness about local domestic violence. It also operates two fantastic local thrift stores. One is **Designer Days Boutique** (5846 Ellsworth Ave., 412/441-0330, www.designerdaysboutique.com, Tues. and Thurs.-Sat. 10 A.M.-5:30 P.M., Wed. 10 A.M.-7 P.M., Sun. 11 A.M.-4 P.M.), a high-end consignment shop where labels including Prada, Louis Vuitton, Chanel, Moschino, and Hermés can often be found. The other is **Thriftique** (7400 Church St., Swissvale, 412/271-0544, www.thriftiquepgh.com, Mon.-Sat. 10 A.M.-6 P.M., Sun. 11 A.M.-4 P.M.), a huge Swissvale thrift store where everything from housewares to furniture to used clothing can be had.

(Contributed by Carrie Ann, a designer and life-stylist based in Pittsburgh and Philadelphia.)

THRIFTIQUE

7400 Church St., Swissvale, 412/271-0544, www.thriftiquepgh.com

HOURS: Mon.-Sat. 10 A.M.-6 P.M., Sun. 11 A.M.-4 P.M.

Map 7

Run by the same organization that operates the upscale Designer Days Boutique in Shadyside, Thriftique is the thrift and consignment store to visit if you're looking for slightly cheaper and more mainstream or "mall" brands: Gap, Banana Republic, Express, Chico, Ann Taylor, and Talbots, for example. Thriftique's greatest asset, however, is probably its size; the store is simply enormous, and aside from men's, women's, and children's clothing and shoes, you'll find everything from furniture to housewares, and from books to toys here. Seniors aged 55 and over save 25 percent on clothing every Monday.

WHO NEW?

5156 Butler St., 412/781-0588, www.who-new.com

HOURS: Wed.-Sat. noon-6 P.M., also by appointment

Map 6

Easily the best place in Pittsburgh at which to track down midcentury decor, Who New? is owned and operated by two men who might best be described as 20th-century design encyclopedias. The shop carries a wide-ranging selection of retro home furnishings, the vast majority from the 1950s through the 1970s, including an incredible selection of vintage barware and kitchen items. The owners are more than willing to bargain, and if you're looking for something specific they don't have, they'll even help you hunt it down. A small selection of new novelties (baby onesies, greeting cards, and toys) is also available.

HOTELS

When it comes time to find a place to stay in Pittsburgh, the good news is that this city has more than enough hotel rooms to accommodate just about any guest for about any length of time. Visit during a large convention, or during the holidays, or even at the beginning or end of a school year, and you're practically assured of finding some sort of vacancy somewhere. Yet it's an unfortunate fact that the variety of accommodation options leaves a bit to be desired. What you'll find in abundance here are mostly corporate-style and chain hotels, most of them pricey. Hotels and guesthouses in Pittsburgh also tend to be clustered together in a handful of neighborhoods, which means you're somewhat limited in terms of where in the city you'll stay.

The backpackers and budget travelers among you will no doubt be disheartened to learn that Pittsburgh's solitary youth hostel, a lovely Hostelling International–sponsored building that was located atop a hill in Allentown, permanently closed its doors in 2003.

But don't trade in your air ticket for a round-trip to Cleveland just yet; there *is* good news in the Steel City lodging scene, most of it revolving around the town's especially quaint bed-and-breakfasts. Visit just about any bed-and-breakfast in the city, in fact, and chances are you'll be pleasantly surprised to find such refined and sophisticated interiors in a town most popularly known for its grittiness and blue-collar history. Do keep in mind, however, that since most bed-and-breakfasts have a very small number of rooms, advance reservations are highly recommended, even in the off-season.

HIGHLIGHTS

LOOK FOR **(** TO FIND RECOMMENDED HOTELS.

(**Best Luxury Hotel:** You'll pay dearly for a room at Downtown's **Fairmont Pittsburgh,** but thanks to the plethora of lavish and grandiose hotel experiences to be had here – upscale guest services, stately rooms with modernist furniture – you won't find anything finer within the Golden Triangle (page 223).

(**Best Room with a View:** Ask for a room on one of the top two floors of Downtown's **Renaissance Pittsburgh Hotel,** and you may be able to take in a pro baseball game from the comfort of your queen-sized mattress. The top floor is the best; just make sure your room faces the Allegheny River (page 224).

(**Best Queer-Friendly Bed-and-Breakfast:** Owned and operated by a wonderfully accommodating couple, Jeff and Karl, **The Inn on the Mexican War Streets** is Pittsburgh's most gloriously decorated residence (page 226).

(**Best Historic Renovation:** No longer just a quaint bed-and-breakfast with a hushed, olde-world European atmosphere, **The Priory** on the North Side is now fully equipped for the modern business traveler. It offers Wi-Fi, meeting rooms, a fitness center, and a complimentary downtown shuttle service (page 227).

(**Best Long-Term Stay:** An artistically decorated inn where stays of a month or more

are encouraged, Bloomfield's **EdenHouse** comes complete with all the modern conveniences of home – and a smartly tricked-out home at that (page 232).

the Fairmont Pittsburgh

COURTESY OF THE FAIRMONT PITTSBURGH

HOTELS

CHOOSING A HOTEL

For any of the Pittsburgh visitors who've come to study or work at a college or area hospital, the university district of Oakland is the obvious choice. Not only does it have a decent number of hotels, it also offers a fair amount of variety. Two Oakland hotels, for instance, offer full suites, and one offers a substantial discount to students.

Just a bit farther east is Shadyside, a relaxed and leafy neighborhood where both the homes and the commercial district are upscale. Here you'll find a number of bed-and-breakfasts;

there's also a decent chain hotel located directly across the street from Shadyside Hospital.

Downtown Pittsburgh, however, is where the majority of the town's tourists and business travelers call it a night. As is the case in most midsize downtowns, pricey chain hotels are the order of the day here. Many Downtown hotels, however, offer a decent mix of telecommuting accessories and on-site eateries, making a weekend in the Golden Triangle as professional and productive as it is entertaining and unique.

Most guidebooks to the region encourage the shoestring traveler to investigate the

HOTELS

PRICE KEY

$ Under $150

$$ $150-250

$$$ Over $250

many chain hotel options near the airport, and while that advice is certainly useful in theory, it does little good for anyone arriving by bus or by train, not to mention anyone without the use of a private vehicle. The artistic-minded Bloomfield bed-and-breakfast known as **EdenHouse** (4069–4071 Liberty Ave., 412/621-1698, www.ironeden.com) is currently the city's most affordable lodging,

with stays of three to six nights at rates as low as $70 per night. For the most part, however, EdenHouse guests are encouraged to stay for at least two nights.

If you'd prefer to stay outside the city, visit www.pittsburghbnb.com, which contains a list of inns and bed-and-breakfasts throughout the Greater Pittsburgh area and its surrounding countryside. The nationwide website www.bed andbreakfast.com is also useful.

For a more comprehensive listing of hotels and motels, cabins, campgrounds, bed-and-breakfasts, and resorts, visit the very useful www.visitpa.com. Also useful for accommodation listings—as well as information about regional events—is www.visitpittsburgh.com.

The rates in this chapter are based on double occupancy in the high season (summer).

Downtown   Map 1

Downtown Pittsburgh is small enough that its entire distance can easily be covered on foot, so when choosing a hotel, there's really not much of a need to consider *where* in Downtown it's located. You can rest assured that shopping, theaters, and restaurants will always be just a brief walk or taxi ride away.

CAMBRIA SUITES PITTSBURGH AT CONSOL ENERGY CENTER $$
1320 Centre Ave., 412/381-6687,
www.cambriasuites.com
A contemporary, all-suite hotel located just steps from the city's newest arena, Cambria Suites Pittsburgh ($179–249) is now the lodging option of choice for anyone attending an event at the CONSOL Energy Center. The 142 rooms here are all non-smoking, and a few even come complete with kitchenettes, hot tubs, and wet bars—not to mention killer city-skyline views. And although Cambria Suites is a chain hotel, it's decked out to resemble an independent, boutique-style inn; the rooms, lobby, and social areas all convey a warm aesthetic.

There's also an on-site fitness center, and free Wi-Fi throughout.

COURTYARD MARRIOTT DOWNTOWN $$
945 Penn Ave., 412/434-5551,
http://marriott.com/property/propertypage/pitcy
As Downtown Pittsburgh's newest hotel, the Courtyard Marriott ($179–289) sits uniquely inside four side-by-side historical buildings. By contrast, Downtown's other lodging options are all stand-alone structures, most of them enormously large. What that equates to is that even though the Courtyard Marriott's buildings have been thoroughly renovated, some interesting architectural details remain, such as the 12- or 14-foot vaulted ceilings found in each room. The fitness room here stays open around the clock, and right next door is the especially popular Sonoma Grille, a contemporary American restaurant with a fantastic wine list. On-site parking is available, and the David L. Lawrence Convention Center is little more than a stone's throw away.

DOUBLETREE HOTEL & SUITES PITTSBURGH CITY CENTER $$

1 Bigelow Sq., 412/281-5800 or 800/222-8733,
http://doubletree.hilton.com

Located in the heart of the Golden Triangle, the Doubletree Hotel ($169–249) sits just steps from the U.S. Steel Tower, the David L. Lawrence Convention Center, and Mellon Bank's headquarters, making it a convenient choice for the busy business traveler. Guests are also welcome to access the hotel's 24-hour business center, which offers free printing, faxing, copying, and high-speed Internet access. The spacious, yet not especially modern rooms all come with work desks, ergonomic chairs, and flat-screen TVs. Also complimentary is access to the adjacent Downtown Athletic Club, a fitness center with an indoor pool and tanning bed.

◖ FAIRMONT PITTSBURGH $$$

510 Market St., 412/773-8800,
www.fairmont.com/pittsburgh

Talk about a welcome reception: With its sleek and minimalist European vibe and its dramatically modern atmosphere, the Fairmont Hotel ($349–369) chain's first Pittsburgh location embodies nearly everything that has been lacking for so long from the city's luxury hotel scene. Located in the heart of Downtown's Cultural District, the 185 rooms here feature floor-to-ceiling windows—many with stunning views—and all the standard touches of a high-end boutique hotel, including iPod stations, brand-name toiletries, and a luxurious collection of the sort of furniture you might expect to see in an IKEA showroom. Guests are also afforded access to the fitness center downstairs. And the on-site Pan-Asian restaurant, Habitat, has consistently earned high scores from area critics. The Fairmont's severely expensive room rates, in fact, may be its only discernable downfall.

HAMPTON INN & SUITES PITTSBURGH-DOWNTOWN $$

1247 Smallman St., 412/288-4350,
http://hamptoninn.hilton.com

Situated literally across the street from the Heinz History Center, there's nothing particularly notable or unique about the Downtown Hampton Inn ($186–229), save for its location on the border of the historic and international Strip District. This is a straight-ahead business traveler's hotel, and as such it comes complete with a convenient business center, as well as a pool and a small gym. The free parking is probably the biggest boon here, although the clean and sizable rooms and the buffet-style breakfasts are also top-notch.

OMNI WILLIAM PENN $$$

530 William Penn Pl., 412/281-7100,
www.omnihotels.com

Known as Pittsburgh's premiere luxury hotel, the Omni William Penn ($229–429) has been welcoming well-heeled guests (including Lawrence Welk and John F. Kennedy) since 1916. Luckily, it's possible to experience the grandeur of the place even if you're not a registered guest: Simply sink into one of the massive lobby's deep couches and gaze upon the many chandeliers and the baby grand. Or, wander

COURTESY OF THE FAIRMONT PITTSBURGH

the Fairmont Pittsburgh's lobby

HOTELS

COURTESY OF ROB MATHENY

the Omni William Penn

into the attached Starbucks, the Tap Room (an English-style ale house), or the Palm Court, a restaurant known for its exquisite cocktails. Rooms are absolutely first-class, too, and come complete with all the modern conveniences, including cherry wood furniture, plush bathrobes, and personalized voicemail.

PITTSBURGH MARRIOTT CITY CENTER ⑤⑤

112 Washington Pl., 412/471-4000 or 888/456-6600, http://marriott.com/property/propertypage/pitdt

Although not necessarily the most conveniently located hotel for those doing daily business in the heart of Downtown, the Pittsburgh Marriott City Center ($189–279) is especially well located for anyone who's come to town specifically to attend an event at the new CONSOL Energy Center; it sits almost directly next door. Celebrity obsessives staying here may even get the chance to spy their favorite star; major musical acts and other performers appearing at Mellon Arena often bunk here because of its obvious convenience. Guest rooms are meticulously decorated, from the carpets to the curtains to the artwork on the walls. And all rooms come equipped with a work desk suitable for the business traveler. Right downstairs is the Steelhead Brasserie and Wine Bar, a popular contemporary American eatery.

◖ RENAISSANCE PITTSBURGH HOTEL ⑤⑤⑤

107 6th St., 412/562-1200, http://marriott.com/property/propertypage/PITBR

Although owned by the Marriott organization, the Renaissance Pittsburgh Hotel ($199–349) is designed to look and feel like a stylish and creatively detailed boutique hotel. With its old-world, European theme, it's one of the few Downtown options for those interested in lodging that lacks the cookie-cutter, corporate feel. Guest rooms, although outfitted with all the conveniences one would find in any Marriott, are smartly decorated as well, and the on-site restaurant, Braddock's American Brasserie, is a locally celebrated European and American fusion spot with an impressive cocktail menu.

HOTELS

COURTESY OF ROB MATHENY

the Westin Convention Center Pittsburgh

Baseball fans should request a room with a PNC Park view.

WESTIN CONVENTION CENTER PITTSBURGH ❸❸❸
1000 Penn Ave., 412/281-3700,
www.starwoodhotels.com/westin

As the name cleverly suggests, the Westin Convention Center Pittsburgh ($325–385) is an ideal lodging choice for any out-of-towner planning to attend the recently remodeled David L. Lawrence Convention Center. In fact, an enclosed skywalk connects the two buildings. The Westin is also home to the Original Fish Market, a fantastic seafood eatery with one of the city's best sushi bars. There's an 8,000-square-foot fitness center as well, complete with a sauna and a lap pool. Rooms here are some of the Downtown area's largest; each one has a view of the central business district. Complimentary transportation to The Andy Warhol Museum and PNC Park is offered. Pets are welcome.

WYNDHAM GRAND PITTSBURGH DOWNTOWN ❸❸❸
600 Commonwealth Pl., 412/391-4600,
www.wyndham.com/hotels/PITWG/main.wnt

Located directly across the street from the entrance to Point State Park, Wyndham Grand Pittsburgh Downtown ($125–514) is the new name of the property that for decades was known as Hilton Pittsburgh; the property is no longer managed by the Hilton corporation. Nevertheless, Wyndham Grand Pittsburgh Downtown is still the largest hotel in the city, with more than 40,000 square feet and 27 different meeting rooms. All 713 rooms boast a phenomenal city view; some gaze out over the park and the three rivers beyond. It's probably worth keeping in mind that the hotel was essentially stripped of the Hilton name due to management conflicts, although fairly extensive interior renovations, at least, were being made at the time of writing. Free Wi-Fi is available.

North Side

Map 1

Thanks in large part to all the recent development around the North Shore, the North Side has lately experienced something of a small hotel boom. If you're here to take in a Steelers or Pirates game, you shouldn't have much trouble securing a bed, although advance reservations are still a good idea in this area. When it comes to bed-and-breakfasts, however, travelers are absolutely awash with choices. There are scores of bed-and-breakfasts in the area, and every last one is creatively decorated and brimming with character. Crossing one of the bridges to Downtown on foot is simple, not to mention a perfect way to get a great view of the city skyline. Yet with all there is to do on the North Side, you can easily spend a long weekend here without ever needing to leave the neighborhood.

HYATT PLACE PITTSBURGH-
NORTH SHORE 💲💲
260 North Shore Dr., 412/321-3000,
www.pittsburghnorthshore.place.hyatt.com

Although it's now the second hotel within shouting distance of PNC Park (the Marriott Springhill Suites is at the field's northeast corner), there's much more to recommend about the city's new Hyatt Place ($149–179) property than its convenient-to-the-ballpark location. The gorgeous contemporary interiors are decidedly boutique-like, and feature 42-inch flat-screen TVs, minimalist furnishings, and soft lighting. Other amenities include oversized sleeper-sofas, a mini-fridge, and all the trappings of a top-notch business hotel: free Wi-Fi, a spacious work area, and two phones. All rooms are smoke-free.

🌙 THE INN ON THE MEXICAN WAR
STREETS 💲💲
604 W. North Ave., 412/231-6544,
www.innonthemexicanwarstreets.com

Without a doubt, this inn ($139–189) is the city's best all-around bed-and-breakfast. Boasting eight individually and uniquely decorated suites, a front porch shaded by stone arches and columns, a gorgeous lobby complete with a baby grand piano, and off-street parking, you just couldn't ask for a lovelier locale. This bed-and-breakfast is gay-owned, gay-friendly, and is patronized largely by gay men and lesbians. Heterosexuals are more than welcome, of course. A phenomenal contemporary American restaurant, Acanthus, is romantically located in a carriage house behind the Inn.

MARRIOTT SPRINGHILL SUITES
NORTH SHORE 💲💲
223 Federal St., 412/323-9005,
http://marriott.com/property/propertypage/PITNS

Because of its location across the street from the Pittsburgh Pirates' PNC Park, the recently constructed Marriott Springhill Suites ($189–219) seems to have been built for the express purpose of housing pro sports fans. Yet it's also true that every tourist destination on the North Side is within walking distance, as is Downtown. Parking is available for $17 a day, and a complimentary shuttle will drop you off and pick you up anywhere within a three-mile radius of the hotel. All suites are equipped with a sofa and a small pantry area. A spa, a heated pool, and a fitness center are also on-site.

THE PARADOR 💲
939 Western Ave., 412/231-4800 or 888/540-1443,
www.theparadorinn.com

Owned and operated by a Pittsburgher who was influenced by a stint in Florida, The Parador ($150) is a Caribbean-themed bed-and-breakfast situated in the unlikely locale of Allegheny West, just up the hill from the Carnegie Science Center. Previously known as the 8,000-square-foot Rhodes Mansion, which was built in 1870, The Parador's many suites and common areas seem to stretch on forever. Each room is decorated and detailed to suggest a different tropical flower, and the lavish 2,000-square-foot ballroom, with its incredibly ornate back bar mirror, must be seen to be believed. At the time of writing, plans for a full beach-themed garden were well under way.

◖ THE PRIORY ⑤⑤

614 Pressley St., 412/231-3338, www.thepriory.com

A 25-room European-style boutique hotel located within walking distance of all the North Side's major attractions, The Priory ($140–235) is a restored 19th-century Benedictine rectory that has been welcoming guests for more than two decades now. Dozens of local and national publications have sung its praises over the years, which shouldn't come as much of a surprise considering its timeless Victorian charm, its truly friendly and personalized service, and a lovely outdoor courtyard. And with its new fitness room, Wi-Fi access, and free North Shore and Downtown shuttle service,

SURF CITY: SLEEPING IN PITTSBURGH ON A SHOESTRING BUDGET

HOTELS

The fact that you are currently using a Moon Handbook significantly increases the possibility that you're already at least somewhat familiar with the hugely popular budget-travel phenomenon and website known as **Couch-Surfing** (www.couchsurfing.org), which may prove to be just the ticket for those lamenting Pittsburgh's truly limited budget-accommodation options. But for those of you who've never heard of it, here's the gist.

The Couch Surfing Project – a verifiable nonprofit organization based in New Hampshire – was founded back in 1999 by Casey Fenton, who at the time was a cash-poor backpacking student. Fenton's visionary idea was rooted in what had long been an unmet need for low-budget travelers the world over: He wanted to create a system whereby travelers who either couldn't afford to sleep in hotels or simply didn't want to sleep in hotels could instead sleep in the homes of fellow travelers around the world. For free. And thanks to the growing popularity of social networking on the Internet – not to mention the age-old concept of crashing on a generous friend's couch – Fenton developed a very simple way to make that happen. To explore the concept yourself, simply log onto the site and sign up for a free account.

Admittedly, the personal profiles you'll find on the CouchSurfing site are quite similar to those found on just about any other flavor-of-the-month social networking site. The difference, however, is that the intention is not to reunite with old friends, but rather to present yourself in such a way that perfect strangers will allow you to actually sleep on their couches – generally for no more than a few days – while you visit their town. The ideal CouchSurfer, of course, returns the favor once his travels are over by hosting other travelers. When it works, this cultural and entirely cash-free exchange tends to epitomize the very best aspects of the budget-travel ethos, which assumes that travelers who live as the locals do will in turn have a much more authentic "experience."

For many travelers, however, the Couch-Surfing concept seems to be fraught with potential peril. And that's exactly why various safeguards – including a home address verification system – have been built into the site. The creation of a city-specific group system was yet another intended safeguard, and Pittsburgh, in fact, is home to a thriving and active CouchSurfing group of its very own. The Pittsburgh group hosts two monthly meetings, including a happy hour get-together at a neighborhood bar, and a potluck, which is generally held at the home of a CouchSurfing member. The Pittsburgh group's website (www.couchsurfing.org; search "Groups" for Pittsburgh) is also a great place for potential visitors to ask questions about the region, to discover useful resources, and hopefully, to make new, real-world friends.

(Contributed by Matt Stroud, a Pittsburgh-based freelance journalist, with additional reporting by Dan Eldridge.)

The Priory is also a wise option for the traveling businessperson looking for something a bit more intimate than the average chain hotel.

RESIDENCE INN NORTH SHORE 💲💲

574 W. General Robinson St., 412/321-2099, www.marriott.com

As is the case with each of the Marriott's hugely popular Residence Inn locations, this recent addition to the tourist-friendly North Shore features comfortably roomy suites with kitchenettes and separate working and sleeping areas ($179–259). Thanks to the contemporary furniture, decor and lighting, though, the rooms here feel much more like well-appointed studio apartments than actual hotel rooms. And yet the real prize is the hotel's location: You'd be hard-pressed to find a spot more conveniently situated to Downtown Pittsburgh without actually staying there. And while on-site parking will set you back $18 daily, the hotel is within easy walking distance of both Heinz Field and PNC Park, as well as a host of new bars and restaurants, and the world-renowned Andy Warhol Museum.

Oakland   Map 2

Oakland is the city's university district, and as such it's naturally home to a number of chain hotels that do a booming business at the beginning and end of every school year. (I recommend booking well in advance if you'll be staying in this neighborhood during the end of August, the beginning of September, the end of April, or the start of May.) Oakland is also a good alternative to Downtown—you'll be surrounded by all the urban amenities here, and both Downtown and the culture-packed neighborhoods of the East End can be easily reached by a quick taxi or bus ride.

FORBES AVENUE SUITES 💲💲

3401 Forbes Ave., 412/325-3900 or 877/335-3900, www.forbesavesuites.net

Offering suites with one, two, or three rooms, Forbes Avenue Suites ($139–215 daily, $700–1,291 weekly, $1,950–3,872 monthly) sits smack-dab in the center of the university district, and according to management, serves mainly two types of clientele: folks affiliated with the surrounding universities (grad students, guest lecturers) or those doing business with the surrounding hospitals (residents, patients' families). The digs here, however, are decidedly grim and with nary a single piece of designer furniture in sight. Yet considering the fact that full-size stoves, ovens, refrigerators, microwaves, dishwashers, and TVs are included, it does serve an important purpose: Should you find yourself in town for a week, a month, or longer, you'll have all the amenities of home without the hassle of a sublet-apartment search. Parking is $10 extra per night, and students receive a 20 percent discount.

HAMPTON INN
UNIVERSITY CENTER 💲💲

3315 Hamlet St., 412/681-1000 or 800/426-7866, www.pittsburghhamptoninn.com

Although South Oakland's Hampton Inn ($159–184) is perfectly located for anyone visiting Magee-Womens Hospital, Carlow College, or the Pittsburgh Playhouse, it should be noted that because of its slightly hidden location in a somewhat confusing part of the city, out-of-towners arriving in their own vehicles will likely get temporarily lost unless they've been given very detailed directions. Conveniently enough, directions can be downloaded from the hotel's website; look for the "hotel fact sheet" PDF link. On the bright side, the Hampton Inn quite often has rooms available when the rest of Oakland is booked solid (at the beginning and end of college semesters, for instance). And although rooms are relatively plain, a daily hot breakfast and a complimentary shuttle service are included. A fitness center and business center are on-site.

HOLIDAY INN SELECT AT UNIVERSITY CENTER $$

100 Lytton Ave., 412/682-6200, www.hiselect.com

If you need to stay in Oakland but would prefer not to be polluted by the noise of the urban jungle, the Holiday Inn Select at University Center ($162–250) would be a wise choice. Located almost across the street from the Cathedral of Learning, the hotel sits a few buildings in from busy 5th Avenue. Rooms are more or less what you'd expect: clean, but with no exciting amenities. There is an indoor pool, however, as well as a restaurant and a small gift shop.

QUALITY INN UNIVERSITY CENTER $

3401 Boulevard of the Allies, 412/683-6100 or 800/245-4444, www.choicehotels.com

Although as a chain it's a bit low-budget and bare-bones, this particular location of Quality Inn ($99–129) is rather nice. It's no boutique hotel, of course, but the rooms and beds are fairly large, and most come complete with small balconies. (Perfect for smokers who've checked into a non-smoking room.) The hotel's real benefit, though, is its location: The Quality Inn is located deeper in South Oakland than any other hotel, so parents visiting college students who live in the neighborhood will be well positioned, even if they've arrived without a car. Extra bonus points: Parking is free, and there's a Panera Bread on the ground floor.

WYNDHAM GARDEN HOTEL $$

3454 Forbes Ave., 412/683-2040, www.wyndham.com/hotels/PITUP/main.wnt

A 198-room, eight-floor hotel in South Oakland, the Wyndham Garden Hotel ($169–269) is a relatively standard spot close to Carlow College, Magee-Womens Hospital, UPMC Presbyterian, and Children's Hospital. On-site you'll find a restaurant, a fitness center, and a complimentary shuttle that will drop off or pick up anywhere within three miles of the hotel. Pets are welcome for an additional $10 charge per day, and six rooms are available for guests using wheelchairs.

FAMILY HOUSE

In late 1983, a small group of doctors and influential community leaders in Pittsburgh noticed a troubling trend taking place in the waiting rooms and hallways of the city's many hospitals: Out-of-town family members of patients undergoing long-term treatment for serious illnesses were sleeping in corridors and plastic chairs for days on end. Sometimes weeks on end. Determined to do something about it, the group formed a nonprofit organization and eventually raised enough money to refurbish an old mansion near the city's main hospital complex. Families of patients with life-threatening illnesses, and in some cases the patients themselves, were welcomed to temporarily move into the mansion at a very reasonable cost. A communal kitchen was built to cut down on the prohibitive expense of eating every single meal at a restaurant.

The popularity of Family House (www.family house.org, 412/647-7777), as the group called its accommodation, soon outgrew the confines of that first mansion. Today the organization has rooms and suites at four separate locales: 514 North Neville Street in North Oakland, 233 McKee Place in South Oakland, 5245 Centre Avenue in Shadyside, and 123 University Place in Central Oakland. All houses offer free shuttles to West Penn Hospital and most UPMC hospitals, as well as libraries, fitness rooms, on-site laundry facilities, TV lounges, cable TV in each room, private phone lines and voice mail in each room, 24-hour security, and most important of all, a warm and caring family environment at very affordable rates.

Single rooms, for instance, are $40 per day, while double rooms cost $50 per day and suites are $60 per day. For more information or to request a room, call or visit the Family House website.

South Side

Map 3

HOTELS

Most Pittsburghers think of the South Side as one of our town's most debaucherous and eclectic neighborhoods. Bars and clubs are everywhere, so if you've come to Pittsburgh primarily to play, sleeping on the South Side makes good sense. For additional good advice about what to see, do, and eat in the area, visit www.southsidepgh.com, www.southsidepitts burgh.com, and www.southsideworks.com.

HOLIDAY INN EXPRESS HOTEL & SUITES 💲💲

20 S. 10th St., 412/488-1130, www.hiexpress.com

The Holiday Inn Express Hotel & Suites ($142–229) is frequently booked. Which isn't to say that it's a particularly special place, just that it is wonderfully located: It sits at the base of the 10th Street Bridge, making a walk into Downtown quite possible. And it's just blocks from the heart of the South Side Flats. Guest rooms are certainly comfortable and clean enough, but if a South Side location isn't important to you, save a few dollars and bunk elsewhere.

MARRIOTT SPRINGHILL SUITES SOUTHSIDE WORKS 💲💲

2950 S. Water St., 412/488-8003, www.marriott.com

Sitting smack-dab in the center of one of the city's best shopping centers—SouthSide Works—and within easy walking distance of East Carson Street's many amenities, the Springhill Suites ($179–289) are home to the sort of rooms that actually do feel a bit like home. Each suite, for instance, comes with a microwave, a fridge, and a wet bar. There's also free Wi-Fi, and a fitness center with a whirlpool, of all things. However, it's the hotel's inventively futuristic design and decor (strikingly similar to that of the W Hotels chain) that make this property so truly enjoyable. The Springhill Suites may be corporate-owned, but its modern design and layout easily

compare with the hippest of boutique hotels. Insider tip: To avoid late-night noise coming from the nearby train tracks, request a room facing away from the Monongahela River.

MORNING GLORY INN 💲💲

2119 Sarah St., 412/431-1707, www.gloryinn.com

A bed-and-breakfast so subtly concealed on a residential street that even most locals don't realize it's there, you might say that the peacefully relaxing Morning Glory Inn ($155–450) is the absolute antithesis of the hard-partying neighborhood it calls home. A lovingly restored 1862 Victorian, this is the South Side's only independent lodging. And trimmed as it is with antiques, period fireplaces, a cozy two-level "Attic Suite," and a wildly popular back garden area where wedding receptions are held most weekends, it's also one of Pittsburgh's better bed-and-breakfasts. Do bear in mind, however, that neither Downtown nor Oakland are within walking distance, regardless of the claims made on Morning Glory's website.

SHERATON HOTEL STATION SQUARE 💲💲💲

300 W. Station Square Dr., 412/261-2932, www.sheraton.com

Should you find yourself booked at the Sheraton Hotel Station Square ($289–339), you may feel somewhat isolated from town. But assuming the weather is nice, reaching the business district is actually quite pleasant—just take a five-minute walk across the Smithfield Street Bridge. The Monongahela Incline leading to Mount Washington is also nearby. And unlike most chain hotels in the city, this one is smartly designed and boasts a beautifully modern lobby. The guest rooms are nicely understated, and there's a fitness room, a pool, and a wonderful steak restaurant—Pittsburgh Rare—on-site.

Shadyside Map 4

The bed-and-breakfasts in Shadyside are all located within walking distance of Walnut Street and Ellsworth Avenue, which is where the vast majority of the neighborhood's shopping, dining, and entertainment options can be found. If you're in town to visit one of the colleges or universities, walking is certainly an option, although you might prefer using a rental car or taxi to get there and back. Most of the bigger East End hospitals are also relatively close by.

THE INN AT 714 NEGLEY 🟢🟢
714 S. Negley Ave., 412/661-0631,
www.theinnsonnegley.com

A restored period home built in the latter part of the 19th century, The Inn at 714 Negley ($180–240) is a wonderfully quaint bed-and-breakfast tucked away in an upscale residential neighborhood. Individual rooms, as well as the inn itself, are professionally decorated with antiques and period furniture; the overall style is a nicely done mixture of country charm and European sophistication. Each room comes with an imported down comforter and either a jetted shower system or whirlpool tub in the bathroom.

SUNNYLEDGE BOUTIQUE HOTEL 🟢🟢
5124 5th Ave., 412/683-5014, www.sunnyledge.com

A historic landmark built in 1886, the Sunnyledge Boutique Hotel ($139–199) is one of the East End's most gorgeous bed-and-breakfast choices. Original oak paneling and fixtures are found throughout, and each of the eight guest rooms is decorated in its own unique and truly elegant Victorian style. Rooms come complete with whirlpool tub, mini-bar, and cable TV, and a library, exercise room, and 24-hour concierge are all on-site. Sunnyledge also features a five-star restaurant, known as the Tea Room, as well as a martini bar.

HOTELS

© DAN ELDRIDGE

The Inn at 714 Negley

Bloomfield and Lawrenceville   Map 6

The Italian district of Bloomfield—conveniently located between the upscale shopping district of Shadyside and artsy, up-and-coming Lawrenceville—doesn't offer much in the way of lodging. Your options are limited to the perfectly comfortable (but still corporate-owned) Courtyard Marriott, or EdenHouse, a sort of bed-and-breakfast for the creative set. Bloomfield is nevertheless one of the city's most authentic neighborhoods, and it's not far from the university and hospital district of Oakland.

COURTYARD MARRIOTT $$

5308 Liberty Ave., 412/683-3113,
http://marriott.com/property/propertypage/PITOK
The Courtyard Marriott ($169–239) sits right on the Shadyside/Bloomfield border, and it's the best choice for anyone visiting patients at the nearby Shadyside Hospital or the UPMC Hillman Cancer Center. It's also conveniently located for anyone visiting family or friends in Bloomfield or Friendship, and it isn't terribly far from North Oakland or East Liberty. The guest rooms, while clean and comfortable enough, aren't much to write home about, although a small indoor swimming pool and a Starbucks are on-site. A parking lot open only to guests is another bonus, although you'll be charged $19.50 a day for the privilege.

[C] EDENHOUSE $

4069-4071 Liberty Ave., 412/621-1698,
www.ironeden.com
Not necessarily a hotel and not quite a bed and breakfast, EdenHouse ($60–175) is a distinctive first for Pittsburgh. A short-term residence owned by two working artists, this gorgeously outfitted home is available for weekly and monthly rentals. (Shorter stays can sometimes be negotiated.) And because it's located in a residential neighborhood, EdenHouse is an ideal choice for travelers interested in experiencing Pittsburgh just as a local would. Accommodation options include the 1,200-square-foot Loft, which sleeps six and features a Jacuzzi and a rooftop garden; the 700-square-foot Apartment, complete with a stove and dishwasher; and the Studio, an efficiency apartment with cable TV, Wi-Fi and a kitchenette. The gorgeous interiors here have a designer vibe and a unique, sophisticated artistic sensibility. And EdenHouse's location in the city's East End is simply unbeatable.

RESIDENCE INN MARRIOTT $$

3896 Bigelow Blvd., 412/621-2200 or 800/513-8766,
http://marriott.com/property/propertypage/PITRO
Located in a rather odd stretch of North Oakland, the Residence Inn Marriott ($169–279) may seem like an impossibly inconvenient place to stay for visitors who've arrived without private vehicles. But the truth is that as the only hotel in the neighborhood, it's perfectly positioned for anyone visiting North Oakland–based friends or family, and a shuttle service to and from central Oakland is complimentary for guests. As for the digs themselves, this is Oakland's only all-suite hotel—as such, rooms come complete with a refrigerator, microwave, toaster, dishwasher, and a full stove and oven. There's also a basketball court, indoor pool, and exercise room on-site, as well as a special outdoor area for pet-walking.

East Liberty and Garfield   Map 6

Until very recently, East Liberty was gang-inflicted and synonymous with danger. Retail growth and creeping gentrification have changed the area to a great degree, although it's still wise to keep your wits about you after dark here. The area is full of galleries and boundary-pushing restaurants and boutiques.

FRIENDSHIP SUITES $

301 Stratford Ave., 412/392-1935, www.friendshipsuites.com

Although technically located in the Friendship/Garfield area, Friendship Suites ($99–149) has a wonderfully convenient (and quietly residential) East End location, and is less than two miles from the university and hospital district of Oakland, as well as the Shadyside shopping district. This is essentially a bed-and-breakfast (minus the breakfast) where spacious, apartment-like suites sit inside a gorgeous Victorian brick home. And although the proprietor doesn't live on-site, he prides himself on top-notch customer service, and is always just a phone call away. Street parking is rarely a problem here, and significant discounts are offered for weekly and monthly stays.

MARRIOTT SPRINGHILL SUITES BAKERY SQUARE $$

134 Bakery Square Blvd., 412/362-8600, www.marriott.com

With a fresh and modernist interior design not unlike that of the recently opened Springhill Suites Southside Works, this 110-room Marriott ($149–219) is located right within East Liberty's much-ballyhooed Bakery Square development, a mixed-use area where upscale retail meshes with corporate office space, including the new Google headquarters. Guests are afforded free use of the adjacent Urban Active Fitness Club, which can be reached via an enclosed walkway. Although considering all the modern conveniences available here—free parking, free Wi-Fi, flat-screen TVs, a heated pool, and suites featuring refrigerators, microwaves, and separate living and work spaces—you may find it difficult to so much as leave the comfy confines of the hotel.

Greater Pittsburgh   Map 7

Assuming you've arrived in Pittsburgh with your own vehicle, staying in Oakmont is a smart compromise between small-town living and the big city. Downtown Pittsburgh is less than a half-hour drive away, yet you'll still feel a peaceful distance from the urban bustle here.

ARBORS BED & BREAKFAST $

745 Maginn Ave., 412/231-4643, www.arborsbnb.com

A 19th-century farmhouse nestled into a wooded and relatively obscure corner of the North Side, Arbors Bed & Breakfast ($95–145) is just minutes from the North Side's commercial district by car. Two rooms and one suite are available; all three are decked out in a fairly traditional "county inn" style, and all come with cable TV and a DVD player. Just off the small downstairs kitchen is the Arbors' sunroom; with its in-floor radiant heat and hot tub, it's undoubtedly the bed-and-breakfast's best feature. The management is particularly friendly and quick to offer sightseeing, nightlife, and dining recommendations.

DOONE'S INN AT OAKMONT $$$

300 Rte. 909, 412/828-0410, www.theinnatoakmont.com

With eight guest rooms, all of them equipped with Wi-Fi and a "sleep machine" programmed with, say, tropical noises or ambient sounds, The Inn at Oakmont ($220–350), as it was formerly

HOTELS

known, is your smartest bed-and-breakfast option if you'd like to be far from an urban neighborhood, but still relatively close to Downtown Pittsburgh via car. A public golf course sits just across the street from the bed-and-breakfast, and, as an added bonus, the charming town of Oakmont is ideal for an afternoon or evening stroll and a bit of window-shopping.

DOUBLETREE PITTSBURGH/ MONROEVILLE CONVENTION CENTER $$

101 Mall Blvd., Monroeville, 412/373-7300, http://doubletree1.hilton.com

Formerly a somewhat disappointing Radisson Hotel, this Doubletree ($126–184) location, which sits just off the Pennsylvania Turnpike, has literally been renovated from the inside out, and it shows. The interiors here are modern and even a touch trendy, which isn't a feature you're likely to find at most other Monroeville-area hotels. Along with the standard pool, hot tub, and fitness center, you'll find Wi-Fi in the rooms and throughout the hotel's public areas. There's also a decent wine bar and a small bistro-style restaurant. You'll definitely need a car to travel around the Monroeville area, however, which is essentially an endless outdoor strip mall filled with chain restaurants and big-box stores.

HILTON GARDEN INN PITTSBURGH/ SOUTHPOINTE $$

1000 Corporate Dr., Canonsburg, 724/743-5000, http://hiltongardeninn.hilton.com

Situated a good 20 miles south of the city in the Washington/Canonsburg area, this is the hotel *par excellence* ($129–219) for business travelers who need to stay within shouting distance of the South Hills suburbs. Amenities here include a 24-hour business center, a small outdoor garden area with a gazebo, a fitness center with a swimming pool and whirlpool, and a grand ballroom that can easily fit 1,000. The rooms and suites here are perfectly clean and accommodating, but fairly standard in terms of style and design. Business travelers will appreciate the two phones—each with two lines—that come standard in every room.

HYATT REGENCY PITTSBURGH INTERNATIONAL AIRPORT $$

1111 Airport Blvd., 724/899-1234, http://pittsburghairport.hyatt.com

Every decent-sized airport in the United States is surrounded by hotels that serve the sort of traveler who, for whatever reason, doesn't need to actually enter the urban center of the city he or she's just flown into. But in Pittsburgh, the Hyatt Regency ($157–209) has introduced a concept you may not have seen before: Because an enclosed walkway attaches the hotel to the airport, lodgers can go from the airport's baggage claim to the hotel's front desk without ever stepping outside. The interior, too, is impressive. Designed to resemble a modern boutique hotel, you'll find detailed and tasteful touches almost everywhere, from the warmly accented lobby to the fitness center. Rooms come with a large desk, dual phone lines, and a dataport.

EXCURSIONS FROM PITTSBURGH

As any serious gridhopper would most likely admit, sometimes the best part about visiting a city is waving goodbye. After all, in order to gain a proper perspective on a place, first you've got to gain some distance. And even those with an unending love of the concrete jungle occasionally need to escape its reach.

Even if you're only planning on being in Pittsburgh for a week or two, I'd still encourage you to consider at least a brief day trip, if not a slightly longer weekend adventure. And while it's probably something of a widespread assumption that the further reaches of Western Pennsylvania don't have much to offer the average traveler, in fact, the exact opposite is true.

Globetrotters the world over have long been visiting the state's Laurel Highlands, and for good reason: Not only does world-famous architecture coexist with the quiet beauty of wooded nature here, but regular ol' fun can be had as well, especially along the banks of the almost-unpronounceable Youghiogheny (pronounced yaw-ki-GAY-nee) River, where some of Pennsylvania's wildest tubing and rafting takes place.

And while art, history, and railroad museums seem to exist in every last nook and cranny of this corner of the world, it's quite likely that you'll experience much more in locales with less institutional flavor. In a booth at a backwoods diner, for instance, where the apple pie and the eccentric locals remind you more of *Twin Peaks* than "America the Beautiful." Or maybe in front of the shelves at an out-of-the-way thrift store, where a stack of ultra-rare vinyl records are waiting for you in a wooden bin and priced at $0.50 each.

© FRANK KOVALCHEK

HIGHLIGHTS

LOOK FOR 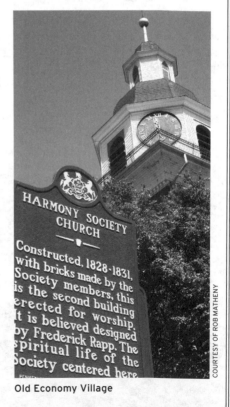 TO FIND RECOMMENDED SIGHTS, ACTIVITIES, DINING, AND LODGING.

Boldest Ode to Local Ingenuity: The Big Mac sandwich was invented by a McDonald's franchise owner in the mid-1960s, and the **Big Mac Museum** in North Huntington is, naturally, the place to show your due respect (page 238).

Best Residential Architecture: Still regarded by critics and professionals alike as one of the finest examples of American residential architecture, **Fallingwater** in Mill Run is quite possibly the most gorgeous – and the most photogenic – of Frank Lloyd Wright's uniquely constructed works of utilitarian art (page 239).

Best Retro Amusement Park: Ligionier's **Idlewild Park** isn't necessarily the place to visit if it's death-defying roller coasters you want. But for a quaintly thrill-packed weekend afternoon, it can't be beat. Bring your "bathing costume" for a trip to the decidedly more modern **Soak Zone,** Idlewild's onsite water park (page 240).

Best River Rafting: Whether you're looking to master some of the country's most vicious Class V white-water rapids, or if you'd simply prefer to float lazily along a slow river in a giant inner tube, you'll find scores of outfitters along the banks of the Youghiogheny in **Ohiopyle State Park** happy to help you do just that (page 241).

Best Landmark: A must-see sight for rail fans the world over, **Horseshoe Curve National Historic Landmark,** a 220-degree curve located outside Altoona at the Kittanning Gap, is still considered an absolutely masterful feat of modern engineering (page 244).

Classiest Tribute to a Local Tragedy: No matter what's on your itinerary, an afternoon at the somber but impressive **Johnstown Flood Museum** is a must. The flood is still considered one of the country's worst-ever natural disasters (page 245).

Best State Park: With its Old Mill and its covered bridge, the forested **McConnell's Mill State Park** in Portersville is as beautifully picturesque as it is welcoming to adventurists (page 249).

Best Blast from the Past: Just a short drive from Downtown Pittsburgh, **Old Economy Village** is the former home of the somewhat bizarre yet fiscally ingenious Harmony Society. The village, located in Ambridge, gives some of the best clues as to how the society lived and worked (page 250).

Old Economy Village

COURTESY OF ROB MATHENY

EXCURSIONS

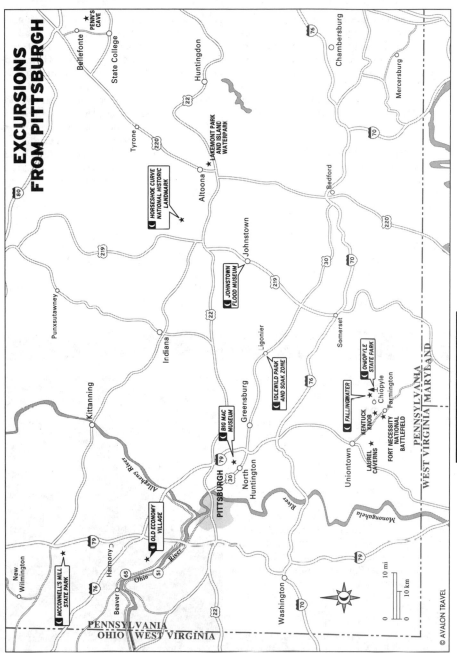

EXCURSIONS FROM PITTSBURGH

PENN'S CAVE
Bellefonte
State College
Huntingdon
Chambersburg
Mercersburg

76

22

80

70

Tyrone

220

LAKEMONT PARK AND ISLAND WATERPARK

HORSESHOE CURVE NATIONAL HISTORIC LANDMARK

Altoona

Bedford

219

Johnstown

JOHNSTOWN FLOOD MUSEUM

220

Punxsutawney

22

219

30

70

Indiana

Ligonier

70

IDLEWILD PARK AND SOAK ZONE

Somerset

Kittanning

Greensburg

76

OHIOPYLE STATE PARK

Allegheny River

BIG MAC MUSEUM

FALLINGWATER

Chiopyle

Farmington

79

KENTUCK KNOB

PENNSYLVANIA

WEST VIRGINIA | MARYLAND

30

North Huntington

FORT NECESSITY NATIONAL BATTLEFIELD

Uniontown

LAUREL CAVERNS

PITTSBURGH

OLD ECONOMY VILLAGE

Monongahela River

New Wilmington

79

MCCONNELL'S MILL STATE PARK

76

Harmony

65

Ohio

51

Beaver

River

79

10 mi

10 km

Washington

70

22

0   10 km

PENNSYLVANIA
OHIO | WEST VIRGINIA

EXCURSIONS

But ultimately, it doesn't much matter which way you explore the outer reaches of Pittsburgh, nor how you decide to have fun. What matters is that you've simply gotten out there. You've explored. You've tried something new. And when the novelty of the rural areas and the tiny little towns begins to wear thin, you know what to do, right? (Hint: Sometimes the best part about visiting the country is waving goodbye.)

PLANNING YOUR TIME

Because Pennsylvania is such a large and sprawling state, it's naturally wise to consult a decent map before simply heading out on the highway. The Keystone State is literally packed with quaint rural areas, small towns that modern time seems to have forgotten, and still-pristine wilderness areas. But it's also heavy with industrial detritus and drab four-lane highways. So do yourself a favor and take the time to sit down with a friendly guesthouse or bed-and-breakfast owner, or a decent state guidebook, before setting out. For comprehensive state and day-trip info, I recommend *Moon Pennsylvania* by Anna Dubrovsky, *Moon Pennsylvania Camping* by Jason Miller and Heidi Ruby Miller, and *Pennsylvania Off the Beaten Path* by Christine O'Toole.

Visitors without a lot of time to spare would probably do best to consider heading toward the nearby Laurel Highlands. Not only can the area be reached quickly by car from Pittsburgh (about an hour's drive), it also offers a wide variety of popular activities, from protected wilderness areas to amusement parks to world-famous works of architecture.

Those with a bit more time on their hands might also consider heading north to the Lake Erie area. Aside from the grandeur of the Great Lake itself, Erie is home to the seven-mile-long peninsula known as Presque Isle State Park. Along the way, there are a number of interesting little towns and unique shopping opportunities located not far from I-79.

Laurel Highlands

Luckily for visitors to Pittsburgh, not only is the Laurel Highlands region relatively nearby, it also contains a wealth of diverse activities. A family of four with differing interests may need to visit four separate sites to keep everyone happy, but for what it's worth, you'll probably find all four of them here. The area's most popular tourist attraction is Frank Lloyd Wright's Fallingwater, but if you're planning to visit the house during a quick day trip, consider leaving a little earlier and mixing in a few side activities along the way.

A massive archive of area activities can be found on the website of the **Laurel Highlands Visitors Bureau** (120 E. Main St., Ligonier, 724/238-5661 or 800/333-5661, www.laurel highlands.org).

SIGHTS
C Big Mac Museum
Pittsburgh boosters are quite fond of reminding visitors that McDonald's iconic Big Mac

Big Mac Museum

© DAVID FULMER

THE JIMMY STEWART MUSEUM

The city of Indiana is a pretty good distance to travel for just one museum, but for hardcore Jimmy Stewart fans, the pilgrimage will be more than worth your while. The now-deceased star of the silver screen grew up in Indiana, and the town boasts a statue of his likeness as well as the Jimmy Stewart Museum (845 Philadelphia St., 3rd floor, 724/349-6112 or 800/835-4669, www.jimmy .org, Mon.-Sat. 10 A.M.-5 P.M., Sun. noon-5 P.M., admission $7 adult, $6 senior, $5 child), which can be found inside the Indiana library and next to its city hall.

The museum contains all manner of movie memorabilia pertaining to Stewart's life, including posters and film clips. There's also a decent gift shop. Don't miss the separate room dedicated to the Stewart family history in Western Pennsylvania – Jimmy Stewart's kin, apparently, have lived in and around the Indiana area since the time of the Civil War.

While at the museum, ask for directions to Jimmy's boyhood home, which remains a private residence. Also ask for directions to the former location of J. M. Stewart & Sons Hardware, his father's store where Jimmy worked as a boy.

sandwich was invented in the region (by franchise owner Jim Delligatti in 1965), and the Big Mac Museum (9051 Rte. 30, North Huntingdon Township, 724/863-9837, www.bigmacmuseum .com, daily 5 A.M.–midnight) is proof positive. Aside from bowing down at the altar of the Big Mac here, by the way, you can also sink your teeth into one, as this is actually a working McDonald's restaurant, and was only recently transformed into a mini-museum. You'll find a life-sized bust of Delligatti himself here, a ridiculously huge (and unnervingly lifelike) Big Mac statue, and all manner of classic McDonald's memorabilia. Whether you're a junk food junkie or a pop culture obsessive, you'll get a kick out of this over-the-top peon to the two all-beef patties. (Take Exit 67 off the PA Turnpike.)

◖ Fallingwater
Declared by architects and critics worldwide as one of the most stunning private structures ever built in the United States, Frank Lloyd Wright's Fallingwater (Rte. 381, Mill Run, 724/329-8501, www.fallingwater.org, Thurs.–Tues. 10 A.M.–4 P.M., admission $18 adult, $12 child) is an absolute must-see for anyone visiting Pittsburgh who also has access to a car. Considering that a mere 90-minute drive from Downtown will get you there, this makes for a fantastic day trip no matter what the season.

Designed in 1935 for the Kaufmann family, who at the time owned one of Pittsburgh's most profitable department store companies, Fallingwater is quite possibly the finest example of Wright's praiseworthy architectural philosophy, which he referred to as "organic architecture": Wright was a staunch believer in the concept that art and nature could coexist peacefully, so when Edgar J. Kaufmann asked for his house to be built next to a favorite waterfall in Mill Run, Wright instead designed it to rest *above* the falls. To see the house from its left or right sides is equally stunning; Wright cleverly built the boxy sandstone shapes and cantilevered levels directly into the sloping earth.

After serving its initial purpose for 26 years (the house was used as a weekend getaway), Fallingwater opened to the public in 1963. Notably, it remains the only important Wright structure in the area open to the public with both its furniture and artwork intact. (Wright was legendary for wishing to control the interior look and layout of the homes he designed.)

Along with regular and in-depth tours, visitors may choose a "Sunset Tour" ($110 pp) or a "Landscape Hike" ($18 pp). Adjacent to the Fallingwater grounds is the 5,000-acre **Bear Run Nature Reserve**— great for hiking and

EXCURSIONS

bird-watching. And Frank Lloyd Wright's **Kentuck Knob** (www.kentuckknob.com)—another innovatively designed residence—is only seven miles away.

Fort Ligonier

Built by the British for protection during the French and Indian War, the historical interest in Fort Ligonier (200 S. Market St., Ligonier, 724/238-9701, www.fortligonier.org, Apr. 15–Nov. 15 Mon.–Sat. 10 A.M.–4:30 P.M., Sun. noon–4:30 P.M., admission adult $8, child $5) is largely due to its seeming impenetrability: During its eight years of existence, the fort's walls were somehow never penetrated.

A full eight acres of the original fort site have been preserved and can be toured today. There's also an impressive onsite museum featuring a French and Indian War art gallery, and a rare collection of pistols once owned by George Washington.

Fort Necessity National Battlefield

If you've already visited the Fort Pitt Museum in Pittsburgh's Point State Park, you may be encouraged to stop by Fort Necessity National Battlefield (1 Washington Pkwy., Farmington, 724/329-5512, www.nps.gov/fone, daily 9 A.M.–5 P.M., admission $5 adult, children 15 and under are free), where the French and Indian War of 1754 first rang out. To start, stop by the battlefield's **visitor center** for a current schedule of activities and to view a short film, *Road to Necessity,* which summarizes the bloody events that took place here. Interactive museum exhibits briefly explain the war as well.

Next, follow a short path to an area known as **Great Meadow.** Nestled into the shadow of the Allegheny Mountains, this is a site of serious historical proportions, as the war actually began here. Visitors feeling a bit restless may want to explore the five miles of hiking trails that surround the site, while history buffs might prefer the seven-mile side trip to **Jumonville Glen** (open daily 9 A.M.–4 P.M., free with paid admission to Fort Necessity National Battle

Field), where George Washington met the French face to face for the very first time.

Ohiopyle State Park, Fallingwater, and Laurel Caverns are all located nearby.

◖ Idlewild Park and Soak Zone

Originally constructed in 1878, Idlewild Park (Rte. 30 East, Ligonier, 724/238-3666, www.idlewild.com, June–Aug. daily 10:30 A.M.–8 P.M., $31.99 general admission, $23.99 senior, free child 2 and under) was during its salad days not much more than a recreational campground with picnic tables and an artificially constructed lake. As the mid-20th century approached, however, Idlewild began attempting to transform itself into an honest-to-goodness amusement park. That plan didn't fully come to fruition until 1983, when the Kennywood Park Corporation bought the company out.

Today, the park consists of seven theme areas, including Olde Idlewild, where the Ferris wheel, the merry-go-round, and other similarly quaint attractions are located, and Soak Zone, a water park with various slides and pools. The five remaining areas, including Mister Rogers' Neighborhood of Make-Believe and Story Book Forest, are considerably tame, and clearly aimed more toward the youngest of guests rather than teenaged coaster fans or anyone seeking thrill rides.

Kentuck Knob

Although it's certainly less visited than Fallingwater, Frank Lloyd Wright's more famous residential cousin that sits only seven miles away, Kentuck Knob (6723 Kentuck Rd., Chalk Hill, 724/329-1901, www.kentuck knob.com, Apr.–Oct. Sun.–Tues. & Thurs.–Sat. 10 A.M.–4 P.M., Wed. noon–4 P.M., Nov. Sun.–Tues. & Thurs.–Sat. 10 A.M.–3 P.M., Wed. noon–3 P.M., tours $18 adult, $12 child) is nonetheless a fascinating and truly unique work of art. Exploring both structures during a day trip from Pittsburgh is certainly possible.

Wright was 86 years old when he designed Kentuck Knob for a family—the Hagans—who had visited Fallingwater a number of times and greatly admired it. Alternately known as "Hagan House" and "The Child of Fallingwater," the house was constructed according to the specifications of a style Wright referred to as "Usonian," which had no attics or basements and was intended to keep building and utility costs low. Derived partly from Wright's Prairie-style homes, the Usonians were relatively small, one-story structures with flat roofs. Kentuck fits that descriptor well, although it also features a number of surprising 60-degree angles; the house was built on a hexagonal grid. (Pay attention while wandering around the house, as the hexagonal theme is repeated throughout.)

Laurel Caverns

Located 50 miles south of Pittsburgh near Uniontown, the 435-acre Laurel Caverns Geological Park (2 Skyline Dr., Farmington, 724/438-3003 or 800/515-4150, www.laurelcaverns.com, May 1–Oct. 31 daily 9 A.M.–5 P.M., tours $11 adult, $10 senior) offers a wealth of family-style activities, including 55-minute guided tours of the sandstone caverns, as well as much more strenuous caving exploration tours lasting as long as three hours. Before or after taking a tour of the caverns, visitors can pay $45 to rappel three times off a 45-foot-high cliff. And for a mere $5 per person there's Kavernputt, an 18-hole miniature golf course inside a 10,000-square-foot artificial cave.

Originally called Laurel Hill Cave, and then Dulaney's Cave, Laurel Caverns is the largest cave in the state of Pennsylvania. It's also the 16th-longest developed cave in the United States; there are a total of 2.8 miles of passages here for visitors to safely explore. According to local historians and anthropologists, the caverns have been explored since the late 1700s and were once used by Native Americans as protection from enemies and the natural elements.

Because the temperature inside the caverns remains steady at about 55°F year-round, visitors are encouraged to bring sweaters or light jackets even on warm summer days.

Ohiopyle State Park

Encompassing just over 19,000 forested acres, Ohiopyle (724/329-8591, www.dcnr.state.pa.us/stateparks/parks/ohiopyle.aspx) provides any number of standard state park activities: biking, trekking, horseback riding, fishing, and even hunting. But without a doubt, the vast majority of Pittsburghers who come here have something else in mind: a white-water boating or white-water rafting trip on the ever-popular Youghiogheny River.

There are all sorts of reasons why Pennsylvanians love the Yough (pronounced yock), but the diversity of the river is certainly at the top of the list. Beginners can easily float down the Lower Yough's Class II rapids, while at the same time, some of the country's most experienced rafters can challenge themselves in the Class IV and V rapids of the Upper Yough, where some of the finest white-water rafting on the entire East Coast takes place. Numerous outfitters in the area rent equipment and offer tours for all levels.

Ohiopyle State Park

© FRANK KOVALCHEK

EXCURSIONS

242   EXCURSIONS FROM PITTSBURGH

Camping at Ohiopyle is a possibility—visit the park's website for detailed information and a campground map. Wooden camping cottages that sleep five people are also available. What's more, Ohiopyle doesn't empty out during the winter months. Snowmobiling, cross-country skiing, and sledding all take place here.

Westmoreland Museum of American Art

One of only three museums in the state that focuses exclusively on American art, the Westmoreland Museum of American Art (221 N. Main St., Greensburg, 724/837-1500, www.wmuseumaa.org, Wed.–Sun. 11 A.M.–5 P.M., Thurs. 11 A.M.–9 P.M., admission $5 adult suggested donation, children free) has been welcoming visitors to Greensburg ever since 1959. Especially in its first two decades, the curatorial team managed to build a rather impressive collection of work by American masters, including paintings by Winslow Homer, Mary Cassatt, and John Singer Sargent. Artists based in Southwestern Pennsylvania have frequently been featured as well.

Along with various paintings and portraiture, items kept in the permanent collection include sculpture, toys, works on paper (such as lithographs and etchings), and decorative arts, which include jugs, cupboards, and other largely utilitarian pieces.

Families visiting the museum might enjoy spending time at KidSpace, a hands-on, interactive room where children can make their own creations while surrounded by pieces from the museum's folk art collection.

RESTAURANTS

Located in downtown Ligonier, the **Ligonier Tavern** (137 W. Main St., Ligonier, 724/238-4831, www.ligoniertavern.com, Mon.–Thurs. 11:30 A.M.–9 P.M., Fri.–Sat. 11:30 A.M.–10 P.M., Sun. noon–8 P.M., $17–24) has three separately designed dining rooms inside a beautifully detailed turn-of-the-20th-century Victorian house. Cuisine here is fairly casual and leans toward American and seafood. Sandwiches, salads, pasta, and chicken entrées are all popular. If the weather is nice, diners can choose to sit outside on the house's second-floor patio. There's also a bakery on-site offering a wide selection of fantastic cakes.

With a name like **Ruthie's Diner** (1850 Rte. 30, Ligonier, 724/238-9930, daily 6 A.M.–9 P.M., $7–11), you can probably guess the sort of food that's on offer here: burgers, sandwiches, and cups of black coffee, for the most part. This is the perfect place to make a pit stop if you're in the midst of road-tripping and searching for the heart of America, or some such romantic notion. And as any local will surely tell you, Ruthie's also serves one of the finest breakfasts in town. Not terribly healthy, of course, but delicious and protein-packed just the same.

Adjacent to the Great Allegheny Passage at the West Newton Trailhead is **The Trailside** (108 W. Main St., West Newton, 724/872-5171, www.thetrailside.com, daily 11 A.M.–11 P.M., $6–10), a casual American-bistro-style eatery serving sandwiches, burgers, and salads. Ask for a table on the outdoor deck, which overlooks the GAP trail and the Youghiogheny River. Free WiFi is available, and an onsite pub offers a decent selection of craft beers.

HOTELS

Roughly a 20-minute drive from Fallingwater is **The Lodge at Chalk Hill** (2920 National Pike, Rte. 40 East, Chalk Hill, 724/438-8880 or 800/833-4283, www.thelodgeatchalkhill.com, $60–199), a lakeside lodge and mountain retreat situated on 37 acres of land. Visitors to Ohiopyle, Fort Necessity, Laurel Caverns, and the Christian Klay Winery will all find their destinations within an easy drive of the lodge. Rooms here are a bit dated and could certainly use a 21st-century makeover, although it's worth noting that the location itself—the lodge grounds as well as the nearby attractions—are what you come here for. Groups and bus tours are welcome here, and there's also an on-site banquet room that can accommodate bridal showers, graduation parties, and the like.

Located along Route 40 in Farmington, the **Stone House Inn** (3023 National Pike, Farmington, 800/274-7138, www.stonehouse inn.com, $97–163) sits a mere two miles from the Fort Necessity Battlefield. Fallingwater, Kentuck Knob, and Ohiopyle are also close.

One of the first inns to open along the National Road, Stone House Inn has been lodging and feeding travelers since 1822. There are seven Victorian-style bed-and-breakfast suites on-site, as well as six modern rooms in the New Zeigler Wing that come complete with whirlpool tub, contemporary furnishings, and other modern conveniences.

A four-star luxury resort, **C Nemacolin Woodlands** (1001 LaFayette Dr., Farmington, 800/422-2736, www.nemacolin.com, $309–3,000) is so lovely that you may decide not to leave the grounds at all. Visitors and guests can indulge in golfing, luxurious spa packages, casual or fine dining, and a wide variety of adventure- or cultural-recreation activities. Lodgers have the choice between six different accommodation options, including a boutique hotel, a classic European-style hotel, a lodge, and a townhouse. Nightly rates are steep, but well worth the unique experiences offered here.

PRACTICALITIES
Visitor Center
The **Laurel Highlands Visitor Bureau** is located at 120 East Main Street in Ligonier; office hours are Monday–Friday 9 A.M.–5 P.M. For directions, call 724/238-5661 or toll-free at 800/333-5661. Information for Fayette, Somerset, and Westmoreland Counties can be collected at the bureau, or you can simply gather the info online at www.laurelhigh lands.org.

Media
The region's largest newspaper is Greensburg's right-leaning *Tribune-Review* (www.pitts burghlive.com), a daily that also publishes a Pittsburgh-specific edition. The affiliated *Daily Courier* (www.dailycourier.com) covers the Connellsville area, while the weekly *Mount Pleasant Journal,* the flagship paper of the Greater Mount Pleasant Area, has been in business since 1873.

Getting There
The majority of the Laurel Highlands' major attractions can be accessed by heading east of the city on U.S. Route 30. Yet since the region is so large, drivers will probably want to have an updated road atlas on hand. Rand McNally's oversized *The Road Atlas* is probably the country's most popular; it can be purchased at most major bookstores, and also includes driving maps of Canada and Mexico.

Greyhound buses regularly travel to a number of cities within the Laurel Highlands region. For more information, call 800/231-2222 or visit www.greyhound.com.

A one-way **Amtrak train** ride from Pittsburgh to Greensburg will set you back $9.

The **Arnold Palmer Regional Airport** (www.palmerairport.com) serves the Greater Greensburg area.

Getting Around
For the most part, visitors to Laurel Highlands would be well advised to arrive with a car or other private vehicle. Contact information for a number of travel and transportation options can be found on the website of the **Laurel Highlands Visitors Bureau** (www.laurelhigh lands.org), including companies that offer organized tours of the area.

Visitors to Greensburg can visit the website of the **Westmoreland County Transit Authority** (www.westmorelandtransit.com) for schedule and fare information.

Altoona, State College, and Johnstown

Even if you're a longtime Pittsburgh resident who knows the Steel City inside and out, if you haven't yet explored much of Johnstown, you may very well find yourself surprised at the fairly large number of activities and sights of interest the town offers. And Johnstown's a simple drive, too: If you're headed east toward the Westmoreland Museum of Art or Idlewild, you're halfway there.

Not much farther to the northeast is Altoona, which is something of an international meeting point for rail fans. (The Railroaders Memorial Museum and the Horseshoe Curve Historic Landmark are both there.) Continue onward to State College, the home of Penn State University. It's a perfectly quaint college town and also home to a number of small museums as well as interesting cave sites, many of which can be explored during guided tours.

For detailed information about Johnstown and Cambria County, visit or write to the Convention and Visitor Bureau at 416 Main Street, Suite 100, Johnstown, PA 15901. Alternately, call 814/536-7993 or 800/237-8590, or visit www.visitjohnstownpa.com. The State College tourism board has an online presence at www.statecollege.com/tourism; the Altoona board's site is at www.altoona.com/tourism.

SIGHTS
Frank & Sylvia Pasquerilla Heritage Discovery Center
Included with the price of admission to the **Johnstown Flood Museum** is admission to the Frank & Sylvia Pasquerilla Heritage Discovery Center (201 6th Ave., Johnston, 814/539-1889 or 888/222-1889, www.jaha.org/DiscoveryCenter/virtualtour.html, daily 10 A.M.–5 P.M., admission $8 adult, $6 student, $7 senior). It tells the stories of the thousands of Southern and Eastern European immigrants who flocked to Johnstown during the last two decades of the 1800s and the first decade of the 1900s.

The museum's main exhibit, *America: Through Immigrant Eyes,* uses a wide selection of interactive media to explain exactly how the immigrants passed their days in Pennsylvania. You'll learn what life was like in Johnstown for a Slovakian butcher, a Russian shopkeeper, and a Hungarian goose farmer, to name just a few. Through an interactive video display, visitors will also view the experience of immigrants being questioned at Ellis Island, and they'll learn about the conditions in Europe that led many to seek a new life elsewhere in the first place.

Other exhibits at the museum show what life was like in the steel mills where many immigrants toiled, while the Generations Theater exhibition includes interviews with both the children and grandchildren of the immigrants. Temporary exhibits can be found on the museum's second floor.

(Horseshoe Curve National Historic Landmark
A longtime favorite of hardcore rail fans who journey to Altoona to visit the Railroaders Memorial Museum is the Horseshoe Curve National Historic Landmark (visitors center at 40th St. and Burgoon Rd., Altoona, 814/941-7960, www.railroadcity.com, Mon.–Sat. 10 A.M.–5 P.M., Sun. 11 A.M.–5 P.M., admission $5 or free with admission to Railroaders Memorial Museum). A legendary railroad curve located about six miles west of Altoona at the Kittanning Gap, the rail's extreme bend is in fact shaped like a horseshoe. Its 220-degree arc was designed by J. Edgar Thomson; it opened to trains in 1854 as a way to significantly reduce the travel time from one end of Pennsylvania to the other. The arc was necessary because of the summit of the Allegheny Mountains, which the track was designed to skirt.

Designated as a National Historic Landmark in 1966, the curve has been a successful tourist attraction for decades. It's wise to stop by the visitors center first, where a number of displays

FLOOD CITY MUSIC FESTIVAL

Should you happen to find yourself in the Pittsburgh area over Labor Day weekend, and should you happen to be a fan of Americana and roots music – blues, zydeco, folk, jazz, and R&B, for instance – you're in luck. That's when the Flood City Music Festival (www.jaha.org/FCMF/performers.html) takes place at the city's Festival Park (90 Johns St., Johnstown), which can be found just across the river from Point Stadium and beside the Cambria Iron Company National Historic Landmark.

Throughout the three days of the festival, which was formerly known as the Johnstown FolkFest, concertgoers can expect to hear roughly 70 hours of live music by bands both world-famous and nearly unknown. Past performers have included Los Lobos, Sleepy LaBeef, Sharon Jones and the Dap-Kings, Brave Combo, Red Elvises, Big Sandy & His Fly-Rite Boys, Robbie Fulks, Southern Culture on the Skids, Buckwheat Zydeco, and R. L. Burnside. And here's the best news of all: The entire thing is free to all. Check the festival's webpage for information about accommodations and driving directions. Free parking is generally available – signs will be posted – and free shuttle buses frequently travel back and forth between parking lots and the festival grounds.

Insider tip: The town's legendary **Inclined Plane** operates free of charge throughout the festival's three days.

Johnstown Flood Museum

Having watched tragedy unfold in New Orleans in 2005, visitors to Southwestern Pennsylvania may find the Johnstown Flood Museum (304 Washington St., Johnstown, 814/539-1889 or 888/222-1889, www.jaha.org/FloodMuseum/oklahoma.html, daily 10 A.M.–5 P.M., admission $8 adult, $6 student, $7 senior) particularly relevant. It documents a massive flooding catastrophe that took place in that city on May 31, 1889, in which 2,209 people perished. Curiously enough, the causes of the disaster were a neglected dam and a massive storm.

Those who make a stop at this especially well-developed museum will have the chance to view a number of artifacts and documents relating to the greatest tragedy ever to befall the city of Johnstown, including a 26-minute Academy Award–winning documentary film that recreates the flood by using archival photos. Also on-site is a relief-map model that uses lights and sound effects to illustrate the flood's path through the Conemaugh Valley. Particularly moving—even disturbing—is the museum's collection of personal artifacts that were recovered after the flood, including a set of keys belonging to a telegraph operator who warned of the dam's impending danger. And also part of the permanent exhibit is an original, renovated "Oklahoma" House. Although they were originally designed for Oklahoma Territory homesteaders, the prefab houses, which measured either 10 by 20 feet or 16 by 24 feet, were also used to shelter refugees of the Johnstown flood.

Visitors can also request information about a downtown Johnstown walking tour, on which many historic buildings that survived the flood can be seen. More information about the tour and a map of the downtown area can both be found on the museum's website.

Johnstown Inclined Plane

Known as the world's steepest vehicular inclined plane, the cable cars of the Johnstown Incline (711 Edgehill Dr., Johnstown, 814/536-1816, www.inclinedplane.org, May 1–Sept. 30 daily 9 A.M.–11 P.M., Oct. 1–April 30 daily

illustrate the construction of the curve. The center also features a gift shop packed with items of interest to the rail fan. From there, guests can ride a funicular railway up to the actual train tracks, or they can choose to hike up the stairway instead.

It's interesting to note that because of the curve's economic importance to the country, a Nazi plan to explode it was in place during World War II.

EXCURSIONS

11 A.M.–11 P.M., tickets $2.25 one way, $4 round-trip) travel a distance of 896.5 feet up the side of Yoder Hill—which has a grade of 70.9 percent—to reach an elevation of 1,693.5 feet. Built by the Cambria Iron Company in 1890 and 1891, the incline was designed specifically so that residents of the hilltop community known as Westmont could easily transport their horses and wagons from ground level to home and back again.

However, on March 1, 1936, the incline served a distinctly different role when, once again, the city suffered a flood. Nearly 4,000 area residents were lifted to dry, higher ground via the incline. The cable cars served the same emergency purpose again on June 20, 1977, during the city's most recent flood.

Visitors to the incline, which was built by Samuel Diescher, the engineer also responsible for building Pittsburgh's Duquesne and Monongahela Inclines, can walk out onto an extended observation deck that offers a rather lovely view of the Johnstown area. A visitors center displays archival photographs of the city and its numerous floods, and from the center's lobby it's possible to view the massive machinery of the incline in action. The James Wolfe Sculpture Trail can be found directly behind the incline.

Lakemont Park and Island Waterpark

Although it first welcomed visitors in 1894 as a trolley park, and then in 1899 as a full-fledged amusement park, Lakemont Park (700 Park Ave., Altoona, 800/434-8006, www.lakemont parkfun.com, call for hours, admission $9.95) isn't a particularly large attraction. There are just a scattering of rides here, including two roller coasters and a go-kart track. Also located on-site and included with the cost of admission is Island Waterpark, complete with slides and pools. Visitors are welcome to enjoy the park's 18-hole miniature golf course and its arcade.

Historically speaking, Lakemont holds two particularly interesting claims to fame: Not only is it the eighth-oldest amusement park in the country, it's also home to the historic

Leap-The-Dips coaster, a wooden ride built in 1902 that is known by roller coaster enthusiasts everywhere as the world's oldest. The figure-eight style design makes for a fairly slow and gentle ride and was given its due respect in 1996 when it was awarded National Historic Landmark status.

Penn's Cave

Known as the country's only all-water cavern, Penn's Cave (222 Penns Cave Rd., Centre Hall, 814/364-1664, www.pennscave.com, call or visit website for hours, cavern tours $15.95 adult, $8.50 child, $14.95 senior, wildlife tours $19.95 adult, $11.50 child, $18.95 senior) is a particularly unique local site. Because the caverns are literally flooded, guided one-hour tours are given by motorboat. Along the way, visitors will see a wide selection of stalagmites, stalactites, and limestone corridors, as well as trout that can often be seen jumping high above the water. (Look out for the stalagmite that bears a striking resemblance to the Statue of Liberty.)

Interestingly, Penn's Cave also offers a 90-minute wildlife tour ($19.95 adult, $11.50 child, $18.95 senior), during which safari buses shuttle visitors throughout the area's 1,500 acres of preserved forests and fields. Mountain lions, wolves, bison, black bears, and wild mustangs are just some of the animals you may encounter.

Railroaders Memorial Museum

One of Western Pennsylvania's most popular railroading attractions, the Railroaders Memorial Museum (1300 9th Ave., Altoona, 814/946-0834, www.railroadcity.com, April–Oct. Mon.–Sat. 9 A.M.–5 P.M., Sun. 11 A.M.–5 P.M., Nov.–Dec. Sat. 9 A.M.–5 P.M., Sun. 11 A.M.–5 P.M., admission $7.50 adult, $5 child, $6 senior) was designed specifically to honor the American railroaders who have contributed significantly to the country's culture and industry. And it makes good sense that the site is located in Altoona: Not only has the city long been known as an important epicenter of rail activity, but the Horseshoe Curve National

Historic Site and the Staple Bend Tunnel (the country's first railroad tunnel), are both located nearby.

Built in 1998, the museum uses a mixture of interactive displays, video presentations, and exhibits to tell the cultural and social story of those who worked in the industry. In other words, the major emphasis here is not on the wheels, gears, and tracks that moved the industry forward, but rather on the people who worked on and alongside the rails throughout the 1920s. And because the light-and-sound exhibits are fairly advanced, the museum feels much more like a place to play than simply a place to drearily read placards and gaze at dusty models.

RESTAURANTS

Conveniently located in Somerset, **The Summit Diner** (791 N. Center Ave., Somerset, 814/445-7154, Sun.–Thurs. 5 A.M.–10 P.M., Fri.–Sat. 5 A.M.–midnight, $6–11) is a 24-hour greasy spoon with surprisingly good food. You'll find it open for business literally every day of the year. The menu is filled with American standards, and the hotcakes here are a local favorite. Assuming this sort of thing is important to you, all the meat is cut and served right in the restaurant's kitchen.

A third-generation family-owned and -operated establishment, **Mel's Restaurant and Bar** (127 W. Patriot St., Somerset, 814/445-9841, www.somersetcounty.com/mels, daily 9 A.M.–2 A.M., $3–9) is the sort of honky-tonk café where one might expect to find a preponderance of gentlemen sporting cowboy hats and chewing tobacco. The menu is a low-budget selection of cheeseburgers, hot dogs, and sloppy joes, and don't be surprised if yours is served on a paper plate. Mel's also boats a 240-square-foot dance floor, live music on the weekend, and a pool table. This is Middle America at its finest, folks.

HOTELS

Just south of Altoona, the **Majestic World Lodge and Retreat** (679 Memory Ln., Portage, 814/693-0189 or 877/365-6972, www

.majesticworldlodge.com) is a family-owned and -operated lodge situated 3,000 feet up in the Alleghenies—one of the highest elevations in the state. The lodge itself is actually a converted, historic barn where guests can gaze out at an elk herd from the comfort of a covered wooden deck. The grounds are absolutely gorgeous, and, incidentally, the snowy winter season is a particularly picturesque time of the year to visit. In spring, the grounds are covered with a carpet of lovely wildflowers.

All rooms are differently designed; rustic types will feel especially at home amongst the patchwork quilts and incredibly creative headboards fashioned from antler horns and cedar logs. Rates begin at $95 a night.

The **Flight 93 National Memorial** (1060 Lambertsville Rd., Stoystown, 814/443-4557, www.flight93memorialproject.org, free, winter daily 9 A.M.–5 P.M., summer daily 9 A.M.–7 P.M.) is close to the lodge in Somerset. Other nearby attractions include the historic **Bedford Village** (220 Sawblade Rd., Bedford, 814/623-1156, www.oldbedfordvillage.com, admission adults $10, senior $9, student $5, daily 9 A.M.–5 P.M.) and the numerous sights and museums of Johnstown. The home field of the **Altoona Curve** (1000 Park Ave., 814/943-5400, www .altoonacurve.com), a minor league baseball club, is roughly a 35-minute drive away.

One of the most gorgeous and unusual places to spend the night in Somerset County, the [**Stone Ridge Bed & Breakfast** (2825 Carpenters Park Rd., Davidsville, 814/288-3931, www.stoneridgebb.com, $150 d) is essentially an A-frame lodge that guests have all to themselves. The grounds couldn't be more romantic—especially during winter. The A-frame comes complete with a stone fireplace, two bedrooms, and two decks, one with a grill. A hot tub is available for use year-round, and the especially rustic surroundings are home to a number of animals, including wild turkey and deer.

Blue Knob, Seven Springs, and Hidden Valley are all relatively close, and downtown Johnstown is only seven miles away.

Located in the East Hills area of Johnstown,

EXCURSIONS

the **Homestead Retreat and Guesthouse** (1077 Crest Ave., Johnstown, 814/539-2273, $75 nightly, $350 weekly, $800 monthly) is a turn-of-the-20th-century farmhouse available for nightly stays or weekly and short-term rentals. Following extensive remodeling, the Homestead resembles nothing more than an actual home. Fans of intimate bed-and-breakfasts can take respite here, enjoying an eat-in kitchen, a TV room, and a grill and campfire area. Smoking is prohibited at the Homestead, although pets are welcomed.

PRACTICALITIES
Tourist Offices
The **Central Pennsylvania Convention & Visitors Bureau** (800 E. Park Ave., State College, Mon.–Fri. 8 A.M.–6 P.M., weekends 9 A.M.–6 P.M., 814/231-1400 or 800/358-5466, www.visitpennstate.org) services State College and offers resources for a variety of outdoor adventures and cultural and sporting events.

Anyone heading to Altoona would be wise to stop by the **Allegheny Mountains Convention and Visitors Bureau** (1 Convention Center Dr., Altoona, 814/943-4183 or 800/842-5866, www.alleghenymountains.com, Mon.–Fri. 8 A.M.–5 P.M.) for tips on lodging, restaurants, and shops.

Those headed to Johnstown should check out the **Johnstown and Cambria County Convention & Visitors Bureau** (416 Main St., Johnstown, Ste. 100, 814/536-7993 or 800/237-8590, www.visitjohnstownpa.com, Mon.–Fri. 8 A.M.–5 P.M., Sat.–Sun. 11 A.M.–3 P.M.), in particular for information on seasonal events.

Media
The daily *Tribune-Democrat* (www.tribune-democrat.com) is the best-known newspaper covering the Johnstown area, while *Johnstown Magazine* (www.johnstownmag.com) digs

deeper into the culture and lifestyles of the region. Pick up a copy of the *Centre Daily* newspaper (www.centredaily.com) for daily news about the Central Pennsylvania area. *State College Magazine* (www.statecollegemagazine.com) celebrates the region in all its glossy, four-color glory. The daily *Altoona Mirror* (www.altoonamirror.com) covers both Altoona and State College.

Getting There
From Pittsburgh, a drive to either Altoona, State College, or Johnstown will require a trip on U.S. Route 22. Those headed to Johnstown will eventually go south on Route 219, while explorers venturing up to Altoona or State College will use Route 220.

Greyhound buses leave the Downtown Pittsburgh depot multiple times a day for State College; the one-way fare is $29. Buses leave twice a day each for Johnstown ($20.75 one way) and Altoona ($41 one way).

Amtrak trains service Altoona ($19 one way).

University Park Airport (www.statecollege airport.org) is located right in State College and is served by a handful of major airlines.

Getting Around
Public transport in the State College area is handled by CATA, the **Centre Area Transportation Authority.** Visit www.catabus .com for schedules and a downloadable PDF of the most recent Ride Guide. To order a taxi in the area, call **AA Taxi** (814/231-8294).

The **Cambria County Transit Authority** (www.camtranbus.com) is responsible for public transportation in Johnstown; when in Altoona use **AMTRAN** (www.amtran.org). For 24-hour **taxi service** in either Cambria or Somerset Counties, call 814/535-4584 or 814/539-1584.

Beaver County and Butler County

The counties of Beaver and Butler sit just north of the city of Pittsburgh and are quite often considered a part of Pittsburgh, especially by the counties' own residents. Old Economy Village and the Harmony Historic District are the big tourism draws—at both sites you can observe the unique and alternative way of living practiced by the now-nonexistent Harmony Society.

For more extensive information, spend some time on the counties' official tourism sites: www.visitbeavercounty.com and www.visit butlercounty.com.

SIGHTS
Harmony Historic District and Harmony Museum

Founded in 1804 and now a National Landmark District, the Harmony Historic District is a relatively small but engaging area where examples of both Harmonist and Mennonite lifestyles can be seen and studied. This walkable area is where the Harmony Museum (218 Mercer St., Harmony, 724/452-7341, www

.harmonymuseum.org, Tues.–Sun. 1–4 P.M., admission $5 adult, $2 child, $4 senior) can be found. At the museum you'll see an example of a communal Harmonist room; also on-site is a Harmonist's wine cellar, accessible by way of a stone-cut staircase. The museum also owns a small collection of Native American artifacts that were discovered in the area.

Other structures of interest in the district include the **Wagner-Bentel House,** which is a brick duplex that was constructed by the Harmonists for two sisters and their families, and the reconstructed **Henry Denis Ziegler log house,** which sits directly across the street from the museum and is made of hand-hewn oak logs.

⬢ McConnell's Mill State Park

Encompassing 2,546 acres of the Slippery Rock Creek Gorge, McConnell's Mill State Park (via I-79 near the intersection of PA 19 and U.S. 422, Portersville, 724/368-8811, open daily sunrise–sunset, free) is named after a logging

EXCURSIONS

Harmony Museum

mill built to channel the creek's water, as well as the water's power. The park has long been a favorite day trip for teenagers living in Pittsburgh's northern suburbs, but considering that it's less than 40 miles from Downtown, it also makes for a worthwhile excursion for city visitors in need of a quick wilderness break.

There are any number of activities to keep you occupied once inside the park. You're almost certain to see rock climbers here, especially if you venture toward Rim Road's climbing area, which sits on the other side of the creek from the Old Mill (where an

---

MOTORDROME SPEEDWAY

NASCAR racing is almost certainly not the first thing that comes to mind when considering a trip to Pittsburgh, a town where sports culture often seems to begin and end with the Pittsburgh Steelers. And yet there it is, a mere 40 miles from the bright lights of Downtown, halfway between Monessen and New Stanton on Route 70: It's known as the Motordrome Speedway (164 Motordrome Rd., Smithton, 724/872-7555, www.motordrome. com), and on Friday nights from April through September, it's the location of the NASCAR-sanctioned Weekly Racing Series, where six different divisions of race cars fly around a mile-long asphalt oval at excessive speeds, much to the delight of screaming fans.

And while Talladega it may not be, there's definitely a good bit of all-American family fun to be had at the Motordrome, where races begin at 7:30 P.M., and where parking, appropriately enough, is always free. You'll see everything from NAPA Late Models to Yellowbook Chargers here, with the vast majority of drivers and racing teams coming from the nearby small towns of Westmoreland County. Special events for kids and families are scheduled regularly, and general admission for adults is rarely more than $12.

---

emergency phone is also located). Head to the intersection of Breakneck Bridge Road and Cheeseman Road to reach the advanced climbing area. White-water rafting and kayaking is also big here, and with seven miles of trails, it would be simple to pass half a day simply exploring the pristine, forested splendor of McConnell's Mill.

The McConnell's Mill Heritage Festival takes place during the third or fourth weekend of September. The operational era of the Old Mill (1852–1928) is celebrated during the festival, and visitors can enjoy activities such as corn grinding demonstrations, mill tours, and old-time musical entertainment.

To reach the park from Downtown, take I-79 to U.S. 19 (Exit 28). Look for signs pointing toward McConnell's Mill Road, where you'll find the park sitting roughly 1,000 feet north of the Route 19 and U.S. 422 intersection.

◖ Old Economy Village

Formerly the home of the 19th-century communal Christian group known as the Harmony Society, the village of Economy, known in its current restored form as Old Economy Village (270 16th St., Ambridge, 724/266-4500, www.oldeconomyvillage.org, Apr. 16–Oct. 31 Tues.–Thurs. 10 A.M.–4 P.M., Fri.–Sat. 10 A.M.–5 P.M., Sun. noon–5 P.M., admission $9 adult, $6 child, $8 senior), was in its day widely recognized as a God-fearing and stoically hard-working place.

The Harmonists fled Germany in the late 1700s due to persecution from the Lutheran Church and went on to purchase 3,000 acres of land in Pennsylvania's Butler County. After moving to Indiana and then returning to Pennsylvania, they settled here; their curious sect is today regarded as one of the country's most successful experiments in economics and alternative living. Completely regardless of gender, the Harmonists shared all manner of village tasks; they also produced everything needed for survival within the confines of the village. And although the society lasted for more than a century, no Harmonists remain today. Why not? The society's members were

COURTESY OF ROB MATHENY

Old Economy Village

all unmarried, and none believed in the concept of procreation. Oops.

Nonetheless, the Harmony Society's history and the Old Economy Village site both make for fascinating studies. Village visitors will have the opportunity to see the society's community kitchen, its cabinet shop and blacksmith shop, a granary, the Economy Post Office, and more.

Prime Outlets

Located in Grove City and about an hour's drive from Downtown Pittsburgh, Prime Outlets (intersection of I-79 and Rte. 208, Grove City, 888/545-7221, www.prime outlets.com, Mon.–Sat. 10 A.M.–9 P.M., Sun. 10 A.M.–7 P.M.) is an almost ridiculously large outlet mall—it covers so much ground, in fact, you may have to return for a second visit in order to see it all. There are more than 140 brand-name outlet stores here, including Juicy Couture, Banana Republic, Dickies, Ecko, J. Crew, and Timberland. Also available are all manner of housewares, home furnishings, children's apparel, lingerie, and luggage.

Unfortunately, hungry shoppers don't have the healthiest options from which to choose; the majority of eateries in the food court are of the Dairy Queen and Pretzel Time variety. There is an Eat 'N Park located nearby, however, where the health-conscious can at least procure a salad.

RESTAURANTS

A Zelie institution since 1810, the **Kaufman House** (105 S. Main St., Zelienople, 724/452-8900, www.kaufmanhouse.com, Mon.–Thurs. 7 A.M.–9 P.M., Fri.–Sat. 7 A.M.–10 P.M., Sun. 11 A.M.–9 P.M., $12–18) has a total of four dining rooms, a coffee shop, and a lounge. And although the restaurant has something of an upscale feel, the appetizers and entrées here are pleasingly all-American, with steaks, chicken, sandwiches, salads, and burgers leading the charge.

A self-described beanery, eatery, brewery, and community center, the **(North Country Brewing Company** (141 S. Main St., Slippery Rock, 724/794-2337, www.northcountrybrew ing.com, Mon.–Thurs. 11 A.M.–11 P.M., Fri.–Sat. 11 A.M.–midnight, Sun. 11 A.M.–10 P.M., $10–23) is close to McConnell's Mill State Park. The on-site brewery is phenomenal, the weekly specials often include wild game, and

EXCURSIONS

the creatively built sandwiches and burgers are exactly what you'd expect to find in a college town: Mouth-watering and especially large. Check the website for live music schedules.

The first six-pack shop to ever grace the streets of Slippery Rock, **B and J Coney Island** (635 Kelly Blvd., Slippery Rock, 724/794-4899, www.bjconeyisland.com, $2–9) sells burgers, fries, and, of course, a wide selection of cold beer.

HOTELS

Particularly popular with golfers, **Conley Resort** (740 Pittsburgh Rd., Butler, 800/344-7303, www.conleyresort.com, $119 and up) offers all guests a complimentary breakfast as well as use of the on-site waterpark, which consists of two slides, a pool, a sauna, a hot tub, and a replica of a pirate ship with its own water cannon. Guests also receive a discount at the resort's golf course. Rooms here are nothing to shout about, but are certainly clean and comfy enough. And since Conley is such a spacious place, it's also a popular spot for business meetings and conferences.

Located on a 175-acre farm in the Butler County town of Renfrew is the **Heather Hill Bed and Breakfast** (268 Rader Scholl Rd., Renfrew, 724/789-7911, www.heatherhillbnb .com, $75–130), where the farm animals range from Peruvian Paso horses to Hereford cattle. The renovated 1821 farmhouse includes four bedrooms, a game room, three wood-burning stoves, and a large country-style kitchen.

Family-run and located just five minutes from Beaver's shopping district, **Willows Inn** (1830 Midland Beaver Rd., Industry, 724/643-4500, www.willowsinnpa.com, $70 and up) has 30 recently remodeled rooms, free wireless access, and famously delicious smorgasbords. There's also a banquet hall and a pub on-site. Penn State's Beaver campus is a 10-minute drive away, and both Geneva College and Old Economy Village are 20 minutes away.

PRACTICALITIES
Tourist Offices
The **Beaver County Recreation & Tourism**

Department, located in the Bradys Run Recreation Facility (526 Bradys Run Rd., Beaver Falls, 724/891-7030 or 800/342-8192, www .visitbeavercounty.com, Mon.–Fri. 8:30 A.M.–4:30 P.M.), offers information on attractions, seasonal events, lodging, and other amenities.

The **Butler County Tourism & Convention Bureau** (310 E. Grandview Ave., Zelienople, 724/234-4619 or 866/856-8444, www.visit butlercounty.com, Mon.–Fri. 8:30 A.M.–4:30 P.M.) provides information on cultural events, sports, local history, and much more.

Media

The *Butler Eagle* (www.butlereagle.com) is a major daily newspaper serving the residents of Butler County. While in Beaver County, pick up the daily *Beaver County Times* (www.times online.com).

Getting There

Driving to both Beaver and Butler Counties from Downtown Pittsburgh is a breeze: Simply take Route 22 west to Route 30 west to reach Beaver. For Butler, head out of the city on I-279 north, which turns into I-79 north. You'll find that the majority of Pittsburgh's Yellow Cab drivers will be all too happy to shuttle you anywhere within the two counties, although be sure to ask about any extra fees you might accrue by traveling outside Allegheny County.

Getting Around

The **Beaver County Transit Authority** (724/728-8600, www.bcta.com) is responsible for operating the region's bus service; schedules, maps, and more can be found its website. For information about travels in and around Butler County, visit the website of **The Bus** (www.thebusbutlerpa.com). Information about various **limousine and taxi services** in Butler County can be found at www.visit butlercounty.com. Or, call the **National Taxi Directory** (www.1800taxicab.com) toll-free at 800/TAXI-CAB (800/829-4222) for further information. The NTD offers telephone numbers of the nearest taxi companies based on the phone number you're calling from.

BACKGROUND

The Setting

Because of the three rivers that wind and wend their way throughout all stretches of the city, and also because of the small hills and deep valleys that seem to appear out of nowhere in this region, the Pittsburgh area is well known as an often difficult-to-traverse part of the country. Yet it's also known as a deeply beautiful place. Much of Southwestern Pennsylvania, as well as much of suburban Pittsburgh, is heavily forested, blanketed with trees and wildlife.

Within Pittsburgh's city limits, however, urban hustle and bustle is in full effect. The majority of the neighborhoods where tourists will find themselves are quite metropolitan; many of the noteworthy East End areas sit side-by-side with lower-income neighborhoods.

GEOGRAPHY AND CLIMATE

Pittsburgh is located in the southwest corner of the state of Pennsylvania, where it sits near the foothills of the Allegheny Mountains. The city rests 696 feet above sea level.

In total, Pittsburgh consists of 58.3 square miles, with 55.6 square miles consisting of landmass and 2.7 square miles consisting of water. In other words, approximately 4.75 percent of the City of Pittsburgh is water.

The city is situated on a land mass known

COURTESY OF VISITPITTSBURGH

as the Allegheny Plateau; this is the area where the city's three rivers—the Allegheny, the Monongahela, and the Ohio—come together at the westernmost tip of the Downtown Pittsburgh area, which is also known as the Golden Triangle.

Pittsburgh is a particularly hilly city, and while it has a continental climate with four seasons, it's also a relatively rainy and snowy place, with approximately 37 inches of rain annually and 43 inches of snow annually.

Pittsburgh's temperature varies widely throughout the year, with the winter months of December, January, and February averaging a low temperature of a chilly 22°F, and the summer months of June, July, and August averaging a high temperature of a rather steamy (and often humid) 82.6°F.

ENVIRONMENTAL ISSUES

Because of the many industrial factories and steel-producing mills that dotted the Pittsburgh cityscape for roughly 150 years, it was inevitable that the town would eventually suffer from the effects of environmental pollution. In fact, during much of the 20th century, the entirety of Pittsburgh was so smoke- and soot-covered that visitors nicknamed it "The Smoky City"; still very much a part of Steel City lore are stories of businessmen leaving the confines of their Downtown offices during the lunch break and returning an hour later to find their white shirts turned dark gray. As a result of the pollution, an alarmingly large number of Pittsburghers living within the city limits at the time suffered from respiratory illnesses. But thanks to the steadfast efforts of one of the city's most popular mayors, David Lawrence, things began to change for the better during the 1950s, as smoke control became a leading local issue.

And although Pittsburgh has a good distance to travel before it becomes a leader in environmental pollution control (emissions from public buses are still a heated issue, for instance), many changes have been made for the better. The locally based Green Building Alliance (www.gbapgh.com) is a nonprofit organization concerned with integrating environmentally responsible design into new area construction. Pittsburgh can now claim the world's first green convention center and the world's largest green building, the David L. Lawrence Convention Center. And partly due to the efforts of the U.S. Green Building Council's Washington, D.C.–based LEED (Leadership in Energy and Environmental Design) program, Pittsburgh is also home to 40 buildings registered under the council's rating system.

History

It's something of a little-known fact that Pittsburgh's history is very much intertwined with that of our nation's first president, George Washington, who first visited the area in 1753. Then a 21-year-old major, Washington surveyed the land at the junction of the Allegheny and Monongahela Rivers (the current location of Point State Park), and wrote that it was "extremely well suited for a Fort; as it has the absolute Command of both Rivers."

Perhaps not surprisingly, the French were also impressed by the city's strategic location at the fork of the three rivers. In 1754, they managed to drive Washington's Virginia militia away, and then built a fort on the site themselves. It was named Fort Duquesne. Four years passed, and the British, led by General John Forbes, managed to defeat the French and reclaim the fort, which was first rebuilt and then renamed. (The wily French had burned the fort to the ground before fleeing.) The new site became known as Fort Pitt, after William Pitt, the English prime minister. On the first day of December, General Forbes named the camp at Fort Duquesne "Pittsburgh."

In 1787, roughly a decade after a heated

WIKIMEDIA COMMONS

lithograph showing Pittsburgh in 1874

dispute between the states of Virginia and Pennsylvania, both of whom wanted to claim Pittsburgh as their own, the Pittsburgh Academy was founded in a small log cabin; this academy would eventually become the University of Pittsburgh. Clearly, Pittsburgh was becoming an outpost to reckon with; the weekly *Pittsburgh Gazette*, the first newspaper to exist west of the Alleghenies, had seen its first issue the year prior. In 1816, Pittsburgh was finally incorporated as a city. By 1820, Pittsburgh's population was just more than 7,000. A decade later, it had grown to more than 12,500.

Pittsburgh had its first experience with major tragedy in 1845, when a fire destroyed roughly a third of the city and left about 12,000 people homeless. Less than a decade later, Pittsburgh's reputation as the "Smoky City" began to grow: The Jones & Laughlin Steel Corporation was founded in 1853. The Clinton iron furnace opened in 1859. And then in 1864, at the age of 29, a Scotsman named Andrew Carnegie decided to join the iron business. He soon became known as the richest man in America. In 1889 he dedicated the region's first Carnegie Library, which still operates in Braddock, and in 1900 he founded the Carnegie Technical School, now known as Carnegie Mellon University.

A true city of industry, Pittsburgh continued cranking through a series of milestones for the next 50 years: The first World Series was played here in 1903; the first motion picture house opened here in 1905; the country's first commercial radio station broadcast from here in 1920. For all its successes, however, Pittsburgh's reputation as an unpleasant place to visit managed to precede it. At the time, the town was known as one of the most polluted cities in America; streetlights were often kept on throughout the day. That all began to change in 1946, though, when Mayor David Lawrence kicked off the city's first official Renaissance, an urban renewal plan that eventually stripped Pittsburgh of its Smoky City image and managed to transform it into the epicenter of medicine, education, and technology that it is today. One of the city's biggest triumphs came in 1953, when Dr. Jonas Salk developed the polio vaccine at the University of Pittsburgh.

Although its total population has declined in recent decades, Pittsburgh continues to march on as a top-ranked metropolis, and in 2010 it was named "America's Most Livable City" by *Forbes* magazine. In 1989, the city elected its first female mayor, the much-loved Sophie

G20 PITTSBURGH SUMMIT

During the last week of September 2009, the G20 Pittsburgh Summit convened, bringing together the third meeting of 20 heads of state to discuss financial markets and the world economy. The event itself was held at the David L. Lawrence Convention Center in Downtown Pittsburgh and it lasted two days: September 24 and 25, a Thursday and a Friday. The event was announced shortly after the April 2009 G20 London summit, and was initially scheduled to be held in Manhattan. Due to a conflict, however, it was rescheduled to be held in Pittsburgh. According to President Barack Obama, Pittsburgh's economic recovery following the collapse of its steel manufacturing sector in the latter half of the 20th century made it a perfect location to hold an economic summit.

A blog post from the *Wall Street Journal* headlined "G20: Why Pittsburgh?" on May 28, 2009, noted that, "By choosing the western Pennsylvania city (unemployment rate 7.6 percent, at last tally) the U.S. is turning to an approach often followed by the Group of Eight, the organization of big industrialized countries."

G8 summits, the article noted, "often have been used as an economic development tool, a way to bring businesses to cities outside the host nation's capital. Italy, for instance, shifted the location of this summer's G8 summit from the island of La Maddalena off the northeast coast of Sardinia to L'Aquila in the Abruzzo region, a town devastated by an earthquake in April."

How's that for a comparison?

Evidently the Pittsburgh Summit was not simply an international event that would put the city's visage on the world stage, but also an opportunity for much-needed revitalization.

The week of the G20, things were tense: News reports had mentioned repeatedly that the city could be targeted by violent anarchists and/or terrorists and that it was likely people could be injured or killed in numerous protests all over the city. The result was a lockdown. Everything closed. From Wednesday afternoon through Saturday, the city was guarded

The Steel City welcomes the world to the 2009 G20 Pittsburgh Summit.

There was a heavy police presence in the city during the week of the G20 Pittsburgh Summit.

by thousands of police officers and national guardsmen from all over the country; windows were boarded up and streets were blocked off. The city's atmosphere that week seemed to fit somewhere between psychotic paranoia and extremely raw naïveté.

Luke Ravenstahl, the city's mayor, told the *New York Times* that the meeting of the world's 20 most powerful economic leaders would dispel the city's "'smoky' image and replace it with the real 'green' image." But outside Ravenstahl's efforts to market the city's environmental renaissance, the real stories were the political protests and the cops.

No one was killed and injuries were minimal, but the weekend following the summit, protests landed more than 100 people in jail. Police fired tear gas and used screeching Long Range Acoustic Devices on students and protestors, and the city's ACLU chapter filed multiple lawsuits against the city for harassing political protestors and stifling First Amendment rights.

As of this writing – about a year after the

event – most of those lawsuits and arrests are still working their way through the legal system. A citizen's review board was appointed by the city, but it has – perhaps unsurprisingly – been largely unsuccessful in revealing any new information about why the city went to such great lengths to stifle pretty much any kind of unplanned activity on that particular week and weekend. Nor has the board managed to discover exactly how far the city went in its efforts to make sure the event went off without a hitch.

Mayor Ravenstahl has declared the event a success in many news outlets, but as time drags on, the ongoing message about the Pittsburgh G20 Summit is not about how Pittsburgh has evolved from a Steel City to a Green City, but how law enforcement from all over the country turned Pittsburgh totalitarian for about 72 hours during the last week of September 2009.

(Contributed by Matt Stroud, a Pittsburgh-based freelance journalist.)

Masloff. And then in 2006, another victory: The Pittsburgh Steelers, whose successful 1970s franchise resulted in the town becoming known as the City of Champions, managed to regain a touch of their former glory by winning a fifth career Super Bowl.

PITTSBURGH TODAY

No one can deny that Pittsburgh made giant leaps in its effort to become a world-class city during the urban redevelopment process known as Renaissance II. Officially begun in 1980, this was when the city saw construction of Three Rivers Stadium and a bevy of Downtown skyscrapers and shopping centers, including USX Tower, Mellon Bank Tower, Oxford Centre, and PPG Place. Pittsburgh's intention was to transform itself from a city of industry into a tech, medicine, and education hub. This was all well and good, until along came the disaster known as Renaissance III.

Led by then-Mayor Tom Murphy, R3 was centered on redeveloping and revitalizing the city's Downtown core, especially the area around Market Square. Pittsburghers weren't fond of Murphy's plan—to drive out decades-old retailers and bring in big-box chains—and ultimately the scheme failed. Today, the abandoned Fifth and Forbes Corridor, as the area is known, is filled with empty storefronts.

As if that weren't enough, Pittsburgh in the early part of the 21st century has been feeling the burn of a serious image crisis, during which many of the town's young and creative types have left in search of brighter opportunities elsewhere. Attempting to halt this flow, a group of corporate and civic leaders in 2002 and 2003 created the Image Gap Committee. Soon, the city had burned through roughly $200,000 in grant money to acquire a new motto, a Pittsburgh font, and even a city-specific color scheme. The so-called Pittsburgh Regional Branding Initiative was widely mocked, and the city's image didn't seem to have improved much as a result.

That all began to change in late 2006, however, when the recently elected Mayor Bob O'Connor unexpectedly died, and was replaced

PPG Place was built during the city's urban redevelopment process known as Renaissance II.

by the city's current mayor, Luke Ravenstahl, who'd been serving as City Council President. At the time, Ravenstahl was just 26 years old—the youngest mayor in the city's history, by a long shot. Naturally, Ravenstahl's entrée to Pittsburgh politics attracted a good deal of media attention, both locally and nationally, and not all of it was positive. Ravenstahl was widely mocked, for instance, after appearing on the *Late Show with David Letterman,* during which he spoke in a pronounced Pittsburgh accent. And yet while his term as mayor has certainly had its controversial moments, the general consensus among average Pittsburghers seems to be that Ravenstahl is doing a decent job for the city, by and large.

Pittsburgh's current economic stability, for instance, is a particularly strong indicator that the city has at least begun the process of getting itself back on track. In fact, quite unlike most other North American metropolitan areas, Pittsburgh has managed to remain economically strong throughout the Great Recession of the late 2000s. Jobs have been lost here at a much slower rate than in other cities of similar size, and the housing market has actually improved over the past few years.

In 2009, Pittsburgh became the subject of nationwide curiosity once again when President Barack Obama and the White House chose the city to host the G20 summit, a meeting of political and financial world leaders. According to the president, the inspirational story of Pittsburgh's economic recovery was a major reason why the city was recommended as a host. Its national reputation as a leader in ecological building practices apparently didn't hurt either, and in fact the summit was held at the David L. Lawrence Convention Center, one of the largest LEED-certified buildings in the world.

All in all, the future is looking decidedly bright for Pittsburgh today. It's a city that recently celebrated its 250th anniversary, and where major construction and urban revitalization projects seem to be popping up quicker than ever. As usual, the future of the city of Pittsburgh can probably best be expressed with one lone punctuation symbol: a question mark.

Government and Economy

GOVERNMENT

Although Pittsburgh was a serious Republican stronghold in the years prior to the Great Depression, the city and its surrounding Allegheny County have largely supported Democratic politicians and ideals in the decades since. The city's support of Democrats initially came about in the 1930s, when immigration to the area was in full bloom, largely due to the huge need for unskilled laborers to populate the area's mills. Indeed, President Franklin Delano Roosevelt's Works Progress Administration proved so popular with the city's largely Eastern European immigrant population that voting Democrat essentially became expected of members of Pittsburgh's blue-collar working class. Today, that tradition continues, and as of November 2008, a little more than 62 percent of Allegheny County's voters were registered as Democrats.

Allegheny County is governed by an elected chief executive (currently Dan Onorato), as well as a 15-member county council.

ECONOMY

Pittsburgh first became an economic powerhouse in the mid-1800s, thanks to the efforts of Scottish immigrant Andrew Carnegie and others involved in the city's iron, steel, and glass industries. The American steel industry suffered a massive collapse in the early 1980s, however, as production began moving to more affordable plants overseas. In an admirable display of its characteristic entrepreneurial and hardworking nature, Pittsburgh steadfastly refused to wither away and took immediate and massive strides to reinvent itself. The city today owes its economic strength to a diverse mixture of healthcare, education, technology, and biotechnology. Finance and tourism also play important roles.

The University of Pittsburgh Medical Center (UPMC) is by far the region's largest employer, with nearly 27,000 employees in Allegheny County alone. West Penn Allegheny Health System and the University of Pittsburgh both employ approximately 10,000 area residents each. Nonetheless, Pittsburgh continues to lead the country in population decline. Although the city claimed 677,000 residents in 1950, today less than 312,000 remain. This likely has much to do with Allegheny County's current per capita income, which rests at $26,140.

A number of *Fortune* 500 and *Fortune* 1000 companies continue to be headquartered in Pittsburgh, including Alcoa, H. J. Heinz, and PPG Industries.

Healthcare

It simply isn't possible to overstate the contribution of the University of Pittsburgh Medical Center to the local economy. Easily the largest employer in Western Pennsylvania, UPMC is also responsible for much of the area's construction boom; the organization spends roughly $250 million annually on construction activity. And because of the patients, families of patients, and investment dollars it attracts from around the county, UPMC estimates that every dollar it spends generates $1.25 for the region itself. Considering that UPMC's annual budget stretches just past $5 billion, it goes without saying that the center's contribution is invaluable for the Southwestern Pennsylvania region.

West Penn Allegheny Health System, the region's second-most important economic leader in the healthcare industry, consists of Allegheny General Hospital, West Penn Hospital, Canonsburg General Hospital, as well as a number of other regional hospitals.

Education

Referred to by some civic boosters as The College City, the greater Pittsburgh area is home to 33 colleges and universities, the most prominent being the University of Pittsburgh (Pitt), Carnegie Mellon University, and Duquesne University. Economically, Pitt is the area's powerhouse; the school pours more than $350 million annually into area businesses whose goods and services keep the behemoth afloat. The university's annual payroll exceeds $530 million, and Pitt is responsible for roughly $200 million in government revenues, such as real estate and sales taxes, each year.

More than 130,000 college and university students matriculate at a Pittsburgh area school each year. Some schools, such as Carlow University, Chatham College, the Art Institute of Pittsburgh, Point Park University, and Robert Morris University, sit right within the city limits. Other schools, such as Seton Hill University, Slippery Rock University, Indiana University of Pennsylvania, and Washington & Jefferson College, are spread throughout the southwestern region of the state.

Technology and Biotechnology

Pittsburgh's tech and biotech industries are much larger and more developed than even most locals realize. Carnegie Mellon University continues to take giant strides in the fields of robotics and software engineering; the school's Federally Funded Research and Development Center spent upward of $43 million in 2003.

Organizations such as the Pittsburgh Lifesciences Greenhouses (a joint venture between Pitt and CMU) have been instrumental in positioning Southwestern Pennsylvania as a bioscience, nanobiotechnology, and robotics leader. Researchers here study neurological disorders, tissue engineering, and drug discovery, among other biotechnology developments.

To stay abreast of local tech news and information, check out the website of the Pittsburgh Technology Council (www.pghtech.org).

People and Culture

POPULATION

In 2009, the U.S. Census Bureau estimated the population of Pittsburgh at 311,647. That figure represents a whopping 6.8 percent population decline from 2000. Women and senior citizens are well represented in Pittsburgh; the population is slightly more than 52 percent female, and 16.4 percent of the population are persons over the age of 65. Twenty-seven percent of Pittsburgh's population is African American, while the local population of Hawaiians and other Pacific Islanders is so small that the group failed to rate on the census report. Nearly 68 percent of all Pittsburghers are Caucasian.

Historically, Pittsburgh has welcomed immigrants since the mid-1700s, the majority being from Southern and Eastern European countries such as Italy and Poland. Pittsburgh saw its largest influx of European immigration during the end of the 19th century and the beginning of the 20th. The majority came in search of work, having heard of Pittsburgh's reputation as an industrial powerhouse. Many of the smaller row houses (or "mill houses") that still stand today in Lawrenceville, the South Side Slopes, and other riverside neighborhoods were first occupied by these Eastern European laborers.

A good number of early immigrants also came to Pittsburgh from Germany and Ireland. The North Side of Pittsburgh, originally a separate city known as Allegheny, is the region where the majority of the city's German immigrants settled, and in the East End neighborhood of Squirrel Hill, Hebrew and Yiddish are still spoken on the streets today.

THE ARTS

Probably because Pittsburgh has for so long been an industrial town with a deeply woven blue-collar temperament, many of the fine arts, performing arts, and visual arts haven't caught on here as quickly or successfully as in other metropolitan cities of equivalent size. And although Pittsburghers tend to vote Democratic, ours is something of a rural-influenced culture. Professional sports are hugely popular; a citywide passion for the Pittsburgh Steelers in particular seems to be the one cultural quirk that unites all Pittsburghers.

For the most part, Pittsburghers are a very proud people; regional pride is something you're likely to encounter over and over again during your stay. Unlike many other metropolitan areas, the majority of Pittsburgh residents have lived in the area their entire lives. In many cases, their parents have as well; grandparents of Pittsburghers in their late 20s and early 30s

PITTSBURGH'S FAMOUS FACES

Regardless of its plain and simple "jus' folks" facade, the Steel City has cranked out an impressive roster of iconic celebrities in fields ranging from music and visual arts to literature and theater. The following is a list of superstars who were either born in the Pittsburgh area or lived and worked here for a significant length of time.

- **Actors and Hollywood players:** F. Murray Abraham, Steven Bochco, Dan Cortese, Ann B. Davis, Jeff Goldblum, Michael Keaton, Gene Kelly, Dennis Miller, Fred Rogers, George Romero, Tom Savini, Jimmy Stewart, Sharon Stone

- **Artists and writers:** Nellie Bly, Rachel Carson, Mary Cassatt, Willa Cather, Michael Chabon, Annie Dillard, Teeny Harris, Philip Pearlstein, Gertrude Stein, Bunny Yeager, Andy Warhol, August Wilson

- **Singers and musicians:** Christina Aguilera, Perry Como, Billy Eckstine, Stephen Foster, Erroll Garner, Henry Mancini, Trent Reznor

were quite often European immigrants. Many of those life-long Pittsburghers, especially those who grew up within the city limits and speak with an accent known as "Pittsburghese" (technically North Midland U.S. English) are referred to as "yinzers." This is generally considered a derogatory term, and shouldn't be used outside of familiar company. To learn about the unique Southwestern Pennsylvania accent, visit www.pittsburghspeech.com and www.pittsburghese.com.

Today, Pittsburgh's arts scene is slowly gaining both traction and national attention. The Pittsburgh Symphony Orchestra has long been noted as being one of the nation's best. And due in large part to the city's extremely low cost of living, young artists and other creative types have been relocating to Pittsburgh—generally in the neighborhoods of the East End—from bigger and more expensive urban areas.

Arts, Crafts, and Folk Traditions

At the Smithsonian-affiliated **Senator John Heinz Pittsburgh Regional History Center** (www.pghhistory.org), scads of interesting facts about Western Pennsylvania's history and heritage can be investigated. The 200,000-square-foot museum includes exhibits about Pittsburgh's glass-making and wood-making heritage; examples of decorative metalwork from a locally based company are also displayed.

At the **Pittsburgh Glass Center** (www.pittsburghglasscenter.org), tours and demonstrations are given in the flame-working and glass-blowing rooms. Classes, private lessons, and studio rentals are available for further study.

At the Strip District's **Society for Contemporary Craft** (www.contemporarycraft.org), works of metal, wood, glass, clay, and fiber can be viewed. Pittsburgh artists are occasionally featured, although the majority of the works displayed were created by artists from around the world.

Pittsburgh Center for the Arts (www.pittsburgharts.org) has frequently changing gallery rooms, as well as a schedule of popular

COURTESY OF VISITPITTSBURGH/ PITTSBURGH GLASS CENTER

You can take glass-blowing classes at the Pittsburgh Glass Center.

classes for both children and adults in ceramics, jewelry making, printmaking, bookbinding, creative writing, and more.

At **Artists Image Resource** (www.artistsimageresource.org) on the North Side, where screen prints and other printed works are displayed, use of the studio's paints and supplies to silkscreen T-shirts, tote bags, or posters is open to the public for a small fee. Open studio nights and times change occasionally; contact 412/321-8664 or info@artistsimageresource.org for more information.

Particularly worthwhile is a day trip to the National Historic Landmark site of **Old Economy Village** (www.oldeconomyvillage .org), the former home of a local installment of the Harmony Society, which was a 19th-century sect of Christianity. Here you can tour the site and experience the Harmonists' lifestyle by participating in candle making, bookbinding, and more.

Literature

Pittsburgh has long had a strong literary history, and, in fact, the University of Pittsburgh was the first institution of higher learning in the United States to offer a Master of Fine Arts degree in creative nonfiction. Pittsburgh author Lee Gutkind spearheads the program; he's also the founding editor of the literary journal *Creative Nonfiction,* which is headquartered in Shadyside.

Pitt's nationally regarded writing program has seen scores of well-known and widely published instructors; writers of note who are currently on staff include the hard-living fiction writer Chuck Kinder, who was one of Raymond Carver's best friends and, according to rumor, was the Pitt professor that the character in Michael Chabon's *Wonder Boys* is based on. (The street that Kinder's character lives on in the *Wonder Boys* film is South Atlantic Street in Friendship.) The poet Toi Derricotte is also a Pitt instructor, as is Faith Adiele, a nonfiction writer and the author of *Meeting Faith: The Forest Journals of a Black Buddhist Nun.*

Renowned poet Jack Gilbert (*Views of Jeopardy, Monolithos*) was born in Pittsburgh in 1925. Author David McCullough, who won the Pulitzer Prize for the masterful biography *John Adams,* is also a Pittsburgh native. And although he has since left town, author John Edgar Wideman (*Brothers and Keepers*) wrote a number of highly-regarded novels about African American life in the Pittsburgh neighborhood of Homewood. Pittsburgher Stewart O'Nan's novel *Everyday People* explored the hardscrabble life of African Americans living in the East End neighborhood of East Liberty.

Possibly better known than all of these authors combined are Pittsburghers Annie Dillard and Gertrude Stein. Dillard's *An American Childhood* examines the events of her childhood in 1950s Pittsburgh. Stein (*The Autobiography of Alice B. Toklas*) was a legendary feminist novelist and playwright who grew up on the city's North Side and eventually settled in Paris.

Music

Possibly Pittsburgh's most famous musician, historically speaking, was Stephen Collins Foster, who lived in Lawrenceville and is buried in Allegheny Cemetery. Foster was a singer, a song leader, and a composer whose first major success was "Oh! Susanna."

Pittsburgh has also produced its share of jazz legends. Although a native of Dayton, Ohio, Billy Strayhorn's music career officially began in Pittsburgh; today he's best known for composing the jazz staple "Take the A Train." The jazz pianist and composer Erroll Garner was born here in 1921; he went on to play with Charlie Parker, among others. Like Gertrude Stein, jazz drummer Kenny Clarke was born here but chose to settle in Paris. He's known as an important innovator of the bebop drumming style. Earl Hines was another well-known jazz pianist also born in Pittsburgh, as was Mary Lou Williams, who worked with Duke Ellington and Thelonious Monk.

Pittsburgh's most legendary jazz venue was the Hill District's Crawford Grill, which still stands today at 2141 Wylie Avenue. Throughout the 1930s, '40s, and '50s, Pittsburgh's Hill District (then known as "Little Harlem") and the Crawford Grill were both well known and respected in prominent African American social circles.

Since the late 1970s, rock 'n' roll—especially the brand of rock now known as "classic rock"—has been favored in Pittsburgh. One of the area's most famous rockers is Joe Grushecky. As a longtime friend of Bruce Springsteen's, Grushecky has been known to bring the Boss to town—unannounced—to perform secret concerts at small clubs. Local musician Donny Iris was a pop and R&B superstar in his own right throughout the 1970s, and the Clarks, a rock group who still perform and record today, have managed to achieve national and even international success.

Of the city's more recent musical talent, the young rapper Wiz Khalifa and the electronic musician Girl Talk (Gregg Gillis) have seen the widest recognition outside Pittsburgh's borders. Other Pittsburgh-based bands of note include Don Caballero, Modey Lemon, Anti-Flag, Rusted Root, and Black Moth Super Rainbow.

Television and Film

For a short while in the 1990s, thanks largely to the efforts of the Pittsburgh Film Office, it seemed as if Southwestern Pennsylvania was on its way to becoming a budget alternative to Hollywood. Vancouver, British Columbia, seems to be claiming that honor for the time being, but movies and the occasional TV show continue to be filmed here with some regularity.

Certainly the city's proudest television accomplishment was the airing of *Mister Rogers' Neighborhood,* a genuine broadcasting treasure hosted by a true American icon, Fred Rogers, who passed away in February 2003. Produced

for 33 years, it was the longest running program ever aired by PBS.

A number of television shows have been set in Pittsburgh but filmed elsewhere, including *Mr. Belvedere,* which followed the trials and tribulations of an upper-middle-class Beaver Falls family; *My So-Called Life,* a hugely popular teen drama that launched the careers of Claire Danes and Jared Leto; *Queer as Folk,* a Showtime series that followed the lives of a group of gay and lesbian friends who frequented the bars on Liberty Avenue; and *The Guardian,* a legal drama that alternated between real shots of Pittsburgh and footage filmed on a California lot.

Pittsburgh's film history has been long and varied. Aside from the 1980s classic *Flashdance,* probably the most important movie filmed in the city remains George Romero's *Night of the Living Dead.* Much of the film, which Romero co-wrote with fellow Pittsburgher John Russo, was filmed in Evans City, which sits about 30 miles north of the Pittsburgh in Butler County. Romero and Russo continue to live in Pittsburgh, as does famed makeup artist Tom Savini, who worked on Romero's *Dawn of the Dead,* a *Night of the Living Dead* sequel that was filmed in the Monroeville Mall. The follow-up film *Day of the Dead* was also filmed in Pittsburgh, although Romero chose to shoot *Land of the Dead* in (gasp!) Canada.

Pittsburgh seems to be a popular setting for frightening films; quite a few scenes from *The Silence of the Lambs* were shot in the Carnegie Museum of Natural History. *Stigmata* was based here and *The Mothman Prophecies* was filmed here.

Other popular movies filmed in and around Pittsburgh include *The Deer Hunter, Wonder Boys,* and *Dogma.*

ESSENTIALS

Getting There

Thanks to its easy-to-navigate Pittsburgh International Airport, its bus and train depots, and its convenient location on I-76 between Chicago and Philadelphia, you shouldn't expect any problems getting into or out of the Greater Pittsburgh area.

BY AIR

More than 14 million travelers each year land at **Pittsburgh International Airport** (PIT) (412/472-5510 or 412/472-3525, www.pitairport.com), which currently holds the distinction of being the fourth-largest airport in the United States. Located 16 miles northwest of Downtown, PIT was one of the first American airports to construct a mammoth, mall-like shopping center on its premises. Along with a collection of more than 100 stores and restaurants, the airport boasts a full-service U.S. Post Office, a nondenominational chapel featuring a daily Roman Catholic mass, and six international gates. Be sure to look out for the gorgeous and appropriately titled Alexander Calder mobile, *Pittsburgh.*

More than a dozen airlines serve Pittsburgh International, including Jet Blue (www.jetblue.com), which flies to New York's JFK and Boston's Logan International Airport. Other

budget airlines serving PIT include AirTran (www.airtran.com), Southwest (www.southwest.com), and USA 3000 (www.usa3000.com), which offers cheap flights to Cancun, Aruba, and the Dominican Republic.

Cheap public transport to and from the airport begins and ends with the **28X Airport Flyer** bus, a bargain at $2.75. The route begins at Carnegie Mellon University before making its way past the University of Pittsburgh, down 5th Avenue in Oakland and into Downtown. Allow 45 minutes if traveling from Oakland, or 30 minutes if traveling from Downtown. Contact **Port Authority** (412/442-2000, www.portauthority.org) for scheduling information. Beware that the first 28X of the day doesn't arrive at the airport until 5:12 A.M., however, so the bus might not be a reliable option if you have an early morning flight. (For domestic flights, allow a minimum of one hour to check in and get through security; allow two hours if you're flying internationally.) The final 28X of the day, which departs from the lower level ground transportation area outside the baggage claim, leaves just past midnight at 11:50 P.M.

A **Yellow Cab** taxi (412/321-8100) will take you to Pittsburgh International at any time of the day or night, but expect to pay around $45 from Downtown, not including a gratuity. Calling Yellow Cab well in advance and booking a taxi is highly recommended, as is booking much earlier than you actually need to: Yellow Cabs in Pittsburgh have a nasty habit of not showing up when they say they will. Should your cab fail to arrive, you'll find a taxi queue outside most Downtown hotels at just about any hour of the day or night.

Your only other transport option to the airport, aside from booking a private car, are the customer courtesy shuttles that run regularly from most Downtown hotels. Inquire at your hotel about this service.

PIT offers a long-term parking lot for travelers who need to leave their vehicles at the airport for days or weeks at a time, although two private companies offer much cheaper rates. **Charlie Brown's Airport Parking** (600 Flaugherty Run Rd., 412/262-4931, www.charliebrownsairportparking.com) charges $6.25 per day or $39.99 per week; the rates at **Globe Transportation** (412/264-4373, www.globeparking.com) are slightly higher at $6.50 per day and $41.50 per week. Coupons offering substantial discounts can be found at both companies' websites, and both companies are open around the clock.

BY TRAIN

Pittsburgh's **Amtrak** station (412/471-6170, www.amtrak.com) is located Downtown at 1100 Liberty Avenue, directly across the street from the recently rebuilt Greyhound bus station, and directly on the border of the Strip District. Trains depart daily for destinations throughout the United States and Canada, although fares on nondirect routes are generally higher than those offered by Greyhound. Trips on Amtrak also tend to take substantially longer than those on the bus—not necessarily a bad thing, as most American train routes pass through surroundings that highway travelers never get a chance to witness.

Popular destinations include Washington, D.C. ($45, 7.5 hours), Philadelphia ($48, 7.5 hours), and New York City ($65, 9 hours).

BY BUS

Located across the street from the Amtrak station at Liberty Avenue and 11th Street, the recently rehabbed **Greyhound** depot (55 11th St., 412/392-6526 or 800/231-2222, www.greyhound.com) features a striking cylindrical glass façade and a huge Greyhound sign, making it conveniently visible from probably a half-dozen blocks away.

The double-decker coaches operated by the British company **Megabus** (www.megabus.com) offer significantly cheaper fares than those offered by Greyhound. They also feature free on-board WiFi, friendlier drivers, cleaner buses, and a younger and more monied clientele. In Pittsburgh, Megabus picks up and drops off passengers outside the David L. Lawrence Convention Center, just north of the intersection of 10th Street and Penn

Avenue. Coaches departing Pittsburgh travel to Philadelphia, New York City, Harrisburg, State College, and Camden, New Jersey. Visit the Megabus website to buy tickets, and to view scheduling and passenger information.

Contrary to popular belief, there is currently one so-called Chinatown bus company serving Pittsburgh. The **Great Wall Line** (www.greatwallbus.com) offers one departure daily from Pittsburgh to New York City. At 12:30 A.M. every Saturday through Thursday night (no Friday departures), buses depart from a sidewalk outside 116 Meyran Avenue in Oakland. They arrive at 143 Division Street in Manhattan the following morning. The 6.5-hour one-way trip costs $45.

Getting Around

PUBLIC TRANSPORTATION

Port Authority Transit (412/422-2000, www .portauthority.org) operates buses, trains, and two inclines within Allegheny County. Bus, train, and incline rides are $2. Transfers cost an extra $0.75; they're generally good for three or four hours and can be used for one ride going in any direction.

The train, known locally as the "T," has four stops in Downtown and another at Station Square. The train also travels through the suburbs of the South Hills; the line ends at South Hills Village Mall. Riding within the "Downtowner Zone," which includes any of the four Downtown stops, is free. The city's two inclines travel up and down Mount Washington. The Monongahela Incline begins across the street from Station Square and discharges passengers on Grandview Avenue. The Duquesne Incline also ends on Grandview Avenue but roughly a mile to the west in the Duquesne Heights district. (This is where Mount Washington's most expensive restaurants are located.) Its street-level station is somewhat inconveniently located along a busy road. If you'd like to ride both inclines, your best bet is to take the Monongahela Incline from Station Square up to Mount Washington, and then walk down Grandview Avenue to the Duquesne Incline. Take the Duquesne down to street level, where you can then walk across a pedestrian bridge to a parking lot. Head toward the river, where you'll find a footpath that conveniently leads back to Station Square.

Weekly and monthly transit passes can be purchased at the **Port Authority Downtown Service Center** (534 Smithfield St., 412/255-1356) or at most Giant Eagle grocery stores.

DRIVING

Because Pittsburgh's public transportation system is relatively reliable, getting by without a car can certainly be done. To fully explore the city's outer reaches, however, a car is a necessary accoutrement. Pittsburgh is a notoriously confusing city to navigate, however, so consider investing in a street atlas. Rand McNally's spiral-bound *Pittsburgh: Street Guide* is a good choice. Also be aware that many neighborhoods within the city limits require all drivers to display a neighborhood-specific parking sticker in their window. If you park without a sticker, you'll need to move your car within one hour to avoid a ticket.

Rental cars are available at various locations throughout the city. At the Pittsburgh International Airport, you'll find rental counters for nine agencies, including **Budget** (800/527-0700, www.budget.com), **Dollar** (800/800-4000, www.dollarrentacar.com), and **Hertz** (800/654-3131, www.hertz.com), on the same level as baggage claim.

TAXIS

Yellow Cab (412/321-8100, www.pghtrans.com/ yellow_cab_pgh.html) is the city's solitary taxi company. Contrary to popular belief, cabs *can* be hailed in Pittsburgh, but only in certain parts of town (Downtown, the South Side, and Station Square are your best bets). If absolutely no cabs are around, try walking to the closest hotel; empty taxis often wait outside for potential passengers. During late-night hours and especially on the weekends, cabs converge en masse on the South Side and at Station Square.

BICYCLING

In 1990, a poll in *Bicycling* magazine ranked Pittsburgh among the 10 worst U.S. cities for cycling. But the biking landscape has lately seen a series of radical changes, thanks especially to **Bike Pittsburgh** (3410 Penn Ave., 412/325-4334, www.bike-pgh.org), a nonprofit cycling and advocacy group committed to making the city safer and more accessible for cyclists. With very few exceptions, Pittsburgh's roadways lack bicycle lanes, so take special care to travel safely on busy or crowded roads. To explore further reaches of the city without the added stress of traffic, download a map of the **Three Rivers Heritage Trail** at www.friend-softheriverfront.org.

DISABLED ACCESS

Yellow Cab operates a special service, **Freedom Coach,** for people in wheelchairs and the otherwise mobility impaired. The company's specially equipped Ford Windstar minivans have a fold-down ramp and rear-entry access, a universal wheelchair tie-down system, and air conditioning with separate backseat controls. Curb-to-curb service is offered. For more information call 412/444-4444 or visit www.pghtrans.com/freedom.cfm.

Tips for Travelers

WEATHER

Depending on whom you ask, the average annual rainfall in Pittsburgh is somewhere between 37 and 40 inches a year, which may or may not mean that the Steel City sees more precipitation than Seattle, an unfounded factoid that you'll likely hear over and over during your stay. But one thing's for sure: Thanks to the hilly topography of the immediate area and the effect of Lake Erie, which sits about 125 miles to the north, Southwestern Pennsylvania is well known as a region with 12 months of wildly unpredictable weather. And what's more, Pittsburgh is not a particularly good place for the depressed: Roughly 200 days of cloud cover are clocked here annually, which means the town once known as "Smoky City" remains one of the cloudiest places in America. (Juneau, Alaska, tops the list.)

Fortunately, however, we do experience four complete seasons in Western Pennsylvania. Summers get good and hot, with the temperature generally hanging between 70 and 80°F (although much hotter days are not uncommon). Winter temperatures settle in somewhere between 20 and 30°F. For detailed day-to-day weather system tracking, log on to the **Weather Channel** online (www.theweatherchannel.com), or take a look at **KDKA**'s local online forecast (weather.kdka.com).

HOURS

Generally speaking, Pittsburgh is a town that rolls up its sidewalks fairly early. Bars here close at 2 A.M., and if business is slow during the week, they may close earlier than that. (Thankfully, business is *never* slow in a Pittsburgh bar on the weekend.) If you're staying in the East End, or anywhere on the South Side, expect the streets to get particularly rowdy about 15 minutes before the bars close on weekend nights. The South Side's East Carson Street in particular can be a frightening place at 2 A.M.; fistfights and police cruisers are not uncommon sights.

Restaurants, too, tend to call it a day fairly early in the evening here. Unlike the fine-dining scenes in cities like Philadelphia, Chicago,

VISIT PITTSBURGH'S NEW WELCOME CENTER

For years now, the city's tourism board, known as VisitPittsburgh, has occupied just one official welcome center in the city. It's a small and rather and underwhelming kiosk located on Liberty Avenue, Downtown, adjacent to the Gateway Center complex. And although it is packed with an absolute wealth of sightseeing brochures, maps, and dining and accommodation info, it's also tiny – not much bigger than a walk-in closet, really. Pittsburghers have long suspected that visitors to our fair city deserved something with a bit more splash and personality.

In late October 2010, that wish was finally realized when the **Greater Pittsburgh Con-** **vention & Visitors Bureau** (412/281-7711, www.visitpittsburgh.com) opened a truly awe-inspiring, 1,000-square-foot visitors center on the ground floor of **Fifth Avenue Place** (120 Fifth Ave., www.fifthavenueplacepa.com), a Downtown skyscraper located a mere stone's throw from the original Liberty Avenue kiosk. Officially known as **Welcome Pittsburgh,** it's the absolute final word on what to do and where to go during your time in the Steel City.

If you're flying into town, you can also stop by the small **VisitPittsburgh booth** at the airport. You'll find it in the Landside Terminal near baggage claim.

or San Francisco, you may be surprised to find that a popular eatery has stopped serving as early as 10 or 10:30 p.m., even on weekends. Always call ahead if your evening has gotten off to a late start.

Downtown Pittsburgh becomes something of a ghost town on weekends, and by about 6 p.m. on weekdays, assuming there are no parades, festivals, or art crawls taking place.

TIPPING

At restaurants, servers should be tipped 15 percent of the check for average service, or 20 percent for exceptional service. At coffee shops, leave the barista a few coins for a simple drink, such as house coffee. If you're ordering a more complicated espresso-based drink, it's not uncommon to leave a dollar. A 15–20 percent tip is also appropriate for taxi drivers, as well as anyone else performing a service for you, such a massage therapist, a hairdresser, or an attendant or manicurist at a spa or salon.

In hotel rooms, you'll often find an envelope with the name of your room's attendant written on the front. If exceptional service is important to you, be sure to leave anywhere from $2–10 a day, depending on the quality of the hotel itself. (Attendants at more expensive hotels expect larger tips, while attendants at budget hotels usually aren't tipped at all.) A hotel concierge should be tipped anywhere between $5–10. If a particularly complicated or time-sensitive service was performed, tip accordingly.

At bars, a minimum tip of a dollar per drink is expected, unless you're ordering a round, in which case you could probably get away with a bit less. Bartenders in Pittsburgh's dive bars don't necessarily expect a dollar a drink, even if the bar in question is particularly popular. Tip well in these busy places, however, and you'll often find that your service improves.

SMOKING

Thanks to the passing of Pennsylvania's Clean Indoor Air Act, Pittsburgh's long-debated smoking ban finally went into effect on September 11, 2008. But because of the law's slightly confusing regulations, it's still legally possible to light up at a number of area bars and restaurants. If a tavern generates less than 20 percent of its revenue from food sales, for instance, smoking is still allowed. Smoking also remains permissible at most private clubs.

Health and Safety

As North American urban areas go, Pittsburgh is a relatively safe place, and locals are almost always more than happy to help a lost, confused, or otherwise disoriented out-of-towner. And while the city does claim a number of higher-crime areas, the majority of these neighborhoods are safe during the day, and most are in obscure enough locales that the average tourist has little chance of stumbling into them.

Neighborhoods in which you'd be wise to keep your wits about you include the North Side, assuming you're north of The Andy Warhol Museum or in the area surrounding the Mattress Factory. (The area known as the North Shore, where PNC Park, Heinz Field, and the Carnegie Science Center are located, is quite safe.) Also take care in the East End. While East Liberty is currently gentrifying and has much to offer visitors, it's still something of a downtrodden locale. Parts of deep Lawrenceville (near the Allegheny River) can be a bit rugged, as can parts of Garfield, including the stretch of the Penn Avenue Corridor between the Allegheny Cemetery and the entrance to East Liberty.

When exploring the Penn Avenue Corridor, avoid entering the residential streets on the side of Penn Avenue that sits opposite Bloomfield.

The Hill District and Uptown should also be avoided after dark, so if you're attending a CONSOL Energy Center event at night, take care to walk back in the direction of Downtown.

HOSPITALS AND PHARMACIES

The majority of Pittsburgh's hospitals and healthcare centers are clustered within the university district of Oakland. These include **UPMC Presbyterian, UPMC Montefiore, UPMC Cancer Institute, Magee-Womens Hospital, The Eye & Ear Institute, Western Psychiatric Institute and Clinic,** and even **The Western PA School for the Blind.** For more information, visit www.upmc.com.

Formerly located in Oakland but now in a colorful new Lawrenceville building at 4401 Penn Avenue is the **Children's Hospital of Pittsburgh** (www.chp.edu).

the Children's Hospital of Pittsburgh

© MATT STROUD

Mercy Hospital is located in between Oakland and Downtown in the Uptown neighborhood, while **Allegheny General Hospital** is located on the North Side, and the **Western Pennsylvania Hospital** is found on Bloomfield's Liberty Avenue. A comprehensive list of every hospital in Allegheny County, which includes links to each hospital's respective website, can be accessed at www.allegheny-county.net/hospital.html. **UPMC Health Plan** is one of the area's most popular and widely used insurance programs. For information, visit www.upmchealthplan.com.

EMERGENCY SERVICES

To call the police, or for fire or medical emergencies, dial 911. For an electrical emergency, dial 412/393-7000. If you have a gas emergency in Pittsburgh, dial 412/442-3095. The Poison Information Center can be contacted at 412/681-6669. For water and sewer emergencies in Pittsburgh, dial 412/255-2429. The toll-free number for PA Crime Stoppers is 800/472-8477. Dial Pittsburgh's non–emergency services phone number, 311, to access information about city government services, and to report non-emergencies such as potholes.

Information and Services

MEDIA AND COMMUNICATION
Phones and Area Codes

On February 1, 1998, after decades of universal use of the 412 area code, Pittsburgh gained a new area code, 724, for telephone numbers outside the city limits. The change affected nearly 1.5 million phone lines. The vast majority of those were outside Allegheny County, although a small number of areas within Allegheny County were affected as well.

Other counties using the 724 area code include Armstrong, Beaver, Butler, Fayette, Greene, Indiana, Lawrence, Mercer, Washington, and Westmoreland Counties, as well as parts of Clarion, Crawford, and Venango Counties. The vast majority of neighborhoods within Allegheny County, which includes the city of Pittsburgh, use the 412 area code. No matter where you're calling to or from, however, you'll always need to dial the appropriate area code before dialing the phone number.

Internet Services

All branches of the **Carnegie Library of Pittsburgh** (412/622-3114, www.clpgh.org) offer free Internet access; a library card is required to get online. Visitors from out of town or abroad can request a temporary library card by showing a state-issued driver's license or a valid passport. The main branch of the Carnegie Library in Oakland conveniently offers free wireless service on its first and second floors. Wireless access is also available at a number of cafés around town, including all seven **Crazy Mocha** locations (www.crazy-mocha.com) and all **Panera Bread** locations (www.panerabread.com). Most major hotels offer free high-speed wireless as well, as does the Pittsburgh International Airport.

Mail and Messenger Services

The **United States Postal Service** maintains post offices in almost every Pittsburgh neighborhood; visit www.usps.com to search for a specific location or call 800/275-8777. For those who prefer specialty shipping options, there are three corporate selections. Both **UPS** (800/742-5877, www.ups.com) and **FedEx** (800/463-3333, www.fedex.com) are handy for sending overnight packages or international shipping; call or go online to find the nearest location. For post office box rentals, **Mailboxes Etc.** (414 S. Craig St., 412/687-6100 or 800/789-4623, www.mbe.com) and **The UPS Store** (1739 E. Carson St., 412/381-7755, www.theupsstore.com) are both reliable alternatives to the USPS. Both stores offer 24-hour mailbox access and a slew of other products and services, such as copying, packaging, and shipping.

IMPORTANT PHONE NUMBERS

SERVICES

- **Lawyer Referral Service:** 412/261-5555
- **Non-emergency city services:** 311
- **Pittsburgh Parking Authority:** 412/560-7275
- **Pittsburgh Public Schools:** 412/622-7920

TRANSPORTATION

- **Amtrak (train):** 800/872-7245 or 412/471-6170
- **Greyhound (bus):** 800/231-2222 or 412/392-6526
- **Pittsburgh International Airport:** 412/472-3525
- **Port Authority Transit (bus and subway):** 412/442-2000
- **Yellow Cab Taxi:** 412/321-8100

UTILITIES

- **Comcast Cable:** 412/771-1300
- **Duquesne Light (electricity):** 888/393-7100
- **Equitable Gas:** 412/395-3050
- **Verizon (Internet):** 412/497-7000

All three of Pittsburgh's bike messenger companies also deliver by car, should you need something picked up or delivered to a location that isn't within realistic cycling distance. The city's largest service is **Jet Messenger** (412/471-4722, www.jetrush.com). Your other choices are **American Expediting Company** (412/321-4546, www.amexpediting.com) and **Quick Messenger** (412/481-5000).

Magazines and Newspapers

Pittsburgh's two daily newspapers include the left-leaning **Pittsburgh Post-Gazette** (www.post-gazette.com) and the conservative **Pittsburgh Tribune-Review** (www.pittsburghlive.com), which also distributes a free evening tabloid, the **Trib PM.** The city's solitary alternative weekly, **Pittsburgh City Paper** (www.pghcitypaper.com), is useful for its arts and entertainment listings, as well as for its well-reported news and feature stories.

Other area newspapers include **Pittsburgh Business Times** (www.bizjournals.com/pittsburgh), which is closely watched by the city's white-collar crowd; **New Pittsburgh Courier** (www.newpittsburghcourier.com), a weekly focusing primarily on African American news and events; **Pittsburgh Catholic** (www.pittsburghcatholic.org), which serves Western Pennsylvania's considerable Catholic population and, tellingly enough, boasts the city's largest circulation; and **Out** (www.outonline.com), a gay and lesbian paper serving the tristate area.

Pittsburgh Magazine (www.pittsburghmagazine.com) is the area's best monthly; it offers feature stories as well as all manner of local arts, food, and travel information. Other area magazines with heavy concentrations of arts and culture coverage include **Pittsburgh Quarterly** (www.pittsburghquarterly.com) and **Whirl** (www.whirlmagazine.com), the latter of which is filled largely with photos of local celebrities flitting about at high-society fundraisers. **Table Magazine** (www.tablemagazine.com) is a quarterly publication dedicated to the Southwestern Pennsylvania food scene; **Edible Allegheny** (www.ediblecommunities.com/allegheny) also covers the Greater Pittsburgh area food scene, with an emphasis on organic foods and sustainable farming practices. **Cue Pittsburgh** (www.cuepittsburgh.com) is an arts and entertainment magazine for the city's gay and lesbian community. Nationally distributed bicycle magazines published in the Pittsburgh area include **Dirt Rag** (www.dirtragmag.com), **Bicycle Times** (www.bicycletimesmag.com), and **Urban Velo** (www.urbanvelo.org).

Pittsburgh has a healthy independent publishing scene. **Creative Nonfiction** (www.creativenonfiction.org) is a highly respected journal published by Pitt instructor Lee Gutkind, who was instrumental in establishing the literary journalism genre. *The New Yinzer* (www.newyinzer.com) is an online literary journal featuring fiction, poetry, and experimental prose; special print issues are occasionally published. *Cafe Racer* (www.caferacermag.com) is a hip motorcycle-culture magazine published by former *Tribune-Review* columnist Mike Seate. *Young Pioneers* (www.youngpioneers.com) is a quarterly publication covering the creative and alternative entrepreneurship scene. It was founded by this book's author, who continues to act as its editor in chief.

Radio and TV

Affiliates of every major network exist in Pittsburgh. The city's PBS station, **WQED** (www.wqed.org), holds the distinction of being the first community-owned station in the country. **PCTV21** (www.pctv21.org) is Pittsburgh's public access station.

The city has a multitude of radio stations; check **Gregory's Radio Guide** (www.gregorysradioguide.com/pittsburg.html) for a decent listing of area stations. Slightly more complete is About.com's listing of Pittsburgh stations (www.pittsburgh.about.com/od/radio).

Some of the more popular area stations include **WDUQ 90.5 FM** (jazz and public radio); **WQED 89.3 FM** (classical and public radio); **WYEP 91.3 FM** (community-supported adult alternative); **WDVE 102.5 FM** (hard rock and classic rock); **3WS 94.5 FM** (oldies); **105.9 The X** (alternative rock); **WTAE 1250 AM** (sports); **Y108 FM** (country); **KDKA 1020 AM** (news and talk); **WAMO 106.7 FM** (hip-hop and R&B); and **WRCT 88.3 FM** (free-form independent music from Carnegie Mellon).

PUBLIC LIBRARIES

Enter a public library anywhere in the city of Pittsburgh, and you're entering not only a sacred monument to learning and growth. You're also passing through an important chapter—so to speak—of Pittsburgh's history.

The Scottish-American industrialist and philanthropist Andrew Carnegie was responsible for the creation of every last library in Pittsburgh, as he was for many other free libraries across the United States and even throughout the world. Without Carnegie's impetus to share the gift of education with the working-class employees of his steel mills, the free public library as we know it likely wouldn't exist today. It is worth noting, however, that not all of Carnegie's employees, who saw their wages lowered so that library construction could go forward, saw fit to return the love. Said one such steel worker in Margaret Byington's *Homestead: The Households of a Mill Town:* "We'd rather they hadn't cut our wages and let us spend the money for ourselves. What use has a man who works 12 hours a day for a library, anyway?"

Good point. Nonetheless, the Carnegie Library system today is a thing of wonder, even if some branches have been shuttered recently because of the city's financial troubles. To find the branch nearest you, visit www.clpgh.org.

The **Carnegie Library of Pittsburgh Main** (4400 Forbes Ave., 412/622-3114) is located in Oakland, directly across from Pitt's Hillman Library; Schenley Plaza separates the two. This main branch recently underwent extensive renovations, and now features free high-speed wireless Internet service on its first and second floors, a magazine room, an outdoor reading deck, and a Crazy Mocha café. The main branch also offers a career services center, an art and music room with an extensive collection of CDs, DVDs, and books on tape, and a superb magazine and newspaper collection.

The **Squirrel Hill** (5801 Forbes Ave., 412/422-9650) branch of the Carnegie Library also underwent renovations recently. The Arthur Lubetz and Associates architecture firm is responsible for the $4.7 million exterior and interior modernist design; the firm has plans to take part in revitalizing every library in the Carnegie system. The **Downtown** (612 Smithfield St., 412/281-5945) and **Homewood** (7101 Hamilton Ave., 412/731-3080) locations have also been recently renovated. Other library branches can be found in **East Liberty**

© DAN ELDRIDGE

Carnegie Library of Pittsburgh Main

(130 S. Whitfield St., 412/363-8232), **Mount Washington** (315 Grandview Ave., 412/381-3380), **Lawrenceville** (279 Fisk St., 412/682-3668), and the **South Side** (2205 E. Carson St., 412/431-0505). Visit www.clpgh.org or any city library location to view a map of the entire 18-branch system.

PLACES OF WORSHIP

Because Pittsburgh is so heavy with Italian and Eastern European immigrants, Catholicism is practically omnipresent. If it's a Catholic church you're after, you won't need to look too terribly hard. In fact, in some neighborhoods (including Bloomfield, where the first edition of this book was written in part), the ringing of church bells can still be heard throughout the day. To plug more effectively into the local scene, pick up a copy of *Pittsburgh Catholic* (800/392-4670, www.pittsburghcatholic.org) at just about any church or chapel, or take a look at the website of the **Roman Catholic Diocese of Pittsburgh** at www.diopitt.org.

The East End neighborhood of Squirrel Hill is one of the largest Jewish neighborhoods on the East Coast; here you'll find nearly two dozen synagogues. **Beth Shalom** (5915 Beacon St.) is one of the neighborhood's most popular. Visit the Pittsburgh page at **ShtetLinks** (www.shtetlinks.jewishgen.org) for a fairly comprehensive list of synagogues in Squirrel Hill and beyond.

The **Jewish Community Center** (5738 Forbes Ave., 412/521-8010, www.jccpgh.org) is located at the corner of Forbes and Murray Avenues in Squirrel Hill. Often referred to by locals as the JCC, here you'll find a fitness center, art classes for children and adults, theater and musical performances, and much more, including the **American Jewish Museum,** which is the sole museum in the western part of Pennsylvania devoted solely to the exploration of Jewish history and culture. And yes, all races, religions, and creeds are welcome at the JCC.

Pittsburgh is also home to the **Sri Venkateswara Temple** (1230 S. McCully Dr., Penn Hills, 412/373-7650, www.svtemple.org), one of the oldest Hindu temples in the

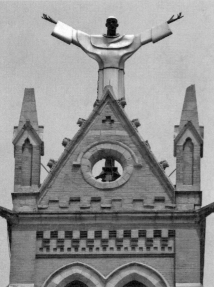

St. Benedict the Moor is one of the 209 parishes in the Roman Catholic Diocese of Pittsburgh.

The Sri Venkateswara Temple is one of the oldest Hindu temples in the country.

country. The Hare Krishna community of **New Vrindaban** (304/843-1600, www.newvrinda-ban.com) is located about an hour's drive from Pittsburgh in Moundsville, West Virginia. Call or visit the community's website for detailed directions.

Buddhists in the Pittsburgh area congregate at Sewickley's **Zen Center of Pittsburgh** (124 Willow Ridge Rd., 412/741-1262, www.deepspringzen.org), a Soto Zen Temple with a resident priest. **Stillpoint** (137 41st St., 412/366-4268, www.stillpointzen.org) is a Soto Zen practice community that gathers regularly in Lawrenceville. The Zen Center of Pittsburgh offers meditation sessions every Wednesday from 6–7:30 P.M. at **Friends Meeting House** (4836 Ellsworth Ave., 412/683-2669), which sits on the border of Shadyside and North Oakland; plan to arrive roughly 20 minutes early.

Muslims in Pittsburgh are well served by the mosque at the **Islamic Center of Pittsburgh** (4100 Bigelow Blvd., 412/682-5555, www

.icp-pgh.org), conveniently located in North Oakland and within easy walking distance of all Oakland universities.

In Pittsburgh, even the tattooed and pierced set has a church to serve their specific needs. **The Hot Metal Bridge Faith Community** (2000 E. Carson St., 412/481-4010, www.hotmetalbridge.com, Sun. worship 11 A.M.) is something of a nondenominational community geared toward people who tend to find standard church services too *standard*. They meet and share meals at the Goodwill Building on the South Side.

To view a brief listing of city and suburban churches for those with Presbyterian, Baptist, Lutheran, or Unitarian leanings, visit www.greaterpittsburgh.com/html/sgp97.html.

MAJOR BANKS

The Pittsburgh area's two largest financial service organizations are **PNC Bank** (www.pncbank.com) and **Citizens Bank** (www.citizensbank.com); the latter bought out the

© DAN ELDRIDGE

PNC Bank

Pittsburgh-headquartered Mellon Bank back in 2001. Both PNC and Citizens have branch locations and ATMs in all reaches of the city. **Dollar Bank** (www.dollarbank.com) is another area bank with numerous locations; the bank's no-fee and no-minimum checking accounts are a popular draw. Other banks you'll encounter around town include **Parkvale Bank** (www.parkvale.com), which claims to offer a personalized banking experience, and **Mars National Bank** (www.marsbank.com), with branches located in the North Hills suburbs. Headquartered in the small Western Pennsylvania town of Hermitage is the **First National Bank** (FNB) (www.fnb-online .com). With over 200 locations in Western Pennsylvania and Northeastern Ohio, FNB is currently the eighth-largest bank in the Pittsburgh region.

First Niagara Bank (www.fnfg.com) became the most recent addition to the city's banking community when it purchased 57 National City branches from PNC. Currently headquartered in Buffalo, New York, the company

also sponsors the outdoor Burgettstown concert venue known as the First Niagara Pavilion, which was formerly known as the Post-Gazette Pavilion, and before that, the Star Lake Amphitheater.

Most major banks can handle foreign currency exchanges even for customers without an account, but be prepared to pay a substantial service charge. Also, be aware that many Pittsburghers still refer to ATMs as "MAC" machines. This is a stubborn holdover from the days of Mellon Bank, which referred to its ATMs as "money access machines."

RELOCATION

If you're thinking about the possibility of making the Greater Pittsburgh area your permanent home, do yourself a favor and spend some time on the comprehensive and educational website (www.alleghenyconference.org/chamber) put together by the Greater Pittsburgh Chamber of Commerce and the Allegheny Conference on Community Development. Here you'll find business resources and demographic information about the area, as well as a cost-of-living calculator, career information, and useful information about life in the region.

Also visit the Chamber of Commerce's website project, www.xplorion.org, which contains loads of information about living, working, playing, and investing in the area. Should you find yourself in Downtown Pittsburgh with a bit of time to kill, wander over to the **Regional Enterprise Tower** at 425 6th Avenue, near the Omni William Penn Hotel. **Xplorion** is located on the ground floor, and the use of computer terminals is free.

Finding a Job

To search the current listings of jobs offered by the City of Pittsburgh, visit the city's site at www.city.pittsburgh.pa.us. You can also call the job hotline at 412/255-2388; listings are updated weekly.

The Pittsburgh Career Connector (http://pghcareerconnector.com) provides job information for those with interest or experience in the business or technology fields.

Other useful online search engines include www.careerbuilder.com, www.monster.com, http://pittsburgh.craigslist.org, and http://hotjobs.yahoo.com. All sites allow job seekers to search for positions by specific region.

The University of Pittsburgh Medical Center has long been one of the city's largest employers. To access its online list of regularly updated open positions, visit http://jobs.upmc.com.

The *Pittsburgh Post-Gazette,* the *Pittsburgh Tribune-Review,* and the *Pittsburgh City Paper* all carry job listings.

Housing

The University of Pittsburgh provides a wonderful service through its **Housing Resource Center.** Apartment listings, roommate matching services, sublets, and housing guides can be accessed even by nonstudents at the center's Off-Campus Living website (www.ocl.pitt.edu). The same site also includes information about purchasing a home in Pittsburgh, how to find the best housing insurance for your needs, and how to pick the right neighborhood. There's even information about local hotels and bed-and-breakfasts, should you find yourself temporarily without a roof over your head. To access the site's very useful list of emergency and non-emergency phone numbers, visit www.ocl.pitt.edu/about/phone.html.

Many Pittsburghers interested in renting, subletting, or finding a prospective roommate do a brisk business on Craigslist. The local site can be accessed at http://pittsburgh.craigslist.org. You might also scan the bulletin boards and message boards throughout the Pitt and CMU campuses; housing notices are often posted here.

Agencies involved in the renting and selling of homes are located in a number of Pittsburgh neighborhoods, especially Shadyside and Squirrel Hill. One particularly popular agency, **Franklin West** (272 Shady Ave., Shadyside, 412/661-1151, www.franklinwest.com), specializes in contemporary apartments and townhouses.

RESOURCES

Suggested Reading

Bell, Thomas. *Out of this Furnace*. University of Pittsburgh Press, 1976. An emotionally wrenching story that tells of the trials and tribulations of three generations of a Slovakian family who immigrated to America and ended up working in the Braddock steel mills.

Chabon, Michael. *The Mysteries of Pittsburgh*. Harper Perennial, 1989. Chabon is a graduate of the University of Pittsburgh and a former employee of Jay's Bookstall; *Mysteries*, his first novel, launched an impressive career. While Chabon's Pulitzer Prize–winning work came years later, this is nonetheless an incredible read about the existential and sexual dilemmas of a group of young adults during their first summer after college.

Dillard, Annie. *An American Childhood*. Harper Perennial, 1988. Dillard ponders her 1950s Pittsburgh childhood in this classic book about growing up, seeing the world anew, and the unavoidable pain of slowly becoming an adult.

Hopper, Justin. *Making the Connections*. The Sprout Fund, 2009. As the gorgeously designed document of a uniquely forward-thinking civic project, *Making the Connections* shares the fascinating stories behind 100 different community projects that were launched as a way to celebrate the city's 250th anniversary. Written by a respected Pittsburgh cultural journalist, this beautiful little product shines a light on the legendary community pride of Southwestern Pennsylvania like no other book before it.

Lorant, Stefan. *Pittsburgh: The Story of an American City*. The Derrydale Press, 1999. Based on decades of tireless research, this heavy, hardcover coffee-table book touches upon nearly every facet of the city's story, from the battles of the mid-1750s to the 1990s. Incredibly detailed and packed with dozens of gorgeous photos, *Pittsburgh* reset the standard for historical and cultural books about cities when it was first published in the 1970s.

O'Nan, Stewart. *Everyday People*. Grove Press, 2001. A fictional tale about gangs, drugs, and the life of hard knocks in East Liberty, a neighborhood that remains troubled and crime-ridden, even while some pockets are quickly becoming gentrified.

Toker, Franklin. *Pittsburgh: A New Portrait*. University of Pittsburgh Press, 2009. A stunningly ambitious look at Pittsburgh as a timeless American city, this heavy volume has now replaced Stefan Lorant's legendary Pittsburgh book as the definitive final word on the Steel City, from its earliest days to modern times.

Various authors. *Pittsburgh Born, Pittsburgh Bred*. Senator John Heinz History Center,

2008. Experience a touch of Steel City pride as you thumb through this engaging coffee-table book, which contains the stories of "500 of the more famous people who have called Pittsburgh home."

Various authors. *Pittsburgh in Words.* Creative Nonfiction, 2008. Published in celebration of the city's 250th anniversary, this magazine-like publication (which was produced by the team behind *Creative Nonfiction,* the local literary journal) features true stories by writers attempting to share and explain the true essence of the Steel City.

Various authors. *Pittsburgh Signs Project.* Carnegie Mellon University Press, 2009. This gorgeously produced book was the final result of a truly ambitious, years-long project during which hundreds of vintage business signs throughout Western Pennsylvania were photographed for posterity's sake. It makes a perfect gift, by the way, for the beloved Pittsburgher in your life.

Wideman, John Edgar. *Brothers and Keepers.* Holt, Rinehart and Winston, 1984. This is one of the most popular books from Wideman, an accomplished author formerly based in Pittsburgh who long chronicled life in the Homewood ghetto. In *Brothers and Keepers,* Wideman waxes poetic about the differences between his life, heavy with learning and culture, and the life of his brother, who is serving a life sentence in jail.

Wilson, August. *Fences.* Samuel French, Inc., 1986. Probably the most legendary play ever penned by Hill District native August Wilson. The story, for which Wilson was awarded the Pulitzer Prize, concerns the struggle of Troy Maxson, a proud black man who can't quite get a grasp on the quickly changing world of the 1960s.

Internet Resources

INFORMATION AND EVENTS

About.com
www.pittsburgh.about.com

A good destination for keeping abreast of upcoming events and local news, About.com's Pittsburgh site also boasts info about finding a job, finding a home, and finding fun things to do with the family.

Carnegie Library of Pittsburgh
www.clpgh.org

The Carnegie Library's website is an absolutely indispensable research site for scholars of all things Pittsburgh. Click the "Research Databases" link on the left-hand side of the "Tools & Research" page, and you'll be directed to a wonderfully detailed collection of Pittsburgh data, be it cultural, historical, or just about anything else.

City of Pittsburgh
www.city.pittsburgh.pa.us

The official City of Pittsburgh site provides information about city parks, tourism, road closures, and city-sponsored events. New residents will appreciate the site's garbage collection schedules, road closure info, and business news.

The College City
www.thecollegecity.com

Particularly useful for its fantastic collection of local links, this site should also be the first stop for any college student interested in area schools. It's also a useful site for new residents and tourists looking to discover the city's more dynamic opportunities.

Global Pittsburgh
www.globalpittsburgh.org

This wonderfully useful site is concerned with connecting Pittsburgh's various international communities. Visitors or new residents from abroad can search for job opportunities, new friends and activities, and information about immigration.

Imagine Pittsburgh
www.imaginepittsburgh.com

Launched as part of a three-year, $3 million marketing campaign to increase awareness of the Pittsburgh area's numerous achievements and its nearly unlimited possibility for growth, this site does a wonderful job of explaining why Pittsburgh is such a unique place. You'll also find links to the helpful tourism sites of 11 surrounding counties.

Never Tell Me the Odds
www.nevertellmetheodds.org

This message board was originally maintained by members of the now-defunct Mr. Roboto Project, a local DIY and punk club. Many threads lean toward the juvenile or self-righteous, but the regular posters are part of a collective clearinghouse of obscure Pittsburgh trivia. If you have a question about the city that you can't find an answer to elsewhere, you might try asking here.

Pittsburghese
www.pittsburghese.com

This is a hilariously good-natured guide to one of North America's most curious regional dialects, Pittsburghese. It includes a glossary, a translator, an audio quiz—even Pittsburghese calisthenics. (Believe me, yinz are gonna need it.)

This Is Happening
www.thisishappening.com

Created with the intention of convincing the young and hip that there are, in fact, interesting and unusual things to do in Pittsburgh, the site is searchable by subject but can be confusing to navigate. You're better off subscribing to the site's free weekly events email, which will conveniently appear in your inbox every Thursday.

VisitPittsburgh
www.visitpittsburgh.com

The Greater Pittsburgh Convention & Visitors Bureau site is where you'll find all the necessary information to plan a vacation or business trip to the Steel City. Essentially a mini–online guidebook, VisitPittsburgh also allows visitors to book hotel and vacation packages. Particularly useful are the suggested itineraries for those interested in taking day trips to the nearby counties and countryside.

NEWS

New Pittsburgh Courier
www.newpittsburghcourier
online.com

The online version of the weekly newspaper geared toward the city's African American community.

Pittsburgh Business Times
http://pittsburgh.bizjournals.com/
pittsburgh

This local edition of the nationwide *Business Times,* a weekly newspaper, is a must-read for local entrepreneurs and corporate types.

Pittsburgh Catholic
www.pittsburghcatholic.org

This widely-read weekly newspaper is published by the Diocese of Pittsburgh. It boasts the largest circulation of any paper in the region.

Pittsburgh City Paper
www.pittsburghcitypaper.ws

The city's solitary alternative newsweekly maintains a huge online archive of feature stories. The website is also indispensible for its comprehensive event listings and many restaurant reviews.

Pittsburgh Indymedia
www.pittsburgh.indymedia.org

This community-based media site is filled with regional news, most with a heavy liberal bias. Pittsburgh's activism community is surprisingly large, and this is where many of them congregate. Information about upcoming protests and antiwar marches can be found here.

Pittsburgh Magazine
www.pittsburghmagazine.com

The website of Pittsburgh's regional monthly magazine offers a wealth of feature stories, an extensive events calendar, thoughtful dining reviews, and more.

Pittsburgh Post-Gazette and *Pittsburgh Tribune-Review*
www.post-gazette.com and www.pittsburghlive.com

Find up-to-the-minute local and national news at the websites of Pittsburgh's two daily newspapers, the liberal and more critically-acclaimed *Post-Gazette,* and the conservative *Tribune-Review,* which publishes a handful of smaller community papers under its Trib Total Media banner.

Pop City
www.popcitymedia.com

This weekly online magazine documents the Pittsburgh experience primarily for the young and active crowd. It features tech, lifestyle, and entrepreneurial news.

BEST PITTSBURGH BLOGS

Behind the Steel Curtain
www.behindthesteelcurtain.com

Pittsburgh is home to an untold number of Steelers fan blogs, and this is one of the very finest.

Boring Pittsburgh
www.boringpittsburgh.com

In its role as an enthusiastic cheerleader for the city, Boring Pittsburgh covers cool and quirky happenings and other events.

Carbolic Smoke Ball
www.carbolicsmoke.com

A sarcasm-littered local news site, this is Pittsburgh's version of *The Onion,* complete with hilariously fake stories.

I Heart Pgh
www.iheartpgh.com

This is a quirky, well-edited, and frequently updated listing of events, especially those with a focus on the arts.

Pittsblog
www.pittsblog.blogspot.com

Local politics and current events from a University of Pittsburgh law professor are featured here.

Pittsburgh Bloggers
www.pghbloggers.org

A blog about local blogs, it's useful largely because of its incredibly extensive collection of links.

Steeltown Anthem
http://steeltownanthem.word press.com

An art, design, and architecture blog with a distinctive *Dwell* magazine sensibility.

That's Church
www.thatschurch.com

Formerly known as The 'Burgh Blog and written by the once-anonymous PittGirl, That's Church is a snarky but intelligent look at life in the Steel City.

Index

Restaurants Index

Nightlife Index

Shops Index

Hotels Index

Acknowledgments

If I had to name the single best aspect of the process of putting together this second edition of *Moon Pittsburgh*—the one thing that made it even more enjoyable than working on the book's first edition—it would almost certainly be the fact that so many different people were willing to help out.

As is almost always the case when I'm working on huge projects with quickly-approaching deadlines, it was my fiancée, Carrie Ann, who helped me stave off many impending panic attacks, and who singlehandedly took on a significant portion of the guide's research tasks. Carrie was also responsible for writing much of this guide's shopping chapter, especially the sections covering men's and women's clothing, arts and crafts, and health and beauty.

Also invaluable was my selfless assistant, the very accomplished Pittsburgh-based journalist Matt Stroud, who helped out by contributing a good number of sidebars, capsule reviews, and photographs. Thanks to Adam Waddell, who contributed photography, and Robert Isenberg, who wrote about the Great Allegheny Passage. Thanks also to Lynne Glover of the Greater Pittsburgh Convention & Visitors Bureau, who supplied a wealth of valuable insider information (along with some of this book's finest photography), and to Mary Carroll, my CouchSurfing.org buddy, who put me up in her Wilkinsburg apartment during my final research stage. A huge thanks to Rob Matheny, an incredibly talented photographer whose work can be seen throughout this entire book. Without your contributions, Rob, this guide would undoubtedly be much less attractive, and nowhere near as interesting.

And finally, an extra special thanks to my parents, Dan and Barbara Eldridge, without whose unconditional love, support, and understanding I would not likely be writing these words. Thanks, guys—I honestly don't know what I would do without you.

www.moon.com

DESTINATIONS | ACTIVITIES | BLOGS | MAPS | BOOKS

MOON.COM is ready to help plan your next trip! Filled with fresh trip ideas and strategies, author interviews, informative travel blogs, a detailed map library, and descriptions of all the Moon guidebooks, Moon.com is all you need to get out and explore the world—or even places in your own backyard. While at Moon.com, sign up for our monthly e-newsletter for updates on new releases, travel tips, and expert advice from our on-the-go Moon authors. As always, when you travel with Moon, expect an experience that is uncommon and truly unique.

MAP SYMBOLS

▦	Expressway	**《**	Highlight	✗	Airfield	⚓	Golf Course
▦	Primary Road	○	City/Town	✗	Airport	**P**	Parking Area
▦	Secondary Road	◉	State Capital	▲	Mountain	▲	Archaeological Site
▦	Unpaved Road	⊛	National Capital	✦	Unique Natural Feature	▮	Church
‑ ‑ ‑ ‑	Trail	★	Point of Interest				Gas Station
⋯	Ferry	•	Accommodation	☜	Waterfall		Glacier
▦	Railroad	▾	Restaurant/Bar	▲	Park		Mangrove
▦	Pedestrian Walkway	■	Other Location	**T**	Trailhead		Reef
▦	Stairs	▲	Campground	⚜	Skiing Area		Swamp

CONVERSION TABLES

°C = (°F - 32) / 1.8
°F = (°C x 1.8) + 32
1 inch = 2.54 centimeters (cm)
1 foot = 0.304 meters (m)
1 yard = 0.914 meters
1 mile = 1.6093 kilometers (km)
1 km = 0.6214 miles
1 fathom = 1.8288 m
1 chain = 20.1168 m
1 furlong = 201.168 m
1 acre = 0.4047 hectares
1 sq km = 100 hectares
1 sq mile = 2.59 square km
1 ounce = 28.35 grams
1 pound = 0.4536 kilograms
1 short ton = 0.90718 metric ton
1 short ton = 2,000 pounds
1 long ton = 1.016 metric tons
1 long ton = 2,240 pounds
1 metric ton = 1,000 kilograms
1 quart = 0.94635 liters
1 US gallon = 3.7854 liters
1 Imperial gallon = 4.5459 liters
1 nautical mile = 1.852 km

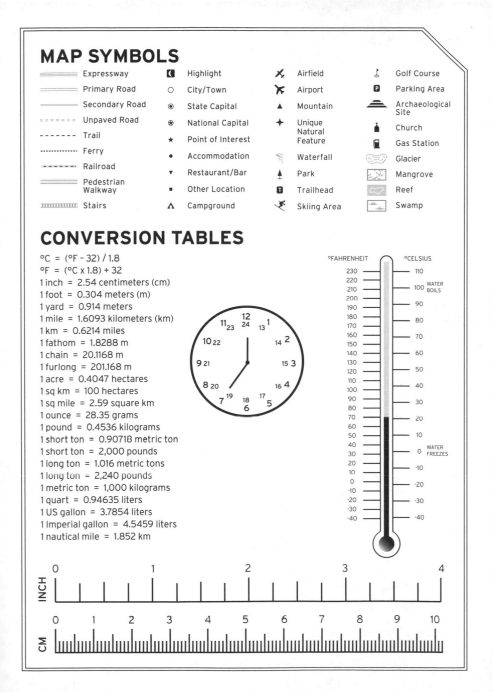

MOON PITTSBURGH

Avalon Travel
a member of the Perseus Books Group
1700 Fourth Street
Berkeley, CA 94710, USA
www.moon.com

Editor and Series Manager: Erin Raber
Copy Editor: Maura Brown
Graphics and Production Coordinator:
   Elizabeth Jang
Cover Designer: Elizabeth Jang
Map Editor: Albert Angulo
Cartographers: Chris L. Hendrick, Kat Bennett,
   Kaitlin Jaffe

ISBN-13: 978-1-59880-730-1
ISSN: 1936-4938

Printing History
1st Edition – 2007
2nd Edition – July 2011
5 4 3 2 1

Front cover photo: Pittsburgh as seen from the
MisterRogers Tribute to Children © David Fulmer

Title page photo: "Cosley Football Player,"
© Ren Netherland, www.animalphotography.com;
dog grooming by Justine Cosley.

Interior color photos: p. 2 (left) Union Station Rotunda
courtesy of VisitPittsburgh, (middle) detail of a house
decoration at Randyland, Mexican War Streets
courtesy of Rob Matheny, (right) eyeball benches
at Agnes R. Katz Plaza (designed by sculptor Louise
Bourgeois) courtesy of Rob Matheny; p. 18 (inset) the
Pittsburgh panther statue © Dan Eldridge, (bottom
left) the Point at night courtesy of VisitPittsburgh,
(bottom right) Kaufmann's clock, downtown, courtesy
of Rob Matheny; p. 19 The Andy Warhol Museum
courtesy of VisitPittsburgh, PNC Park with statue
of J.P. "Honus" Wagner (sculptor Frank Vittor)
courtesy of Rob Matheny; p. 20 courtesy of Rob
Matheny; p. 21 © The Waffle Shop; p. 22 © Gino Santa
Maria/123rf.com; p. 23 courtesy of National Aviary/
VisitPittsburgh; p. 24 courtesy of Rob Matheny

Photos from Flickr Creative Commons members
are used according to the following license: http://
creativecommons.org/licenses/by/2.0/

Printed in Canada by Friesens

KEEPING CURRENT

If you have a favorite gem you'd like to see included in the next edition, or see anything
that needs updating, clarification, or correction, please drop us a line. Send your
comments via email to feedback@moon.com, or use the address above.